WITHDRAWN

The Making of the Presidential Candidates 2004

The Making of the Presidential Candidates 2004

Edited by
William G. Mayer

ROWMAN & LITTLEFIELD PUBLISHERS, INC.
Lanham • Boulder • New York • Toronto • Oxford

9177374

KSG- PPP 343

ROWMAN & LITTLEFIELD PUBLISHERS, INC.

Published in the United States of America
by Rowman & Littlefield Publishers, Inc.
A wholly owned subsidary of The Rowman & Littlefield Publishing Group, Inc.
4501 Forbes Boulevard, Suite 200, Lanham, MD 20706
www.rowmanlittlefield.com

P.O. Box 317, Oxford OX2 9RU, UK

British Library Cataloguing in Publication Information Available

Library of Congress Cataloging-in-Publication Data

The making of the presidential candidates 2004 / edited by William G.
Mayer
    p.   cm.
Includes bibliographical references and index.
ISBN 0-7425-2918-5 (cloth : alk. paper) — ISBN 0-7425-2919-3 (pbk. :
alk. paper)
    1. Presidents—United States—Nomination.   I. Mayer, William G., 1956–
JK521.M35   2003
324.5'0973—dc21   2003009735

Printed in the United States of America

∞ ™ The paper used in this publication meets the minimum requirements of American
National Standard for Information Sciences—Permanence of Paper for Printed Library
Materials, ANSI/NISO Z39.48-1992.

To Our Children

Natalie and Thomas Logan Mayer
Katherine Noelle and Daniel Christopher Busch
Nathaniel and William Tenpas
Taylor E. Dark IV
Matthew Cornfield
Elizabeth and Natalie Shribman
Philip and Geoffrey Smith

Contents

Preface   ix

1   The Front-Loading Problem   1
Andrew E. Busch and William G. Mayer

2   Financing Presidential Nominations under the BCRA   45
Anthony Corrado and Heitor Gouvêa

3   The Basic Dynamics of the Contemporary Nomination Process:
An Expanded View   83
William G. Mayer

4   How Incumbent Presidents Run for Reelection   133
Kathryn Dunn Tenpas

5   From Resistance to Adaptation: Organized Labor Reacts to a
Changing Nominating Process   161
Taylor E. Dark III

6   The Net and the Nomination   199
Michael Cornfield and Jonah Seiger

7   Only a Lunatic Would Do This Kind of Work: A Journalist's
Perspective on the Perspective of Journalists   229
David M. Shribman

8   The Perils of Polling in New Hampshire   245
Andrew E. Smith

9   The Emerging International Trend toward Open Presidential
       Primaries: The American Presidential Nomination Process in
       Comparative Perspective   265
       James A. McCann

Index   295

About the Contributors   305

Preface

This is the third in a quadrennial series of books about the presidential nomination process. Though the title is new (the first two volumes were called *In Pursuit of the White House* and *In Pursuit of the White House 2000*), this book is intended to serve the same objectives: to present a broad overview of the presidential nomination process through a detailed examination of some of its most significant components, and to showcase some of the most interesting work now being done on the politics of presidential selection.

Besides its title, this book features one other innovation. Ever since the series was launched during the 1996 election cycle, it had been my hope that, in addition to including articles from academic analysts of the nomination process, I could persuade thoughtful practitioners to reflect upon and write about their experiences with the presidential selection system. Chapter 7 in this book is the first fruit of that aspiration: a wonderful essay by David Shribman, executive editor of the *Pittsburgh Post-Gazette* and a Pulitzer Prize–winning reporter and columnist, that examines the special perspective that journalists bring to the coverage of presidential campaigns—and how their perspectives, goals, and work habits differ from those of political scientists. (As a further sign of the substantial gulf between the journalistic and academic cultures, David was the only contributor to this book who got his chapter to me in advance of the original deadline.)

All of the contributors to this book would like to express our enormous gratitude to the folks at Rowman & Littlefield, who took on this project at a rather late stage and still managed to bring the book out on time. Our particular thanks go to Jennifer Knerr, Renee Legatt, and Alden Perkins.

Eleven years ago, when my first book was published, perhaps the greatest source of satisfaction was the opportunity it gave me to express my gratitude and love to my family. Four books later, this is still the case. Trying to be a husband and father has only made me more conscious of all that I owe to my parents,

Mary Rose and Joseph Mayer, and to my siblings and their families: Joe, Rita, Lauren, and Joseph Michael Mayer; Mary Beth, Joe, Allie, and Kate King; Jack; Tom; and Rosemary, Scott, Andy, Steve, Dana, and Renee Kryk.

To be born into such a family is an extraordinary joy. To marry into one that has been equally loving and supportive seems almost profligate. This is the first book I have had published since the death of my mother-in-law, Natalie Logan. No one was more extravagant in her praise of everything I wrote. As I told her on a number of occasions, one reason I could never be a stand-up comic is that I can't imagine ever telling a mother-in-law joke. I will never forget her gentle, loving presence and the wholehearted way she welcomed me into her family. My love and thanks also to Maury Logan; Brian, Coralee, Adam, and Katie; Nancy; and Maureen, Bill, Andrew, and Christina Ferrari.

Most of all, I wish to express my love and devotion to my daughter Natalie, who gave her daddy a needed respite from political science by getting him to read all four of the Harry Potter books; my son Thomas, whose current literary tastes run more to lift-the-flap books, but with whom one day I hope to share the pleasures of football and Sherlock Holmes; and my wife Amy Logan, my favorite reading companion, who has made my life so immeasurably richer.

1

The Front-Loading Problem

Andrew E. Busch and William G. Mayer

Of all the major institutions and processes in contemporary American government, perhaps none has been as consistently controversial as the presidential nomination process. The basic rules governing delegate selection and convention decision-making were completely rewritten in the early 1970s, and from the moment the "reforms" first took effect, they faced a firestorm of criticism. The new rules were attacked from almost every conceivable angle: for producing candidates who were ideological extremists or not very experienced or just plain mediocre; for weakening the parties and empowering the news media; for making nomination campaigns longer and more expensive; for producing convention delegates who were unrepresentative of the party rank-and-file; for conferring disproportionate power on Iowa and New Hampshire; for emphasizing campaigning over governing; for almost entirely excluding party leaders and top elected officials from the decision-making process; for undermining the support that a president could expect to receive from members of his own party within Congress and the executive branch; and for accentuating potential sources of party division and thus making it more difficult for the parties to present a united front in the general election.[1]

The subject of this chapter is a relative latecomer to the list of faults and derelictions, but by the final years of the twentieth century, it had emerged as perhaps the single most-criticized feature of the entire process. Front-loading is what might be called a "second-order" effect of the new nomination rules. It did not become a major problem until the new system had been in operation for two or three election cycles and its basic tendencies and incentives had started to become apparent. Unfortunately, this also means that front-loading has probably

1

not yet run its course. Where most other features of the contemporary nomination process have now reached a point of stability, there are, as we will see, strong reasons to think that front-loading will get worse.

The rules of the presidential nomination process are, as a general matter, a pretty arcane subject: of some concern to the party officials who must write them and the campaign managers who must live under them, but not very interesting to anyone else. By the mid-1990s, however, a quite large number of political commentators and observers had taken notice of front-loading and, with a singular degree of unanimity, deplored its effects on the presidential selection process. In 1996, the system that resulted from front-loading was described as "madness," "insane," "warped and virtually mindless," "absurdly accelerated," "self-defeating," "debilitating," a "high speed demolition derby," and a "parody of participatory democracy" in which "candidates have rushed through the country like passengers late for a connection."[2] In 2000, various commentators called the nomination process "a sound-bite saturated sprint," a "stampede," a "disaster for democracy," "absurd," a "mosh pit," "terrible," "dangerously irrational," a "mutant game of hopscotch," a "freight train," and a "crazy-quilt system" that produced a "lemming-like rush."[3]

The purpose of this chapter is to provide a broad overview of the front-loading issue: what it is, why it developed, and what consequences it has for the nomination process as a whole.

THE RISE OF FRONT-LOADING

Front-loading is the name that has been given to an important recent trend in the presidential nomination process, in which more and more states schedule their primaries and caucuses near the very beginning of the delegate selection season. The result is a nomination calendar in which a large proportion of the delegates are selected within a few weeks after the process formally commences, as opposed to having the primaries and caucuses spread out evenly or having them concentrated near the end of the process.

Perhaps the best way to demonstrate the nature and significance of this development is to compare two presidential primary calendars: one from the period before front-loading began, the second showing front-loading at its zenith. Table 1.1 shows the schedule of Democratic primaries held in 1960 (the Republican calendar was all but identical). The first presidential primary that year took place in New Hampshire, on March 8. There were no other primaries during the remainder of March. Then, in each of the first three weeks in April, a single primary was held. Not until week 8 (that is, seven weeks after New Hampshire) did two primaries take place on the same day. Put another way, of the 648 delegates to the 1960 Democratic National Convention who were selected or bound by primary, only about a third had been selected by the end of the eighth week of

Table 1.1 Calendar of Democratic Presidential Primaries in 1960

Week	Dates	States Holding Primaries (date)	Number of Delegates Selected	Cumulative Number Selected	Cumulative Percentage Selected
Week 1	March 6–12	New Hampshire (3/8)	10	10	2
Week 2	March 13–19	None	—	10	2
Week 3	March 20–26	None	—	10	2
Week 4	March 27–April 2	None	—	10	2
Week 5	April 3–9	Wisconsin (4/5)	30	40	6
Week 6	April 10–16	Illinois (4/12)	50	90	14
Week 7	April 17–23	New Jersey (4/19)	40	130	20
Week 8	April 24–30	Massachusetts (4/26)	40		
		Pennsylvania (4/26)	60	230	35
Week 9	May 1–7	Alabama (5/3)	29		
		Distr. of Col. (5/3)	9		
		Indiana (5/3)	33		
		Ohio (5/3)	63	364	56
Week 10	May 8–14	Nebraska (5/10)	15		
		West Virginia (5/10)	24	403	62
Week 11	May 15–21	Maryland (5/17)	23		
		Oregon (5/20)	17	443	68
Week 12	May 22–28	Florida (5/24)	29	472	73
Week 13	May 29– June 4	None	—	472	73
Week 14	June 5–11	California (6/7)	80		
		New York (6/7)	86		
		South Dakota (6/7)	10	648	100

Note: Table includes all primaries used to select or bind delegates, regardless of whether or not they included a presidential preference vote. In Illinois, New York, and Pennsylvania, some delegates were chosen by primary, others at a state convention; only the delegates chosen by primary are included in this table.

primaries. At the other end of the spectrum, the 1960 version of "Super Tuesday," when California and New York both held their primaries and about a quarter of the primary delegates were selected, did not take place until week 14, at the very *end* of the primary season.

Compare this now to the calendar the Republicans used in 1996, as shown in table 1.2. Once again, the process began in New Hampshire (some things haven't changed). But there was one primary held later that week, four more in the week after that, nine in week 3, seven in week 4, four in week 5, and three more, including California, in week 6. By the end of week 6, in short, the Republicans had held 29 primaries. Of all the delegates that were selected or bound by primary in 1996, fully 77 percent had been chosen after just six weeks. In 1960, by contrast, there were just three primaries held in the first six weeks, which together selected 14 percent of all the primary delegates.

For those seeking a more systematic measure of this trend, tables 1.3 and 1.4 present, for every presidential election year between 1952 and 2000, two summary indicators of how front-loaded the delegate selection process was: the num-

Table 1.2 Calendar of Republican Presidential Primaries in 1996

Week	Dates	States Holding Primaries (date)	Number of Delegates Selected	Cumulative Number Selected	Cumulative Percentage Selected
Week 1	Feb. 18–24	New Hampshire (2/20)	16		
		Delaware (2/24)	12	28	2
Week 2	Feb. 25–March 2	Arizona (2/27)	39		
		North Dakota (2/27)	18		
		South Dakota (2/27)	18		
		South Carolina (3/2)	37	140	9
Week 3	March 3–9	Colorado (3/5)	27		
		Connecticut (3/5)	27		
		Georgia (3/5)	42		
		Maine (3/5)	15		
		Maryland (3/5)	32		
		Massachusetts (3/5)	37		
		Rhode Island (3/5)	16		
		Vermont (3/5)	12		
		New York (3/7)	93	441	28
Week 4	March 10–16	Florida (3/12)	98		
		Louisiana (3/12)	9		
		Mississippi (3/12)	33		
		Oklahoma (3/12)	38		
		Oregon (3/12)	23		
		Tennessee (3/12)	38		
		Texas (3/12)	123	803	51
Week 5	March 17–23	Illinois (3/19)	59		
		Michigan (3/19)	57		
		Ohio (3/19)	67		
		Wisconsin (3/19)	36	1022	65
Week 6	March 24–30	California (3/26)	165		
		Nevada (3/26)	14		
		Washington (3/26)	18	1219	77
Week 7	March 31–April 6	None	—	1219	77
Week 8	April 7–13	None	—	1219	77
Week 9	April 14–20	None	—	1219	77
Week 10	April 21–27	Pennsylvania (4/23)	66	1285	81
Week 11	April 28–May 4	None	—	1285	81
Week 12	May 5–11	Dist. of Col. (5/7)	14		
		Indiana (5/7)	30		
		North Carolina (5/7)	58	1387	88
Week 13	May 12–18	Nebraska (5/14)	9		
		West Virginia (5/14)	18	1414	89
Week 14	May 19–25	Arkansas (5/21)	20	1434	91
Week 15	May 26–June 1	Idaho (5/28)	18		
		Kentucky (5/28)	26	1478	93
Week 16	June 2–8	Alabama (6/4)	40		
		New Jersey (6/4)	48		
		New Mexico (6/4)	18	1584	100

Note: Table includes all primaries used to select or bind delegates, regardless of whether or not they included a presidential preference vote. In Idaho, Illinois, Indiana, Louisiana, Nebraska, New York, Pennsylvania, and Washington, some delegates were chosen by primary, others by caucus; only the delegates chosen by primary are included in this table.

Table 1.3 Two Summary Measures of Front-Loading in the Democratic Primaries, 1952–2000

A. Number of Primaries Held during Each Week of the Primary Season

Week	1952	1956	1960	1964	1968	1972	1976	1980	1984	1988	1992	1996	2000
1	1	1	1	1	1	1	1	1	1	1	1	2	1
2	1	1	0	0	0	1	1	1	0	1	1	0	0
3	0	0	0	0	0	1	1	3	5	0	4	9	0
4	2	1	0	0	1	0	1	1	1	16	8	7	0
5	1	1	1	1	0	1	1	2	1	1	2	3	0
6	1	1	1	1	0	0	0	3	1	0	1	1	14
7	2	2	1	1	1	0	2	0	1	1	0	0	6
8	1	2	2	2	1	2	0	0	0	1	3	0	1
9	4	4	4	4	4	6	0	1	0	0	0	0	0
10	2	2	2	3	2	2	2	0	3	1	0	1	2
11	0	0	2	1	0	2	4	4	4	1	1	0	0
12	0	1	1	1	2	2	2	2	2	3	3	3	0
13	2	4	0	3	3	0	2	1	0	2	2	2	0
14	0		3		1	4	6	3	0	1	1	1	3
15	1				1	0	3	8	5	0	2	1	2
16						1	3			0	6	4	1
17										4			2
18													0
19													5

B. Cumulative Percentage of Delegates That Had Been Selected by the End of Each Week during the Primary Season

Week	1952	1956	1960	1964	1968	1972	1976	1980	1984	1988	1992	1996	2000
1	1	1	2	1	2	1	1	1	1	1	1	1	1
2	6	6	2	1	2	5	5	6	1	1	1	1	1
3	6	6	2	1	2	14	9	14	18	1	9	26	1
4	13	10	2	1	8	14	17	22	27	42	31	46	1
5	22	18	6	6	8	17	19	36	29	49	41	60	1
6	27	24	14	11	8	17	19	43	41	49	43	74	47
7	53	39	20	18	15	17	35	43	49	51	43	74	65
8	60	44	35	33	22	30	35	43	49	54	56	74	71
9	80	64	56	53	43	50	35	51	49	54	56	74	71
10	86	68	62	61	49	53	47	51	56	63	56	81	79
11	86	68	68	66	49	62	55	61	74	70	62	81	79
12	86	72	73	71	58	65	57	64	77	79	68	87	79
13	99	100	73	100	84	65	66	66	77	81	70	89	79
14	99		100		89	86	73	70	77	83	72	91	86
15	100				100	86	76	100	100	83	75	92	88
16						100	100			83	100	100	89
17										100			92
18													92
19													100

Table 1.4 Two Summary Measures of Front–Loading in the Republican Primaries, 1952–2000

A. Number of Primaries Held during Each Week of the Primary Season

Week	1952	1956	1960	1964	1968	1972	1976	1980	1984	1988	1992	1996	2000
1	1	1	1	1	1	1	1	1	1	1	1	2	1
2	1	1	0	0	0	1	1	2	0	1	1	4	1
3	0	0	0	0	0	1	1	3	5	1	4	9	1
4	2	1	0	0	1	0	1	1	1	15	8	7	2
5	1	1	1	1	0	1	1	2	1	1	2	4	2
6	1	1	1	1	0	0	0	3	2	0	1	3	13
7	2	2	1	1	1	0	2	0	1	1	0	0	6
8	1	1	2	2	1	2	0	0	0	1	4	0	1
9	1	4	3	3	3	5	0	1	0	0	0	0	0
10	2	2	2	3	2	2	2	1	4	1	0	1	2
11	0	0	1	1	0	2	4	4	4	1	1	0	0
12	0	1	1	1	2	2	2	2	2	3	3	3	0
13	2	4	0	3	3	0	2	2	1	2	2	2	0
14			3		1	4	6	3	0	1	2	1	3
15					1	0	2	8	5	1	3	2	2
16					1	3	3		1	0	5	3	1
17										3	1		3
18										1			0
19													4

B. Cumulative Percentage of Delegates That Had Been Selected by the End of Each Week during the Primary Season

Week	1952	1956	1960	1964	1968	1972	1976	1980	1984	1988	1992	1996	2000
1	3	2	2	2	1	2	1	1	2	1	1	2	1
2	8	7	2	2	1	7	4	6	2	3	2	9	2
3	8	7	2	2	1	14	9	14	18	5	12	28	4
4	17	11	2	2	7	14	15	20	24	49	36	51	9
5	26	19	8	7	7	17	19	30	26	54	44	65	13
6	33	25	16	15	7	17	19	37	37	54	46	77	49
7	61	40	23	22	16	17	30	37	43	56	46	77	68
8	68	41	40	36	22	28	30	37	43	59	56	77	72
9	78	61	56	53	38	50	30	42	43	59	56	77	72
10	84	67	63	61	44	55	42	48	58	65	56	81	78
11	84	67	66	64	44	64	52	57	72	70	60	81	78
12	84	71	71	70	53	68	55	61	75	78	66	88	78
13	100	100	71	100	77	68	64	68	77	80	67	89	78
14			100		86	90	75	72	77	82	71	91	84
15					100	90	78	100	99	83	75	93	86
16					100	100	100		100	83	99	100	87
17										99	100		92
18										100			92
19													100

ber of primaries that were held during each week of the primary season; and the cumulative percentage of delegates that had been selected by the end of each week. As these figures show, in the years between 1952 and 1968, the system was actually quite *back-loaded*. The primary season always began slowly, with a small number of primaries in March and, usually, a few weeks in which there were no primaries at all. Most presidential primaries took place during a span of about seven weeks stretching from late April through early June.

And then, in a rather short period of time during the late 1960s and the early 1970s, the rules of the presidential nomination process were almost entirely rewritten. The revolution began on August 27, 1968, when the Democrats, on the second day of their national convention, narrowly approved a vaguely-worded resolution that, as ultimately interpreted, endowed a commission set up by another resolution with a quite broad mandate to rewrite the party's delegate selection rules. By 1972, that commission had achieved an almost complete transformation of the basic ground rules of the presidential selection process. Byron Shafer, who wrote an award-winning history of that commission, has called it "the greatest systematic change in presidential nominating procedures in all of American history."[4] One of the few aspects of the nomination process that the Democrats' commission did not attempt to refashion was campaign finance. But two years later, Congress filled the void, passing legislation in 1974 that radically altered the ways in which presidential campaigns could raise and spend money. The U.S. Supreme Court would later call this act "by far the most comprehensive reform legislation ever passed by Congress concerning the election of the President, Vice-President, and members of Congress."[5]

The new rules had a number of important and immediate effects on the presidential selection process.[6] But as can be seen in tables 1.3 and 1.4, front-loading actually took a while to get going. In the first few elections of the new era, there was a significant increase in the *number* of primaries, but the clustering or pacing of these primaries (which is what front-loading measures) changed rather modestly. It was, in fact, not until the early 1980s that the problem first started to attract the attention of party officials, campaign strategists, or reporters. Front-loading took a huge leap forward in 1988, driven by the formation of the southern "Super Tuesday," when sixteen states held their primaries on a single day in early March. Because Super Tuesday did not appear to meet its organizers' major objectives, including greater attention to the South and the nomination of a more moderate Democratic candidate, in 1992 some of these states moved to different, generally later dates. This left the 1992 calendar slightly less front-loaded than the 1988 calendar—but the retreat turned out to be temporary. By early in the 1996 election cycle, it was clear that front-loading would soar to unprecedented heights, this time promoted by California's decision to move its primary from its traditional date in early June to the final Tuesday in March. The result, as we have seen, was a calendar that seemed just a few steps short of a national primary, with 29 primaries held in the first six weeks.

In the early stages of the 2000 election cycle, it appeared that front-loading would get significantly worse. Again, California was an important part of the story. After finding that a late March primary did not greatly increase its role in the presidential nomination process (the 1996 Republican race was effectively settled several weeks earlier), in 1998 California took the logical next step, moving its primary to the *first* Tuesday in March, the earliest date permitted under Democratic party rules. It was joined there by ten other states, including New York, Ohio, and every New England state except New Hampshire, in an event variously dubbed "Titanic Tuesday" and the "Bicoastal Blowout." There were three other primaries scheduled for later that week and then, on the second Tuesday in March, six southern and border states would go to the polls, including both Texas and Florida.

Yet, one last-minute decision had the effect of significantly opening up the beginning of the 2000 delegate selection calendar and making it, by our measures, actually somewhat *less* front-loaded than the calendars of 1988, 1992, and 1996. When California moved its primary to March 7, most observers assumed that the New Hampshire primary would take place in the final week or two of February. (In 1996, for example, it had been held on February 20.) But after a bit of preliminary maneuvering, in late September, 1999, New Hampshire finally announced that it would hold its first-in-the-nation primary on February 1. Though its significance was not immediately appreciated, New Hampshire's decision imparted a quite different dynamic to the beginning of the 2000 delegate selection season. Instead of a situation in which, as the *New York Times* put it, "candidates coming out of the New Hampshire race in February will *immediately* be forced into a massive, bicoastal campaign," now, suddenly, five weeks separated the New Hampshire primary and the California–New York extravaganza.[7]

The parties filled these five weeks in different ways. Since Democratic party rules forbid any states except Iowa and New Hampshire from holding a delegate selection event before the first Tuesday in March, the five-week gap remained just that: not a single Democratic primary or caucus took place during this period.[8] Republican national rules were more permissive, so a handful of states jumped into the void, ultimately creating a calendar that had at least some pretensions to a gradual beginning. In the end, there was only one Republican primary in each of the two weeks immediately after New Hampshire, and two each in the two weeks after that. And most of these primaries took place in small or medium-sized states.

As we write this chapter, in early 2003, it is impossible to say with any assurance just what the nomination calendar for the 2004 election cycle will look like. Many of the more important scheduling decisions will not be made until mid- or even late 2003. But one important decision, taken by the Rules and Bylaws Committee of the Democratic National Committee in November, 2001, strongly suggests that the 2004 calendar, in both parties, will be significantly *more* front-loaded than the one used in 2000.[9]

In 2000, as we have just noted, there was an important disjunction between what the Democratic and Republican parties' national rules said about the scheduling of primaries and caucuses. Democratic rules specified that, except for Iowa and New Hampshire, no state could hold a caucus or primary before the first Tuesday in *March*. Republican rules prohibited states from holding a caucus or primary before the first Monday in *February*. The result was that, between February 1 and March 7, there were six Republican primaries and two Republican caucuses—but not a single, binding Democratic event of any kind. In the opinion of many Democrats, this "ceded the spotlight to the Republicans for an entire month" and thus put their party at a "competitive disadvantage."[10] Hence, in formulating their delegate selection rules for the 2004 election, the Democrats moved the start of their window up a month to match that of the Republicans.

At a minimum, this decision will almost certainly increase the level of front-loading in the Democratic calendar. In 2000, the six states that held Republican primaries between February 1 and March 7 either held no Democratic primary or a purely advisory one (i.e., one that played no role in delegate selection). In 2004, any states in this position will very likely hold binding Democratic primaries at the same time as the Republican ones.[11] More importantly, a lot of states were discouraged from holding their primaries in February because of the prohibition in the Democratic rules. The state of California, in particular, was determined in 2000 to vote at the earliest feasible date, before either party's race was settled. Yet, had they tried scheduling their primary on February 8, the week after New Hampshire, they would have been faced with the prospect of either holding a second state-wide primary for Democrats one month later or forcing state Democrats to select their delegates through a separate, caucus procedure. As a result, California set its 2000 primary for March 7, the earliest date allowable under *both* parties' rules; ten other states, including New York, made the same calculation. In 2004, it is difficult to believe that many of these states will not try to move their primaries up a few weeks. James Roosevelt, the cochair of the Democratic rules committee, offered an especially gloomy prognosis: "My speculation is that more and more states will move to the earliest date the parties allow. We are moving toward a de facto national primary."[12]

EXPLAINING FRONT-LOADING

Why has the shape of the delegate selection calendar changed so dramatically over the last three decades? Why did so many states try to move their primaries and caucuses to earlier dates in the nomination season? The single, proximate cause that lies behind most recent state scheduling decisions is a phenomenon best described as "New Hampshire envy." In simple terms, New Hampshire envy is the perception that New Hampshire, because it holds the first primary in the nation, derives a substantial array of political and economic benefits from that position and plays a highly significant role in determining who ultimately wins the major-party presidential nominations, despite the fact that it is a very small state and is, in important ways, not particularly representative of the country as a whole. As more and more states became aware of all the advantages accruing to New Hampshire—and after 1976, Iowa as well—they, too, naturally came to believe that it would be to their benefit if they could either vote on the same day as New Hampshire or, if that wasn't possible, at least schedule their primary or caucus somewhere near the start of the delegate selection calendar.

The benefits that New Hampshire and Iowa derive from their privileged position in the presidential selection process fall into five principal categories:

1. *Press Coverage.* From the moment that political scientists first began to apply content analysis to media coverage of the presidential nomination process, one of their first and most consistent findings has been the extent to which that coverage is dominated by New Hampshire and Iowa. In one of the best studies of this kind, Michael Robinson and Margaret Sheehan counted up the number of stories devoted to a particular primary or caucus that were run on the CBS Evening News and the United Press International (UPI) wire service between January 1 and June 6, 1980. As shown in table 1.5, in both outlets Iowa and New Hampshire each received about 14 percent of the total coverage, well ahead of every other state, including such big primary states as Illinois, Pennsylvania, California, and New York.[13]

2. *Attention from the Candidates.* Whether as cause or as effect of this coverage, New Hampshire and Iowa also receive a lot more attention from the candidates than other states do. The campaigns, for example, spend a lot more money in these two states than they do almost anywhere else. The personal campaigning of the candidates is also concentrated to an extraordinary degree in Iowa and New Hampshire, particularly during the so-called invisible primary period that precedes the formal delegate selection season.

3. *Influence on the Nomination Race.* All this press coverage, not surprisingly, has an effect on public opinion. At a time when almost all delegates are selected by ordinary voters participating in primaries and caucuses, the results in New Hampshire and Iowa can dramatically reshape the standings in a contested nomination race. Candidates who win or do "better than expected" in these two states generally see a large increase in their support across the country; candidates who lose frequently see their stock tumble. When John McCain won the New Hampshire primary in 2000, the number of Republicans who supported him for their party's nomination immediately jumped from 15 percent to 34 percent in the national polls.

4. *Economic Benefits.* Holding the first caucus and the first primary also brings a host of economic benefits to Iowa and New Hampshire. Besides all the candidate campaign spending mentioned above, there is the far larger

amount of money spent by reporters and media organizations, plus a great deal of free publicity for the states' resorts, tourist attractions, and industries. A recent report by the Library and Archives of New Hampshire's Political Tradition estimates the total economic impact of the 2000 primary on that state's economy to be $264 million.[14]

5. *Special Policy Concessions.* Finally, though it is difficult to quantify, it seems clear that both Iowa and New Hampshire receive a diverse array of what might be called "special policy concessions" as a result of their privileged positions in the presidential nomination process. As candidates spend time in these two states and talk to their voters and political leaders, they are made especially sensitive to each state's problems and concerns. In a similar vein, when incumbent presidents face contested races for renomination, they generally shower Iowa and New Hampshire with all sorts of discretionary funds and favorable bureaucratic decisions.[15]

There is little doubt, then, that Iowa and New Hampshire derive an impressive set of advantages from being the *first* caucus and the *first* primary. But what about states that are merely *early*? If a state knows that it will not be the very first in line, does it matter if it votes or caucuses in, say, mid-March rather than mid-May?

The answer is that early states do, on the whole, benefit from moving to the front. Consider, for example, how much attention the candidates pay to each state. The best way of quantifying how much campaigning occurs in each state is to follow the money. Since 1974, the Federal Election Commission has compiled data on the total amount of money the presidential candidates have spent in all fifty states and the District of Columbia. For each contested nomination race between 1980 and 1988, we have used these figures as the dependent variables for a series of regression equations. There were five independent variables in each equation, the most important of which for our purposes was the date on which the state held its primary or caucus, measured as the total number of days that had passed since the first delegate selection event. (The other four variables were the number of delegates each state had, whether it used a primary or caucus to select its delegates, and separate dummy variables for Iowa and New Hampshire.) Table 1.6 shows the results for the Democratic and Republican nomination races of 1980 (similar results were obtained for the Democratic contest in 1984 and both the Democratic and Republican races of 1988).

The date coefficient was large and statistically significant in every one of these equations. Even with the singular effects of Iowa and New Hampshire taken out of the picture, moving up the date of a primary or caucus paid off at a rate between $4,000 and $12,000 per day. In 1980, a state that moved its primary up by one month (30 days) could expect that total candidate spending, in both parties combined, would increase by about $486,000. A state that moved from early June to mid-March could expect about $1,360,000 in additional spending. To

Table 1.5 Media Coverage of the 1980 Presidential Primaries and Caucuses, by State

CBS Evening News

	Number of News Seconds	Percentage of the Total	Seconds per Delegate[a]
Iowa	2940	14	33.8
New Hampshire	2815	14	68.7
Illinois	2000	10	7.1
Pennsylvania	1950	9	7.3
New York	1515	7	3.7
Massachusetts	1450	7	9.5
California	1205	6	2.5
Wisconsin	1165	6	10.7
Ohio	915	4	3.8
Maine	795	4	18.5

UPI

	Number of Column Inches	Percentage of the Total	Inches per Delegate[a]
New Hampshire	774	15	18.9
Iowa	679	13	7.8
Pennsylvania	366	7	1.4
Illinois	349	7	1.2
Michigan	342	7	1.5
New York	307	6	0.8
Wisconsin	271	5	2.5
California	183	4	0.4
South Carolina	172	3	2.8
Massachusetts	160	3	1.0

[a] Based on the total number of delegates each state sent to both the Democratic and Republican national conventions.

Source: Michael J. Robinson and Margaret A. Sheehan, *Over the Wire and On TV: CBS and UPI in Campaign '80* (New York: Russell Sage Foundation, 1983), 176–77.

put these figures in perspective, the median spending per state in 1980 was just $291,000. In a similar way, a second series of regression equations that examined how much coverage each state received on the national television evening news programs found that coverage was clearly correlated with a state's position in the campaign calendar. Later states suffered in comparison to earlier states.[16]

As a general matter, then, front-loading occurs because states believe—correctly—that holding their primaries and caucuses near the start of the delegate selection season provides them with important benefits, such as increased attention from the candidates and increased press coverage. Yet, this conclusion

Table 1.6 Effect of Primary or Caucus Date on Total Campaign Spending per State in the 1980 Nomination Races

A. 1980 Democratic Race

Variable	Coefficient	Standard Error
Date of primary or caucus	− 4,500	968***
Number of delegates	3,987	461***
Primary states	214,701	69,288**
Iowa	535,504	216,555**
New Hampshire	575,920	216,700**
Constant	236,380	83,754

$R^2 = .76$
Adj. $R^2 = .73$
$N = 51$
Median spending per state = $88,368

B. 1980 Republican Race

Variable	Coefficient	Standard Error
Date of primary or caucus	− 11,708	2,491***
Number of delegates	9,612	2,624***
Primary states	723,710	230,587**
Iowa	782,178	571,046
New Hampshire	177,389	553,745
Constant	615,023	254,334

$R^2 = .58$
Adj. $R^2 = .52$
$N = 42$
Median spending per state = $202,998

* $p < .05$
** $p < .01$
*** $p < .001$
Note: The dependent variable in both equations is the total amount of money spent in each state by all candidates for that party's presidential nomination who filed state spending reports with the Federal Election Commission.

is plainly not a complete explanation of the front-loading phenomenon. In particular, New Hampshire envy, by itself, fails to explain why front-loading occurred *when* it did. New Hampshire, after all, has been holding the first primary in the nation since at least 1952.[17] Yet, as we have just seen, front-loading did not begin to emerge as a major trend until the early 1980s. What was it, then, that finally set front-loading in motion?

The answer, we believe, was the wholesale restructuring of the rules of presidential politics that took place in the early and mid-1970s. The new rules changed the presidential nomination process in a variety of ways; but three such changes deserve special attention here, for each helped upset the equilibrium that had held the old nomination calendar in balance, eliminating most of the incentives that had once existed for holding late primaries and caucuses and dramatically increasing the importance of going early.

First, unlike the system that preceded it, the reformed nomination process tended to select very few delegates who were uncommitted and thus free to make their choice at the convention. The vast majority of delegates today are selected in ways that explicitly commit them to vote for a particular candidate. In contested nomination races held between 1952 and 1968, 35 percent of the delegates, on average, were still uncommitted on the weekend before the convention. In the races since 1980, only 6 percent of the delegates were selected on an uncommitted basis.[18]

Second, the new rules, particularly the campaign finance laws, have had the effect of forcing a large proportion of the candidates to withdraw from the race just days or weeks after the delegate selection process formally begins. In the pre-reform period, candidates who got into the race generally stayed in the race—at least to the end of the primary season, usually all the way up to the actual convention balloting. Beginning in about 1976, however, one starts to see the emergence of a quite different pattern. Candidates who did poorly in one or two early contests—in particular, the Iowa caucuses and the New Hampshire primary—were withdrawing from the field just days after the race had formally commenced. In 1984, for example, there were eight major candidates for the Democratic presidential nomination. By the middle of March, less than three weeks after New Hampshire, five of the eight were already out of the race. In 1988, every one of George Bush's Republican opponents except Pat Robertson had dropped out by the end of March. In 1992, three of five Democratic contenders had withdrawn by the end of the third week in March.

With more and more delegates being selected on a committed basis, and with fewer candidates still in the race to divide up these committed delegates, a third change was almost inevitable: one of the presidential candidates would clinch the nomination well before the convention opened. Under the old rules, the leading candidate at the end of the primaries had generally accumulated only about 40–70 percent of the number of delegates he needed to win the nomination. Even on the eve of the convention, the eventual winner had usually not yet won enough commitments to put him over the top. Contemporary nomination contests clearly move to a different dynamic. In every contested nomination race since 1980, one candidate has secured a majority of the delegates by the final day of the primary season. While the convention still serves a number of functions—putting together the platform, reuniting the party, selling the candidate to a national television audience—it does not play any real role in choosing the party standard bearer.

Up through 1968, in short, a state that wanted to "get something" out of the presidential nomination race—whether that something was patronage, attention from the campaigns and the media, or the nomination of a particular candidate—could secure these benefits from the bargaining and maneuvering that came *after* the primaries. And thus, late-voting states still had an important role in the process. The new nomination rules, by contrast, eliminated this kind of post-primary bargaining. Everything of significance, from the states' perspective, took place during the increasingly brief period in which the nomination was being decided. And the only way to have an effective voice in that decision was to move to the front of the calendar.

THE CONSEQUENCES OF FRONT-LOADING: EFFECTS ON VOTER LEARNING AND DECISION-MAKING

Should anyone except the candidates and their campaign managers care about front-loading? What effects does it have on the dynamics of the presidential nomination process?

The principal problem with front-loading is that it greatly accelerates the voters' decision process, and thus makes the whole system less deliberative, less rational, less flexible, and more chaotic. It will probably strike some readers as strange to see the American presidential nomination process described as reaching a decision too *quickly*. This is, after all, a system in which almost every serious presidential aspirant except an incumbent president must announce his or her candidacy in the late winter or early spring of the year *before* the election. (In fact, most contenders have been laying the groundwork for their campaign for months or even years prior to their official announcement.)

The problem is that too much of this campaigning occurs while none of the voters are paying attention—and too little when they finally start to become interested. To get a better sense of what the voters know about presidential candidates and when and how much they learn, consider the data in table 1.7. Over the last several election cycles, CBS News and the *New York Times* have periodically asked national samples of registered voters if their opinion of each of the major presidential contenders was "favorable, not favorable, undecided" or if they hadn't "heard enough about [the candidate] yet to have an opinion." Table 1.7 shows the results for the 1992 and 1996 election cycles.[19]

A number of significant conclusions emerge from these data. First, when the invisible primary begins—usually several months after the midterm elections— most presidential candidates are almost entirely unknown to most of the potential electorate. This statement applies not only to those obscure non-entities with little or no previous governmental experience who somehow see fit to run for president; it is also true of people with distinguished careers as governors or senators, whom informed observers universally regarded as serious and legitimate candidates for the White House. In October, 1991, more than 75 percent of all

Table 1.7 Voter Knowledge of the Presidential Candidates during the Invisible Primary and Primary Seasons

"Is your opinion of _____ favorable, not favorable, undecided, or haven't you heard enough about _____ yet to have an opinion?"

1992 Democratic Nomination Race

	Favorable	Not Favorable	Undecided	Haven't Heard Enough
Bill Clinton				
Oct. 15–18, 1991	7%	5%	8%	80%
Jan. 6–8, 1992	11	6	14	69
Feb. 19–20	24	26	30	19
Feb. 26–March 1	20	31	30	18
March 26–29	24	41	27	8
April 20–23	26	40	28	6
Jerry Brown				
Oct. 15–18, 1991	11	21	15	51
Jan. 6–8, 1992	9	26	12	52
Feb. 19–20	8	28	22	41
Feb. 26–March 1	8	27	21	41
March 26–29	18	31	27	24
April 20–23	15	47	20	18
Paul Tsongas				
Oct. 15–18, 1991	6	7	8	78
Jan. 6–8, 1992	6	10	11	73
Feb. 19–20	28	11	25	36
Feb. 26–March 1	25	18	25	31
March 26–29	28	21	23	26
April 20–23	25	17	26	32
Bob Kerrey				
Oct. 15–18, 1991	8	4	11	77
Jan. 6–8, 1992	7	7	17	69
Feb. 19–20	10	12	25	53
Feb. 26–March 1	11	16	26	46
Tom Harkin				
Oct. 15–18, 1991	8	5	8	78
Jan. 6–8, 1992	5	7	14	74
Feb. 19–20	7	15	21	57
Feb. 26–March 1	7	20	23	50

1996 Republican Nomination Race

	Favorable	Not Favorable	Undecided	Haven't Heard Enough
Bob Dole				
Feb. 22–25, 1995	40%	23%	22%	15%
Aug. 5–9	30	24	24	21
Oct. 22–25	26	28	25	20
Dec. 9–11	25	29	21	24
Jan. 18–20, 1996	24	35	22	18
Feb. 22–24	23	42	24	10
March 10–11	25	35	23	17
Pat Buchanan				
Feb. 22–25, 1995	10	28	28	34
Aug. 5–9	11	28	24	36
Oct. 22–25	12	33	22	32
Dec. 9–11	11	40	24	24
Jan. 18–20, 1996	11	44	23	22
Feb. 22–24	19	48	22	10
March 10–11	12	51	18	18
Lamar Alexander				
Feb. 22–25, 1995	4	3	8	84
Aug. 5–9	4	4	5	85
Oct. 22–25	5	8	10	76
Dec. 9–11	6	10	10	74
Jan. 18–20, 1996	5	9	13	71
Feb. 22–24	14	18	22	45
Phil Gramm				
Feb. 22–25, 1995	14	13	20	52
Aug. 5–9	12	17	19	52
Oct. 22–25	13	22	19	45
Dec. 9–11	12	25	20	43
Jan. 18–20, 1996	13	26	24	37
Richard Lugar				
Aug. 5–9, 1995	5	4	10	79
Oct. 22–25	7	6	12	74
Jan. 18–20, 1996	5	10	15	69
Steve Forbes				
Oct. 22–25, 1995	8	9	14	67
Dec. 9–11	7	10	16	67
Jan. 18–20, 1996	14	16	23	46
Feb. 22–24	10	37	25	28
March 10–11	14	31	22	33

Source: All polls conducted by CBS/*New York Times*.

registered voters openly admitted that they did not know enough about Bill Clinton, Paul Tsongas, Bob Kerrey, or Tom Harkin to provide an evaluation of them; another 10 percent said they were "undecided." Jerry Brown, who had run for president in two previous elections and served as governor of the nation's largest state, was somewhat better known. Yet, even in his case, 51 percent of those surveyed said they hadn't heard enough about him to form an opinion. Similarly, as of August, 1995, about 80 percent of the public had heard next to nothing about Lamar Alexander and Richard Lugar; 52 percent drew a blank on Phil Gramm. Pat Buchanan, who had run for president four years earlier and received considerable exposure as a television commentator, was unknown to about a third of the public—and another 28 percent said they were undecided about him. Only in the case of Bob Dole, Senate majority leader and two-time presidential candidate, could a majority of registered voters actually give him a rating (favorable or unfavorable).

Second, the general public learns remarkably little during the invisible primary. They do learn *something*: in almost every case, the number saying that they haven't heard enough about a candidate does decline over time. But it declines very slowly. In February, 1995, 84 percent of the CBS/*Times* sample said they hadn't heard much about Lamar Alexander. In January, 1996, after eleven months of almost constant campaigning, 71 percent still said they hadn't heard enough about Alexander to form an opinion about him. The trend is similar for Gramm, Buchanan, and Lugar—and for Brown, Harkin, Kerrey, and Tsongas in 1992. In every case, public familiarity with the candidate grew at the rate of about 1 percent per month. Of all the candidates shown in table 1.7, only Bill Clinton in 1992 and Steve Forbes in 1996 were able to get their names out to a somewhat larger segment of the electorate during the invisible primary.

When the caucus and primary season finally begins, the pace of voter learning dramatically accelerates. From mid-January to mid-February, every candidate in table 1.7 succeeded in making himself known to a substantially larger segment of the potential electorate. Yet, given the low levels of information from which the public starts, and the highly compressed schedule of primaries that results from front-loading, this process of educating the public, it appears, never gets all that far along. Many major presidential candidates—including, in table 1.7, Tom Harkin, Bob Kerrey, and Lamar Alexander—exit the race with almost half of all registered voters still saying that they haven't heard enough about them to form an opinion.

How might this situation have changed if these nomination races had not come to an end so quickly? To answer this question, we need to look at data from races that did *not* end a few weeks after New Hampshire and on candidates who, although not initially well-known, stayed in the race to the bitter end. Table 1.8 shows the public's assessment of two such candidates: Gary Hart in 1984 and Michael Dukakis in 1988. What is noteworthy about these results is how much voter learning occurred *after* the first round of primaries and caucuses. As of

Table 1.8 The Growth of Voter Familiarity with Gary Hart in 1984 and Michael Dukakis in 1988

	Favorable	Not Favorable	Undecided	Haven't Heard Enough
Gary Hart				
Jan. 14–21, 1984	6%	10%	13%	71%
Feb. 21–25	15	15	19	50
March 5–8	37	7	19	36
March 21–24	41	12	19	28
April 23–26	36	19	26	18
June 23–28	39	19	23	18
Michael Dukakis				
May 5–6, 1987	12	4	13	70
Oct. 18–22	21	9	14	56
Nov. 20–24	14	8	23	55
Jan. 17–21, 1988	17	6	22	54
Feb. 17–21	34	9	18	39
March 19–22	39	12	22	25
May 9–12	49	7	22	22
July 5–8	40	6	36	15

Note: Figures for Hart are based on all registered voters; figures for Dukakis are based on registered voters who identify with the Democratic party.

Source: All polls conducted by CBS/New York Times.

early March, 1984, a week after Hart's breakthrough victory in New Hampshire—*when Hart was actually leading Mondale in many national polls*—fully 36 percent of all registered voters still said they hadn't heard enough about Hart to form an opinion about him. Not until late April did this figure fall below 20 percent. Similarly with Dukakis: In a poll conducted immediately after the New Hampshire primary, Dukakis had a clear lead over the rest of the Democratic field—yet 39 percent of all Democratic registered voters said they didn't know enough about the Massachusetts governor to express an opinion about him. In early May, when Dukakis had all but clinched his party's nomination, 22 percent still said they hadn't heard very much about him.

Thus far, our analysis of voter learning has been limited to questions that ask if the voters know enough about the candidates to "have an opinion" about them. But this is, to say the least, a very low standard against which to evaluate voter knowledge. Undoubtedly, many of those who said they did have a favorable or unfavorable opinion of a particular candidate did so on the basis of only the most superficial impressions, without much solid information about the candidate's policies, past record, or personal abilities. How much do the voters know about these more substantive matters—and when do they learn it?

The best available answer to these last two questions comes from an analysis of the 1984 Democratic nomination race conducted by Henry Brady and Richard

Johnston, that made use of a special national survey that interviewed about 75 people every week throughout the election year.[20] At one level, Brady and Johnston found that, very soon after Hart's victory in New Hampshire, most survey respondents were willing to provide answers when asked about Hart's positions on the issues or his rating on various personal traits, such as intelligence, compassion, and leadership. On closer inspection, however, there was considerable reason to doubt how much the public really knew about Hart. On the one hand, Brady and Johnston found that evaluations of Hart, when compared with those given to better-known figures such as Reagan and Mondale, were quite *unstable*, varying a good deal from week to week depending on the latest news reports or recent events in the campaign. Public assessments of Hart were also, in this early period, relatively *undifferentiated*. Unlike Reagan and Mondale, who were seen as strong on some personal traits and weak on others, most respondents tended to give Hart uniformly good or bad ratings, no matter what specific trait or ability was being asked about.

As the campaign progressed, evaluations of Hart became more solidly grounded. That is to say, the public's view of him became both more stable and more differentiated. But the progress on both dimensions was fairly slow. Specifically, Brady and Johnston estimate that it would have taken 20 weeks for Hart's image to become as stable as Mondale's, and 30 weeks for the public to develop as differentiated an image of Hart as they held about Mondale. The problem, of course, was that the entire 1984 delegate selection season lasted just 16 weeks.

In the end, Brady and Johnston argued that one of the major weaknesses of the presidential nomination process as it existed in 1984 was that it forced primary voters to register their judgments too quickly, before they knew very much about all of the major candidates. But compared to more recent nomination races, the 1984 contest actually proceeded at a quite slow and leisurely pace. The battle between Hart and Mondale lasted for about three and a half months (from the middle of February to the first week in June). By contrast, the competitive phase of the 1996 Republican race took less than one month. In 2000, the first showdown between Bush and McCain came in New Hampshire, on February 1. On March 9, a little more than five weeks later, McCain announced his withdrawal.

In a front-loaded system, in short, voters are forced to reach a final decision about their party's next presidential nominee in a remarkably short period of time. The evidence strongly suggests that they do so on the basis of fairly shallow and superficial knowledge about many of the top candidates—and no knowledge at all about some major contenders. Equally important, front-loading makes it all but impossible for the voters to reconsider their initial judgment if new information becomes available. In 1984, many Democrats who jumped on the Hart bandwagon moved back to Mondale once they had learned more about Hart's convoluted personal history and the specific kinds of policies he favored. In 1996, any second thoughts that Republican voters entertained about Bob Dole as he fell further and further behind Bill Clinton in the polls came after Dole had already locked up the nomination.

POOR QUALITY CAMPAIGNS

Besides greatly compressing the effective decision-making period, front-loading also affects the quality of the campaign and thus further complicates the voters' task. During the crucial weeks immediately after New Hampshire, when most primaries are being held and the race is being decided, the campaign, according to most observers, becomes increasingly superficial and non-substantive.

Though it is unrealistic to expect every primary state to get the kind of sustained attention and intensive, face-to-face campaigning that occurs in Iowa and New Hampshire, it is not unreasonable—it actually occurred, to a fair extent, in 1976, 1980, and 1984—for the candidates to be able to campaign in just one or two states per week. If not exactly a model of deliberative democracy, a campaign of this nature at least allows the candidates some opportunity to address special state or regional concerns, hold rallies, speeches, and debates in front of local audiences, be interviewed on local television, and so on. But such activities become considerably more difficult if the candidates are required to campaign in five or eight states in a single week. The role of campaign volunteers also declines as the primary schedule becomes more compressed.[21]

Concerns of this sort first became widespread in the campaign that preceded Super Tuesday in 1988. When a group of southern state legislators first launched the effort to organize a southern regional primary, one of its principal objectives was to force the major presidential candidates to address distinctively southern issues and interests. So far as we can tell, no one seems to believe that it actually accomplished this goal. The weeks immediately preceding Super Tuesday were frequently described as a "tarmac campaign," in which the candidates flew frenetically from one airport to another, rarely venturing beyond the parking toll gates—and thus rarely making contact with real people and their concerns.

In 2000, the campaign that preceded the March 7 extravaganza, when eleven states held their primaries, was described this way:

> The candidates are largely bypassing the small and medium-sized states and concentrating on the larger states, such as New York and California, that have the most delegates. Even there, some critics charge that the candidates don't linger long enough to create much of an impression on voters, or generate substantive debate on issues. In place of the candidates, voters in some states are seeing only their surrogates. . . . And without the candidates, voters can't press them on local issues important to them.[22]

A far-flung, multistate campaign also places a severe strain on the media who cover the candidates. As *Newsday* editor Noel Rubinton noted on the morning of March 7, 2000: "The press is struggling mightily. . . . This year's primary campaign has demanded incredible speed and juggling on the part of the press. But these same attributes are often at odds with quality reporting and constructive political discourse. . . . [Front-loading] guaranteed that the race would be a travel marathon and scheduling meltdown for the candidates, the media, and ultimately the voters."[23]

EFFECTS ON CANDIDATE CHOICE 1:
LOCKING IN THE FRONT-RUNNER

Besides making the nomination process more chaotic and less well-informed, it is widely alleged that front-loading also has important consequences for the types of candidates who are ultimately nominated. Indeed, since front-loading first became a significant issue in the mid-1980s, there have actually been two, quite different theories as to what type of candidate was likely to benefit from the new delegate selection calendar.

The more popular of these two theories, especially over the last several election cycles, has been that front-loading works to the advantage of the front-runner. With so many primaries and caucuses jammed together, the argument goes, the only kind of candidate who can run effectively—who can campaign in five or ten different states every week—is someone who is already well-known and well-financed. Someone who is not a first-tier candidate—even though he may be quite experienced and have a solid base of support within the party—cannot participate in what is, for all practical purposes, a national campaign.

If the results of the last several nomination races do not actually *prove* this theory, they are, at the very least, clearly consonant with its basic prediction. When the new nomination rules first went into operation in the early 1970s, one of the first and most widely-accepted conclusions about the new system was that it greatly advantaged the candidacies of outsiders, insurgents, and other non–front-runners. As political scientist Jeanne Kirkpatrick put it in 1979, "In the past only a predictable number of people who established positions of leadership within the party could win. . . . The moral of the Carter and McGovern experiences is that anyone can win."[24]

Though the image of a wide-open nomination process still persists in some quarters,[25] the record speaks strongly to the contrary. While Kirkpatrick's statement was an accurate description of how the process seemed to work in the 1970s, Jimmy Carter was, as it turned out, the last real long-shot candidate to win a presidential nomination. Without much fanfare, a system once thought to be quite favorable to outsiders and insurgents has evolved into one that almost invariably confers the presidential nomination on the pre-election front-runner.

Consider, in particular, the data in table 1.9. There, we use two criteria to identify the front-runner in each contested nomination race since 1972: who was leading in the last national poll of party identifiers conducted before the Iowa caucuses; and who had raised the most money in the year before the election. The moral of table 1.9 is clear: whatever may have happened back in the 1970s, over the last two decades the American presidential nomination process has not been notably kind to the ambitions of long-shots and outsider candidates. Of all the candidates who have been nominated since 1980, *every one* of them can plausibly be regarded as, if not *the* front-runner, at least as one of the top-tier candidates. In eight of ten cases, one candidate was leading in both the pre-election polls and the fund-raising derby—and in *every* such case, that candidate went on to win his party's presidential nomination.

We are not claiming, we want to emphasize, that front-loading is solely responsible for the increased success rate enjoyed by recent front-runners. A number of other factors are clearly at work.[26] But if the task confronting long-shot presidential candidates has never been easy, front-loading makes their lives even more difficult, in at least two major ways.

1. *Front-loading makes it more difficult for non–front-running candidates to maintain a reliable flow of campaign funds.* As befits a long-shot candidate, Jimmy Carter raised a relatively small amount of money in the year before the 1976 election: $989,000, as compared to $2.2 million for Henry Jackson and $2.9 million for George Wallace. But Carter's inability to raise a lot of money early in the

Table 1.9 The Fate of Front-Runners in Contested Nomination Races, 1972–2000

Race	Candidate Leading in the Last National Poll Taken before the Iowa Caucuses	Candidate Raising the Most Money Prior to the Election Year	Eventual Nominee
1972 Democratic	Humphrey	n.a.[a]	McGovern
1976 Democratic	Humphrey	Wallace	Carter
1976 Republican	Ford	Reagan	Ford
1980 Democratic	Carter	Carter	Carter
1980 Republican	Reagan	Connally	Reagan
1984 Democratic	Mondale	Mondale	Mondale
1988 Democratic	Hart	Dukakis	Dukakis
1988 Republican	Bush	Bush	Bush
1992 Democratic	Clinton	Clinton	Clinton
1992 Republican	Bush	Bush	Bush
1996 Republican	Dole	Dole	Dole
2000 Democratic	Gore	Gore	Gore
2000 Republican	Bush	Bush	Bush

[a] Accurate data on pre-election year fund-raising are not available until the 1976 election cycle.
Source: Poll results are taken from the Gallup Poll; fund-raising totals are based on FEC reports.

election cycle did not prove to be an insurmountable obstacle to his eventual success. The Carter campaign's fund-raising strategy—in fact, it was their strategy for dealing with just about every important resource—was to start small and build on their early successes. They *did* have enough money to wage a vigorous campaign in Iowa and New Hampshire, and if successful there, they believed, they could then raise the money necessary to contest the next round of primaries, which, if they kept winning, would allow them to raise more money for still later primaries, and so on through the final primaries and on into the convention.

To a remarkable extent, the Carter campaign was able to make this strategy work. And so, to a lesser extent, were George Bush in 1980 and Gary Hart in 1984—two other long-shot candidates from this period who caught fire in the early going. What needs to be emphasized, however, is that in order to raise money in this way, Carter and the other long-shots needed a delegate selection calendar that began in a reasonably slow and gradual manner. In Carter's case, his first significant win came in the Iowa caucuses on January 21.[27] He then had five full weeks to reap the financial benefits of that victory before the next major contest, the New Hampshire primary, which took place on February 24. There was just one primary per week in the four weeks after New Hampshire, and only one of those (the Florida primary on March 9) was really central to Carter's plans. There were two major primaries on April 6—but then nothing in the two weeks after that. At every stage of the primary and caucus season, in short, Carter had time to raise money from contributors who were impressed by his latest triumph(s), and then apply that money to the next round of primaries.

Front-loading, by contrast, imparts a very different rhythm to the nomination race. Now when a long-shot candidate wins in Iowa or New Hampshire, there is very little time available for raising all of the money that is necessary for waging even a minimally competitive campaign in the dense cluster of primaries that comes immediately after New Hampshire. Given the $1,000 limit that federal law imposed on individual contributions (at least up through 2000), fund-raising in a presidential nomination race is almost inevitably a slow and labor-intensive process. Given that reality, it is almost impossible, in a period of one or two weeks, to raise a large amount of money, deposit it in the bank, and then actually spend it in a productive way.

For a revealing illustration of how front-loading can wreak havoc on the finances of a long-shot candidate, consider the case of Lamar Alexander in 1996.[28] For a candidate who never received more than 4 percent of the vote in the national polls, Alexander had put together an exceptionally strong financial team, including six of the last seven Republican National Finance chairs. With a lot of effort, that team managed to raise $11.5 million in 1995. But the 1996 race also required a great deal of early spending. By the beginning of the delegate selection season, Alexander would later write, "we were running on empty."[29]

All of that early campaigning finally paid off, however, in Iowa. In the final week before the caucuses, Gramm and Forbes both faded and Alexander finished third—or as the media almost always described it, "a strong and surprising third." Suddenly, Alexander was a hot story on television and in the newspapers, with a real prospect of winning New Hampshire. In the first four days after Iowa, according to one newspaper tracking poll, Alexander's vote in New Hampshire jumped from 5 percent to 18 percent.[30] Equally important, the Iowa results breathed new life into the campaign's finances. Beginning three days after Iowa, Alexander has written, "contributions started rolling into our Nashville head-quarters at the rate of $100,000 a day *without events*."[31]

Unfortunately, this money came too late to do him any good in New Hampshire: any television ads that would run on the Saturday, Sunday, or Monday before the primary had to be purchased by Friday. The result was that Alexander was largely absent from the airwaves in the final days of the New Hampshire campaign. Bob Dole, as the front-runner, was not so financially strapped, and he used his money to run a series of ads attacking Lamar Alexander. According to reports later filed with the Federal Election Commission, the Dole campaign spent $459,000 in New Hampshire during February, as compared to just $94,000 for Alexander. Dole's ads did exactly what they were supposed to do: blunting Alexander's momentum just enough so that he came in third, 7600 votes behind Dole.

Even after its disappointing finish in New Hampshire, the Alexander campaign continued to raise money at the rate of $100,000 a day. But impressive as that figure might have been under other circumstances, it simply wasn't enough to allow Alexander to run a competitive campaign in the highly front-loaded calendar of 1996, in which 21 states held their presidential primaries in the three weeks after New Hampshire. At one point, the Alexander high command estimated that it needed $2.6 million to keep itself going during these three weeks.[32] But $100,000 a day over a three-week period comes up a half million dollars short of this figure.[33] The result was that Dole continued to outspend Alexander whenever his campaign felt the need to do so. In the critical South Carolina primary, for example, Dole spent $685,000 during February and March, versus $250,000 for Alexander. As it turned out, Alexander was never a serious factor in any primary after New Hampshire. On March 6, he withdrew from the race.

The moral of this story should be clear: In a front-loaded system, there just isn't time to win in Iowa or New Hampshire and then raise the money for the next round of primaries. To take advantage of an early breakthrough, a candidate has to have assembled a large war chest *before* Iowa, and given the federal contribution limits, long-shot candidates can rarely do this. The result in recent years is that whenever a non–front-runner wins (or does better than expected) in Iowa and New Hampshire, he usually finds himself significantly outspent and out-campaigned by the front-runner in the next round of primaries. This, in brief, is what happened to Dick Gephardt in 1988, Paul Tsongas in 1992, and Lamar Alexander in 1996.

2. Front-loading greatly increases the organizational demands upon the non–front-runners. Running for president has always been something of an organizational nightmare, requiring every campaign to navigate its way through 51 distinct delegate selection events, each with its own set of laws, rules, customs, and constituencies. When the primaries and caucuses were concentrated near the *end* of the delegate selection season, however, these tasks were considerably more manageable, for the simple reason that they did not all have to be confronted at once. In organization as in fund-raising, second-tier candidates had the luxury of starting small. In the early stages of the campaign, they only needed to be organized in a small number of states: Iowa, New Hampshire, and perhaps three or four other states with early primaries. If successful in these early events, the non–front-running campaign would then have time to organize and prepare for later primaries. This, in particular, was the pattern of the Carter campaign in 1976.

Front-loading forces candidates to adopt an early battle plan that is considerably more ambitious. Given the current shape of the delegate selection calendar, every candidate who hopes to do well in Iowa and/or New Hampshire must also be prepared, the moment the votes in New Hampshire have been counted, to run a full-scale, national campaign. While this sudden transformation poses a number of challenges for a campaign, it puts an especially severe strain on the campaign organization. Grassroots organizations, of the kind that do door-to-door campaigning or conduct get-out-the-vote drives, simply cannot be put together overnight. If they do not already exist on the day before New Hampshire, they will almost certainly never get established. Though every presidential campaign conducted in a nation of 200 million eligible voters must inevitably rely to a great extent on the mass media, front-loading makes the nomination phase of the campaign even more media-centered and, thus, more remote from the typical voter.

From the perspective of a presidential campaign (which is not the only relevant perspective), establishing an extensive grass-roots organization is helpful but probably not essential. A candidate who is receiving lots of favorable coverage in the media or advertising heavily on television may be able to win a primary or caucus even if he has little or no on-the-ground presence in a state.[34] But certain other organizational tasks cannot be ignored or sloughed off on the media. In particular, every presidential campaign must make sure that it meets two important requirements in every major primary state.

First, the candidate must actually be listed on the ballot. Though write-in campaigns are not unheard of in presidential nomination races, it is obviously much easier to win votes if the candidate's name appears on the official ballot.[35] What a candidate must do to qualify for a primary ballot varies from state to state. In about 40 percent of the states, most candidates are automatically granted ballot access: a state or party official is required, by law, to put together a list of the "major" or "nationally recognized" candidates seeking a party's presidential nomination and then to include all of them on the primary ballot.[36] There remain, however, a considerable number of states where campaigns must take a more active role in securing ballot access: filing a petition with a few thousand signatures and/or paying a qualifying fee. While such requirements are generally not very onerous,[37] the important point is that the filing deadlines usually occur several months before the primary. In 1996, by the time the New Hampshire primary took place on February 20, the filing deadlines in 30 other states had already passed. For second-tier and long-shot candidates, who are generally short of funds and staff, meeting these filing requirements is at least a nuisance and sometimes a major burden.

Though most second-tier candidates do manage to make it on the ballot in almost every state, many fail to surmount a second hurdle: filing delegate slates. The problem here is a rather technical one (though no less important for that) and concerns how it is that states that hold presidential primaries actually choose specific persons to serve as national convention delegates. In many states, particularly those that use the so-called direct election system, state law requires each candidate to have a complete list of potential delegates put together *before* the primary takes place. If the campaign neglects to run delegates pledged to its candidate in a particular district, they cannot win delegates in that district—no matter how well they do in the presidential preference vote.

The best example of a campaign that failed to meet the challenge of filing full delegate slates—and suffered for its failure—is the Hart campaign in 1984. In the month and a half immediately after New Hampshire, there was a succession of big-state primaries—including Florida, Illinois, and Pennsylvania—all of which used direct election delegate selection systems. Because of their position in the calendar, the deadline for filing delegate slates in each of these states came before the New Hampshire primary, when Hart was still limping along at one percent in the national polls and his campaign was struggling just to stay afloat. The upshot was that in every one of these states, the Hart campaign was unable to file complete delegate slates—and thus won significantly fewer delegates than it might have in a less front-loaded system.

In Florida, for example, the front-running Mondale campaign filed full delegate slates in all of Florida's nineteen congressional districts—but the Hart organization was unable to field a single candidate for delegate in eight districts and had incomplete slates in five others. The result was that while Hart beat Mondale 39 percent to 33 percent in the preference vote, it was Mondale who scored a plurality of the delegates, winning 61 to Hart's 52 (9 others were uncommitted).[38] Our estimate is that if Hart had filed full delegate slates in every district, the delegate count would have been Hart 87, Mondale 34. The pattern is similar in Illinois, where Hart filed complete delegate slates in just seven of 22 congressional districts and partial slates in three others. Had Hart filed full slates, we estimate that he probably would have won 21 more delegates in Illinois, Mondale 20 fewer. Given how close the 1984 nomination race turned out to be—when

Mondale finally declared victory on the day after the last round of primaries, he had just 7 more delegates than the minimum number needed for nomination—these discrepancies are not trivial.

The good news for Democrats is that the difficulties associated with filing delegate slates have been largely eliminated. In 1996, the Democrats added a provision to their national delegate selection rules which requires states using presidential primaries to allocate delegates according to the presidential preference vote, and specifically allows candidates who haven't filed full slates before the primary to choose any additional delegates they are entitled to through a "special post-primary procedure."[39] But nothing similar exists in the Republican party, where direct election primaries continue to pose a substantial burden for the non–front-runners.

There is, in the end, a certain irony in criticizing the presidential nomination process on the grounds that it is *too* favorable to front-runners. For it was not so many years ago that most commentators (including most political scientists) were attacking the process for precisely the opposite reason: that it didn't do enough to advance the candidacies of the nationally known and those with long records of service to the parties, that it gave too much of an advantage to the outsider and the insurgent. Yet, the contradiction between these two viewpoints may be more apparent than real.

On the one hand, there is much to be said for a system that does not deliberately stack the deck in favor of outsiders and insurgents, as seemed to be the case with the nomination process of the 1970s. The presidency of Jimmy Carter, in particular, could not help but raise questions about the wisdom of giving a major-party presidential nomination to someone who was almost entirely unknown to most voters—and even to a substantial segment of his own party's leadership—just twelve months earlier. So not all front-runners are bad. Indeed, many became front-runners for the eminently sensible reason that they spent years earning the trust and support of other party leaders. A nomination process that favors front-runners, then, is not the worst thing in the world.

Yet, there is, we think, some happy medium between a system that nominates Carter-type candidates and one that poses so many difficult, perhaps insurmountable, obstacles to the non–front-runners. Our argument, simply put, is that not all front-runners are the best possible nominees or would make the best possible presidents. Sometimes candidates become front-runners simply because they are flamboyant or famous or controversial, or because they happened to do well in the last nominating cycle. What a good nomination process requires—and the present system seems to lack—is some measure of flexibility: some capacity to question and test the front-runner, to ask if he really is the right person for the circumstances facing the party and the country, to ensure that he is not nominated *merely* because he is the front-runner. And the more front-loaded the system becomes, the more it loses this flexibility.

EFFECTS ON CANDIDATE CHOICE 2: THE CASE OF THE UNSTOPPABLE MOMENTUM

All the evidence we have to date, then, suggests that front-loading tends to help the front-runner. But a second possibility has also been entertained by a number of commentators: that in some circumstances, front-loading might propel a little-known outsider all the way to his party's nomination, before the public or the press has any real opportunity to learn much about him or to conduct a thorough assessment of his strengths and weaknesses.

The sort of scenario these commentators have in mind is, in many ways, quite familiar: A candidate with very little previous exposure in national politics somehow manages to pull off an upset victory in the New Hampshire primary. Suddenly, this candidate is the hottest thing in American politics: a fresh face with, at least for the moment, no blemishes. Eventually, of course, this early glow will start to fade: the media will do more detailed and more balanced reporting about the candidate and his record; his inevitable errors and shortcomings will come out; his opponents will begin to counterattack. The problem, under a heavily front-loaded system, is that this new information, these second thoughts, may come too late. By the time the doubts set in, the new candidate may already have locked up the nomination.

Lest the scenario we have just described be dismissed as entirely fanciful, consider the candidacy of Gary Hart in the Democratic nomination race of 1984. As is well-known, Hart went from an asterisk to a front-runner in essentially eight days. After finishing a quite distant second in the Iowa caucuses, he received a huge wave of publicity and press attention that enabled him to come from far behind in the polls and post a comfortable win in New Hampshire. Suddenly, the entire Democratic race was turned upside down: Hart was now the front-runner and the previously unstoppable Mondale campaign was close to collapse.

Eventually, Mondale recovered, won a string of important primaries, and went on to become the party nominee. But—and this is the key point—it took *time*. As one media scholar concluded about the press's behavior in the first few weeks after Iowa, "Hart's coverage [during this period] was virtually free of any harsh criticism, unflattering issues, or cynical commentary."[40] Indeed, it wasn't until about a week and a half after New Hampshire that the initial infatuation with Hart began to wear off. Fortunately for Mondale, under the 1984 delegate selection calendar, he did have at least a little bit of time. In the week immediately after New Hampshire, there was just one Democratic caucus and a single, nonbinding presidential primary. There were five more primaries in the week after that, but two were in states (Alabama and Georgia) that were unusually strong for Mondale.[41]

And so, barely, Mondale managed to hang on. But what if the primary calendar had been more front-loaded? What if, as in the 1996 Republican race, there were four primaries in the week immediately after New Hampshire and nine more in the week after that? A strong case can be made that under this sort of calendar, Hart would have wracked up enough victories in the two weeks after New Hampshire to establish a commanding lead in the delegate count and compel Mondale to withdraw from the race.

This "outsider breakthrough" scenario, as we have already noted, is, to date, entirely hypothetical. And for reasons developed in the previous section, riding a wave of momentum all the way through to the nomination is not, in the end, as simple as it sounds. But enough candidates have come close—to Hart's name, one could add those of Lamar Alexander and, possibly, Paul Tsongas and John McCain—to suggest that this possibility needs to be taken seriously, especially because its implications are so plainly troubling. Whatever may be said against individual front-runners, the length of the invisible primary generally guarantees that they will have received at least some measure of public and media scrutiny by the time the first delegates are selected. Long-shots and outsiders, by contrast, are much less well-known—not only to voters, but often to the reporters who are supposed to cover them. As we argued at the end of the previous section, a good presidential selection process ought to allow for second thoughts, for reconsideration, for the possibility that initial impressions may be wrong. And the more front-loaded the system becomes, the less opportunity we all have to do this.

THE "ENTRY FEE" AND CANDIDATE ATTRITION

Front-loading also constrains the voters' options in another important way: by limiting the number of candidates who get into the race at all. If candidates cannot count on raising the money they need *after* Iowa and New Hampshire, as we have argued earlier, the logical corollary is that they need to have raised a great deal of money before the delegate selection season begins—and that candidates who cannot raise money in such large quantities may simply decide not to run. In the leadup to both the 1996 and 2000 nomination races, it was widely argued—by both participants and pundits—that in order to have any chance of running a competitive campaign, a candidate had to raise between $20 and $25 million before a single delegate was selected.[42] While this is obviously only an estimate, this is a case where the perception may be as important as the reality, scaring off candidates who believe they cannot raise this sum of money.

Two points are worth noting about this "entry fee." First, only two types of candidates can generally be expected to raise such money in advance of actually winning a few primaries: wealthy, self-financed candidates like Steve Forbes; and well-connected political insiders such as George Bush, Phil Gramm, Bob Dole, and Al Gore. Second, political money is a finite resource, so only a few candidates in any given election cycle will be able to reach such heights of fund-raising. Prior to the recent changes in the federal contribution limits, one Republican fund-raiser had estimated that the current system required a candidate to find a minimum of 20,000 contributors, each of whom would give $1,000, from a donor pool of no more than 50,000 possible contributors.[43] Several putative Republican candidates in the 2000 election cycle testified that Bush's fund-raising success was less important for the use Bush made of it than for the way it sucked money out of the political world like a vacuum sucking air out of a sealed room. Lamar Alexander, for one, argued that, "The problem is not that Bush has raised too much, it's that nobody else can raise enough to compete."[44]

Consequently, many candidates who could have made a viable, if not successful, run for their party's nomination two decades ago are now preemptively driven from the race. Some prospective candidates, calculating the improbability that they will be able to reach the minimum threshold for competitiveness, simply stand aside from the outset. Others make the effort, find their situation hopeless, and quickly remove themselves from the race.

A number of factors enter into a potential candidate's decision to get into or stay out of a presidential nomination race, so it is difficult to say for certain how many candidates were kept out of the contest just because of front-loading. But both parties' experience in the 2000 nomination races is surely sufficient to set off some alarm bells. On the Democratic side, the long- and well-established tradition is that whenever a Democratic president isn't running for reelection (and sometimes, even when one is), there is always a large and vigorous field of contenders. In 2000, by contrast, Al Gore had just one opponent: former New Jersey Senator Bill Bradley. So far as we can determine, there is no other case in the history of the Democratic party where an open-seat presidential nomination race attracted just two candidates. Perhaps this was because, as the incumbent vice president, Gore was seen as such a prohibitive favorite. Yet it is worth noting that, in late 1998 and early 1999, when a number of other Democrats were debating whether to get into the race, there was a widespread perception that while Gore brought a number of strengths to the campaign, he also had a number of shortcomings. He was generally regarded as a wooden and uninspiring campaigner and he had been tarnished by the Clinton fund-raising scandals. It is also instructive to compare Gore's experience with that of George Bush, Sr., when he sought his party's nomination as the incumbent vice president in 1988. Unlike Gore, Bush had five major opponents, including the Senate Minority Leader (Bob Dole), a former secretary of state (Alexander Haig), a former congressman and governor (Pete DuPont), and a congressman who had co-authored the Reagan tax cut and was a favorite of the conservative movement (Jack Kemp).

On the Republican side, a much larger number of candidates got into the 2000 race, in the sense that they publicly declared their intention to seek the Republican presidential nomination. But an unusually large number—6 of 12 announced candidates—also exited the race months before the first caucuses were held in Iowa. Among the early retirees were a number of candidates who clearly deserved a more extended hearing, including Lamar Alexander, Elizabeth Dole, House Budget Committee chairman John Kasich, and former vice president Dan Quayle.

COMPROMISED PARTICIPATION

When the McGovern-Fraser Commission first launched the effort to rewrite the rules of the presidential nomination process in the late 1960s, it did so on the basis of an apparent mandate to "give all Democratic voters a full, meaningful, and timely opportunity to participate in the selection of delegates, and, thereby, in the decisions of the Convention itself."[45] Thirty years later, one of the most widely criticized features of the system the reformers spawned is precisely its effect on the extent and quality of voter participation.

As the primary and caucus calendar has become more front-loaded, it has become routine for nomination races to be settled in the early spring. Even with front-loading, this means that lots of states select their delegates at a time when everything of significance has already been decided. In 1996, Robert Dole was widely declared to have a lock on the Republican nomination after winning all eight of the primaries that were held on March 5.[46] All of his major opponents except Pat Buchanan had withdrawn by March 14; Dole finally secured a mathematical majority of his party's national convention delegates on March 26. Depending on which of these dates one chooses to emphasize, at least 12—and possibly as many as 25—states voted after the race was already over. In 2000, 25 states held their primaries after both Bradley and McCain had officially withdrawn.

What effect does this sort of "early closure" have on voter participation rates? To answer this question, table 1.10 shows voter participation rates in the 1996 and 2000 presidential primaries, broken down by the date on which the primaries were held.[47] Once again, New Hampshire emerges as a special case. If the Granite State's voters receive an extraordinary amount of attention from the candidates and the media, they at least appear to recognize the significance of the role they have been assigned and turn out at a far higher rate than occurs in almost every other state.

Putting New Hampshire aside, voter turnout rates declined as the primary season progressed in two of the three races examined here. In the 2000 Republican race, those primaries held between February 8 and March 7 attracted, on average, about 26 percent of the potential Republican electorate to the polls. For primaries held after John McCain's withdrawal on March 9, the average turnout was 16 percent. In 1996, average Republican turnout fell from 22 percent in primaries held between February 24 and March 2, to 18 percent in primaries held during the remainder of March, and then to 14 percent in the April, May, and June primaries. In the 2000 Democratic contest, by contrast, there was actually

Table 1.10 Primary Turnout by Date in 1996 and 2000

Date	Average Turnout	(No. of States)
1996 REPUBLICAN		
New Hampshire (Feb. 20)	42%	(1)
February 24–March 2	22	(5)
March 5–26	18	(22)
April 23–June 4	14	(12)
2000 REPUBLICAN		
New Hampshire (Feb. 1)	52	(1)
February 8–29	26	(6)
March 7	26	(11)
After March 9	16	(23)
2000 DEMOCRATIC		
New Hampshire (Feb. 1)	40	(1)
March 7	17	(11)
After March 9	16	(22)

no difference in turnout between those states that voted while Bill Bradley was still actively contesting the race and those that voted after Bradley's withdrawal. Perhaps most voters had concluded that the Democratic race was effectively over well before March 7.[48]

THE OTHER SIDE OF THE LEDGER

Such is the case against front-loading. Is there anything to be said in its defense?

Perhaps the most common argument made in defense of front-loading—or at least cited as a mitigating factor—is that clustering the primaries and caucuses at the beginning of the delegate selection season helps bring an early end to the nomination contest, and thus gives the parties more time to heal any wounds caused by a hard-fought nomination campaign and present a united front for the general election. A party that is deeply divided over its presidential nominee, according to this argument, almost invariably loses in November. Though front-loading obviously doesn't prevent intra-party divisions, it does make sure that they are not unduly prolonged and gives the parties ample time to undo the damage. As a subcommittee of the Democratic National Committee noted in a recent report:

> The most important part of any primary/caucus schedule is that it needs to identify a strong Democratic nominee early and lead to a Democratic victory in the general election. . . . Consequently, criticism about a front-loaded schedule has to be weighed against a process that seems to be working well. In the last few cycles, the

current system has allowed the Democratic Party to identify its presumptive nominee early. As a result, the process has helped the Party unify behind its nominee and focus its resources on the general election.[49]

This line of thinking has also been supported by a number of academic specialists in the parties and elections subfield, who have put forward a body of research often referred to as the "divisive primary hypothesis." According to this theory, having to go through a long and divisive nomination race severely scars whichever candidate eventually wins the nomination, and thus makes it more difficult for him to achieve victory in the general election. One of the most vigorous exponents of this argument has been political scientist Martin Wattenberg:

> One of the key features of the candidate-centered age is the increasingly difficult task of unifying a political party in November when the various factions within it have been competing so long. Internal animosities stirred up by the reformed nomination process are more likely to continue to hurt the nominee in November. These animosities hurt a candidate not only with his own party's voters but with Independents and the opposition party as well. After all, if members of the candidate's own party find fault with their nominee why should those outside the party view him favorably? . . . A successful presidential campaign now depends on wrapping up the nomination faster and with less lingering bitterness than the opposition . . .[50]

By significantly shortening the nomination contest, then, front-loading may help promote party unity for the fall campaign.

Two points should be made in response to this argument. In the first place, as we have argued in considerable detail elsewhere,[51] there is very little good evidence to show that having a divisive nomination race really does harm a party or candidate in the general election. More precisely, what evidence has been cited in defense of the theory comes from a misspecified model. According to the divisive primary hypothesis, divisions within the party are *created* by a contested nomination race. Rival candidates for the nomination essentially manufacture differences and disagreements that have little or no basis in anything real but that, once excited, linger on to haunt the party in the general election. In our view, it makes considerably more sense to assume (or at least to allow for the possibility) that divisive nomination races are more effect than cause: that bitter, hard-fought nomination races simply *reflect* and *reveal* the problems and divisions that already exist within a party. Divisive primaries may thus be correlated with a weak performance in the general election, but the relationship is spurious. Analyzed from this perspective, most of the evidence offered in support of the divisive primary hypothesis evaporates.

As an example of these two different approaches to the question, consider the Democratic nomination race of 1972. At first glance, the basic facts of this race might be seen as supporting the divisive primary hypothesis. Three strong and ideologically distinct candidates fought it out through the preconvention campaign, with the eventual winner, George McGovern, receiving just 25 percent of the total primary vote. And several months later, McGovern went down to one of the most lopsided defeats in the history of American presidential elections. But can we therefore conclude that the first circumstance caused the second?

A different interpretation seems to us distinctly more plausible. The Democrats began the 1972 election sharply and crucially divided over two major issues: race and the Vietnam war. The 1972 campaign emphatically did not create these two divisions. The war had been a source of substantial intraparty disagreement for at least six years prior to 1972; race had been threatening to split the Democrats since the 1940s. Against this background, it is no wonder that the Democrats endured such a remarkably divisive nomination race—and then saw so many Democrats defect to the opposition in November. Indeed, what would have been truly shocking is if the 1972 nomination process had been a calm and unifying affair.

Second, even if the evidence supporting the divisive primary hypothesis were a good deal stronger than it is, this would not necessarily mean that the parties would be better off bringing their presidential nomination races to a premature conclusion. Whatever benefits accrue to a party from a shorter nomination contest need to be balanced against all the potential harms associated with front-loading. In particular, as we have argued earlier, front-loading greatly increases the likelihood that a party will settle on a nominee before receiving a full discussion of his strengths and weaknesses, and before many of his leading rivals have been given an adequate opportunity to make their case to the voters.

In 1992, for example, Ron Brown, then the chairman of the Democratic National Committee, intervened in the Democratic nomination race at several points, in an attempt to bring it to an early conclusion.[52] While Brown's actions perhaps played some role in promoting greater party unity for the general election, it may have done so at a significant cost, pushing the Democrats to rally around a candidate (Bill Clinton) with a number of major personal flaws, many of which may have hurt the party in 1992 and in subsequent elections. It is, in short, an open question as to whether Brown's desire for a quick decision really helped his party in the long run. At the very least, we would argue, there needs to be an appreciation of the costs as well as the (alleged) benefits of shortening the nomination race.

IN SEARCH OF A SOLUTION

Any attempt to untangle the consequences of front-loading must contend with the complexity of presidential nominations, the small number of cases from which to draw conclusions, and the fact that some consequences have already manifested themselves (for example, the high "entry fee" and the effective disfranchisement of half of the states) while others are thus far only hypothetical (the potential for runaway momentum to nominate a little-known contender). But all the evidence to date—and all the consequences it is reasonable to expect in the future—argue quite strongly, in our view, that the effects of front-loading on American presidential politics are almost entirely negative. While a small number of arguments have been made in favor of front-loading, all of them are flawed, we think, in a variety of important ways.

Given all the arguments that can and have been mounted against front-loading, it is a good question why nothing effective has yet been done to reverse or even significantly mitigate it. What alternatives are there to front-loading? Why have none of them been implemented? How to cope with front-loading is an enormously complicated question, a full discussion of which would require another book (a book we have actually written).[53] For the moment, we will simply state two broad conclusions.

First, perhaps the most important reason that nothing has yet been done about front-loading is that there simply are no easy or obvious solutions available. A lot of remedies have been proposed, to be sure, but all of them are unlikely to solve the problem or would carry serious, negative consequences of their own—or both.

One of the few such reforms that has actually been given a trial was a "bonus delegate" scheme that the Republicans used for the first time in the 2000 election cycle.[54] Under the new rule, states got more delegates if they held later primaries and caucuses. Specifically, states holding their primaries or caucuses between March 15 and April 14 had the size of their national convention delegation increased by 5 percent; states holding their primaries or caucuses between April 15 and May 14 got 7.5 percent more delegates; while states selecting their delegates on May 15 or later received a 10 percent bonus. The Republican plan was an interesting experiment, nicely consonant with basic party principles. Unfortunately, it had one major drawback: it didn't work. In the lead-up to the 2000 nomination race, twice as many states moved their Republican primary or caucuses forward in the calendar as moved them in the opposite direction. Given all the benefits states received from going early, the promise of a few extra delegates simply wasn't enough to change the basic calculus.

Perhaps the most commonly-proposed remedy for front-loading is to move to a system of regional primaries, in which the states would be divided into a number of groups based on their geographic location, with the states in each region voting on one particular day. It is, however, by no means clear that a regional primary system would actually solve most of the problems associated with front-loading. In most regional primary proposals, states are divided into a quite small number of regions, usually between four and six. This means that on the first day of the nomination season, all candidates would be required to mount campaigns in eight or twelve states at once—which effectively guarantees that most of the problems associated with front-loading would continue. Front-runners would still have enormous advantages, the entry fee would be little altered, and campaign quality probably would not improve much.

Another serious problem associated with regional primaries is that they would confer a significant advantage on any candidate who happened to be particularly strong in whatever region went first. Region is a very important variable in explaining primary outcomes. Almost every recent presidential candidate has done significantly better in one region than in the others. In 1976, for example, Gerald Ford won 60 percent of the vote in the average northeastern primary, as against 35 percent in the average western primary. In the same year, Jimmy Carter won, on average, 62 percent of the vote in the South, 35 percent in the Northeast, and 21 percent in the West.

Which region goes first could thus have very important implications for which candidate gets nominated. If the 1976 Republican nomination contest had begun with a western regional primary, it might have dealt a severe blow to Gerald Ford's candidacy, while a process that began with an eastern regional primary might have greatly lengthened the odds against Ronald Reagan. In 1992, Bill Clinton's candidacy would likely have been doomed if the southern states had voted last: for the first five weeks of that year's delegate selection season, Clinton didn't win a single primary or caucus outside the South.

Even if we could somehow determine the perfect plan for dealing with front-loading, however, a second major obstacle would remain: Figuring out a way to implement and enforce the new system. One of the greatest barriers to reforming the presidential nomination process has always been the extreme fragmentation of authority over that process. A remarkable number of different agents play some part in making the rules, including the national parties, state parties, the federal government, state governments, and the courts. And for some of the more ambitious reform proposals, it is not clear that *anyone* has the authority to do what the proposals would require.

Who, for example, has the power to establish and administer a regional primary system? Many of the more prominent regional primary proposals call for the system to be created by ordinary federal legislation. Yet it is far from clear that the federal government has the constitutional authority to tell the political parties how to nominate their presidential candidates or to tell the states when to hold their primaries. Certainly there is nothing in the plain text of the Constitution that gives the national government that power.

Other would-be reformers look to the national parties as the proper agencies for restructuring the primary calendar. But though recent court decisions have given the national parties fairly sweeping powers to govern their own internal affairs, their capacity to compel obedience from state parties or state legislatures is considerably more limited. In this regard, the only concrete power the national parties have—their sole real enforcement tool—is their control over the seating of convention delegates. If a state selects its delegates in a way that the national party believes violates that party's delegate selection rules, the party can refuse to seat those delegates at its national convention. In practice, however, this can be a difficult power to wield. Would any national party, for example, seriously consider denying seats to the entire California delegation on the grounds that that state had held its primary in the wrong week?

Front-loading, in short, is a tough nut to crack. Journalists and political practitioners first began to take notice of the problem in the early 1980s. Two decades later, front-loading is a much more prominent theme in discussions of the presidential nomination process—yet for all the hand-wringing and lamentation, the problem has gotten a good deal worse and very little has actually been done to alleviate it. It will not surprise us greatly if, twenty years from now, that is still the case.

NOTES

1. For a sampling of some of the best critiques of the contemporary presidential nomination process, see Anthony King, "How Not to Select Presidential Candidates: A View from Europe," in *The American Elections of 1980*, ed. Austin Ranney (Washington, D.C.: American Enterprise Institute, 1981); James I. Lengle, *Representation and Presidential Primaries: The Democratic Party in the Post-Reform Era* (Westport, Conn.: Greenwood, 1981); James W. Ceaser, *Reforming the Reforms: A Critical Analysis of the Presidential Selection Process* (Cambridge, Mass.: Ballinger, 1982), esp. chap. 4; Nelson W. Polsby, *Consequences of Party Reform* (New York: Oxford University Press, 1983); Scott Keeter and Cliff Zukin, *Uninformed Choice: The Failure of the New Presidential Nominating System* (New York: Praeger, 1983), esp. chap. 8; Thomas E. Mann, "Should the Presidential Nominating System Be Changed (Again)?" in *Before Nomination: Our Primary Problems*, ed. George Grassmuck (Washington, D.C.: American Enterprise Institute, 1985); and James W. Davis, "The Case against the Current Primary-Centered System," in *Choosing Our Choices: Debating the Presidential Nominating System*, ed. Robert E. DiClerico and James W. Davis (Lanham, Md.: Rowman & Littlefield, 2000).

2. Ronald Brownstein, "GOP Leaders Fear That Frantic Pace of Primaries Leaves Voters Out in Cold," *Los Angeles Times*, March 11, 1996, A5; Gerald F. Seib, "Primary Issue: If It's Broke, Why Not Fix It?" *Wall Street Journal*, March 20, 1996, A16; William Safire, "Primary Reform Now," *New York Times*, March 28, 1996, A25; and David S. Broder, "Primary Madness," *Washington Post*, March 3, 1996, C7.

3. "Democrats Delinquent," *Washington Post*, May 27, 2000; Fred Brown, "And the first may be the least," *Denver Post*, February 2, 2000, 2D; Ken Foskett, "So many primaries, so little time . . ." *Atlanta Constitution*, February 24, 2000, 18A; Liz Halloran, "Primaries: Who Ordered This Chaos?" *Hartford Courant*, March 3, 2000, A1; "Primary reforms," *St. Petersburg Times*, March 14, 2000, 8A; Noel Rubinton, "Eye on the Media: Speed Cuts Depth in Campaign Coverage," *Newsday*, March 7, 2000, A35; Jack W. Germond and Jules Witcover, "Looking Ahead to 2004," *Baltimore Sun*, March 22, 2000, 21A; "Primary Responsibility," *Los Angeles Times*, May 4, 2000, B10.

4. Byron E. Shafer, *Quiet Revolution: The Struggle for the Democratic Party and the Shaping of Post-Reform Politics* (New York: Russell Sage Foundation, 1983), 28.

5. See *Buckley v. Valeo*, 424 U.S. 1 (1976), at 7.

6. For a fuller discussion of the rules changes and what effects they had on the presidential selection process, see Michael G. Hagen and William G. Mayer, "The Modern Politics of Presidential Selection: How Changing the Rules Really Did Change the Game," in *In Pursuit of the White House 2000: How We Choose Our Presidential Nominees*, ed. William G. Mayer (New York: Chatham House, 2000), 1–55.

7. *New York Times*, September 5, 1998, A10 (emphasis added).

8. There were three advisory Democratic primaries held between February 1 and March 7, but since they played no role at all in the delegate selection process, they were, with one exception, roundly ignored by both the candidates and the media. The exception was Washington state, where Bill Bradley, faced with the prospect of losing all eleven primaries on the first Tuesday in March, made a last-ditch effort to pump some momentum into his campaign, though without any noticeable effect.

9. The decision by the Rules and Bylaws Committee needed to be approved by the full Democratic National Committee; that approval came in mid-January, 2002.

10. Both phrases are quoted from a letter that Terry McAuliffe, chairman of the Democratic National Committee, wrote to the *Wall Street Journal*, February 14, 2002, A21.

11. When the new window was approved by the Democratic National Committee, DNC chairman Terry McAuliffe said that Democrats in South Carolina, Michigan, and Arizona were "almost certain" to hold their primaries on the same date as their Republican counterparts. See *Washington Post*, January 20, 2002, A4.

12. As quoted in David S. Broder, "Democrats push up calendar on presidential primaries," *Boston Globe*, November 28, 2001, A25.

13. Michael J. Robinson and Margaret A. Sheehan, *Over the Wire and On TV: CBS and UPI in Campaign '80* (New York: Sage, 1983), 174–80. For similar results in other years, see William C. Adams, "As New Hampshire Goes . . ." in *Media and Momentum: The New Hampshire Primary and Nomination Politics*, ed. Gary R. Orren and Nelson W. Polsby (Chatham, N.J.: Chatham House, 1987), 42–59; and S. Robert Lichter, Daniel Amundson, and Richard Noyes, *The Video Campaign: Network Coverage of the 1988 Primaries* (Washington, D.C.: American Enterprise Institute, 1988), 12–14.

14. See Library and Archives of New Hampshire's Political Tradition, *First in the Nation: The New Hampshire Primary: What It Means to the State and the Nation* (Concord, N.H., 2001).

15. On the general way that presidents use their control over the executive branch to reward states and constituencies that are important to their reelection, see Kathryn Dunn Tenpas, *Presidents as Candidates: Inside the White House for the Presidential Campaign* (New York: Garland, 1997), 78–83 and 89–94.

16. For further details about the regression equations discussed in the last two paragraphs, see William G. Mayer and Andrew E. Busch, *The Front-Loading Problem in Presidential Nominations* (Washington, D.C.: Brookings Institution, forthcoming), chap. 3.

17. New Hampshire has actually been holding the first presidential primary in the nation since 1920, but up through 1948, New Hampshire did not have a presidential preference or "beauty contest" line on its ballot. The primary was used only as a mechanism for selecting national convention delegates. It was thus difficult for the media to interpret the results as a victory or defeat for any particular candidate. The "beauty contest" line was added to the ballot by state law in 1949.

18. These figures are based on the delegate counts maintained by major media organizations, particularly the Associated Press. For further details, see Mayer and Busch, *Front-Loading Problem*, chap. 3 and appendix C.

19. We use data from these two election cycles because they most completely cover the invisible primary period. In other years, the question wording was changed in the middle of the series or the question was never asked at important points in the campaign or coverage of the full field of candidates was not as thorough.

20. The survey referred to is the "Continuous Monitoring" component of the 1984 American National Election Study. The study discussed in the next several paragraphs is Henry E. Brady and Richard Johnston, "What's the Primary Message? Horse Race or Issue Journalism?" in *Media and Momentum: The New Hampshire Primary and Nomination Politics*, ed. Gary R. Orren and Nelson W. Polsby (Chatham, N.J.: Chatham House, 1987), 127–86.

21. On this last point, see Ronald B. Rapoport and Walter J. Stone, testimony before the RNC Advisory Commission on the Presidential Nominating Process, as reprinted in *Nominating Future Presidents: A Review of the Republican Process* (Washington, D.C.: Republican National Committee, 2000), 145.

22. Foskett, "So many primaries."

23. Rubinton, "Eye on the Media."

24. As quoted in *Congressional Quarterly Weekly Report*, June 16, 1979, 1168.

25. For example, in a book on political reform published in 1996, G. Calvin Mackenzie argued, "[The contemporary presidential nomination] process has a strong tendency to promote the candidacies of outsiders who have little or no Washington experience and who are often strangers to the leading members of their own party." See Mackenzie, *The Irony of Reform: Roots of American Political Disenchantment* (Boulder, Colo.: Westview, 1996), 50.

26. One such factor is simply that, after the new rules had been in operation for an election cycle or two, the candidates became more familiar with them and understood better what they had to do in order to win. See William G. Mayer, "Forecasting Presidential Nominations," in *In Pursuit of the White House: How We Choose Our Presidential Nominees*, ed. William G. Mayer (Chatham, N.J.: Chatham House, 1996), 60–64.

27. As is well-known among political junkies, Carter didn't actually win the Iowa caucuses—he came in second to the uncommitted vote. But with a remarkable degree of unanimity, the media interpreted it as a win.

28. The following account draws on Lamar Alexander, "Off with the Limits," *Campaigns & Elections*, October/November 1996, 32–35; Anthony Corrado, "Financing the 1996 Elections," in *The Election of 1996: Reports and Interpretations*, ed. Gerald M. Pomper (Chatham, N.J.: Chatham House, 1997); *New York Times*, February 19, 1996, A11; and *Washington Post*, February 21, 1996, A14.

29. Alexander, "Off with the Limits," 33.

30. For polling data on the 1996 New Hampshire primary, see William G. Mayer, "The Presidential Nominations," in *The Election of 1996: Reports and Interpretations*, ed. Gerald M. Pomper (Chatham, N.J.: Chatham House, 1997), 40–42.

31. Alexander, "Off with the Limits," 33 (emphasis in original).

32. The figure is cited by two different Alexander campaign officials in *Washington Post*, February 21, 1996, A14.

33. Actually, it comes up almost a million dollars short of this figure, since Alexander's estimate of $100,000 a day specifically excluded Sundays.

34. There are many examples to prove this statement, but one of the most compelling is the Maine Democratic caucuses of 1984. Well before the caucuses took place, the Mondale campaign had invested heavily in establishing an extensive network of supporters and party activists throughout the Pine Tree State. They also had the support of almost all of the state's labor unions and Democratic elected officials. Hart, by contrast, had a skeleton organization at best. Yet, because Maine came four days after New Hampshire, Hart beat Mondale there 50 percent to 45 percent. See Jack W. Germond and Jules Witcover, *Wake Us When It's Over: Presidential Politics of 1984* (New York: Macmillan, 1985), 171–74.

35. The 1996 Rhode Island Republican primary provides a nice test of the effect of ballot access. Because of its early filing deadline, a number of major Republican candidates, including Pat Buchanan and Steve Forbes, did not get on the Rhode Island ballot, which had a substantial effect on the votes they received there. In every other primary held on March 5, Buchanan won at least 15 percent of the total vote. In Rhode Island, where he could only get write-ins, Buchanan received just 2.6 percent of the vote. Similarly, Forbes won an average vote of 15.8 percent in the seven states where he was listed on the ballot, as compared to 0.9 percent in Rhode Island.

36. Though this type of provision invests a party or elected official with a certain amount of discretion in determining who qualifies as a "nationally recognized" candidate, in general it appears that this criterion is interpreted rather liberally and that all plausible nomination candidates are usually included on the ballot. The only recent candidate who seems to have had a major problem in this regard was David Duke in 1992. For understandable reasons, many state Republican parties did not wish to acknowledge Duke as a member of their party, much less a serious candidate for their party's presidential nomination, and hence kept him off their state ballot.

37. Since 1996, the Democrats have had a provision in their national party rules which stipulates that no state may require a candidate to submit more than 5,000 signatures or pay a filing fee of more than $2,500 in order to have his name listed on the presidential primary ballot.

38. Jesse Jackson also won one delegate. The count reported here includes all announced commitments and changes up through the final assignment of at-large delegate seats by the Florida Democratic Committee in early May. It is also based only on those delegates selected through the primary; i.e., it excludes superdelegates. See *New York Times*, May 6, 1984, 26; and May 19, 1984, 8.

39. The rule for the 2004 Democratic National Convention reads as follows: "A presidential candidate or his/her authorized representative(s) should act in good faith to slate delegate and alternate candidates; however, in any event, if a presidential candidate (including uncommitted status) has qualified to receive delegates and alternates but has failed to slate a sufficient number of delegate and alternate candidates, then additional delegates and alternates for that preference will be selected in a special post-primary procedure." See *Delegate Selection Rules for the 2004 Democratic National Convention* (Washington, D.C.: Democratic National Committee, 2002), Rule 12C.

40. William C. Adams, "Media Coverage of Campaign '84: A Preliminary Report," *Public Opinion* 7 (April/May 1984), 11.

41. Mondale also benefited from a quirk in the way the media reported the results of

the March 13 delegate selection events. For details, see Germond and Witcover, *Wake Us When It's Over*, 195–200.

42. See, for example, *Congressional Quarterly Weekly Report*, February 25, 1995, 630; April 22, 1995, 1124; and January 23, 1999, 197; *Time*, April 27, 1998, 36; and *New York Times*, December 5, 1998, A8; January 12, 1999, A17; and January 22, 1999, A17.

43. Jackie Calmes, "Campaign 2000: Dole's Exit Reflects Rocketing Costs of Presidential Race," *Wall Street Journal*, October 21, 1999.

44. As quoted in *New York Times*, January 18, 2000, A21. See also Harold W. Stanley, "The Nominations: The Return of the Party Leaders," in *The Elections of 2000*, ed. Michael Nelson (Washington, D.C.: CQ Press, 2001).

45. The mandate is quoted from the beginning of the commission's report; see Commission on Party Structure and Delegate Selection, *Mandate for Reform* (Washington, D.C.: Democratic National Committee, 1970), 9.

46. The coverage in America's two largest weekly newsmagazines offers a good example. In its March 18 issue (the first published after the March 5 primaries), *Time* called Dole "the presumptive nominee" and said that the previous week marked "the unofficial start of the general election." In its issue of the same date, *Newsweek* didn't even bother to talk about what had happened in the March 5 primaries, instead featuring a lengthy story about the upcoming battle between Dole and Clinton. See *Time*, March 18, 1996, 38–44; and *Newsweek*, March 18, 1996, 22–25.

47. The turnout data in table 1.10 are calculated using a "normal vote"–based estimate of the eligible electorate in each state. In brief, this method uses past election results to compute the proportion of Democratic and Republican voters in every state, which is then multiplied by the voting age population in the state. For a good explanation and defense of the method, see Barbara Norrander, "Measuring Primary Turnout in Aggregate Analysis," *Political Behavior* 8 (1986): 356–73. In table 1.10, the normal vote is based on an average of the last three presidential elections and the last six congressional elections.

48. Participation in the March 7 Democratic primaries may also have suffered from the fact that not a single Democratic delegate selection event of any type had been held since the New Hampshire primary on February 1, thus leaving the public and media to give their attention entirely to the Republican race. As noted earlier, this was one reason why the Democrats decided in late 2001 to move up the start of their delegate selection window.

49. Rules and Bylaws Committee of the Democratic National Committee, *Beyond 2000: The Scheduling of Future Democratic Presidential Primaries and Caucuses* (Washington, D.C.: Democratic National Committee, April 29, 2000), 11.

50. Martin P. Wattenberg, "The Republican presidential advantage in the age of party disunity," in *The Politics of Divided Government*, ed. Gary W. Cox and Samuel Kernell (Boulder, Colo.: Westview, 1991), 40, 42.

51. See William G. Mayer, *The Divided Democrats: Ideological Unity, Party Reform, and Presidential Elections* (Boulder, Colo.: Westview, 1996), chap. 3. See also Lonna Rae Atkeson, "From the Primaries to the General Election: Does a Divisive Nomination Race Affect a Candidate's Fortunes in the Fall?" in *In Pursuit of the White House 2000: How We Choose Our Presidential Nominees*, ed. William G. Mayer (New York: Chatham House, 2000), 285–312.

52. On Brown's attempts to shorten the 1992 nomination race, see *New York Times*,

May 18, 1991, 7; October 23, 1991, B2; November 14, 1991, B7; January 21, 1992, A21; and March 27, 1992, A1.

53. The following pages are an attempt to summarize the argument of chaps. 5–7 in Mayer and Busch, *Front-Loading Problem*.

54. For a detailed account of this task force, see Andrew E. Busch, "New Features of the 2000 Presidential Nominating Process: Republican Reforms, Front-Loading's Second Wind, and Early Voting," in *In Pursuit of the White House 2000: How We Choose Our Presidential Nominees*, ed. William G. Mayer (New York: Chatham House, 2000), 57–86.

2

Financing Presidential Nominations under the BCRA

Anthony Corrado and Heitor Gouvêa

The 2004 presidential election will be the first conducted under the campaign finance rules established by the Bipartisan Campaign Reform Act of 2002 (BCRA), the first major piece of federal campaign finance legislation to be adopted in more than twenty years.[1] The act, more commonly known as the McCain-Feingold bill in recognition of its principal congressional sponsors,[2] went into effect on November 6, 2002.[3]

The BCRA principally imposes restrictions on two forms of unregulated financial activity that have grown rapidly in recent elections: party soft money and candidate-specific issue advocacy electioneering.[4] Soft money, which is the unregulated money parties raise from individuals, corporations, and labor unions in unlimited amounts, is banned at the national level by the BCRA. The law also severely restricts its use at the state level for federal election–related activities. Issue advocacy electioneering, which is a form of advertising that features but does not expressly advocate the election or defeat of a federal candidate, is brought within the scope of federal regulation. The law broadens the definition of "federal election activity" to encompass broadcast advertisements that feature federal candidates and are targeted at a specific candidate's electorate in close proximity to an election. The new definition seeks to ensure that such ads sponsored by party committees and non-party groups are financed with monies subject to federal contribution limits and disclosure requirements.[5]

The BCRA makes no major revisions in the rules governing presidential candidates. It does not change the ways candidates are required to finance their campaigns, nor does it alter the regulations governing the presidential public funding system. In fact, the only change that will directly affect presidential candidates is a provision that doubles the amount an individual may contribute to a candidate from $1,000 per election to $2,000. Yet, despite this general acceptance of the status quo, the BCRA is likely to have a major effect on the financial strategies used in presidential nomination contests and may have the unintended consequence of diminishing the role of public funding in presidential elections.

This chapter examines the potential effects of the BCRA on the financing of presidential nomination campaigns. It begins by reviewing the regulations the BCRA leaves intact, which were established by the Federal Election Campaign Act of 1974 (FECA), and the influence these regulations have had on the dynamics of presidential campaign finance. It next considers the possible consequences of the BCRA in light of the financial practices that have characterized recent nomination contests. In particular, it examines the ways in which the BCRA's higher contribution limit (a provision that is expected to be upheld in the initial constitutional challenges to the law)[6] might alter the dynamics of presidential fundraising, and considers how candidates and party committees might adapt their strategies in light of the BCRA's new restrictions.

THE REGULATORY STRUCTURE

The basic regulatory framework for the financing of presidential elections was established by the campaign finance reforms adopted in the wake of the Watergate scandal in the mid-1970s. The FECA and its subsequent amendments imposed contribution limits and disclosure requirements on presidential campaigns, and created an innovative program of voluntary public funding for all stages of the presidential selection process. This program provides taxpayer-supported subsidies to presidential candidates in primary and general elections, as well as grants to national party committees to help pay the costs of national nominating conventions. In exchange for these benefits, candidates who accept public funding agree to abide by campaign spending ceilings and to limit their own personal contributions to their campaigns. The revenue for this program comes from a tax checkoff on individual federal income tax forms, which was originally set at $1 for individual filers ($2 for couples filing jointly) and was increased to $3 ($6 for those filing jointly) in 1993.

These reforms were designed to reduce the influence of private contributions in the presidential nominating process by requiring candidates to finance their campaigns from limited donations and by encouraging them to solicit small donations that could be matched with public funds. To accomplish these objectives, the law placed a limit of $1,000 per election on the amount an individual may contribute to a candidate and $5,000 per election on the amount a political action committee (PAC) may contribute. It also provided candidates with an incentive to solicit smaller contributions by establishing a public subsidy program that matches individual contributions of up to $250 on a dollar-for-dollar basis with taxpayer funds.

To qualify for this matching subsidy, a candidate has to raise at least $5,000 in donations of $250 or less in twenty states. A candidate must also limit personal contributions to his or her own campaign to no more than $50,000 and agree to abide by spending limits. Once a candidate has qualified for the subsidy, any eligible individual contribution received after January 1 of the year before the election can be matched with public dollars, with the first payments made to the candidates on January 1 of the election year.[7]

Candidates who accept public funds are subject to an aggregate expenditure ceiling, as well as state-by-state limits. The aggregate ceiling was set in 1974 at a base amount of $10 million, with a quadrennial adjustment for inflation based on the Consumer Price Index (CPI) and a "fundraising exemption" that allows a candidate to spend an additional 20 percent of the base amount to pay for fundraising costs. This exemption was included in recognition of the higher costs that would be incurred to solicit the smaller donations from a broad base of donors that were required under the FECA's contribution limits.

Under the original provisions of the FECA, each candidate was also allowed to raise an unlimited additional amount that was exempt from the ceiling to pay the legal and accounting costs incurred to comply with the law. However, in 2000, the Federal Election Commission (FEC) changed this rule and adopted a "compliance exemption" that permits a candidate, while engaged in active campaigning, to spend an amount equal to 15 percent of the overall ceiling to cover the costs of compliance. Thereafter, during the period when a campaign is over and winding down, any funds spent on salary and overhead are considered exempt compliance expenditures that are not counted against the spending limit.[8]

Because the spending limit is tied to the rate of inflation, the overall amount a candidate for the presidential nomination may spend from the start of a campaign through to the party nominating convention grows in each successive election. In 1976, the first election conducted with public funding, the base limit was $10.9 million, plus $2.2 million for fundraising costs, for a total cap of $13.1 million.[9] By 2000, the base limit had reached $33.8 million and, with fundraising costs included, the overall cap totaled $40.5 million. When the $5.1 million in exempt compliance spending is included, the aggregate limit in 2000 reached $45.6 million, or about three times the amount permitted more than twenty years ago.[10] Assuming a 2 percent rate of inflation, the aggregate spending limit in 2004, including the allowances for fundraising and compliance costs, will be approximately $50 million.

In addition to this aggregate ceiling, publicly funded candidates must also adhere to limits on spending in each state. These ceilings are based on a 1974 formula that allows 16 cents times a state's voting age population plus adjustments for inflation, with a minimum limit of $200,000, which is also adjusted for inflation. In 2000, these state limits ranged from a minimum of $675,600 in a low population state such as New Hampshire or Delaware, to $13.1 million in California.[11]

These state limits, however, are of less importance to the conduct of presidential campaigns than the aggregate limit on total spending. Since 1976, the state caps have affected candidate spending only in a few states that vote at the start of the delegate selection process, such as Iowa, New Hampshire, and South Carolina.[12] In the vast majority of states, candidates never even approach the state caps. Even so, by the mid-1980s, candidates were using a variety of accounting gimmicks and other complex schemes to spend more money than permitted under the state cap in the crucial early contests. For example, campaigns allocated a share of their in-state expenses to fundraising costs, attributed a portion of salaries and overhead to exempt compliance costs, stationed staff and made purchases in bordering states (so the costs could be allocated to Vermont or Massachusetts rather than New Hampshire), and developed complicated formulas for allocating expenditures on media, polling, and telemarketing to more than one state. These legal subterfuges made state expenditures particularly hard to monitor and the ceilings difficult to enforce.

The FEC responded to these practices by loosening state spending restrictions. In 1991, the agency liberalized its rules to exempt large categories of spending from the state limits. These exempted expenditures, however, are still counted against the aggregate spending limit. Under the revised rules, expenses are allocable against a state spending limit only if they fall within one of five specific categories: media expenses, mass mailings, overhead expenses, special telephone programs, and public opinion polls. This excludes many state campaign–related expenditures from the state caps, including all fees associated with the placement of television, radio, and print advertisements, a candidate's expenses while traveling in a state, and the salaries or fees of some national staff personnel and consultants who are active participants in a state campaign. The rules also allow candidates to treat up to 50 percent of their allocable expenditures in a particular state as exempt fundraising costs, and 10 percent of their administrative costs as exempt compliance spending.[13] As a result of these revisions, the state caps have become increasingly porous and ineffective constraints on candidate spending.

A presidential hopeful who takes full advantage of the exemptions in the law can easily spend more than twice the amount established by the state cap in Iowa or New Hampshire. Yet, even with this leeway, these limits still pose strategic difficulties for publicly funded candidates. Because the caps are based on voting age population, they bear no relation to the relative importance of states in the presidential nominating process. Iowa, the initial gateway on the road to the nomination, has a cap of $1.1 million, which is lower than that of 29 other states. New Hampshire, widely acknowledged to be the most important state primary, is among the states with the lowest expenditure limit.[14] Candidates, especially prospective frontrunners who are expected to do well in these initial contests, face enormous pressure to spend money in these states in order to gain a victory that may launch a successful candidacy, or at least meet the expectations of the political community, thereby surviving the winnowing process that results from these early contests. They therefore have a strong incentive to spend as much as possible in these states in hopes of gaining a relative advantage over opponents. Consequently, they continue to seek out new ways of circumventing the limits in an attempt to maximize their chances for victory.

The strategic concerns posed by the state limits are even more compelling in regard to the aggregate limit. This overall ceiling on candidate spending has had a major influence on the financial strategies employed in recent nomination contests, and has spurred many of the innovative financial practices that have characterized recent campaigns.

In each successive election conducted under the public funding program, the aggregate expenditure ceiling has become an increasingly acute problem, particularly for the nominee who emerges from a competitive race. The problem stems from the fact that, over time, the sum of money permitted under the cap has become increasingly inadequate given the practical realities and costs of a presidential campaign. The parameters established by the FECA were always somewhat arbitrary, as indicated by the significant disparity between the aggregate limit and the cumulative total of the 50 state limits. For example, in 2000, the aggregate limit with all exemptions included was $45.6 million. But if all of the state caps are added together the total is more than $113 million. Candidates are thus allowed to spend less than half of the amount called for by the state ceilings.

Nonetheless, the provisions of the law could accommodate the financial demands of the nominating process in the late 1970s and early 1980s. But campaign costs have risen more rapidly than inflation, so the adjustments that have been made in the aggregate limit have not kept pace with the actual costs of campaigning. More importantly, the law was passed soon after the McGovern-Fraser reforms changed the rules of the presidential selection process and encouraged states to move to primaries as the principal means of determining voters' presidential preferences. The spending limit was thus established a decade before the front-loading of the delegate selection calendar began and long before the emergence of the current nominating process in which more than half of the delegates in each of the major parties are chosen by the middle of March.[15] The spending limit was not adopted with such an intensive, front-loaded process in mind.

Paradoxically, one consequence of the more compact formal selection process has been a lengthening of the period encompassed by the campaign. As an increasing number of state contests have moved into the early weeks of the primary calendar, candidates have been forced to begin campaigning earlier and earlier. The changes that have taken place demand an early start, because candidates need more time to meet the growing financial demands of a process that now requires a multi-state campaign organization before the election year has even begun.

These operational effects of the delegate selection process were compounded by the incongruent FECA regulations governing spending and contribution limits. While the spending limits were adjusted for inflation, the contribution limits were not. Thus, while the total amount a candidate was permitted to spend rose from about $13 million in 1976 to almost $46 million in 2000, the maximum allowable individual contribution remained static at $1,000. During this period, the real purchasing power of a $1,000 gift declined to less than $300 due to the effects of inflation. Consequently, in each succeeding election, candidates had to devote more time to fundraising in order to generate the increasingly large number of contributions needed to raise the amount they were legally allowed to spend under the aggregate limit.

This emphasis on early fundraising has been intensified by the rules of the matching funds program, since contributions raised in the pre-election year are eligible for matching. Candidates therefore attempt to raise as much money as possible in the pre-election year to maximize the amount of their respective initial matching payments, which can provide an important inflow of campaign cash in the weeks leading up to the initial face-offs in Iowa and New Hampshire.

Finally, the changes in the selection schedule have also extended the length of the "back end" of the process, since the period of time between the effective end of the primaries (the point at which a candidate has secured enough delegates to win the race) and the national nominating conventions has also increased. In the first few elections conducted under the FECA, the nominees involved in competitive races typically wrapped up the nomination toward the end of the delegate selection process in late May or early June. Thus, in 1976 through 1984, the "bridge" period between the effective end of contested nomination battles and the start of the conventions lasted less than two months. By 1996 and 2000, this bridge period had grown to five months, as the nomination in each party was essentially determined before the end of March.

Prospective nominees have filled this gap by beginning their general election campaigning earlier than in the past. By shifting to a general election orientation as soon as possible, a presidential hopeful reduces the risk of losing any momentum that may have been gained from a primary victory and minimizes the possibility of ceding a political advantage to a more aggressive general election opponent. This approach also allows a candidate to frame the public dialogue about the issues in the race, rather than relinquish it to an opponent, a factional group within either of the major parties, or some special interest group, all of whom have an incentive to try to influence the issue agenda in the presidential campaign during the months leading up to the convention. As a result, candidates now begin their general election campaigning even before the formal primary period has ended, and continue to campaign throughout the summer months.

Under FECA regulations, general election spending technically does not begin until the convention has formally approved a party nominee.[16] So most of the electioneering costs incurred during the bridge period between the end of the primaries and the national convention must be allocated against the aggregate spending limit that governs campaigning during the prenomination period. Although the FEC has allowed candidates to attribute some pre-convention expenditures to general election planning and overhead, it is generally the case that any monies spent on politicking and almost all of the monies spent to maintain a campaign operation must be counted against the aggregate nomination spending limit. In other words, the FECA's conception of how to distinguish primary from general election expenditures no longer applies in practice. Its outmoded notion of when the general election begins is one more aspect of the law that makes it difficult for presidential aspirants to conduct viable campaigns within the parameters of the FECA's aggregate spending limit.

COPING WITH THE LIMITS

The conflicting pressures of the regulatory structure, requiring on the one hand an early start to campaigning and on the other restraints on spending, have compelled candidates to adopt innovative financial strategies. They have also encouraged parties and other political organizations to participate in the financing of presidential elections in ways that were not contemplated—or were thought to be prohibited—when the FECA was adopted. These responses have undermined the efficacy of the FECA regulations and created the need for the new prohibitions contained in the BCRA. They also shed light on the ways the law has influenced the financial activity in presidential campaigns and provide insight into the strategies to be used by the candidates in 2004.

The Private Funding Option

In principle, the simplest solution to the problems posed by the public funding regulations is not to participate in the program. A candidate who forgoes public funds is freed of any spending limits and can raise and spend as much money as possible, so long as the funds conform to the source and contribution restrictions of the FECA. Few candidates, however, have chosen this option. And only one major party candidate, Republican George W. Bush in 2000, has done so and won the party nomination.

In practice, public matching funds have been such an invaluable source of revenue that most candidates are unwilling, or even unable, to seek the presidency without this benefit. Since 1976, this program has provided about $315 million to 84 primary candidates, including nine minor party contenders, and more than

$1 billion in all, when general election payments and convention subsidies are included.[17] On average, public matching funds have made up about a third of the total campaign monies available to major party candidates seeking a presidential nomination. Candidates who have emphasized the solicitation of small, matchable contributions, including such diverse contenders as Republican Ronald Reagan in 1980, Democrat Jesse Jackson in 1988, Democrat Jerry Brown in 1992, and Republican Patrick Buchanan in 1996, have received an even higher proportion of their campaign revenues from public funds, with the shares reaching 40 to 45 percent. Those who have placed a greater focus on the solicitation of larger contributions, including such well-established contenders as then–Vice President George H. W. Bush in 1988, then-President Bill Clinton in 1996, and then–Senator Robert Dole in 1996, have received from 25 to 30 percent of their total receipts from public funds.[18]

Because the amount a candidate is allowed to raise and spend has increased with each election cycle, the dollar amount of this public subsidy has grown significantly. During the 1980 campaign, President Jimmy Carter accrued $5.1 million in matching funds in his bid for renomination, while his opponent, Republican Ronald Reagan, surpassed all major party contenders by qualifying for $7.3 million in public money.[19] By 1996, the amounts received by the two major party nominees, President Clinton and Republican Robert Dole, had grown to $13.4 million and $13.5 million, respectively.[20] In 2000, the Democratic nominee, then–Vice President Al Gore, received $15.5 million in public money, while his major challenger, former Senator Bill Bradley, received about $12.5 million. On the Republican side, Senator John McCain, who emerged as the top challenger to George Bush, accrued about $14.5 million in matching dollars (see table 2.1).[21]

Given the sums that can be accrued from public funding, it is not surprising that most candidates have been willing to participate in this program. Less well known candidates, especially insurgents challenging established party leaders, generally lack the broad-based donor support needed to generate the substantial sums of money needed to launch and sustain a viable candidacy. These individuals have a strong incentive to accept public funding since they have the greatest need for the supplemental revenue this subsidy can provide. Better known or more established candidates also have had a strong incentive to participate. A major contender would have to solicit several thousand additional contributions to replace the monies obtained from public funds. For most candidates, the replacement of such a large sum is a daunting task. It is much more efficient and cost effective to accept the public money and the corresponding spending limits than it is to raise the additional millions of dollars that would be needed to replace the revenue provided by the subsidy.

Beyond the money involved, most candidates have also been unwilling to forego public funding due to their concerns about the potential political consequences. Public funding stands as the hallmark of the campaign finance reform

Table 2.1 Presidential Prenomination Campaign Receipts, 2000

Candidate	Total Adjusted Receipts[a]	Individual Contributions	PAC Contributions	Public Funds	Candidate Personal Funds
Democrats					
Al Gore	$49,408,081	$33,930,296	$0	$15,456,081	$0
Bill Bradley	42,220,218	29,270,624	0	12,462,045	18,219
Republicans					
George Bush	95,541,540	92,291,250	2,021,342	0	0
Steve Forbes	48,147,976	5,755,150	0	0	42,330,000
John McCain	45,212,723	28,141,463	404,599	14,635,682	0
Alan Keyes	13,110,267	8,226,755	10,100	4,871,767	0
Gary Bauer	12,753,624	7,912,984	6,000	4,890,212	0
Dan Quayle[b]	6,317,916	4,083,201	43,200	2,087,748	0
Elizabeth Dole[b]	5,127,532	5,001,335	118,292	0	735
John Kasich[b]	3,191,083	1,702,668	77,224	0	0
Lamar Alexander[b]	3,085,631	2,301,747	80,383	0	666,417
Orrin Hatch	2,559,300	2,146,182	189,516	0	0
Robert Smith[b]	1,618,878	1,522,128	17,070	0	4,680
Totals	$328,294,769	$222,285,783	$2,967,726	$54,403,535	$43,020,051

Source: Federal Election Commission, as of December 31, 2000.
[a] Total receipts include transfers from previous campaigns, loans, and other revenues.
[b] Withdrew from the race before the end of 1999 and the issuance of public match payments.

movement of the 1970s, and most presidential hopefuls do not want to risk being cast by their opponents or the press corps as an "anti-reform" candidate. This is especially true among Democrats, since the more liberal voters who participate in their party's selection process are generally considered to be supportive of public funding. Candidates have thus perceived a political benefit in the acceptance of public funds, given the belief that a failure to participate in the program may reduce their voter support.

Accordingly, only one Democrat to date has seriously considered opting out of the program. In 1996, then-President Bill Clinton faced no serious challenger in his bid for renomination and considered opting out in order to avoid the spending limits. In the fall of 1995, Clinton's campaign advisors wanted to engage in an expensive early advertising campaign to bolster his support in a number of targeted general election battlegrounds. But Clinton's strategists recognized that the spending limit could not accommodate such a strategy, since it would leave Clinton with little ability to spend money campaigning for most of the rest of the primary period.[22] Clinton, however, decided to participate in the program for political reasons: he hoped to garner general election support from independents and those who cast their ballots in 1992 for the Reform Party nominee, multimillionaire H. Ross Perot. These voters were perceived to be in favor of campaign finance reform and Clinton did not want to risk alienating them by

deciding to refuse public funding so he could spend more than the amount permitted by the expenditure cap.[23] Clinton's choice was also undoubtedly influenced by the decision made by campaign advisors that the ad campaign could be
financed by the Democratic party, instead of the campaign, and thus could be
conducted without being allocated against the presidential expenditure ceiling
(see discussion below).

Since Clinton chose to take public funds, the only major party candidates who
have refused this subsidy have been competitors for the Republican party nomination.[24] In the first five elections conducted under the FECA, only one major
party candidate, Republican John Connally in 1980, chose to forego public funding. Connally, who was philosophically opposed to public funding, refused the
subsidy to avoid the spending ceiling in key states, where he hoped to compete
with prospective front-runner Ronald Reagan by outspending him.[25] His strategy, however, did not work, as he spent about $12.7 million in search of a victory
in one of the early states, but failed to garner much of the vote and ended up
winning only one delegate.[26]

In 1996, two Republican challengers decided to use their personal resources to
try to capture the Republican presidential nomination. Malcolm "Steve" Forbes
and Maurice Taylor, both wealthy businessmen, eschewed public matching funds
so they could spend unlimited amounts of their own money in pursuit of the
party standard. Their strategies followed the approach used by independent candidate H. Ross Perot in 1992, who relied on his personal wealth to mount a general election candidacy in which he eventually spent about $63 million out of his
own pocket.[27] Taylor spent $6.5 million, mostly in Iowa and New Hampshire, in
a short-lived effort to launch a candidacy. Forbes was more successful, spending
more than $37 million of his own wealth and presenting a major challenge to
Bob Dole.[28] Forbes spent lavishly in Iowa, New Hampshire, and a few other early
states, outspending Dole by substantial amounts. But Dole had the resources
needed to overcome Forbes' challenge and secured the nomination before the
end of March. Forbes' spending, however, forced Dole to spend large sums early
in the process, leaving the nominee with little left to spend under the expenditure
cap during the bridge period from April through July.[29]

In 2000, Forbes ran again, this time spending more than $42 million out of
his own pocket, but even this sum was not enough to compete with the resources
available to George Bush, who had established himself as the clear front-runner
by the beginning of the election year.[30] Consequently, Forbes failed to do well in
Iowa and New Hampshire, and ended up dropping out of the race soon after the
first wave of selection contests was over.

Two other Republicans, Representative Robert Dornan in 1996 and Senator
Orrin Hatch in 2000, refused public funds for philosophical reasons. Dornan and
Hatch opposed the use of taxpayer money to pay for political campaigns, but
their individual decisions had no bearing on the dynamics of the presidential

race. Neither one of these candidates raised a meaningful amount of money or mounted a viable campaign.[31]

That Forbes was able to wage a viable nomination campaign without public funding highlights one of the criticisms often levelled against the current campaign finance system—that it gives a strategic advantage to wealthy candidates who are able and willing to spend large sums of personal money on a campaign.[32] Such self-funded candidates can avoid the rigors of fundraising and operate free of any spending constraints. Moreover, they can afford the type of national campaigning needed to develop name recognition and have their messages heard by the public. However, as the experience in presidential elections has demonstrated, these advantages do not necessarily translate into electoral victory. Self-financed candidates usually lack the broad base of donor support that tends to reflect electoral support. As a result, although they find it easier to mount a campaign, they do not significantly outperform other well-funded candidates.[33]

Among those candidates who have decided not to accept public funds, Bush stands out as unique. Bush is the first presidential nominee since the FECA was adopted to opt out of the public matching funds program and finance a major party nomination campaign solely with private contributions and without any personal funds. His ability to raise money, which was well-established months before the first matching payments were to be issued, was certainly a major factor in his decision to opt out. His choice also was undoubtedly influenced by Dole's experience in 1996 and the prospect of running against Forbes, who could spend unlimited sums of his own money in early contests (and did). Bush did not want to find himself in a position comparable to Dole's: he did not want to win the nomination only to find himself constrained by the spending limit and unable to continue an aggressive campaign throughout the summer months, especially since his opponent was likely to be the incumbent Vice President Al Gore.[34]

Bush is also the only candidate to refuse public funds and prove capable of raising more money than the amount established by the aggregate spending limit for candidates who accept matching funds. In all, Bush raised more than $95 million for his nomination campaign, more than twice the amount permitted under the spending limit. He raised far more than he would have received from public matching payments, which might have totaled between $12 million and $14 million.[35] About two-thirds of this $95 million, $67.6 million, was raised before the start of the election year.[36] Even more remarkable was the fact that most of his campaign money, about $60 million, came from donors who contributed the $1,000 maximum. No previous presidential candidate had ever received even one-third of this amount from $1,000 donors.

Bush was able to finance a winning nomination race because he entered the contest with an extraordinary fundraising base. In his two winning gubernatorial campaigns in Texas, he raised a total of $41 million, so his home state provided a solid foundation for financial success.[37] Bush also relied on the well-established fundraising network that had supported his father, former President Bush, which encompassed an estimated 50,000 donors.[38] In addition, Bush began in 1998 to recruit a large group of fundraisers, who came to be known as the Pioneers, who each agreed to be responsible for raising $100,000 by identifying ten individuals who would each give $1,000 and who would then in turn find ten others to do the same. By the end of the nomination campaign, this pyramiding effort had produced more than 200 Pioneers who were responsible for soliciting more than $20 million.[39]

Bush thus began with a financial base comparable to that of an incumbent president, and he was able to capitalize on this financial support as a result of the dynamics of the selection process. By September of 1999, he had already raised $57 million, including more than $12 million from Texas donors.[40] This sum tripled his initial fundraising goal of $20 million for 1999 and surpassed the total amount permitted under the expenditure limit governing publicly funded candidates by more than $11 million. It also established him as the clear winner of the "money primary" that is an essential part of the "invisible primary" that takes place in the pre-election year.[41] Bush's total dwarfed the total receipts of other candidates and caused many of his opponents to drop out of the race before the end of December 1999. Having established himself as the candidate to beat and likely winner of the nomination, Bush gathered additional momentum and garnered another $10 million in the fourth quarter of 1999 alone.[42]

With his fundraising totals greatly exceeding the sum allowed by the public funding spending limit, Bush only had to consider the potential political ramifications of private funding, and these were not very significant. Forbes had already decided to forego public money, thus providing Bush with a rationale for his decision to opt out. In addition, the conservative voters who tend to form the base of the Republican presidential primary electorate were not perceived to be strong supporters of taxpayer-funded elections. Finally, any political risk of being cast as "anti-reform" for foregoing public funds was less of a concern than the risk inherent in accepting the spending limit and thereby constraining the type of campaign he could run between March and July. In the end, Bush's decision to conduct a wholly privately financed campaign was an easy one to make.

Early Fundraising and the Role of Large Donors

The scope of Bush's fundraising makes comparisons with other candidates difficult, but his financial strategy did reflect two of the general patterns that have characterized recent presidential nomination campaigns: the growth of early fundraising and an emphasis on large contributions.

As has been noted, the financial demands of the presidential selection process necessitate an early start to campaign fundraising. By 1996, this need had become a strategic imperative, since the increasingly compact delegate selection calendar permitted little time for concerted fundraising efforts once the formal primary period began. Moreover, with more than half of the delegates selected by mid-March, the nomination process was likely to yield a nominee after a relatively short period of voting. Candidates who hoped to be competitive had to amass the resources needed to wage viable campaigns in a number of states simultaneously. And the sum they had to amass was substantial. In advance of the 1996 and 2000 elections, most political practitioners and informed observers were estimating that a candidate would have to raise $20 million to $25 million in the year before the election in order to meet the costs of the front end of the delegate selection process.[43]

Candidates responded to this strategic imperative by concentrating their fundraising efforts in the year before the election. As noted in tables 2.2 and 2.3 below, the leading candidates in the presidential race in 1996 and 2000 solicited more than $20 million in the year before the election, which represented more than 75 percent of the total sum they received in private contributions for the entire campaign. In other words, exclusive of public matching funds, the vast majority of the money raised in presidential nominating contests is now raised well before any voting has taken place. And the percentage would be even higher if the monies solicited in the election year in the weeks before the Iowa caucuses were included.

In 1996, for example, then-President Clinton, who was unchallenged in his bid for renomination, raised $25.8 million by the end of December of 1995, which represented 89 percent of the total of $29.1 million of non-public funding that he received during his entire prenomination campaign (see table 2.2). Among the Republicans, the leaders in the 1995 money chase, Senators Bob Dole and Phil Gramm, each took in more than $20 million. Dole led all Republican contenders in early fundraising with a take of $24.6 million, or only $1.2 million less than President Clinton. Gramm raised $20.8 million, including $4.8 million that he transferred from his senatorial campaign committee, while another aspirant, former Tennessee governor Lamar Alexander, raised more than $10 million. Almost half of Alexander's total (47 percent) came from donors from his home state.[44] The amounts generated by Dole and Alexander, who survived the winnowing process in Iowa and New Hampshire, represented 78 percent of all the private money they received during the campaign, while Gramm's total represented 97 percent of his private funding.

In 1996, Patrick Buchanan was the only major contender who did not receive most of his private funding before the start of the election year. In this regard, he was the exception that proved the rule. Buchanan, a well-known conservative who had sought the Republican nomination in 1992 and had an established base of direct-mail donors, performed well in New Hampshire, which led to a surge in contributions in the weeks after the primary.[45] This influx of cash allowed Buchanan to continue campaigning after New Hampshire, but he still lagged well behind Dole in financial resources. Dole relied on the war chest he had built up

Table 2.2 Early Fundraising, 1996 Prenomination Campaign

Candidate	1995 Receipts (in million $)	1995 Receipts from $1,000 Donors (in million $)	% from $1,000 Donors	Total Campaign Receipts w/o Public Money (in million $)	% of Total Raised in 1995
Democrats					
Clinton	25.8	15.2	59	29.1	89
Republicans[a]					
Dole	24.6	14.3	58	31.6	78
Gramm[b]	20.8	8.5	41	21.4	97
Alexander[c]	10.2	7.0	69	13.1	78
Buchanan	7.2	0.4	6	16.0	49
Lugar[c]	4.6	1.7	37	5.0	92
Keyes	1.7	0.08	5	3.5	49
Dornan	0.2	0.01	5	0.3	67

Source: Based on data available from the Federal Election Commission. Number of $1,000 donors based on analysis by the authors.

[a] Does not include Arlen Specter and Pete Wilson, who withdrew from the race prior to December 31, 1995. Also omits Steve Forbes and Maurice Taylor, who were self-financed candidates. By the end of 1995, Forbes had given $16.5 million to his campaign and raised $1.5 million in private contributions. Taylor had given $4.5 million to his campaign and raised $25,400.

[b] Includes $4.8 million transferred from Senate committee. If this amount is excluded, the percentage of funds raised in 1995 from $1,000 donors is 53 percent.

[c] 1995 receipts adjusted to deduct loans repaid with public matching funds.

early in the process to recover his lead after New Hampshire and wrapped up the nomination in the next few weeks.

Candidates in the 1996 election cycle not only sought to raise large sums in the preelection year, but they sought to do so as efficiently as possible. While the FECA's public funding provisions were designed to encourage candidates to emphasize the solicitation of small contributions that could be matched with public money, well established candidates with extensive donor bases have chosen instead to emphasize contributions of the maximum amount permitted under the FECA in an effort to amass as much money as possible as quickly as possible. This approach helps to reduce the costs of fundraising, since the solicitation of these larger contributions is generally much cheaper than prospecting for small donations through direct mail and telemarketing. It also minimizes the amount of time and effort a candidate has to devote to the burdensome task of raising money. The emphasis on larger donors thus represents a logical response to the strategic problems posed by the rules governing the current selection process. Accordingly, well-known candidates have sought to exploit their established donor bases by emphasizing the solicitation of $1,000 contributions. Those who have most successfully implemented this strategy have emerged as the winners of the money primary and gone on to win the presidential nomination.

To determine the role of $1,000 donors, an analysis was conducted of each of the individual contributions disclosed by the 1996 and 2000 major party presidential candidates during the primary period. Under the disclosure regulations established by the FECA, candidates are required to disclose every contribution of $200 or more; in a few instances, lesser known candidates who raised relatively small sums included some donations of less than $200 in their disclosure reports. Each of the individual contributions reported by these candidates was reviewed to identify multiple contributions by the same donor (e.g., instances where an individual donor made two $500 contributions or a $250 and $750 contribution for a total gift of $1,000). A data file was then created containing the aggregate amount given by each donor. These aggregate gifts were then sorted by date to determine the timing of the amount contributed. The analysis did not include Steve Forbes, since he basically self-financed his campaigns in both 1996 and 2000.

This analysis provided data on the role of $1,000 *contributors*, as opposed to $1,000 *contributions*, in the early fundraising efforts of presidential aspirants.[46] As the data in table 2.2 indicate, the candidates who raised the most money in the year before the 1996 election were those who had the most success in attracting $1,000 donors. Indeed, the leading candidates raised more than half of their total 1995 receipts from donors who each gave a total of $1,000. As might be expected, then-President Clinton had the greatest success in soliciting these large donors, raising 59 percent of his money ($15.2 million) from $1,000 donors. Similarly, then-Senate Majority Leader Dole raised 58 percent of his early money ($14.3 million) from large givers. Gramm and Alexander also generated most of their early money from big givers. Alexander raised less than half of the amount raised by Dole, but almost 70 percent of the $10 million he did solicit came from $1,000 donors. Gramm received more than 40 percent of the $20.8 million he reported from big givers. But when the monies transferred from his senate campaign committee are excluded (since the sources of these monies are not included in the presidential disclosure reports) and only the funds solicited after Gramm declared his presidential candidacy are considered, the share of his 1995 receipts that came from $1,000 donors rises to 53 percent. Thus, the five top fundraisers in 1995 each raised more than half of their money from those who gave the maximum permissible contribution.

Conversely, lesser known aspirants and ideological candidates (i.e., candidates whose support is concentrated among very liberal or conservative voters) failed to raise much money early in the process. These aspirants lacked broad donor bases or had to rely on the smaller gifts typically contributed by ideological donors,[47] which made it difficult, if not impossible, to raise the sums needed to wage viable campaigns in the initial wave of selection contests. With little prospect of catching the frontrunners in the money race, a number of these financially strapped candidates in 1996 and 2000 dropped out of the race even before the start of the election year.

Thus, the ability to solicit large individual contributions was a crucial factor in determining the relative financial success of candidates early in the 1996 election. Candidates who enjoyed substantial support from big givers were able to raise the sums needed to emerge as serious candidates in the invisible primary period. Those who could not were cast as unlikely winners who lacked the resources needed to compete effectively. In general, establishment candidates were able to separate themselves from ideological challengers and insurgent candidates as a result of their ability to garner large numbers of $1,000 gifts.

A similar pattern characterized the early financial activity of the major party candidates competing in the 2000 election. The one notable difference was that the leading candidates raised even more money in the pre-election year and an even larger share from $1,000 donors than did their counterparts four years earlier. As noted in table 2.3, the two contenders for the Democratic nomination, Al Gore and Bill Bradley, each raised more than $27 million in 1999, thus surpassing the amount solicited by then-President Clinton in 1995. These 1999 receipts represented more than 80 percent of total private contributions Gore received during the course of the campaign and more than 90 percent of Bradley's. What was most impressive about their early fundraising, however, was their success in attracting large donors. Gore and Bradley each received more than $18 million from $1,000 donors, which constituted 67 percent of their total 1999 receipts. This success reflected the extensive donor bases each of these candidates had developed over the years, as well as the perceived competitiveness of the race in the early stages of the contest.

Gore and Bradley both raised more money in the pre-election year than any previous presidential candidate. But their efforts were overshadowed by Bush's extraordinary performance. The unprecedented nature of Bush's fundraising is indicated by the figures in table 2.3. Bush raised more than Gore and Bradley *combined* in 1999 and more than twice the sum achieved by Dole in the comparable period four years earlier. Moreover, in part due to the efforts of his Pioneers, Bush received almost $50 million, or 74 percent of his total 1999 receipts, from $1,000 donors. No previous presidential hopeful had ever come close to developing such an extensive large donor base. Bush's $1,000 donors alone provided more than enough revenue to outdistance the funds available to his closest challenger, Steve Forbes, who had given close to $29 million of his personal wealth to his campaign by the end of 1999 and raised an additional $5.2 million from other donors.

Senator John McCain of Arizona, who did not compete in the Iowa caucuses and emerged as Bush's principal challenger only after an upset victory in the New Hampshire primary, also raised a substantial amount of early money, amassing a total of $15.5 million before the end of 1999, or about $5 million more than Lamar Alexander had achieved as the "third place" candidate in the 1996 money primary. But he did not raise most of his money in the pre-election year. McCain received about half of his total funds from private contributions in 1999, with only about 35 percent coming from $1,000 donors (if the amount transferred

Table 2.3 Early Fundraising, 2000 Prenomination Campaign

Candidate	1999 Receipts (in million $)	1999 Receipts from $1,000 Donors (in million $)	% from $1,000 Donors	Total Campaign Receipts w/o Public Money (in million $)	% of Total Raised in 1999
Democrats					
Gore	27.8	18.6	67	33.9	82
Bradley	27.5	18.3	67	29.7	93
Republicans[a]					
Bush	67.6	49.8	74	95.5	71
McCain[b]	15.5	5.4	35	30.6	51
Bauer[c]	6.8	1.1	16	7.9	86
Hatch	2.3	1.0	43	2.6	88
Keyes[c]	3.3	0.2	6	8.2	40

Source: Based on data available from the Federal Election Commission. Number of $1,000 donors based on analysis by the authors.

[a] Does not include Lamar Alexander, Elizabeth Dole, John Kasich, Dan Quayle, or Robert Smith who withdrew from the Republican race prior to December 31, 1999. Also does not include Steve Forbes, who relied on personal funds. By the end of 1999, Forbes had given $28.7 million to his campaign and raised $5.2 million.

[b] Includes $1.96 million transfer from Senate committee. If this amount is excluded, the percentage of funds raised in 1999 from $1,000 donors is 40 percent.

[c] 1999 receipts adjusted to deduct loans repaid with public matching funds.

from his Senate campaign committee is excluded, the share from $1,000 donors rises to 40 percent). He was thus the only major contender in 2000 to deviate from the early fundraising pattern typical of serious candidates.

McCain was able to raise a substantial amount of money during the primaries, and thus build on his early success, due to the emergence of the Internet as a vehicle for campaign fundraising. McCain's unexpected victory over Bush in New Hampshire led to a surge of support for his candidacy, and encouraged thousands of individuals to visit his campaign's website and make a contribution electronically. In the week after his victory, the campaign received about $1.4 million via the Internet, primarily in small contributions. Since most of these gifts were eligible for matching funds, these contributions produced $2 million in revenue. By the end of the month, McCain had received $3.7 million in Internet donations, and thus had the funds needed to wage aggressive campaigns in targeted states in early March.[48] By the middle of March, McCain had raised a total of $45.2 million, including public matching funds, which allowed him to spend the maximum sum permitted by the aggregate spending limit. But even this amount was not enough to compete with the resources available to Bush, and by the third week of March, the Republican nomination battle was effectively over.

That Buchanan in 1996 and McCain in 2000 were exceptions to the general pattern that prevailed in the past two elections can also be discerned from a broader analysis of the financial activity that took place in these contests. In general, the reliance on large donors that characterizes early fundraising has been a feature of the nomination campaign as a whole. Indeed, a disproportionate share of the money raised in presidential nomination campaigns, particularly among the leading candidates, now comes from $1,000 donors. Moreover, this reliance on large donors has increased over the past two election cycles.

As noted in table 2.4, almost half of the money received from individual donors in the 1996 presidential nomination campaign came from those who gave the legal maximum. In all, there were more than 57,600 individuals who gave $1,000 during the 1996 primary election, and these donors were responsible for 47 percent of the funds raised from individual contributions. The eventual nominees received at least half of their private funding from $1,000 donors. Clinton solicited about 15,681 maximum gifts, and these donors were responsible for 55 percent of his total receipts from individual contributions. Dole also did well in raising large donations, soliciting more than 14,875 maximum contributions. These donors provided Dole with 50 percent of his total individual receipts. Among the most financially successful candidates, only Buchanan received more money from small donors than large donors. Those who gave $1,000 (approxi-

Table 2.4 Percentage of Total Individual Receipts from $1,000 Donors, 1996 Presidential Nomination Campaign

Party	Candidate	Adjusted Individual Contributions (in million $)	Amount from $1,000 Donors[a] (in million $)	% of Individual Contributions from $1,000 Donors
Republican				
	Dole, R.	29.8	14.9	50
	Gramm	15.9	8.6	54
	Buchanan	15.5	1.0	6
	Alexander	12.6	8.6	68
	Wilson	5.6	4.0	71
	Lugar	4.8	1.9	40
	Forbes	4.2	2.0	48
	Keyes	3.5	0.08	2
	Specter	2.3	1.1	48
	Dornan	0.3	0.02	7
	Taylor	0.03	0.02	67
Democrat				
	Clinton	28.3	15.7	55
Total		122.8	57.9	47

Source: Based on data obtained from disclosure reports filed by the candidates with the Federal Election Commission. Number of $1,000 donors and corresponding amount of money received from these donors based on an analysis conducted by the authors.

[a] Includes some donors who are listed as contributing more than $1,000.

mately 894 individuals in all) provided him with only 6 percent of the money he received from individual donations.

In 2000, the share of contributed funds coming from $1,000 donors was even higher (see table 2.5). In this year, large donors were responsible for more than half of the money contributed by individuals (54 percent). There were more than 118,000 individuals who gave the legal maximum in 2000, and half of these individuals gave $1,000 to George Bush. In all, Bush solicited an astounding 59,279 maximum donations, or about as many as all of the 1996 candidates combined or all of the other candidates in 2000 combined. And he was not the only candidate focused on large gifts. Both Gore and Bradley received more large gifts than Clinton had in 1996, and raised a greater share of their contributed funds from this source. Gore received about 19,289 maximum gifts, or about 3,500 more than Clinton, which provided 57 percent of his total individual funding. Bradley solicited 18,345 maximum gifts, or about 2,600 more than Clinton, which provided him with 63 percent of his individual revenues. So even if Bush is excluded from the compilations, the role played by large donors was substantial. Overall, without Bush, the candidates received more than $59 million from $1,000 donors, which represented about 46 percent of their total receipts from individual contributions.

The only serious 2000 contender not to receive the lion's share of his funding from large gifts was McCain, who raised about 36 percent of his total individual funds from this source. In this regard, the financial dynamics of his campaign differed from those of other recent competitive candidates. In all, McCain received slightly more than 10,000 maximum gifts, with about 5,400 of these donations received in 1999 and the other 4,600 during the course of the rest of the campaign.

The Problem of Spending Limits

While the dynamics of McCain's fundraising did not conform to the characteristic pattern of serious contenders, the dynamics of his spending did. Like competitive candidates in other recent contested races for the presidential nomination, McCain effectively reached the aggregate spending ceiling long before the end of the primaries. In fact, if he had performed better on Super Tuesday and won enough state contests to continue his battle with George Bush, he would not have been able to do so without violating the expenditure limit. By the third week of March, McCain had basically spent the amount permitted by the law. Had he decided to go on, he would have had to cut his national campaign operation to the bare bones, stop all paid advertising, and minimize all campaign travel. In short, he would have had to pull up stakes in the midst of a hotly contested race that had captured national attention.

McCain decided to suspend his candidacy before having to face the full conse-

Table 2.5 Percentage of Total Individual Receipts from $1,000 Donors, 2000 Presidential Nomination Campaign

Party	Candidate	Adjusted Individual Contributions (in million $)	Amount from $1,000 Donors[a] (in million $)	% of Individual Contributions from $1,000 Donors
Republicans				
	Bush	92.3	59.3	64
	McCain	28.1	10.1	36
	Keyes	8.2	0.5	6
	Bauer	7.9	1.4	18
	Forbes	5.8	1.8	31
	Dole, E.	5.0	3.0	60
	Quayle	4.1	1.5	37
	Alexander	2.3	2.0	87
	Hatch	2.1	1.1	52
	Smith	1.5	0.08	5
Democrats				
	Gore	33.9	19.3	57
	Bradley	29.3	18.4	63
Total		220.6	118.5	54

Source: Based on data obtained from disclosure reports filed by the candidates with the Federal Election Commission. Number of $1,000 donors and corresponding amount of money received from these donors based on an analysis conducted by the authors.
[a] Includes some donors who are listed as contributing more than $1,000.

quences of the expenditure ceiling. But his experience highlights another major problem in the presidential finance system that has been evident for some time: the inadequacy of the expenditure ceiling. Since at least the mid-1980s, the presumptive nominees, particularly those who have emerged from competitive contests, have found it increasingly difficult to finance campaign activities in the period leading up to the convention due to the constraints of the expenditure limit. In the 1980s, the presumptive nominees effectively reached the limit (i.e., their total expenditures, including anticipated operational costs for the remaining period leading up to the convention, equaled the amount permissible under the cap) by late May or early June. These candidates, including Democrat Walter Mondale in 1984, Republican George H. W. Bush in 1988, and Democrat Bill Clinton in 1992, had to reduce their spending and limit their campaigning in the final months of the prenomination campaign in an effort to avoid exceeding the limit.[49] Mondale and Bush each ended up surpassing the limit, and thus had to pay a penalty after the election for violating the law.[50]

In more recent elections, this problem has become even more severe as the combination of heavy early spending and a longer bridge period have combined to make it nearly impossible for a candidate in a competitive contest to have sufficient spending authority left after the effective end of the primaries to continue campaigning. In 1996, for example, the presumptive Republican nominee, Robert Dole, reached the limit months before the party's national convention. By the end of March, Dole had spent $29.3 million of the $30.9 million base spending limit and had little room left under the aggregate cap.[51] At the same time, his prospective opponent, incumbent President Bill Clinton, who was unchallenged in his bid for renomination, had about $20 million left to spend.[52]

Similarly, in 2000, Al Gore won the Democratic nomination with surprising ease, yet by the end of March he was already facing the constraints of the spending cap. (Gore's opponent, Bill Bradley, withdrew from the race in the second week of March, yet still spent $42 million against the $45.6 million cap. He, too, would have been restricted by the limit had he won the nomination.) Although Gore had about $11 million in spending room remaining at the end of March, this sum basically represented the costs of maintaining his campaign infrastructure through July. He had no room left to spend substantial sums on active campaigning. His prospective opponent George Bush, however, was free of the spending limit and continued to spend large sums on campaigning, while raising about $20 million in additional money after he had wrapped up the nomination.[53]

The Parties Respond

The inability of presidential nominees to continue to campaign aggressively once the nomination is decided has encouraged the party committees to campaign on their respective nominees' behalf. In 1996 and 2000, party committees spent tens of millions of dollars on advertising in support of their respective standard bearers in the months before the conventions. None of these expenditures was subject to the candidate expenditure ceilings and soft money was used to pay most of the costs.

The parties were able to circumvent the spending and contribution limits by conducting candidate-specific "issue advocacy advertisements" on behalf of their prospective nominees. These ads were considered exempt from federal regulation because they did not include such words as "vote for," "elect," or "defeat."[54] Accordingly, the parties argued that they could spend unlimited amounts on issue advocacy advertising, including ads that featured their presumptive nominees, and pay for them in part with soft dollars.

This innovative tactic began with the Democrats, who conducted a massive issue advertising effort in 1995 to bolster President Clinton's prospects in advance of the 1996 election. Clinton's political advisors and national party committee officials concluded that such advertising was not "campaign spending" and thus could be carried out beyond the scope of the expenditure limits governing Clinton's campaign. In this way they solved the strategic problem of how to accept public funding yet spend large sums on early advertising without breaking the spending limit. By June of 1996, the Democratic National Committee (DNC) and Democratic state party committees had spent more than $34 million on issue ads, including at least $22 million of soft money.[55]

In the summer of 1996, the Republican National Committee (RNC) relied on the Democratic precedent to intervene in the presidential race and support Dole with an issue advertising campaign of its own. In May, the RNC chairman, Haley Barbour, announced a $20 million advertising effort to "show the differences between Dole and Clinton and between Republicans and Democrats on the issues facing our country."[56] By the start of the general election, the party had spent $18 million advocating Dole's candidacy.[57] Because of the spending limit, Dole was forced to become a surrogate of the party committee. He relied on party advertising to distribute his message, and what little campaigning he did largely consisted of appearances at party fundraisers or other events. The party even helped to maintain his organization by placing 44 members of his campaign staff on various party payrolls.[58]

In 1996, this party advertising was a highly controversial and legally questionable practice that helped to spur the demand among advocates of campaign finance reform for statutory restrictions on this type of electioneering. But in the aftermath of the 1996 election, no enforcement actions were taken to discourage this practice. Consequently, both parties in 2000 relied even more heavily on issue advertising to provide a form of "bridge financing" to their respective nominees. These efforts were facilitated by the extraordinary sums of soft money raised by both parties, which totaled more than $495 million by the end of the election cycle, or almost twice as much as the amount raised four years earlier.[59]

From the beginning of June through the middle of September, the Democratic and Republican party committees spent an estimated $48 million on issue advertisements in support of their respective presidential nominees. The Democrats were the first to begin advertising and spent an estimated $25.7 million during the bridge period in support of Al Gore. Like Dole in 1996, Gore had insufficient spending authority remaining after he wrapped up the nomination to finance any advertising on his own, and thus was relegated to a dependence on the party apparatus for all broadcast communications. What was more remarkable was the Republican response. Even though Bush was not hampered by the limits and had plenty of money available to spend, the party still decided to intervene on his behalf and took primary responsibility for responding to the Democrats' advertising. Over the course of the summer, the party spent an estimated $22.3 million on issue ads in support of Bush.[60] This sum compared to about $3 million spent on advertising by the Bush campaign during this bridge period, most of which was spent in July on media related to the convention.[61]

These party expenditures highlighted the inadequacy of FECA restrictions by suggesting that the actual costs of campaigning could not be accommodated under its obsolete ceilings. At the same time, they made a mockery of the FECA's contribution and spending limits. The ability of party committees to supplement the financing available to a presumptive nominee in effect turned the public funding program into a system of "floors without ceilings." The public funding provided the candidates who accepted this subsidy with a floor of support, but placed no effective ceiling on the amounts spent in support of a particular candidate. Once a nominee reached the limit, the party simply assumed the burden of financing campaign-related activity and continued to spend without concern for any cap considerations. More importantly, the practice eviscerated the FECA's restrictions on the sources of funding used to pay for election-related activity, since parties could use soft money solicited from sources prohibited from making contributions to presidential candidates in amounts not permitted under federal law to finance the major share of the costs of these advertising campaigns. As a result, by the end of the 2000 election cycle, the limit on presidential campaign spending was essentially a matter of how much the parties were able to raise and willing to spend to capture the Oval Office.

THE EFFECT OF THE BCRA

In adopting the BCRA, Congress largely, and to some extent deliberately, avoided discussion of the presidential nominating process, since most legislators did not want to become enmeshed in a debate over public financing and spending limits. Consequently, the statute treated the symptoms of the presidential system rather than the cause of the disease: it took action to restrict the practices that have arisen in response to the inadequacies of the public funding regulations, but did nothing to rectify the underlying shortcomings and strategic incentives that gave rise to these innovations in the first place. As a result, the law will not resolve the deeply rooted problems that have long been evident in the public funding program. Instead it is likely to exacerbate many of the trends that have become a cause for concern in recent elections.

Higher Contribution Limits

Only one provision of the BCRA will affect presidential candidates directly: the law increases the maximum amount an individual may contribute to a candidate from $1,000 per election to $2,000, and adjusts this amount in subsequent elections for inflation. This change, which is likely to withstand judicial scrutiny,[62] will make it easier for candidates to raise money. It will help lesser known candidates raise seed money from their small bases of support to launch a campaign, but it will provide the greatest benefit to well known candidates who can successfully solicit large numbers of maximum contributions. The new limit will allow incumbent presidents and other well established contenders to amass substantial sums more quickly and efficiently than they have in previous elections and provide these candidates with additional resources. The amount of additional money they will be able to garner will depend on how successful they are in convincing those who now give $1,000 to give even more. It will therefore encourage established candidates to solicit an even greater share of their campaign funds from large donors than they have in the past, and thereby increase the shift away from small donor fundraising that has characterized recent contests.

As the leading candidates take advantage of their ability to receive larger sums from well-heeled donors, lesser known aspirants, ideological contenders, and insurgent candidates will fall further and further behind in the money race. Assuming that the patterns exhibited in 1996 and 2000 will continue, and there is no reason to believe that they will not, the $2,000 limit will make it even less likely that a dark horse contender or insurgent candidate will emerge as a serious competitor for the nomination.

For example, as noted above, in 1996 and 2000 the financial advantage gained by the leaders in the money chase during the invisible primary was principally a result of their success in raising $1,000 contributions. This relative advantage is likely to increase under the BCRA, since candidates who rely on small donors are unlikely to be able to match the increased revenues that well established candidates can realize as a result of the higher contribution limit. In other words, on a relative basis, well established candidates are likely to receive more from donors giving between $1,000 and $2,000 than less established candidates are likely to raise from small donors, even if their efforts are highly successful. The new law will thus broaden the revenue gap between well-established and less-established contenders, thus enhancing the prospect that aspirants in the latter category will be significantly outspent in a nomination campaign. Take, for example, the case of the 1996 Republican contest. In that race, Dole received $14.9 million from $1,000 donors. If only 30 percent of these contributors had increased their gift to $2,000, Dole would have raised an additional $4.5 million. In contrast, Buchanan would have received only $300,000 in additional funding under a similar scenario.

By broadening the gap between candidates who can rely on large donors and those who cannot, the BCRA will exacerbate the stratifying effects that fundraising has in differentiating candidate prospects, making it even more difficult for less well-funded candidates to make the political case that they have a realistic chance of advancing a competitive candidacy. It thus enhances the importance of fundraising during the invisible primary that takes place before the start of the formal selection process. As in the 1996 and 2000 Republican primaries, in 2004 and beyond it is likely that the money race will have a substantial winnowing effect on the field, pressuring candidates who cannot keep pace with the finances of the leading contenders to drop out of the race before the election year has even begun.

Furthermore, the new law is likely to produce a selection process in which prospective front-runners who accept public funds will essentially raise the total amount they will be allowed to spend in the year before the election, with no room to raise additional funds thereafter. The leading candidates in contested nomination races are already raising more than 75 percent of their funds from individuals in the year before the election. In the 2000 Democratic contest, both candidates raised more than 80 percent of their total individual receipts during this period. With the added revenue that will be provided by donors giving more than $1,000, these percentages will climb even higher, and it is likely that the leaders will basically accrue the amounts they will be allowed to spend before the Iowa caucuses convene.

In the context of the 2004 election, the greatest beneficiary of the $2,000 limit will be President George Bush, who will be able to capitalize even further on his extraordinary fundraising base. As was the case for other recent incumbents, Bush is expected to seek renomination in an uncontested race. Given his experience in 2000, it is generally expected that he will do so without accepting public funds. Bush will thus be in a position to raise even more money than he did four years ago, which will provide him with a substantial financial advantage over any prospective Democratic opponent.

How much Bush will be able to raise is impossible to determine with any certainty, but the expansion of his campaign war chest, at a minimum, is likely to be substantial. If Bush does run unopposed and if his levels of political support do not drop precipitously, he should retain the donor base he established in his first run for the White House. This base, which consists of more than 59,000 donors who gave $1,000 in 2000, is expected to give significantly more money in 2004 with the higher contribution limit. While all of these donors will not "double up" in 2004, a sizable proportion most likely will. According to one survey of the pool of presidential donors, about 33 percent of Bush's $1,000 contributors in 2000 report that they would give more money if the contribution limits were raised.[63] If these intentions were to be actualized, and those donors who express a willingness to give more were to contribute the maximum permissible amount, Bush would receive about $20 million in additional receipts *from his current large donor base*. When this sum is added to the $59.3 million he received from large donors in 2000, the total represents a base of almost $80 million. When combined with the monies Bush received from donors of lesser amounts, which was roughly $35 million in 2000, his total potential receipts in 2004 for the prenomination campaign alone would be about $115 million, or more than twice the $50 million that a publicly funded candidate would be permitted to raise and spend. And this represents a conservative estimate of the president's fundraising potential. If Bush also received larger contributions from his donors who gave less than $1,000 in 2000 or is able to expand his fundraising base significantly, he would raise much more. For example, if half of his $1,000 contributors in 2000 were to give $2,000 in 2004, his fundraising total would rise to more than $135 million.

The Role of Party Funding

Whatever the total resources eventually at the president's command, the expectation that he will once again choose to conduct a privately funded nomination campaign and spend well beyond the amount permitted publicly funded candidates is certain to influence the strategic thinking of his prospective opponents. It is likely to ensure that Bush will not face a major challenge from within his own party, since such challenges are rare in the first place (since 1980 no incumbent president has faced a serious intra-party challenge) and Bush's anticipated war chest will further discourage such a possibility. More importantly, it will give cause to his potential Democratic opponents to give more deliberate consideration to the option of foregoing public funds. This consideration will be strengthened by the effects of the BCRA, which diminish the incentives to accept public funds.

Prior to the 1996 election, those contemplating a presidential bid could safely assume that all contenders, particularly the major contenders, would accept public funds and be subject to campaign spending limits. Aspirants could therefore anticipate that every candidate would be pursuing a similar financial strategy and that the eventual winners of the nomination in each party would be conducting campaigns on a relatively level playing field with respect to campaign spending. Since the 1996 election, the strategic calculus has become more complex. At first, candidates had to confront the problems posed by a *self-funded* candidate free of any spending limit. Now, they also have to consider the possibility of a *privately funded* candidate capable of spending more than the amount allowed by the public funding ceiling.

One option available to candidates under BCRA is to accept public funds and rely on party support to continue campaigning once the spending limit is reached. In this scenario, candidates would be following the financial patterns established in 1996 and 2000. However, in 2004 and beyond party organizations will have to use a somewhat different strategy than that employed in previous nomination campaigns, since they will no longer be able to use soft money to buttress the prospects of their presidential hopeful.

Two provisions of the BCRA will have a significant effect on the financial practices of party committees during the bridge period between the end of the primaries and the national nominating conventions. The first of these reforms, a ban on soft money, will have the largest effect, since it prohibits party committees from using unregulated money to finance activities that will directly benefit a presidential candidate, including the type of broadcast advertising both parties conducted in 1996 and 2000 prior to the national nominating conventions. All party advertising conducted in connection with the presidential race will thus have to be financed with hard money raised in compliance with federal contribution limits.

The law also requires party committees to decide at the time of nomination whether to support their nominees with coordinated expenditures or independent expenditures. Coordinated expenditures are monies spent by party committees in coordination with a candidate; party officials can work with a candidate to determine how and where the monies will be spent. Independent expenditures, in contrast, are monies spent by party committees without input from a candidate; the parties alone determine how and where the monies will be spent. Both types of spending must be financed with federally regulated funds, but when parties act in coordination with a candidate the amount they are allowed to spend is limited. In 2000, the limit was $13.7 million for each party, a sum that will rise to an estimated $15 million in 2004.[64] If parties act independent of a candidate, the amount they are allowed to spend is not limited.[65] Once a party committee, such as the Democratic or Republican National Committee, engages in coordinated spending on behalf of a candidate, all expenditures by affiliated national and state party committees are considered to be coordinated expenditures subject to the limit.

Although this provision is principally designed to affect general election spending, it will shape the approach party committees take in supporting a prospective nominee in advance of the convention. Prior to the adoption of the BCRA, parties could exercise either of these options and could even begin coordinated spending on behalf of the presumptive nominee prior to the convention. But parties instead chose the issue advocacy alternative that could be financed with soft money. With soft money funding no longer an option, parties will now have to make a choice as to how they will conduct their hard money expenditures in support of a candidate. Given that the limits on coordinated spending are lower than the actual amounts spent by each of the major parties on issue advertising during the bridge period in 2000, it is probable that parties will choose to spend money independently during this period in future races, and perhaps even continue this approach in the general election.

The provisions of the BCRA thus allow party committees to continue to serve as a failsafe for presidential aspirants constrained by the campaign spending cap. Looking ahead to 2004, this consideration will be particularly relevant for Democrats, since challengers in this party, which will feature an open nomination contest, are the most likely to be running under public funding restrictions and thus the most likely to need party support to help ease the problems created by the spending limit. That the party is prepared to provide such relief was indicated by Terence McAuliffe, the national party chairman, who announced early in 2003 the party's intention to form a special "presidential trust fund" to raise money that will be used to assist the party's nominee.[66]

How much will be available for this purpose, and whether it will be enough to mitigate Bush's financial advantage, remains to be seen. The Democrats will not be able to match Bush's spending, or the combined spending of the president's campaign and the Republican National Committee, should the party decide to help the president, as was the case in the summer of 2000. The ban on soft money

will reduce party revenues significantly, especially among Democratic committees, which received 47 percent of their funding in 2000 from soft money contributions. The Democrats must find ways to improve their hard money
fundraising, since they have traditionally lagged far behind the Republicans in
hard money resources.[67] Their support for the presidential nominee will depend
on the amount of hard money the party can raise under the BCRA's revised party
contribution limits, which increase the amount an individual may contribute to
a national party committee from $20,000 per year to $25,000 per year, indexed
for inflation, and raise the total annual amount an individual may contribute to
all candidates, parties, and PACs from $25,000 per annum (or $50,000 every two
years) to $95,000 per two-year election cycle.[68] It will also depend on the party's
willingness to devote resources to the presidential race in contrast to other electoral contests. Even so, the Democrats should be able to provide substantial support to their presumptive nominee in 2004, although perhaps not as much as the
$25 million the party spent in the summer of 2000.

The Diminished Role of Public Funding

Even if party organizations continue to provide support to their presidential
nominees, this tactic would be, at best, a stopgap measure. It would not resolve
the problems created by the current spending limits. Nor would it eliminate the
incentives that might lead candidates to forego public funds altogether during
the nomination stage of the presidential selection process. Party spending would
only benefit the presumptive nominee in each party, since the party is unlikely
to get involved in a nomination contest until a winner has emerged. And even
in the case of the nominee, the party option is a less desirable alternative to that
of being able to spend one's own campaign money. There is no guarantee that a
party acting independently of its nominee will craft a message or frame an ad in
a way that is acceptable to the candidate. Most candidates would prefer to control
their own destiny by exercising control over any broadcast messages or other
expenditures. This preference is best realized when expenditures are made by a
candidate's campaign committee.

So even with the possibility of party support, there are reasons why candidates
would prefer to be able to spend money without spending constraints. To date,
candidates have had to balance this desire against the benefits to be obtained by
accepting public funding, and the vast majority have chosen the public funding
option. But the BCRA changes this calculus. Instead of strengthening the incentives in favor of the public option, it will provide candidates with greater incentives to forego public subsidies.

In this regard, the most important aspects of the BCRA are the lacunae in the
law, rather than its specific provisions. While the new statute increases the individual contribution limit, it does not correspondingly increase the $250 ceiling

for matching contributions. The relative value of this public subsidy will therefore drop from one-quarter of a maximum contribution (the first $250 of $1,000) to one-eighth ($250 of $2,000). The law also fails to increase the aggregate expenditure limit or provide some other form of relief from this unrealistically low ceiling. It thus fails to reduce the financial pressures faced by candidates.

The combination of higher contribution limits, unadjusted matching amounts, and unchanged spending limits will lead to a decline in the relative importance of public money in the funding of nomination campaigns. Candidates who succeed in raising large amounts from maximum contributions under the BCRA will receive less public money than candidates did in the past, and public funding will make up a significantly smaller share of their total campaign receipts. For example, in 2000, the leading publicly funded candidates raised about 30 percent of their total receipts from matching funds, or an average of roughly $14 million. Gore received $15.5 million in public funds, which represented 31 percent of his total receipts. If Gore had been running under the terms of the BCRA and we assume that a third of his 19,000 large donors would have given $2,000, he would have received an additional $6 million in private contributions. Assuming that he would have raised approximately the same total amount of money (due to the constraints of the spending limit), his share of receipts from public funds would have declined significantly. He would have received a minimum of $1.5 million to $2 million less in public subsidies and perhaps as much as $3 to $4 million less, since the added revenue from gifts between $1,000 and $2,000 also would produce no additional public money.

Accordingly, the BCRA's regulations are likely to provide presidential candidates, especially an incumbent president or established politicians perceived to be prospective front-runners, with greater incentives to forego participation in the public funding program. Such candidates, who should be able to raise sizable numbers of maximum contributions successfully, will receive a larger share of their campaign monies from private funds; depending on the circumstances, the proportion of campaign receipts generated through public funding is likely to decline to less than 25 percent. This, combined with the pressure Bush will place on prospective opponents to follow his lead and be free of the spending limits, will force Democratic candidates in 2004 to consider whether a wholly privately funded campaign is a viable option. If Bush is reelected, candidates in 2008 will face similar pressures, since the open race in each party will encourage some contenders to try to break free from the pack by foregoing public funding restrictions.

Whether any Democrat will be able to forego public funds is an open question. The Democratic field will consist of a number of well-established candidates: possible contenders include former vice presidential candidate and current Senator Joseph Lieberman of Connecticut, Senator John Kerry of Massachusetts, Senator John Edwards of North Carolina, and former House Minority Leader Richard Gephardt. Given the expected level of competition in the 2004 race, one or more of these candidates will certainly consider whether a strategic advantage could be achieved by refusing public funds. But to pursue this option success- fully, a candidate will need the benefit of a number of favorable circumstances.

To run without public funds, a candidate would have to believe that he or she is capable not only of replacing the monies that would be generated by the public subsidy, but of raising substantially more than the spending limit permits. If a candidate could not raise substantially more than the amount established by the spending limit, the refusal of public funds would make little strategic sense, since the candidate would be taking on a significant additional fundraising burden with relatively little added spending capacity to show for it. But raising the sum needed to meet this objective is not an easy task. Even with the diminished role of public funding, the leading candidates can expect to receive as much as $10 million or more from public coffers. The replacement of these monies would entail significant fundraising costs and would require the solicitation of thou- sands of additional contributions. At a minimum, a candidate would have to raise more than 5,000 additional $2,000 contributions to amass this sum. In 2000, fewer than 38,000 Democrats gave $1,000 in a competitive race. Any of the Democrats considering a run for the White House in 2004 would have to expand the traditional donor base in presidential races significantly in order to raise enough money to make a privately financed campaign a viable possibility.

A candidate who wanted to pursue the private funding option would thus have to carry out successfully a two-phase fundraising operation. In the first phase, which would take place throughout the year before the election, a candidate would have to raise enough private money to finance campaign operations in the early caucus and primary states without having to rely on public funding. During this period, a candidate would seek to raise at least $30 million to $40 million. Then, once the nomination race was over, a second phase would begin in which the presumptive nominee would appeal to party supporters, including those who supported other candidates in the nomination contest, in an effort to raise the funds needed to finance a campaign from the effective end of the nominating process through to the convention. The goal of this phase would be to raise sig- nificantly more than the amount that would have been available to spend under the expenditure limit of the public funding program.

Alternatively, a candidate could refuse public funds and rely on personal resources. This would be a realistic option for a viable contender able and willing to supplement privately solicited contributions with millions of dollars of per- sonal money. Of the candidates who are expected to seek the Democratic nomi- nation, Senator Kerry, whose wife is an heiress to the Heinz company fortune, is the most likely to consider this option. If he emerged by the end of 2003 as a serious contender with a realistic chance of winning the nomination, he might decide to forego public funds and rely on his personal wealth to supplement his fundraising, with the hope of gaining a victory that could be the basis for further fundraising. Kerry would have to weigh the political consequences of such an approach, given his long-standing support for public funding, but party members might be willing to accept a candidate who eschews public funds in the context of a race against the privately funded Bush.

A privately funded candidacy without the benefit of personal resources would only be likely if a candidate demonstrated notable political strength, just as Bush did in 2000. Specifically, a candidate would have to emerge from the field as a consensus front-runner well before the Iowa caucuses and raise enough money in the pre-election year to be able to conduct campaigns in the early contests without public money. To effectuate this strategy, a candidate would have to surpass prospective opponents in early fundraising by a substantial margin, and rely on this early fundraising to drive most opponents out of the race or at least convince the electorate that they will not be competitive. That candidate would also have to raise enough money in the pre-election year to conclude that a level of spending well in excess of the spending cap is a realistic possibility. The BCRA thus provides candidates with a strong incentive to behave in ways that will exacerbate the emphasis on early fundraising and make the invisible primary even more draconian than it has been in recent elections.

Finally, a candidate seeking to rely on private money would probably have to secure the nomination relatively quickly, claiming victory after the first few selection contests. By wrapping up the nomination early in a race that is not so divisive or rancorous that it serves to alienate supporters of losing candidates, the presumptive nominee would be provided with the opportunity to capitalize on the momentum gained from a victory and appeal to partisan interests to stimulate a surge in fundraising that would provide the monies needed to compete against President Bush through to the party convention. While this scenario is unlikely to produce a Democratic contender who could match Bush's war chest, it would almost certainly yield a challenger capable of spending substantially more than the limit, particularly if the nominee proved capable of securing contributions from those who supported other candidates during the primaries.

CONCLUSION

The BCRA will exacerbate the emphasis on early fundraising and large donor contributions that has been evident in recent presidential elections. The law's higher contribution limits and failure to reform the public funding program will serve to diminish the role of public monies in nomination campaigns and provide candidates with even greater incentives to opt out of the program. Prospective frontrunners and other well-established hopefuls, who already have an incentive to refuse public funds due to the inadequacy of the spending limits, will feel even greater pressure to refuse the matching subsidy, since they will have to conduct their campaigns under the assumption that at least one of their opponents is likely to choose the private funding option. If a growing number of candidates decide to follow the model established by President Bush and non-participation in the matching funds program becomes more commonplace, the public financing system will become less relevant to presidential politics.

The BCRA will thus undermine the objectives the FECA sought to achieve. It will not reduce the emphasis on fundraising in presidential elections, encourage candidates to rely on small donors in the financing of their campaigns, enhance political competition, or limit the role of private contributions in the presidential selection process. Instead, it will encourage candidates to place even greater emphasis on the solicitation of large gifts, and make early fundraising in the invisible primary an even more important factor in winnowing candidates from the field.

In the longer term, the effects of the BCRA may alter the dynamics of presidential fundraising in such a way as to produce two tiers of candidates. One tier will consist of well-financed, privately funded establishment candidates or self-financed millionaires. The other will consist of publicly funded insurgent candidates or less well known contenders. The latter group is likely to lag far behind their more established opponents in the money race, and thus find it increasingly difficult to mount competitive bids for the Oval Office. In this scenario, the presidential nomination race would become an even more money-driven process than has been the case in recent elections.

If public funding is to continue to be an important source of funding in presidential campaigns, additional reforms will be necessary. The aggregate expenditure ceiling needs to be much higher to reflect the actual financial demands of the modern nominating process. The aggregate ceiling also should be simplified by incorporating the fundraising and compliance exemptions into the base limit and eliminating the state caps. In addition, the amount of an individual's total contributions eligible for matching should be increased. At a minimum, the sum eligible for matching should be changed from $250 to $500 to maintain the relative value of this subsidy under a $2,000 contribution limit. Such an increase, however, could not be accommodated by the current tax checkoff revenues, which barely met the needs of the candidates in 1992, 1996, and 2000.[69] So further reforms to guarantee the future fiscal solvency of the Presidential Election Campaign Fund will also be required.

The enactment of the BCRA represents a major step in the effort to address the problems of the presidential campaign finance system. But it is only a first step. As the effects of the BCRA become manifest, the fundamental problems in the presidential public funding system will intensify and the demands for additional reform will become more pronounced. The BCRA will thus serve to reinvigorate, rather than resolve, the debate over the financing of presidential campaigns.

NOTES

The authors wish to acknowledge the support of The Pew Charitable Trusts, which provided support for the research on which this chapter is based. The opinions expressed herein are those of the authors and do not necessarily reflect the views of The Pew Charitable Trusts.

1. Public Law 107–155, 116 Stat. 81 (2002). The bill was signed into law by President George Bush on March 27, 2002. Hereafter cited as BCRA.

2. The legislation was sponsored by Senators John McCain, an Arizona Republican, and Russell Feingold, a Wisconsin Democrat. A companion bill in the House was sponsored by Republican Christopher Shays of Connecticut and Democrat Martin Meehan of Massachusetts.

3. Most of the provisions of the new law went into effect on this date. The increased contribution limits, however, did not go into effect until January 1, 2003.

4. "Soft money" is the common term used to refer to the contributions raised by party committees from individuals, corporations, and labor unions that are not subject to federal contribution limits. Candidate-specific issue advocacy advertisements are ads that feature federal candidates, but do not "expressly advocate" the election or defeat of a candidate by using such words as "elect," "support," "defeat," or "vote for." Such ads are not subject to federal campaign finance regulations. For background on these forms of funding, see Anthony Corrado, Thomas E. Mann, Daniel R. Ortiz, Trevor Potter, and Frank J. Sorauf, eds., *Campaign Finance Reform: A Sourcebook* (Washington: Brookings Institution Press, 1997), especially chapters 6 and 7.

5. See, in particular, Section 101 of the BCRA. For background on the law and a summary of its major provisions, see Joseph E. Cantor and L. Paige Whitaker, *Bipartisan Campaign Reform Act of 2002: Summary and Comparison with Existing Law*, Congressional Research Service Report for Congress (Washington: Library of Congress, 2002); and Robert F. Bauer, *Soft Money, Hard Law: A Guide to the New Campaign Finance Law* (Washington: Perkins Coie, 2002).

6. The constitutionality of the BCRA's major provisions is being challenged at the time of this writing. More than 80 plaintiffs in a dozen separate lawsuits challenged the law. These actions have been consolidated into one case, *McConnell v. Federal Election Commission*, Civ. No. 02–582 (D.D.C. 2002).

7. To ensure that the availability of matching funds does not encourage a candidate who is unlikely to win to remain in the race, the regulations state that a candidate who fails to receive at least 10 percent of the vote in two consecutive primaries is no longer eligible to accrue public funds after 30 days. 26 U.S.C.§9033(c). The 10 percent rule only applies to primaries; it does not include a candidate's performance in a presidential preference caucus. The FEC has interpreted this provision to mean two consecutive primaries in which a candidate is entered on the ballot, as opposed to two consecutive primaries as determined by the delegate selection calendar. A candidate is allowed to ask the FEC to exclude particular primaries for purposes of determining that candidate's continuing eligibility for matching funds. See Federal Election Commission, *The Presidential Public Funding System* (Washington: April 1993), 11–12. This understanding has had little effect on the distribution of matching funds in major party nomination contests, since the front-loaded primary calendar essentially requires candidates to contest primaries on a weekly basis once the formal selection process has begun.

8. FEC, "FEC Announces 2000 Presidential Spending Limits," press release, March 1, 2000.

9. Anthony Corrado, *Paying for Presidents* (New York: Twentieth Century Fund Press, 1993), 102.

10. FEC, "FEC Announces 2000 Presidential Spending Limits."

11. FEC, "FEC Announces 2000 Presidential Spending Limits."

12. Corrado, *Paying for Presidents*, 56.

13. 11 CFR 106.2 and FEC, *Record* 17 (September 1991), 2–5. See also, Herbert E. Alexander and Anthony Corrado, *Financing the 1992 Election* (Armonk, NY: M. E. Sharpe, 1995), 28–30.

14. FEC, "FEC Announces 2000 Presidential Spending Limits."

15. William G. Mayer, "The Presidential Nominations," in Gerald M. Pomper, ed., *The Election of 2000* (New York: Chatham House, 2001), 12–14.

16. In 2000, the FEC modified its regulations with respect to the allocation of expenses between the primary and general election. This change was adopted to add flexibility to campaign spending that occurs between June 1 of the election year and the date a candidate is nominated. Under the revised regulations, salary and overhead expenses incurred during this period may be attributed to the general election rather than the primary, but the amount allocated cannot exceed 15 percent of the limitation on primary election expenditures. See 11 CFR §9034.4(e) and FEC, *General Election Supplement to the Financial Control and Compliance Manual for Presidential Primary Candidates Receiving Public Funding* (Washington: June 2000), 4.

17. Congressional Research Service, *The Presidential Election Campaign Fund and Tax Checkoff: Background and Current Issues* (Washington: Library of Congress, March 2000). The authors have updated the figures for 2000 provided in this report with the most recent FEC data.

18. Anthony Corrado, *Campaign Finance Reform: Beyond the Basics* (New York: Century Foundation Press, 2000), 61.

19. Corrado, *Paying for Presidents*, 107. These figures represent the amounts paid to the candidates during the campaign, prior to any repayments. Post-election repayments reduced these amounts to $5 million for Carter and $6.3 million for Reagan.

20. Figures based on data obtained from the FEC on the receipts of presidential candidates in the 1996 prenomination campaign through December 31, 1996.

21. FEC, "FEC Approves Matching Funds for 2000 Presidential Candidates," press release, September 19, 2000, 1.

22. John Aloysius Farrell, "Clinton Campaign Mulls Private Funding," *Boston Globe*, August 28, 1995, 1; Dick Morris, *Behind the Oval Office* (New York: Random House, 1997), 138–153; and Bob Woodward, *The Choice* (New York: Touchstone Books, 1996), 234.

23. Farrell, "Clinton Campaign Mulls Private Funding."

24. A number of minor party candidates have also decided not to accept public funds or have failed to qualify for the subsidy. For example, the Libertarian party nominee in each election has not attempted to qualify for matching funds, due to the party's opposition to taxpayer-funded elections.

25. Herbert E. Alexander, *Financing the 1980 Election* (Lexington, Mass.: Lexington Books, 1983), 194–195.

26. Alexander, *Financing the 1980 Election*, 195; and Gerald M. Pomper, "The Nominating Contests," in Gerald M. Pomper et al., *The Election of 1980* (Chatham, N.J.: Chatham House, 1981), 13.

27. Alexander and Corrado, *Financing the 1992 Election*, 128–130.

28. FEC, "Presidential Candidate Summary Report [1996]," available at: *http://www.fec.gov/pres96/presmstr.htm* (viewed January 7, 2003).

29. Ruth Marcus, "Dole Nears Finance Limit for Primaries," *Washington Post*, February 24, 1996, A1; and Stephen Labaton, "Dole's Campaign Nears Limit on Spending for the Primaries," *New York Times*, March 22, 1996, A21.

30. FEC, "Receipts of 1999–2000 Presidential Campaigns through July 31, 2000," available at: *http://www.fec.gov/finance/precm8.htm* (viewed January 7, 2003); and Mayer, "The Presidential Nominations," 30–31 and 34.

31. Dornan raised less than $350,000 for his presidential campaign. Hatch raised less than $3 million.

32. In 1992 Perot received the highest share of the vote given to a third party candidate in the presidential general election since 1912, when Theodore Roosevelt ran as the nominee of the Progressive Party. In 1996 Forbes emerged as a major contender for the Republican nomination and waged a highly competitive race against front-runner Robert Dole.

33. For a discussion of the issues associated with self-financed candidates and their relative electoral performance, see Jennifer A. Steen, "Beyond Huffington: Personal Spending in Congressional Elections," paper prepared for presentation at the Annual Meeting of the Midwest Political Science Association, Chicago, Illinois, April 2000. See also Jennifer A. Steen, *Money Isn't Everything: Self-Financing Candidates in U.S. House Elections, 1992–1998*, Ph.D. Dissertation, University of California-Berkeley, 2000, available at: *http://ist-socrates.berkeley.edu/~jsteen/* (viewed December 24, 2002).

34. John C. Green and Nathan S. Bigelow, "The 2000 Presidential Nominations: The Costs of Innovation," in David B. Magleby, ed., *Financing the 2000 Election* (Washington: Brookings Institution Press, 2002), 58–59.

35. These estimates represent projected amounts Bush might have received if he had chosen to participate in the public funding program and had received 25 to 30 percent of his revenues from matching funds, which is usually the case for well-established candidates like Bush. Given his emphasis on large donations in his fundraising efforts, his public monies would have most likely been on the lower end of the range.

36. These figures are based on data files provided to the authors by the FEC for the receipts of presidential candidates through December 31, 1999, and through December 31, 2000.

37. Michael Isikoff, "The Money Machine," *Newsweek*, January 24, 2000, 48.

38. Don Van Natta Jr., "Early Rush of Contributions Opened the Floodgates for Bush," *New York Times*, January 30, 2000, A20.

39. Isikoff, "The Money Machine"; and Mike Allen, "Pioneers Pointing the Way for Bush," *Washington Post*, March 3, 2002, A5.

40. Van Natta, "Early Rush of Contributions."

41. The "invisible primary" is the term commonly used to describe the campaigning that takes place during the long period leading up to the voting in Iowa and New Hampshire. During this period, candidates vie to become the perceived front-runner in the race. See, among others, Emmett H. Buell Jr., "The Invisible Primary," in William G. Mayer, ed., *In Pursuit of the White House* (Chatham, N.J.: Chatham House, 1996), 1–43.

42. "Bush Adds $10M to His Record Campaign Fund," *Boston Globe*, December 31, 1999, A18.

43. See, among others, Mark Shields, "High-Stakes Presidential Poker," *Washington Post National Weekly Edition*, February 14–20, 1994, 28; Mayer, "The Presidential Nominations," 15; and Thomas B. Edsall, "First Democratic Race is for Cash," *Washington Post*, December 31, 2002, A6.

44. Wesley Joe and Clyde Wilcox, "Financing the 1996 Presidential Nominations: The Last Regulated Campaign?" in John C. Green, ed., *Financing the 1996 Election* (Armonk, NY: M. E. Sharpe, 1999), 48.

45. Joe and Wilcox, "Financing the 1996 Presidential Nominations," 55–56; and Anthony Corrado, "The Changing Environment of Presidential Campaign Finance," in William G. Mayer, ed., *In Pursuit of the White House* (Chatham, NJ: Chatham House, 1996), 228–229.

46. To carry out this analysis of individual *contributors*, as opposed to individual *contributions*, we built a data file containing all of the individual contributions disclosed to the FEC by the major party candidates in the 1996 and 2000 presidential prenomination campaign and separated them by candidate. In all, this pool encompassed approximately 1.6 million separate contributions. We then cross-matched these files via computer with files obtained from the FEC that included listings by candidate of all contributions refunded or returned to donors in order to adjust the donor files for any contributions that were not retained by the candidate. In many instances, the refunded contributions represented amounts that exceeded the $1,000 maximum (e.g., a donor who had already given an aggregate of $1,000 made an additional contribution of $250) or were made from sources prohibited under federal law (e.g., a donor who made a contribution via a check written on a limited partnership account or small business account instead of from a personal account). In some instances, candidates reported adjustments to correct errors (e.g., contributions listed as $10,000 instead of $1,000). We did, however, find a relatively small number of donors whose aggregate gifts totaled more than $1,000 with no accompanying refund or adjustment. In these instances, we recorded the person who made the contribution as a $1,000 donor.

Once the files were adjusted for these refunds and returns, donor files were matched for common name and address. Where there was a variation in the identified source of a possible multiple donor (e.g., separate contributions with one record adding "Jr." to a name, or the same name with a street address in one record and P.O. box in another), the gifts were not aggregated. Three additional reviews were conducted on a case-by-case basis to review possible matches for small variations that did not call into question the source of the contribution (e.g., instances where a male name and address matched up but one file included "Mr." while the other did not, or instances where numbers in a zip code had been transposed). Our method allowed us to match up more than 95 percent of the multiple contributions reported for each candidate. However, because we were basically limited to disclosed contributions of $200 or more our methodology could not detect individuals who might have given $1,000 by making ten $100 contributions or four contributions of $200 and two contributions of $100. Even so, we believe that there are relatively few donors who give $1,000 in this manner and that for the purposes of our analysis, the lack of such $1,000 donors in the data set does not materially alter our findings. To the extent that there are other donors who gave $1,000 in smaller, undisclosed sums, the addition of such donors only serves to strengthen our argument.

47. For a discussion of the financial activity of ideological candidates in presidential campaigns and their reliance on small contributions, see Clifford Brown, Jr., Lynda Powell, and Clyde Wilcox, *Serious Money: Fundraising and Contributing in Presidential Nomination Campaigns* (New York: Cambridge University Press, 1995).

48. Anthony Corrado, "Financing the 2000 Elections," in Gerald M. Pomper, ed., *The Election of 2000* (New York: Chatham House, 2001), 102.

49. Corrado, *Campaign Finance Reform*, 64.

50. Corrado, *Paying for Presidents*, 56.

51. Labaton, "Dole's Campaign Nears Limit on Spending for the Primaries"; and Scott E. Thomas, "The Presidential Election Public Funding Program—A Commissioner's Perspective," testimony presented at the public hearings of the Task Force on Financing Presidential Nominations, Campaign Finance Institute, Washington, D.C., January 31, 2003, 6.

52. Ruth Marcus, "Spending Solution Tantalizingly Close; Dole Looks Forward to $62 Million," *Washington Post*, May 21, 1996, A6.

53. Corrado, "Financing the 2000 Elections," 105.

54. The distinction between "express advocacy" and "issue advocacy" as a standard for determining Congress's authority to regulate campaign finance was made by the Supreme Court in its landmark 1976 decision in *Buckley v. Valeo* (424 U.S. 1). For background, see Trevor Potter and Kirk L. Jowers, "Issue and Express Advocacy," available at *http://www.brookings.edu/dybdocroot/gs/cf/sourcebk/IssueExpressAd.pdf* (accessed January 2, 2003).

55. Common Cause, "Statement of Common Cause President Ann McBride at News Conference Asking for Independent Counsel to Investigate Campaign Finance Activities of Clinton, Dole Campaigns," press release, October 9, 1996, 7.

56. Republican National Committee, "RNC Announces $20 Million TV Advertising Campaign," press release, May 16, 1996.

57. Thomas, "The Presidential Election Public Funding Program," 6.

58. Thomas, "The Presidential Election Public Funding Program," 6.

59. FEC, "FEC Reports Increase in Party Fundraising for 2000," press release, May 15, 2001.

60. The estimates of party spending in the 2000 cycle included in this paragraph are based on the detailed analysis of party expenditures found in Anthony Corrado, Sarah Barclay, and Heitor Gouvêa, "The Parties Take the Lead: Political Parties and the Financing of the 2000 Presidential Election," in John C. Green and Rick Farmer, eds., *The State of the Parties*, 4th ed. (Lanham, Md.: Rowman & Littlefield, 2003), 107–109.

61. The $3 million figure is based on an analysis by the authors of the media expenditures reported by the Bush for President Committee on its monthly disclosure reports filed with the Federal Election Commission.

62. In recent cases, the Supreme Court has upheld contribution limits and demonstrated some deference to Congress as regards the appropriate level of these limits, so long as a contribution limit is not set so low as to make it difficult for candidates to raise the funds needed to wage a meaningful campaign. See *Buckley v. Valeo* and *Nixon v. Shrink Missouri Government PAC*, 528 U.S. 377 (2000).

63. The surveys noted here were conducted by a group of political scientists led by John Green of the University of Akron. See Alexandra Cooper et al., "With Limits Raised, Who Will Give More? The Impact of the BCRA on Individual Donors"; and Anthony Corrado and John C. Green, "The Impact of the BCRA on Presidential Campaign Finance: 2004 and Beyond," both in Michael J. Malbin, ed., *Life After Reform: When the Bipartisan Campaign Reform Act Meets Politics* (Lanham, Md.: Rowman & Littlefield, forthcoming).

64. FEC, "FEC Announces 2000 Party Spending Limits," press release, March 1, 2000. The estimate for 2004 is based on a 2 percent annual rate of inflation.

65. Independent spending by party committees in support of federal candidates was upheld by the Supreme Court in *Colorado Republican Federal Campaign Committee v. Federal Election Commission*, 518 U.S. 604 (1996), generally known as *Colorado I*. In *Federal Election Commission v. Colorado Republican Federal Campaign Committee*, 533 U.S. 431 (2001), generally known as *Colorado II*, the Court upheld the limits on party coordinated spending.

66. "Democrats Start Presidential Fund," Associated Press news release, January 31, 2003, available at *http://www.nytimes.com/aponline/national/AP-Campaign-Finance.html* (accessed February 1, 2003).

67. In the 2000 election cycle, the Democrats raised $190 million less than the Republicans in hard money; in 2002, $180 million less. See FEC, "FEC Reports Increase in Party Fundraising"; and FEC, "Party Fundraising Reaches $1.1 Billion in 2002 Election Cycle," press release, December 18, 2002.

68. These changes in the contribution limits are found in Section 307 of the Act. The $95,000 aggregate limit on the amount an individual may contribute in each two-year election cycle includes one sub-limit for contributions to candidates and another for contributions to parties and PACs. Under the new law, individuals can give a maximum of $37,500 in total contributions to candidates every two years, and a maximum of $57,500 in total contributions to party committees and PACs, of which no more than $37,500 can be made up of contributions to state and local party committees or PACs. These sub-limits are indexed for inflation.

69. According to data available from the FEC, the Presidential Election Campaign Fund had a balance of about $4 million after the 1992 election, $3.7 million after the 1996 election, and about $16 million after the 2000 election, due largely to Bush's decision not to accept public matching funds. The amount of public money disbursed in the 2000 election was $210 million.

3

The Basic Dynamics of the Contemporary Nomination Process

An Expanded View

William G. Mayer

There is no simple way to determine how many people run for president every four years, but the number is surely substantial. Perhaps the closest thing in American politics to an official registry of presidential candidates is maintained by the Federal Election Commission (FEC). Since 1974, anyone who spends at least $5,000 on his or her own presidential campaign is required to file a statement of candidacy with the FEC; many other individuals who will not actually spend that much nevertheless notify the FEC just to be safe or because they like the sense that this somehow makes them an "official" presidential candidate. Whatever the explanation, every four years the FEC receives a staggering number of filings: 262 in the 1992 election cycle, 265 in 1996, 232 in 2000.[1]

From the perspective of the average voter, a more relevant question is how many of these presidential candidates are "major" or "serious." This obviously is a more exclusive club, yet its numbers are also quite sizable. The precise number, of course, depends on what one means by these terms and what sorts of things one believes a candidate should be required to do or show in order to merit such labels. Though these are unavoidably subjective questions, there are some reasonable and widely-used criteria available to help answer them: how much support a candidate has in the polls; his previous governmental experience (any sitting governor or U.S. senator who runs for president should probably be classified as a major candidate, no matter what else he has going for him); the way his candidacy is treated by the media or other political elites; the number of states in which he is listed on the ballot (primary or general election). Taking such things into account, every recent election cycle has produced, according to most observers, between ten and fifteen major *declared* presidential candidates. One could also make a good case for adding in another five or ten names per cycle, to take account of all the people who conducted preliminary or "exploratory" campaigns but shut them down once it became apparent that there was no particular demand or support for their candidacy.

However large the initial field of possibilities, the reality is that by late August of the election year—and probably a lot earlier—most Americans will be trying to decide between just two persons: a Democrat and a Republican. Such, in a nutshell, is the purpose and effect of party nominations: they define and limit the effective choices of the voters. The purpose of this chapter is to provide a broad overview of how that delimiting process takes place, by describing and documenting the basic dynamics of the contemporary presidential nominating process. In particular, I focus on the issue of how it is that the process finally settles upon a candidate: how and why it is that one candidate rather than another finally wins the nomination. Over the last two decades, I will argue, the American presidential nomination process, once widely thought of as an almost uniquely turbulent and unpredictable enterprise, has in fact usually operated in a quite regular and predictable fashion. And while every election has its new wrinkles and novel situations, most of what transpires in the 2004 election cycle will, in all likelihood, have clear and obvious parallels in the races that preceded it.

AN INITIAL MODEL

The analysis begins with a nomination forecasting model that I first proposed almost ten years ago.[2] Though contemporary observers often depicted the presidential nomination process as an almost uniquely chaotic and unpredictable enterprise, a closer look at the record, I argued, strongly belied this image. In fact, there were two indicators, both available before any of the primaries and caucuses had taken place, that correctly predicted which candidate would win his party's presidential nomination in six of the preceding seven contested nomination races.[3]

The first of these indicators was the candidates' relative standing in polls of the national party electorate. Well before any of the national convention delegates are actually selected—in fact, quite soon after the conclusion of the previous presidential election—pollsters regularly ask national samples of Democrats and Republicans whom they would like to see nominated as their party's candidate for president. As shown in table 3.1, if one focuses on the last poll taken before the start of delegate selection activities—meaning, in most years, the last poll before the Iowa caucuses—the candidate leading in that poll went on to win

Table 3.1 National Poll Standings and Pre-Election Year Fund-Raising Results as Predictors of Presidential Nominations

A. Poll Standings

Year	Party	Candidate Leading in the Last Poll before the Iowa Caucuses	Eventual Nominee
1980	Republican	Reagan	Reagan
1980	Democratic	Carter	Carter
1984	Democratic	Mondale	Mondale
1988	Republican	Bush	Bush
1988	Democratic	Hart	Dukakis
1992	Republican	Bush	Bush
1992	Democratic	Clinton	Clinton
1996	Republican	Dole	Dole
2000	Republican	Bush	Bush
2000	Democratic	Gore	Gore

B. Fund-Raising Totals

Year	Party	Candidate Raising the Most Money Prior to the Year of the Election	Eventual Nominee
1980	Republican	Connally	Reagan
1980	Democratic	Carter	Carter
1984	Democratic	Mondale	Mondale
1988	Republican	Bush	Bush
1988	Democratic	Dukakis	Dukakis
1992	Republican	Bush	Bush
1992	Democratic	Clinton	Clinton
1996	Republican	Dole	Dole
2000	Republican	Bush	Bush
2000	Democratic	Gore	Gore

the nomination in six of the seven contested nomination races held between 1980 and 1992.

The second indicator was the candidates' relative success in raising money. Under the federal campaign finance laws that were enacted in 1974, every active presidential candidate is required to make periodic reports to the Federal Election Commission indicating how much money he or she has raised and spent for the campaign. As is also shown in table 3.1, the leading money raiser during the pre-primary campaign—more precisely, the candidate who had raised the largest amount of money as of December 31 of the year *before* the election—went on to win the nomination in six of seven cases.

Since that article was published, the country has seen three contested presidential nomination races—*and both indicators worked perfectly in every case.* The relevant data for both 1996 and 2000 are shown in table 3.2.

To put these results in a more mathematically tractable form, and to allow for easier comparison with work on general election forecasting, I then combined these two indicators into a regression model that generates a numerical prediction of each candidate's performance in the presidential nomination race. The dependent variable in this equation is the percentage of the total vote won by each candidate in all presidential primaries held by that candidate's party during the nomination season. In the 2000 Republican contest, for example, a total of 17,156,117 votes were cast in 42 different primaries. George Bush received 10,844,129 of those votes, or 63.2 percent; John McCain had 5,118,187, or 29.8 percent; and so on.

Two independent variables are used to predict these primary vote shares. The first is the percentage of party identifiers who supported each candidate in the

Table 3.2 Presidential Nomination Predictors in the 1996 and 2000 Nomination Races

Presidential Nomination Preferences of National Party Identifiers		Total Net Receipts through the End of the Year before the Election	
1. 1996 Republicans			
Dole	47%	Dole	$24,611,816
Forbes	16	Gramm	20,758,066
Gramm	8	Forbes	17,973,910
Buchanan	7	Alexander	11,516,266
Alexander	3	Buchanan	7,222,685
Lugar	3	Lugar	5,903,326
Keyes	1	Keyes	1,405,570
2. 2000 Republicans			
Bush	63%	Bush	$67,630,541
McCain	19	Forbes	34,150,997
Forbes	6	McCain	15,532,082
Bauer	2	Bauer	8,761,166
Keyes	1	Keyes	4,483,505
Hatch	1	Hatch	2,285,829
3. 2000 Democrats			
Gore	60%	Gore	$27,847,335
Bradley	27	Bradley	27,465,950

Sources: Poll results are taken from the Gallup Poll, surveys of January 26–29, 1996; and January 17–19, 2000. Fund-raising totals are derived from the individual candidate reports submitted to the Federal Election Commission.

last national Gallup Poll taken before the start of delegate selection activities. The second is the total amount of money each candidate raised before the election year, divided by the largest amount of money raised by any candidate in that party's nomination race. Again using the figures from the 2000 Republican race as an example, the most successful fund-raiser in that contest was George Bush, who raised $67,630,541. Bush thus receives a score of 100 on this variable. Steve Forbes, who raised $34,150,997, gets a score of 50.5, because he raised 50.5 percent of Bush's total; McCain, with net receipts of $15,532,082, is given a score of 23.0.[4]

Table 3.3 shows three different versions of this forecasting equation.[5] The first version, which is taken from the original article, is based on the data from 1980 through 1992. The second, which adds in the data from 1996, was used to forecast the 2000 nomination races. The third version also adds in the figures from 2000 and can, if anyone sees fit, be used to forecast the 2004 elections. The forecasts that were generated for 1996 and 2000—and the actual results—are shown in table 3.4.

The fund-raising variable is not statistically significant in any of these equations, but the poll-standings variable clearly is and accounts for about 70 percent of the variance in the final primary vote shares. For reasons that will be explored later in this chapter, Dole, Buchanan, McCain, and Gore all did somewhat better than the model forecast; Forbes (in both years), Gramm, and Bradley fared less well than the model predicts. Yet the forecasts do mirror the general shape of these races as they ultimately turned out; in particular, the model does correctly forecast the winner in all three contests.

One final point is worth noting about this model: It is limited to *declared* presidential candidates. Put another way, besides predicting each candidate's share of the total primary vote, the model also contains a second, implicit prediction: that only candidates who make an active, public, organized effort to win the nomination have any real chance of getting it.[6] This has not always been the case.

Table 3.3 Baseline Model for Predicting Primary Vote Shares

Regression Coefficients	1980–1992	1980–1996	1980–2000
National poll standings	.94 (.14)	.99 (.13)	1.05 (.11)
Total funds raised	.02 (.08)	.00 (.07)	−.02 (.06)
Constant	1.31 (3.37)	1.61 (3.00)	1.75 (2.57)
R^2	.70	.72	.78
Adjusted R^2	.69	.71	.77
SEE	11.93	11.37	10.80
N	38	45	53

Notes: Dependent variable is the percentage of the total primary vote won by each candidate in all presidential primaries held by that candidate's party during the nomination season.
Figures in parentheses are the standard errors of the coefficients.

Table 3.4 Baseline Model Forecasts for the 1996 and 2000 Nomination Races

	Predicted Vote	Actual Vote	Error (Actual-Predicted)
1. 1996 Republicans			
Dole	47.5%	58.5%	11.0
Buchanan	8.5	21.6	13.1
Forbes	17.8	10.2	−7.6
Alexander	5.1	3.5	−1.6
Lugar	4.6	0.9	−3.7
Gramm	10.5	0.5	−10.0
Keyes	2.4	3.2	0.8
2. 2000 Republicans			
Bush	64.0%	63.2%	−0.8
McCain	20.4	29.8	9.4
Forbes	7.6	0.8	−6.8
Bauer	3.6	0.4	−3.2
Keyes	2.6	5.3	2.7
Hatch	2.6	0.1	−2.5
3. 2000 Democrats			
Gore	61.0%	75.7%	14.7
Bradley	28.3	19.9	−8.4

Before the rules of the presidential nomination process were rewritten in the early 1970s, a number of candidates won their party's nomination even though they spent most of the nomination season sitting on the sidelines—not entering a single primary or even formally announcing their interest in the job until just before the convention. The evidence of the last six election cycles, however, strongly suggests that candidacies of this sort are no longer possible. Since 1980, no unannounced or late-starting[7] candidate has ever received even one percent of the total votes cast in the primaries or one-half of one percent of the votes recorded on any presidential roll-call ballot taken at the national conventions.

Much of the rest of this chapter involves attempts to extend and elaborate this basic model. Before turning to that endeavor, however, I wish to call attention to two important conclusions that derive from this model, conclusions that plainly contradict what was, at least until quite recently, the almost universally accepted wisdom about how the presidential nomination process worked.

First, *the contemporary presidential nomination process has gradually evolved into a system that is highly favorable to front-runners.* In the first two nomination races that were held after the Democrats rewrote their delegate selection rules in the early 1970s, the Democratic party nominated candidates who were definitely *not* the pre-election front-runners. George McGovern in 1972 and Jimmy Carter in 1976 both began the primary and caucus season as decided long-shots. Neither had ever been supported by more than 6 percent of his party's identifiers in any national poll conducted prior to the Iowa caucuses, nor did either candidate rank among his party's top money-raisers. When George Bush, Sr., came close to repeating this feat in 1980, a consensus quickly emerged that the new process was unusually well-disposed to the political fortunes of outsiders, insurgents, and relative unknowns.

It wasn't just the press and the pundits who reached this conclusion. The same verdict was pronounced in some of the very best academic writing on the subject. One of the best-known models of the primary election process is that of Henry Brady and Richard Johnston. As they conclude in the very last sentence of their article: "The lesson, then, of this analysis is that being the favorite is a mixed blessing, and one might better be a newcomer with media appeal and a little luck in Iowa or New Hampshire."[8] Larry Bartels ended his award-winning book on presidential primaries on a similar note. Characterizing the current system as one with a "remarkable openness to new candidates," he added, "In many political systems positions of party leadership are earned through decades of toil in the party organization. In contemporary American politics the same positions are sometimes seized, almost literally overnight, by candidates with negligible party credentials and very short histories as national public figures."[9] James Ceaser, who approached these issues from a more historical and theoretical perspective, pronounced a similar verdict: "When the effects of sequence in the primaries and the influence of the media are taken into consideration, the nominating campaign often becomes not simply a test among established national contenders, but an occasion for outsiders to make their reputation during the campaign itself. In this respect, the current system is more open than the pure convention system and the mixed nominating system."[10]

Whatever may have happened in 1972 or 1976, a very different sort of outcome has occurred in every race since then. In the last ten contested nomination races, the candidate who won was the front-runner—or at least *one* of the frontrunners—before any of the delegates were selected. To say the least, this is not a system characterized by its openness to new faces.

Second, if the pre-race front-runner usually wins, then *momentum is not the overwhelming force that it is frequently portrayed to be.* This is not to say that momentum no longer occurs or is entirely without consequences. Later in this chapter, in fact, I will provide at least one plausible way of estimating its net effect. But over the last two decades, the limits on momentum seem much more striking than its potency.

Momentum can be compared to a roller-coaster ride: It provides a lot of thrills and excitement, but in the end, it leaves us pretty much where we started out. And so it is in presidential politics: After all the effects of momentum have come and gone, the person who starts out ahead almost always finishes ahead. Put another way, if you're interested in figuring out why John McCain went from 15 percent to 34 percent in the national polls within five days of his New Hampshire victory, momentum clearly provides the best explanation. But if your main interest is in determining who finally gets nominated and who doesn't, momentum just isn't of very much help. Not since Jimmy Carter in 1976 has a momentum-driven candidacy been successful.

CANDIDATE EMERGENCE DURING
THE INVISIBLE PRIMARY

However successful this model is in forecasting the nomination winner, it obviously is not the whole story. To the contrary, the preceding analysis positively begs at least one major question. If major-party presidential nominations are usually won by the person who is the front-runner at the end of the invisible primary, how does one become such a front-runner? How is it that one person breaks out of the pack of declared presidential candidates?

To answer this question, I have conducted an intensive analysis of the surveys of national party identifiers that are conducted throughout the invisible primary period.[11] Because of their accessibility, reliability, and methodological consistency, I have tended to rely on polls conducted by the Gallup Organization, but I also made use of similar surveys conducted by a wide variety of other survey research firms.[12] I have defined the invisible primary in the broadest possible terms, as beginning on the day after the preceding presidential election. In the 2000 election cycle, in other words, the invisible primary extended from November 6, 1996 to January 23, 2000 (the Iowa caucuses took place on January 24). For those who want a more detailed look at these data, the Gallup results for all of the contested nomination races between 1980 and 2000, along with some general comments about the methodology of such polls, are provided in an appendix to this chapter.

The ten nomination races being considered here break down into four categories, which are set out in table 3.5.

The first category consists of three nomination races in which one candidate led all of his competitors from wire to wire: one candidate, that is to say, was clearly ahead in the polls throughout the *entire* invisible primary period. The three candidates who fit this description are George Bush in 1988, Bush again in 1992, and Al Gore in 2000. Each was ahead in the first poll conducted after the preceding election, was still ahead in the final poll before the Iowa caucuses—and then triumphed in the primaries and at the convention.

So far as I can determine, the first national poll conducted about the 2000 Democratic nomination race was a survey by Yankelovich Partners on March 11–12, 1997. That poll showed Gore already dominating the field. Offered a choice among six potential candidates—Al Gore, Dick Gephardt, Bob Kerrey, John Kerry, Bill Bradley, and Jesse Jackson—41 percent of the country's Demo-

Table 3.5 How Candidates Emerge as Front-Runners in Contested Nomination Races, 1980–2000

1. Eventual Nominee Leads the Polls throughout the Entire Invisible Primary

Bush in 1988
Bush in 1992
Gore in 2000

2. Eventual Nominee Establishes an Early Lead among the Declared Candidates; His Strongest Potential Rival Decides Not to Run

Reagan in 1980
Mondale in 1984
Dole in 1996
Bush in 2000

3. Eventual Nominee Becomes the Front-Runner Late in the Invisible Primary Period

Carter in 1980
Clinton in 1992

4. Eventual Nominee Becomes the Poll Leader during the Primary and Caucus Season

Dukakis in 1988

crats chose Gore; his nearest competitor, Jesse Jackson, had just 15 percent. The first Gallup survey on the race, in early September, 1997, had it Gore 47 percent, Jackson 13 percent. Gallup asked the same question twenty more times over the next twenty-eight months, varying the list of candidates as different contenders tested the waters or dropped out, and Gore led every time, by an average margin of 29 percentage points. Though Bradley did narrow the race somewhat in the closing months of 1999, Gore's lead over the former New Jersey senator was never smaller than 12 percentage points.

In many respects, Gore was simply revisiting the path trod by George Bush, Sr., twelve years earlier. The resemblance is, of course, no accident: Both were sitting vice presidents, serving under relatively popular presidents who were, because of the Twenty-second Amendment, legally unable to run for reelection. In late December, 1984, less than two months after Ronald Reagan was re-elected, Penn and Schoen asked a national sample of Republican identifiers which of five candidates was their "first choice" for the 1988 nomination. Bush won 40 percent of the votes; his nearest competitor, Senate Majority Leader Howard Baker, received just 20 percent. In the first Gallup sounding, in June, 1985, Bush's vote was little changed, but Baker, who had chosen not to run for reelection in 1984, saw his standing in the polls enter into a sharp decline.[13] By January, 1987, the GOP race was shaping up as a two-man contest, with Bush clearly in the lead, Bob Dole, the new Senate Majority Leader, in second place, and everybody else lagging well behind. One year later, on the eve of the Iowa caucuses, that was still the case.

The survey record on the 1992 Republican nomination is considerably thinner, but the data that are available clearly suggest that this race, too, belongs in the first category. The problem, of course, is that up until quite late in the invisible primary period, the 1992 Republican race was expected to be uncontested and, thus, hardly a fit subject for extensive polling. Indeed, through the first two and a half years of the Bush presidency, I have been able to locate just one question about the 1992 Republican nomination, from a March, 1990, Gallup Poll. Fortunately, its results bear out what everyone pretty much suspected at the time. Simply put, Bush was the overwhelming favorite of the Republican rank-and-file. Fully 65 percent wanted him to be their party's presidential candidate in 1992; no other of the eight candidates mentioned received more than 7 percent.

In late 1991, however, two candidates who were granted at least some measure of credibility by the media entered the race against Bush: television commentator and former presidential speechwriter Pat Buchanan; and former Louisiana state representative and Ku Klux Klan leader David Duke. At least in the polls, neither even came close to denting Bush's lead. In three separate Gallup surveys conducted between December, 1991, and early February, 1992, Bush was supported, on average, by 85 percent of Republicans, as compared to 9 percent for Buchanan and 4 percent for Duke.

The second category in table 3.5 includes four races in which the eventual nominee also ran strong in the polls almost from the very beginning. In each of these cases, however, the nominee-to-be did face serious competition from one other potential candidate. In every case, though, that chief rival ultimately decided not to run for president, leaving the eventual nominee as the clear front-runner. Perhaps the best way to describe this category, then, is to say that the eventual nominee established an early lead in the polls *among those candidates who actively sought the nomination*, and then maintained that lead through the rest of the invisible primary. The four candidates in this category are Ronald Reagan in 1980, Walter Mondale in 1984, Robert Dole in 1996, and George Bush in 2000.

A good example of this pattern is the Republican nomination race of 1996. The first national survey on this race was a Hart-Breglio poll for NBC News and the *Wall Street Journal*, conducted between December 12 and 15, 1992. The leader in that poll, with 20 percent of the vote, was Jack Kemp, one of the few members of the outgoing Bush administration who had received positive notice during Bush's final year in office. But right behind Kemp—in a statistical tie, in fact—was Robert Dole, at 19 percent. James Baker, the former secretary of state who was then serving as Bush's chief of staff, had 12 percent, while Vice President Dan Quayle received 10 percent. Over the next year and a half, however, Kemp, Baker, and Quayle were sitting on the sidelines, while Dole emerged as one of the most visible leaders of the opposition to Bill Clinton. By August, 1993, a poll conducted for *U.S. News & World Report* had Dole solidly in first place, 11 percentage points ahead of his nearest competitor. Kemp, by contrast, had slipped to third place, 16 points behind Dole.

By the early spring of 1995, after Kemp and Quayle had both announced that they would not be candidates for the 1996 nomination, Dole had opened up a huge lead over every other announced candidate. An April, 1995, Gallup survey found that 46 percent of the nation's Republicans said that Dole was the candidate they would be "most likely to support" for their party's next presidential nomination, as compared to just 13 percent for Phil Gramm and 8 percent for Pat Buchanan.

There was one candidate, however, who ran competitively with Dole through at least part of the 1996 invisible primary season: former chairman of the Joint Chiefs of Staff Colin Powell. As shown in table 3.6, how well Powell fared against Dole varied over the course of the campaign. In the second half of 1993 and through most of 1994, polls showed Dole slightly ahead of Powell—by about 6 percentage points, on average. (Dole's lead was not just a product of sampling error, however: he was ahead of Powell in every one of the six surveys conducted during this period.) In early 1995, Dole opened up a much larger lead over the former general. Surveys taken between late March and early June all had Dole trouncing Powell by about 25 points. In the fall of 1995, however, Powell benefited from a huge wave of publicity surrounding the release of his autobiography and the accompanying book tour. With just one exception, polls taken between mid-September and early November—Powell finally declared that he would not be a candidate on November 8—showed Dole with, at best, a single digit lead over Powell. In two polls, Powell was actually ahead of Dole.

All told, I have been able to locate 26 polls from the 1996 invisible primary period that matched Dole and Powell as rival candidates for the 1996 Republican nomination (in every case, the question also named a number of other potential candidates). Dole led Powell in 23 of these surveys (though in some cases the difference was less than the margin of sampling error), Powell led Dole twice, and in one survey they were tied. There is, then, no compelling reason to think that Powell would have bested Dole even if he had entered the nomination race. The important point is that Powell was the only candidate who even threatened to dislodge Dole from the front-runner's position. Without Powell in the race, the Senate majority leader had, by early 1995, established a large lead over every other announced candidate and then maintained that lead until the beginning of the actual caucus and primary season.

In a similar way, the only candidate who challenged Ronald Reagan during the 1980 invisible primary was eventual non-candidate Gerald Ford. Reagan generally (though not invariably) beat Ford in questions that named the full field of potential Republican candidates. But Gallup also asked a series of what it called "showdown" questions, in which respondents were asked to say whom they

Table 3.6 Matchups of Robert Dole and Colin Powell during the 1996 Invisible Primary

Organization	Sampling Dates	Dole	Powell	Difference (Dole-Powell)
Tarrance-MLL[a]	Aug. 29–31, 1993	36%	25%	11%
Hart-Teeter[b]	Oct. 22–26, 1993	28	25	3
Gallup[c]	March 28–30, 1994	20	13	7
Harris[d]	Aug. 2–4, 1994	17	12	5
PSRA[e]	Sept. 29–30, 1994	33	24	9
Gallup[c]	Oct. 7–9, 1994	25	23	2
Harris[f]	Dec. 9–14, 1994	29	14	15
Hart-Teeter[f]	March 4–7, 1995	37	27	10
Marist[e]	March 27–29, 1995	42	17	25
Harris[d]	April 14–20, 1995	42	15	27
Hart-Teeter[b]	April 21–25, 1995	44	20	24
Hart-Teeter[f]	June 2–6, 1995	48	22	26
PSRA[c]	June 8–11, 1995	42	17	25
Yankelovich[c]	June 21–22, 1995	43	22	19
Harris[d]	July 13–16, 1995	38	20	18
Harris[d]	Aug. 31–Sept. 3, 1995	31	19	12
PSRA[e]	Sept. 14–15, 1995	37	22	15
Hart-Teeter[f]	Sept. 16–19, 1995	34	31	3
Gallup[c]	Sept. 22–24, 1995	31	31	0
Yankelovich[c]	Sept. 27–28, 1995	25	29	−4
ABC/WP[c]	Sept. 28–Oct. 1, 1995	31	22	9
CBS[g]	Oct. 12–14, 1995	41	23	18
CBS/NYT[g]	Oct. 22–25, 1995	29	34	−5
Hart-Teeter[f]	Oct. 27–31, 1995	38	34	4
Yankelovich[e]	Oct. 31–Nov. 6, 1995	32	24	8
Gallup[c]	Nov. 6–8, 1995	34	33	1

[a] Asked of Republican registered likely voters
[b] Asked of Republicans, Republican-leaning independents, and pure independents
[c] Asked of Republicans and Republican-leaning independents
[d] Asked of Republicans and independents
[e] Asked of Republicans and Republican-leaning independents who were registered to vote
[f] Asked of Republicans
[g] Asked of Republican primary voters

Sources: Tarrance-MLL = The Tarrance Group and Mellman, Lazarus, and Lake; PSRA = Princeton Survey Research Associates; ABC/WP = ABC News and the *Washington Post*; CBS/NYT = CBS News and the *New York Times*.

would support if the 1980 Republican contest "narrows down to Gerald Ford and Ronald Reagan." In this type of question, Ford generally beat Reagan. Whichever question one considers a better measure of voter sentiment on this race, the essential point, of course, is that Ford never did get into the race and that among those candidates who did get in, none came close to challenging Reagan's hold on the Republican rank-and-file.

For the first two years of the 1984 invisible primary period, the clear front-runner in polls about the Democratic nomination race was Senator Edward Kennedy, who had also run for his party's nomination in 1980. In an April, 1982, survey, for example, Gallup found that 45 percent of all Democratic identifiers wanted to see Kennedy as their party's next presidential candidate. The second-place finisher, Walter Mondale, was supported by just 12 percent. On December 1, 1982, however, Kennedy announced that he would not be running for president in 1984. Less than two weeks later, a new Gallup survey showed that Mondale was now the front-runner. The former vice president won the backing of 32 percent of his fellow partisans; in second place, with 14 percent, was John Glenn. Every other potential candidate was in single digits. Fourteen months later, on the eve of the Iowa caucuses, that was still pretty much the pecking order.

Against this background, the presidential odyssey of George Bush in 2000 seems, in many ways, strikingly familiar. Like Bob Dole in 1996, Bush was not the leader in the very first poll conducted on the 2000 nomination race. A Hart-Teeter survey conducted between December 5 and 9, 1996, found Colin Powell at the head of the Republican pack with 37 percent, followed by Jack Kemp, the party's 1996 vice presidential candidate, at 20 percent, and Bush at 19 percent. A Harris survey in January, 1997, showed Bush in fourth place, backed by just 7 percent of all Republicans, trailing Powell, Kemp, and even Dan Quayle. By the early spring of 1997, however, Bush was already starting to move up in the polls. In late April of that year, a Hart-Teeter survey that did not include Powell's name in its list of prospective candidates had Bush now leading the field, with 24 percent of the vote, followed by Kemp with 17 percent and Elizabeth Dole with 16 percent. Surveys through the rest of 1997 that used the same set of candidates produced highly similar results. Bush was always in the lead, supported by 20–25 percent of Republican identifiers, with Kemp, Dole, and Quayle all clustered about 5–10 percentage points behind him.

It was during 1998 that George Bush clearly began to put some distance between himself and the rest of the Republican field. A May, 1998, Gallup survey found Bush now supported by 30 percent of the nation's Republicans, while Elizabeth Dole was still stuck at 14 percent and Kemp and Quayle had slumped to 9 percent. In an October Gallup poll, it was Bush 39 percent, Dole 17 percent, Quayle 12 percent (Kemp's name was not included in the question). A September, 1998, Hart-Teeter survey showed Bush with an even larger lead. The Texas governor was favored by 41 percent of all Republicans, while Kemp had the support of just 11 percent and Dole had 10 percent.

As the preceding discussion has already suggested, the candidate who ran best against Bush during this period—the only candidate who ever really threatened his position as the early front-runner—was Colin Powell. Given the widespread assumption that Powell would probably not be a presidential candidate in 2000, I have been able to locate only six polls from the 2000 invisible primary period that included both Bush and Powell's names. The results for all six are shown in table 3.7. In late 1996 and early 1997, Powell ran well ahead of every other Republican hopeful, Bush included. By early 1998, however, Powell's star had

Table 3.7 **Matchups of George Bush and Colin Powell during the 2000 Invisible Primary**

Organization	Sampling Dates	Powell	Bush	Kemp	Quayle
Hart and Teeter[a]	Dec. 5–6, 1996	37%	19%	20%	—[c]
Harris[b]	Jan. 9–13, 1997	36	7	14	11
Gallup[a]	Apr. 11–13, 1997	37	14	15	11
Harris[b]	Oct. 15–19, 1997	28	9	12	8
Opinion Dynamics[b]	March 10–11, 1998	15	29	5	5
Harris[b]	July 17–21, 1998	24	20	5	7

[a] Asked of Republicans and Republican-leaning independents
[b] Asked of Republicans
[c] Quayle's name was not included in this survey

started to fade, while Bush's was in the ascendant. A March, 1998, Opinion Dynamics poll had Bush beating Powell, 29 percent to 15 percent, though a July Harris survey had Powell narrowly besting Bush, 24 percent to 20 percent. Unfortunately, that seems to have been the last time that a question of this type was asked. As in the 1996 race, then, the available evidence does not provide much ground for confidence that Powell would have won even if he had thrown his hat in the ring. His decision to stay out, however, clearly did remove one more obstacle in the path of the Bush juggernaut.

THE EXCEPTIONS

The most striking conclusion to emerge from this analysis is how early in the election cycle most eventual nominees were established as their party's front-runner. In seven of the ten cases considered here, the nominee-to-be had opened up a sizable lead over every other eventual candidate by, *at the latest*, one month after the preceding midterm election—more than a year, in other words, before the start of the actual delegate selection activities, at least a year and a half before the opening of the national conventions.

The exceptions to this general pattern are of two types. Two of the exceptions—Jimmy Carter in 1980 and Bill Clinton in 1992—*did not become front-runners until relatively late in the invisible primary.* Up until the final two months before Iowa, Carter and Clinton had quite unimpressive polling numbers, but both then leaped ahead of the competition in December of the year preceding the election and January of the election year.

It is a remarkable commentary on Jimmy Carter's tenuous grip on his own party and the rocky course of his tenure in the White House that by late March, 1978, barely fourteen months into his presidency, Carter was, at least according to the polls, not the front-runner for the next Democratic presidential nomination. Matched up against five other leading Democrats, Carter was supported by just 29 percent of his fellow partisans. The leader in that poll was Edward Kennedy, and over the next year or so, Kennedy's lead grew significantly larger, to the point that, by the summer of 1979, he was preferred to Carter by almost a three-to-one margin both in head-to-head matchups and when other Democratic hopefuls such as Jerry Brown were included in the question.

In retrospect, it seems clear that Kennedy's lead was artificially, misleadingly high. On the one hand, he was benefiting from the aura that had long surrounded his family's name, an aura that, at the time, largely transcended partisan and ideological categories. In a July, 1979, survey, for example, Gallup found Kennedy beating Carter within every major demographic category in the Democratic party, with strikingly little variation. Even among southern Democrats, Kennedy led by a 58 percent to 37 percent margin. In an October, 1979, Gallup Poll, 36 percent of all Democrats described Kennedy's "political position" as right of center, as against just 44 percent who located him (correctly) to the left of center.[14] The early dynamics of the 1980 campaign also aided Kennedy. Throughout the first ten months of 1979, Carter's weaknesses and shortcomings were at the center of popular and press attention, while the principal storyline involving Kennedy concerned how popular he was and how many people wanted him to run for president.

There is good reason, then, to think that once Kennedy became an official candidate and his real policy views became more widely known, his lead would decline somewhat.[15] But there was nothing inevitable about how far and how fast Kennedy's numbers fell. In mid-October, 1979, the nation's Democrats preferred Kennedy to Carter, 60 percent to 30 percent. By early January, 1980, just two and a half months later, Carter was leading Kennedy, 51 percent to 37 percent. The principal reason for this abrupt turnaround is not hard to identify. In the final two months of 1979, Carter's political fortunes benefited from two major foreign policy crises. On November 4, the American embassy in Teheran was seized by Iranian students who took 65 Americans hostage; on December 27, the Soviet Union invaded Afghanistan. In the predictable way that the American public rallies around the president during a time of international stress,[16] Carter's approval ratings, which had been hovering in the high 20s and low 30s since May, 1979, soared to 58 percent in mid-January, 1980. His standing vis-à-vis Kennedy closely parallels his approval ratings.[17] Absent events in Iran and Afghanistan, it is difficult to believe that Carter would have beaten back Kennedy's challenge.[18]

The rise of Bill Clinton in late 1991 and early 1992 is less easy to explain. The Gulf War of January-February, 1991, made the lead-up to the 1992 Democratic nomination contest quite different from every other out-party race considered here. On the one hand, the active campaign simply started a lot later. Where most contemporary presidential candidates officially launch their campaigns in the late winter or early spring of the year before the election, by early September, 1991, the Democrats had only one declared candidate. Even more striking was the fact that all of the putative front-runners—every Democrat who ranked among the leaders in early polls of the national rank-and-file—ultimately decided *not* to make the race. Mario Cuomo, Jesse Jackson, Lloyd Bentsen, Dick Gephardt, Al Gore, Bill Bradley, George McGovern, and Sam Nunn all decided they had other commitments or thought there was too little chance of beating George Bush.

The result was that, when the Democratic nomination race finally began to take shape in the fall of 1991, it lacked a real front-runner. The leader in the polls was Jerry Brown, the only candidate who had previously run for national office, but compared to almost every other race considered here, Brown had, at best, a weak grip on the top spot. In two different Gallup Polls—one in mid-September, the other in early November—only 21 percent of the nation's Democrats wanted Brown to be their next presidential standard bearer, a level of support far below that enjoyed by Kennedy in 1979, Mondale in 1983, or Gore in 1999. The other five candidates each received between 5 and 10 percent of the vote.

Between mid-October, 1991, and late January, 1992, however, Bill Clinton gradually emerged from this tightly clustered pack. Again, I have tried to find every national survey from this period that included a question on the Democratic nomination race; the results are shown in table 3.8. By early January, these polls indicate, Clinton was all but tied with Brown; and by the end of January, the Arkansas governor had opened up a 20-percentage-point lead over every other declared candidate. From October through mid-January, Clinton's gradual rise in the polls is probably attributable to the fact that (a) he was receiving more press coverage than any other candidate; and (b) much of that coverage was strikingly favorable.[19] What finally sent Clinton soaring past all his competitors, however, was the controversy that erupted in late January over his marital infidelities. The episode began on January 17, when a tabloid called *The Star* published a front-page article claiming that Clinton had had at least five extramarital affairs while serving as governor of Arkansas. The story was quickly picked up by the mainstream media, and soon began to dominate coverage of the campaign. On January 26, in an attempt to stem the damage, Clinton and his wife appeared on a special "60 Minutes" program that was aired immediately after the Super Bowl, to answer questions about the matter.

On January 16, just before the original *Star* article appeared, a Yankelovich Clancy Shulman poll showed Brown and Clinton in a dead heat, each supported by 22 percent of the Democratic electorate. By early February, four separate polls showed Clinton leading the rest of the field by margins of between 16 and 26 percentage points. How this controversy came to work to Clinton's advantage is unclear, especially since in New Hampshire, it seems to have had quite the opposite effect, sending the Clinton campaign into a sharp decline while pouring new life into that of Paul Tsongas. In part, Clinton's soaring numbers in the national polls may have been a simple matter of publicity and name recognition: By the time the dust had settled, Clinton was far and away the best known of the Demo-

Table 3.8 The Emergence of Bill Clinton during the 1992 Invisible Primary

Organization	Sampling Dates	Clinton	Brown	Kerrey	Tsongas	Harkin
Gallup[a]	Sept. 13–15, 1991	6%	21%	5%	5%	6%
Hart-Teeter[b]	Sept. 20–24, 1991	5	11	6	5	6
CBS/NYT[c]	Oct. 15–18, 1991	5	12	7	2	3
Hart-Teeter[b]	Oct. 25–29, 1991	9	21	8	5	4
Gallup[a]	Oct. 31–Nov. 3, 1991	9	21	10	7	10
CBS/NYT[c]	Nov. 18–22, 1991	6	11	7	2	6
Hart-Teeter[b]	Nov. 20–21, 1991	8	20	7	5	6
LA Times[a]	Nov. 21–24, 1991	9	20	5	4	4
Hart-RSM[b]	Dec. 6–9, 1991	10	18	7	4	8
Harris[d]	Dec. 26–30, 1991	15	23	7	3	6
Gallup[a]	Jan. 3–9, 1992	17	21	11	6	9
CBS/NYT[c]	Jan. 6–8, 1992	14	13	7	2	3
YCS[a]	Jan. 16, 1992	22	22	10	8	7
Hart-Breglio[b]	Jan. 17–21, 1992	20	19	7	7	5
CBS/NYT[c]	Jan. 22–25, 1992	22	13	9	10	4
YCS[a]	Jan. 30, 1992	41	17	9	6	6
ABC/WP[e]	Jan. 30–Feb. 2, 1992	37	21	8	7	6
Gallup[a]	Jan. 31–Feb. 2, 1992	42	16	10	9	9
LA Times[a]	Jan. 31–Feb. 2, 1992	30	12	7	7	7

[a] Asked of Democrats and Democratic-leaning independents who were registered to vote
[b] Asked of Democrats, Democratic-leaning independents, and pure independents who were registered to vote
[c] Asked of Democratic registered voters who usually vote in Democratic primaries
[d] Asked of Democrats
[e] Asked of Democrats and Democratic-leaning independents
Sources: CBS/NYT = CBS News and the *New York Times*; Hart-RSM = Peter Hart and Research/Strategy/Management; YCS = Yankelovich Clancy Shulman; ABC/WP = ABC News and the *Washington Post*.

cratic candidates. Clinton may also have gotten some credit for the resilience and determination he showed in continuing his campaign, and perhaps some support from those who saw him as the victim of media excess. Whatever the exact cause(s), the result is clear: By the eve of the Iowa caucuses, Clinton had a large lead in the polls of Democratic identifiers.

The final category in table 3.5 is the one envisioned in the classic accounts of momentum: a candidate who is not the front-runner at the end of the invisible primary, but manages to do well in some of the early primaries and caucuses, which then propels him to a lead in the national polls, further success in the primaries, and ultimately the nomination. What is striking is that this last category includes just one candidate: Michael Dukakis in 1988.

The early poll leader in the 1988 Democratic nomination race was Gary Hart, who had narrowly lost the nomination to Walter Mondale in 1984. In April, 1987, about two months after Mario Cuomo had officially declared that he would not be a candidate, a Gallup Poll showed Hart supported by 46 percent of Democratic identifiers, as compared to 18 percent for Jesse Jackson and single-digit numbers for everybody else. In early May, however, the *Miami Herald* revealed that Hart had spent a night in his Washington, D.C., townhouse with a sometime model named Donna Rice. Five days later, Hart dropped out of the race.

For the next seven months, the 1988 Democratic race, like the party's 1992 contest, lacked a clear front-runner. In first place, according to four different Gallup Polls, was Jesse Jackson, but like Jerry Brown in 1992, Jackson was never supported by more than 22 percent of his fellow partisans. The rest of the vote was divided among six other announced Democratic candidates,[20] none of whom seems to have been very well known outside of his own home state, with an unusually large number of respondents (about 40 percent) saying they were undecided. To further confuse matters, on December 15 Hart re-entered the race, and probably just because he was better known than all the other candidates except Jackson, immediately resumed his lead in the polls. Yet the Donna Rice affair had clearly done its damage: In nine different polls conducted during January, 1988, Hart was favored, on average, by just 22 percent of the nation's Democrats, about half the support he had had before exiting the race (see table 3.9).

So Dukakis was not the clear front-runner in the 1988 Democratic nomination race on the eve of the Iowa caucuses. Yet neither was he a prohibitive long-shot. To begin with, Dukakis was, as noted in table 3.1, his party's leading fund-raiser

Table 3.9 National Survey Results for the 1988 Democratic Nomination Race between Hart's Re-entry and the Iowa Caucuses

Organization	Sampling Dates	Hart	Jackson	Dukakis	Simon	Gephardt
YCS[a]	Dec. 17, 1987	30%	22%	14%	7%	4%
Gallup[b]	Dec. 17–18, 1987	31	13	10	10	2
YCS[a]	Jan. 3–6, 1988	28	17	11	13	4
Harris[c]	Jan. 7–26, 1988	19	15	15	8	6
Gallup[b]	Jan. 8–17, 1988	25	19	10	8	4
CBS/NYT[d]	Jan. 17–21, 1988	23	17	6	9	4
ABC/WP[b]	Jan. 17–23, 1988	26	28	11	11	4
NBC/WSJ[e]	Jan. 20–22, 1988	18	14	9	7	7
Gordon Black[f]	Jan. 21–28, 1988	17	13	13	7	9
Gallup[g]	Jan. 22–24, 1988	23	15	16	9	9
NYT[d]	Jan. 30–31, 1988	18	16	8	6	4

[a] Asked of registered voters likely to vote in a Democratic primary or caucus
[b] Asked of Democrats and Democratic-leaning independents
[c] Asked of Democrats and independents who were registered to vote
[d] Asked of registered Democratic primary voters
[e] Asked of Democrats who are likely to vote in a Democratic primary or caucus
[f] Asked of Democrats
[g] Asked of Democrats and Democratic-leaning independents who are registered to vote

Sources: YCS = Yankelovich Clancy Shulman; CBS/NYT = CBS News and the *New York Times*; ABC/WP = ABC News and the *Washington Post*; NBC/WSJ = NBC News and the *Wall Street Journal*; NYT = *New York Times*.

during 1987. In fact, he raised almost twice as much money during the invisible primary as any of his competitors.[21] Even in the polls, as shown in table 3.9, Dukakis generally finished second or third, just behind Hart and Jackson. If, as was widely assumed at the time, Hart would falter once the actual caucus and primary season began and Jackson's support was intense but quite narrow, Dukakis was well-positioned to pick up the pieces.

At the risk of generalizing on the basis of just three cases, the preceding analysis underlines the difficult challenge facing any candidate like Bill Bradley or John McCain, who hopes to win a presidential nomination for which they are not the early front-runner. To derail an early front-runner, it would appear, takes a special set of circumstances.[22] Kennedy's defeat is primarily attributable to one of the worst U.S. foreign policy crises in the final quarter of the twentieth century. The 1988 Hart campaign was wrecked by the personal self-destructiveness of the candidate. The 1992 Democratic nomination race, I think it fair to say, never really had an early front-runner: Of the candidates who did decide to run for president that year, none had a clear and commanding lead over the rest of the field. Of course, every presidential campaign has its unique occurrences and unexpected twists. If the McCain and Bradley strategists were hoping that something similar might happen in 1999 or 2000, it was not entirely an exercise in wishful thinking. The point is that they probably did need something well out of the ordinary: Merely running a good campaign, history suggests, would not be enough.

ENTER IOWA AND NEW HAMPSHIRE

Having examined how candidates become—or fail to become—front-runners, I now want to extend the analysis in the opposite direction. As the results in table 3.4 indicate, the basic model discussed in the first section of this chapter does correctly forecast the eventual nominee and perhaps says something useful about the general shape of the race. Yet some of the individual predictions are clearly rather wide of the mark.[23] What accounts for these errors?

One obvious place to look is the events that lead off the delegate selection calendar. Compared to other types of elections, perhaps the most distinctive feature of presidential primaries is that they occur sequentially. While the states in a general election all vote on the same day, presidential primaries take place over a period of approximately four months. Under such an arrangement, it would not be surprising to find—indeed, it is probably to be expected—that the voting in later primaries is affected by what happens in earlier primaries.

The general term for such an effect, of course, is momentum. Though I have argued earlier that momentum has somewhat more limited effects than has generally been supposed, it clearly does have some impact. In this section, I want to make an attempt to incorporate the effects of early momentum into the basic model, to see what difference it makes and how much total effect it has on the final outcome.

To be more specific: If there is one moment when nomination races genuinely do seem up for grabs, it is at the very beginning of the delegate selection calendar, when two events dominate the proceedings: the Iowa caucuses and the New Hampshire primary. To what extent do these two states rearrange the basic structure of the race? How much more predictable does the race become once these two states have had their say?[24]

For a preliminary answer to these questions, consider table 3.10, which shows, for each of the ten races being analyzed here, the nomination preferences of national party identifiers at three points in time: just before the Iowa caucuses; in between Iowa and New Hampshire (where such a poll is available); and immediately after New Hampshire. Particularly when compared to the relative stability of the national polls during the invisible primary, it is striking how much impact these two events have generally had on the shape of the national race. In six of the ten races, one candidate gained at least 15 percentage points in the national polls on the basis of his performance in Iowa and/or New Hampshire.

What happens when we add Iowa and New Hampshire into the basic forecasting model? In order to answer this question properly, one other issue needs to be addressed: In what form are the results of Iowa and New Hampshire incorporated into the results of later primaries? When we say that voters in states like California, Illinois, and Ohio are "influenced by" what has happened in Iowa and New Hampshire, what exactly are they reacting to? It seems clear, to begin with, that what matters is *not* the raw, unadjusted vote percentage received by each candidate. In 2000, for example, Bill Bradley received 45.6 percent of the votes cast in the New Hampshire Democratic primary, a percentage substantially higher than that received by Jimmy Carter in 1976, Gary Hart in 1984, or Paul Tsongas in 1992. Yet, all indications are that Bradley received far less benefit from that showing than any of these other candidates.[25] In some fashion, then, these raw percentages are adjusted or discounted because of the special circumstances and conditions that accompany a given election.

Obviously, one thing that matters is the order in which the candidates finish. Carter, Hart, and Tsongas all gained a lot from New Hampshire because they won that state's primary; Bradley's vote totals were seen as much less impressive for the simple reason that Al Gore beat him. In multi-candidate races, it also probably helps to come in second, since that at least allows a candidate to project himself as the principal opponent of the winner.

Yet, there is clearly a lot more to the story than this. In many cases, what seems to matter is not who wins or loses in an absolute sense, but whether a candidate does better or worse than "expected." In 1984, to take a particularly celebrated example of this phenomenon, Walter Mondale posted one of the most dominating victories in the history of the Iowa caucuses, yet seems to have received almost no benefit from that showing because it was so widely expected. The can-

Table 3.10 Effect of Iowa and New Hampshire on the Presidential Nomination Preferences of National Party Identifiers, 1980–2000

	Last Poll before Iowa	Poll(s) between Iowa and New Hampshire		First Poll after New Hampshire	Total Change
1980 Democrats[a]					
Carter	51%	63%	61%	66%	+15%
Kennedy	37	29	32	27	−10
1980 Republicans[a]					
Reagan	41	32	47	55	+14
Baker	14	8	8	9	−5
Connally	13	11	8	3	−10
Bush	9	32	25	25	+16
1984 Democrats					
Mondale	43	57		31	−12
Glenn	16	7		7	−9
Jackson	12	8		7	−5
Hart	1	7		38	+37
1988 Democrats					
Hart	17	9		7	−10
Dukakis	13	16		22	+9
Jackson	13	12		14	+1
Gephardt	9	20		13	+4
1988 Republicans					
Bush	43	38		39	−4
Dole	24	32		30	+6
Robertson	6	10		7	+1
Kemp	4	5		5	+1
1992 Democrats					
Clinton	42	—[b]		41	−1
Brown	16	—[b]		7	−9
Kerrey	10	—[b]		6	−4
Tsongas	9	—[b]		31	+22
1992 Republicans					
Bush	84	—[b]		78	−6
Buchanan	11	—[b]		20	+9
Duke	4	—[b]		*	−4

Table 3.10 (continued)

	Last Poll before Iowa	Poll(s) between Iowa and New Hampshire	First Poll after New Hampshire	Total Change
1996 Republicans				
Dole	47%	—[b]	41%	− 6%
Forbes	16	—[b]	8	− 8
Buchanan	7	—[b]	27	+ 20
Alexander	3	—[b]	14	+ 11
2000 Democrats				
Gore	60	67	65	+ 5
Bradley	27	21	24	− 3
2000 Republicans				
Bush	63	65	56	− 7
McCain	19	15	34	+ 15
Forbes	6	7	2	− 4

[a] In 1980, there were 36 days between Iowa and New Hampshire. In all other years, there were just 8 days between the two events.

[b] No national poll with a nomination preference question was asked in between Iowa and New Hampshire in 1992 and 1996.

*Indicates the candidate was supported by less than one-half of one percent of the survey respondents.

Sources: 1980, 1992, 1996, and 2000 results are taken from the Gallup Poll; 1984 results are from CBS/ *New York Times*; 1988 results are taken from surveys conducted by Gordon S. Black.

didate whose campaign was buoyed by Iowa in 1984 was Gary Hart, who finished more than 30 percent behind Mondale, yet performed better than most observers had anticipated he would.

So expectations matter. The problem, from the perspective of model-building, is finding a plausible way to operationalize this hypothesis. We need, that is to say, a reasonable way to determine how well each candidate was expected to run in Iowa or New Hampshire, as a standard against which to compare their actual showing. Yet, the more one studies this subject, the more clear it becomes that a quite large number of factors enter into these expectations judgments, many of which are probably idiosyncratic to a particular race and candidate.

As a general proposition, expectations seem to be based primarily on how well each candidate is perceived to be doing in the race as a whole. This, for example, explains why Hart's Iowa showing was regarded as such a significant story in 1984. Hart won 16 percent of the delegates to the next round of caucusing at a time when he was pulling just 3 percent in the national polls. By contrast, Mondale's 49 percent in the Hawkeye State exactly matched his standing in Gallup's most recent national survey and thus raised few eyebrows. Similarly, Buchanan's second-place showing in the 1992 New Hampshire primary was widely regarded as a victory because he won 37 percent of the vote, far higher than the 11 percent he was then receiving in the national polls.

Yet there are also lots of exceptions and qualifications to this generalization. Richard Gephardt's 1988 Iowa victory, for example, was substantially discounted because he came from a neighboring state. On the surface, Steve Forbes's showing in the 2000 Iowa caucuses would seem to resemble Gary Hart's situation in 1984: Forbes came in second to George Bush (a quite strong second, in fact), and Bush's victory had long been expected. Yet Forbes, so far as one can tell, got little benefit from that performance, partly because Bush's principal rival in the national polls (John McCain) had skipped Iowa, partly because most reporters and commentators thought that Forbes had little real chance of winning the nomination. In New Hampshire, most of these same factors come into play—but the Iowa results are also taken into account. In 1988, George Bush seems to have gained a lot from his New Hampshire victory: Even though he was the early front-runner, his front-runner credentials had been badly tarnished by his third-place finish in Iowa. The same thing happened to Ronald Reagan in 1980.

In the end, I have tried to measure the impact of Iowa and New Hampshire by creating, for each event, three pairs of variables.

1. A pair of dummy variables that designate the winners in Iowa and New Hampshire, respectively.
2. A second pair of dummy variables that designate the second-place finishers in Iowa and New Hampshire, *but only in multi-candidate races*. As indicated earlier, the logic behind this variable is that in a crowded field, the second-place candidate at least establishes himself as the principal opponent of the front-runner, a designation that may be of considerable value in upcoming primaries.
3. A measure of how well each candidate finished in Iowa and New Hampshire *relative to expectations*. This variable is derived by taking the candidate's actual showing in each state and subtracting from it the candidate's current standing in the national polls of party identifiers.[26]

The equation that results, *estimated for all races except those held in 1992*,[27] is shown in table 3.11. Three points are worth noting. First, to no one's great surprise, the earliest delegate selection events do have a substantial effect on the final results of a contested nomination race. Adding in the results of Iowa and New Hampshire increases the adjusted R^2 in the forecasting equation by .10 (i.e., the new variables explain an additional 10 percent of the total variance). More importantly, the final forecasts become substantially more accurate. For the original equation, the mean absolute prediction error for all 45 candidates is 7.9: the average forecast, in other words, was off by 7.9 percentage points. With the New Hampshire and Iowa results added in, the mean absolute error falls to 5.3 points.

Second, what seems to matter, according to table 3.11, is how the candidates actually finish, *not* how they finish relative to prior expectations. There are two ways of interpreting this result. One is that, as I have already conceded, I simply may not be measuring expectations very accurately. Alternatively, it may be that,

Table 3.11 Primary Forecasting Model with Iowa and New Hampshire Taken into Account

Independent Variables	Coefficient	Standard Error
National poll standings	0.95	0.21***
Pre-election year fund-raising	−0.05	0.06
First place finish in Iowa	−12.65	12.80
Second place finish in Iowa	−0.46	5.08
Iowa finish relative to expectations	0.06	0.22
First place finish in New Hampshire	26.79	5.41***
Second place finish in New Hampshire	17.18	9.47*
New Hampshire finish relative to expectations	−0.08	0.18
Constant	0.33	2.18

$R^2 = .90$
Adj. $R^2 = .87$
SEE = 7.84
N = 45

* $p < .05$
*** $p < .001$
Note: Equation excludes both parties' nomination races in 1992.

particularly when it comes to New Hampshire, reporters and commentators have become somewhat more suspicious of expectations judgments and are therefore increasingly reluctant to second-guess the hard, mathematical results that get registered in the voting booths. In 1968 and 1972, the media received a lot of criticism for turning New Hampshire victories by Lyndon Johnson and Edmund Muskie into losses, based on the highly debatable notion that these candidates had run "worse than expected." Just as one might have anticipated, in subsequent nomination races many campaigns actively tried to manipulate these expectations, downplaying their chances before the primary and then painting their actual showing in the rosiest possible terms. As a result, media reports on New Hampshire have tended in recent years to focus more closely on the actual results: wins are wins and losses are losses. Over the last six election cycles, the only candidate who managed to convert a New Hampshire loss into a perceived victory was Pat Buchanan in 1992.[28] While many other candidates have tried to duplicate this feat, there is no evidence that they were successful.

THE ROLE OF IOWA

The third and perhaps most surprising result in table 3.11 is that the capacity of early delegate selection events to affect the final outcome of a presidential nomination race is due *entirely* to New Hampshire. The two coefficients that measure the order of finish in New Hampshire are both large and statistically significant. After controlling for everything else, a win in the New Hampshire primary increases a candidate's expected share of the total primary vote by a remarkable 26.8 percentage points. Even a second-place finish in New Hampshire (in a multi-candidate race) increases a candidate's final vote totals by 17.2 percent. By contrast, the two coefficients that measure the impact of Iowa are both statistically insignificant. According to one of them, a win in Iowa actually *reduces* a candidate's expected total vote in the primaries. The general finding that New Hampshire substantially outweighs Iowa, it is worth adding, stands up quite well to changes in specification. For example, if we drop the four dummy variables in table 3.11 that designate the first- and second-place finishers in Iowa and New Hampshire, and measure the effects of these two events solely by comparing each candidate's finish relative to expectations, the New Hampshire variable still turns out to be large and statistically significant, while the Iowa variable is both small and insignificant.

One of the clear messages of this analysis, then, is that Iowa has substantially less impact than New Hampshire on the final outcome of a contested nomination race. Yet Iowa is not quite as impotent as a superficial reading of table 3.11 might suggest. The key to understanding the role of Iowa in the presidential nomination process is to recognize that the coefficients in table 3.11 show the effect of Iowa *holding New Hampshire constant.* Iowa does have an impact on many races, but that impact is mediated through New Hampshire. The general set of relationships that governs the earliest stages of the presidential nomination process is shown in figure 3.1. What is important about Iowa, according to this model, is that it sets the table for New Hampshire. Iowa influences New Hampshire; and New Hampshire and the national poll standings, in turn, affect the final distribution of votes in the presidential primaries. Put another way, a candidate who does well in Iowa puts himself in a somewhat better position to do well in New Hampshire. But if that doesn't occur—if a strong showing in Iowa is *not* followed up by a good performance in New Hampshire—the Iowa result will probably not help the candidate much in the long-run.

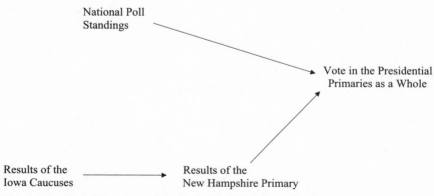

Figure 3.1   Causal Structure of the Early Presidential Nomination Process

How much effect do the Iowa caucuses have on the New Hampshire primary? This question is difficult to answer succinctly. Consider the data in table 3.12. For each of the eight nomination races being considered here (again, I exclude 1992), this table shows the results of: a poll of New Hampshire voters conducted just *before* the Iowa caucuses; a second New Hampshire poll conducted shortly *after* Iowa; and the final results of the New Hampshire primary. It is clear, at a minimum, that New Hampshire listens to Iowa: In *every* race shown here, the polls in New Hampshire show movement in response to the Iowa caucus results. In a fair number of instances, however, that movement turns out to be very short-lived. In 1988, for example, Bob Dole's win in Iowa, coupled with a fairly weak showing by front-runner George Bush, vaulted Dole into first place in the Granite State polls. But in the last few days before the primary, Bush mounted a strong counterattack that, in combination with a rather lackluster campaign by Dole, put the vice president back in front. When the two changes are added together, the final New Hampshire results ended up very close to what the polls were showing on the day before Iowa.

Something very similar happened in the 2000 Democratic race. Al Gore trounced Bill Bradley in the Iowa caucuses, 63 percent to 35 percent; as a result, Gore's lead in New Hampshire, which had been just 5 percent before Iowa, widened to 16 percent by the end of the week. In the last few days before the primary, however, Bradley finally regained his footing and began to respond to the attacks Gore had been making on him for the last several months. That effort significantly narrowed Gore's lead, but ultimately fell short. As with the Republicans in 1988, the final Democratic vote totals in the 2000 New Hampshire primary look remarkably similar to what the polls had been showing just before Iowa.

Yet, there clearly are cases where Iowa has had a more lasting effect on New Hampshire. The best example of this occurred during the 1984 Democratic nomination race. In the week before Iowa, a *Washington Post*/ABC News tracking poll in the Granite State showed Walter Mondale with a substantial lead over the rest of the Democratic field. Mondale had 37 percent of the vote, to 20 percent for John Glenn and just 13 percent for Gary Hart. Immediately after finishing second in Iowa, however, Hart's support began to climb. By election day, Hart had 37 percent of the vote, while Mondale had slipped to 28 percent and Glenn was down to 12 percent. In 1996, the results in Iowa buoyed the New Hampshire campaigns of Pat Buchanan and Lamar Alexander, while dooming those of Phil Gramm and Steve Forbes.

The erratic, idiosyncratic way that the results in Iowa have influenced the course of events in New Hampshire necessarily makes it difficult to model that process. Though I have been tempted at times to introduce a host of new distinctions and qualifications, I have chosen in the end to estimate a model similar to the one in table 3.11. Specifically, the final vote in New Hampshire is hypothesized to be a function of four variables:

Table 3.12 Effect of the Iowa Caucuses on the Vote in New Hampshire

	Poll of New Hampshire Voters Just before Iowa	Poll of New Hampshire Voters Just after Iowa	Final New Hampshire Primary Results
1980 Republicans			
Reagan	43%	39%	50%
Bush	24	43	23
Baker	10	6	13
Anderson	6	2	10
(N)	(200)	(275)	
1980 Democrats			
Carter	35	54	47
Kennedy	31	36	37
Brown	11	5	10
(N)	(372)	(231)	
1984 Democrats			
Hart	13	22	37
Mondale	37	39	28
Glenn	20	14	12
Jackson	10	7	5
(N)	(526)	(343)	
1988 Republicans			
Bush	36	28	38
Dole	26	32	28
Kemp	13	13	13
DuPont	9	11	10
Robertson	6	10	9
(N)	(501)	(457)	
1988 Democrats			
Dukakis	43	40	36
Gephardt	12	16	20
Simon	13	16	17
Jackson	6	6	8
(N)	(503)	(455)	
1996 Republicans			
Buchanan	16	22	27
Dole	24	25	26
Alexander	5	18	23
Forbes	20	13	12
(N)	(400)	(400)	

Table 3.12 (continued)

	Poll of New Hampshire Voters Just before Iowa	Poll of New Hampshire Voters Just after Iowa	Final New Hampshire Primary Results
2000 Republicans			
McCain	43%	36%	48%
Bush	34	37	30
Forbes	13	15	13
(N)	(620)	(587)	
2000 Democrats			
Gore	50	56	50
Bradley	45	40	46
(N)	(487)	(466)	

Sources: Survey data are taken from: 1980 Republicans: Decision Making/Information poll for the Reagan for President campaign, survey of January 11–12; Research Analysis Corporation, survey of January 24–27, as reported in *Boston Globe*, February 3, 1980. 1980 Democrats: Blake and Dickinson survey of January 16–19, as reported in *Boston Globe*, January 22, 1980; Research Analysis Corporation, survey of January 22–24, as reported in *Boston Globe*, January 27, 1980. 1984 Democrats: ABC/*Washington Post*, surveys of February 13–20 and 21–23. 1988 Republicans: ABC/*Washington Post*, surveys of February 1–7 and 11–13. 1988 Democrats: ABC/*Washington Post*, surveys of February 1–7 and 11–13. Data for 1984 Democrats, 1988 Republicans, and 1988 Democrats are all taken from Kenneth E. John, "The Polls: 1980–1988 New Hampshire Presidential Primary Polls," *Public Opinion Quarterly* 53 (Winter 1989): 590–605. 1996 Republicans: KRC Communications Research, surveys of February 10–11 and February 16, as reported in *Boston Globe*, February 12, 1996 and February 17, 1996. 2000 Republicans: Gallup Poll, surveys of January 21–23 and 25–27, as reported in *Gallup Poll Monthly*, January, 2000, 39. 2000 Democrats: Gallup Poll, surveys of January 21–23 and 25–27, as reported in *Gallup Poll Monthly*, January, 2000, 41.

1. The candidate's standing in the New Hampshire polls just before Iowa (i.e., the first column of figures in table 3.12).[29]
2. A dummy variable that designates the winner of the Iowa caucuses.[30]
3. A second dummy variable that designates second-place finishers in Iowa in multi-candidate races.
4. A measure of how well each candidate finished in Iowa relative to expectations, calculated in the same way as the expectations variables in table 3.11.

The result is shown in table 3.13. In general, according to this model, candidates who won the Iowa caucuses got little or no benefit in New Hampshire from that showing. The benefits from Iowa have tended to go to the second-place finisher. After controlling for the candidate's pre-Iowa standing in the polls, a second-place finisher could expect to increase his share of the New Hampshire primary vote by about 7 percentage points. Since the winner of the New Hampshire primary in these eight races received, on average, just 42 percent of the vote, a 7-point boost is not insignificant. As the preceding discussion has tried to make clear, however, that 7-point figure is an average, that masks a considerable amount of variation. Hart's second-place finish in Iowa helped boost his New Hampshire vote by 24 percentage points; in 1996, Pat Buchanan gained 11

Table 3.13 Regression Model for the Effects of Iowa on New Hampshire

Independent Variables	Coefficient	Standard Error
New Hampshire poll just before Iowa	0.99	0.07***
First place finish in Iowa	1.19	2.74
Second place finish in Iowa	7.06	2.92**
Iowa finish relative to expectations	0.09	0.09
Constant	0.29	1.32

$R^2 = .88$
Adj. $R^2 = .87$
SEE = 5.78
N = 45

** p < .01
*** p < .001
Notes: Dependent variable is the percentage of the total vote a candidate received in the New Hampshire primary.
Equation excludes both parties' nomination races in 1992.

percent between Iowa and New Hampshire. By contrast, finishing second to George Bush in the 2000 Iowa caucuses brought no apparent gain to Steve Forbes, in New Hampshire or anywhere else.

Overall, even the effect of Iowa on New Hampshire is somewhat weaker than I had initially anticipated. Some candidates in the Granite State have clearly benefited from running strong in Iowa, but for many others, the gains were small and fleeting.

CONCLUSION

The major purpose of this article has been to describe the basic dynamics of the contemporary presidential nomination process. My findings in that regard can be summarized in the form of four major propositions.

1. Its initial reputation notwithstanding, the contemporary presidential nomination process is actually quite favorable to front-runners. In all of the last ten contested nomination races, the eventual nominee was either (a) leading in the national polls of party identifiers at the beginning of the delegate selection season; or (b) had raised more money than any other candidate in the year before the election. In eight of ten cases, the nominee-to-be led in *both* the polls and the fund-raising derby.
2. Most front-runners establish themselves in that position at a quite early point in the election cycle. Most recent nominees were leading the national polls for at least a year before the first delegates were selected.
3. Though momentum is not the overwhelming force that it is sometimes portrayed to be, strong showings in the earliest caucuses and primaries do have a clear and significant effect on a candidate's fortunes.

4. Of the two highly-publicized events that lead off the delegate selection calendar, the New Hampshire primary towers over the Iowa caucuses in its impact on recent nomination races.

While these conclusions have a number of important implications for campaign strategy during the 2004 nomination season, perhaps the most intriguing concerns the role of the Iowa caucuses. For if the analysis in the last section is correct, a candidate short of time or money might be able to skip Iowa entirely and find that his campaign's long-term prospects of success are essentially unaffected.

As it turns out, the 2000 election cycle provided what comes close to being an experimental test of this hypothesis, for the two major challengers to the front-runners, Bill Bradley on the Democratic side and John McCain on the Republican, chose to deal with Iowa in very different ways. After concentrating much of his early campaigning in New Hampshire, Bradley decided late in 1999 to mount a major effort in Iowa as well. Iowa had never looked like particularly fertile ground for Bradley's message, and the caucus format would only seem to magnify all the advantages that Gore derived from his support among unions and party officials. But the conventional wisdom going into the 2000 campaign held that *both* Iowa and New Hampshire were essential proving-grounds for the serious national candidate and Bradley chose not to put this maxim to the test. Instead, he spent $2.2 million and half of January campaigning in Iowa. The most important penalty Bradley paid for that decision was not the decisive drubbing he suffered in the Hawkeye State but all the time diverted from New Hampshire, where he had been running basically even with Gore since the early fall. There is no way to prove, of course, that Bradley would have won New Hampshire even if he had concentrated his efforts there—but it almost certainly would have helped and, as it was, Bradley only lost the state by 6,000 votes.

John McCain chose the path that Bradley rejected. McCain completely ignored Iowa and instead devoted all of his considerable energy to New Hampshire, holding a total of 114 town meetings in the Granite State. There is, to say the least, no indication that the lack of an Iowa campaign handicapped McCain in New Hampshire. As can be seen in table 3.12, McCain's support in New Hampshire did drop a bit in the days immediately after Iowa, but it had recovered by week's end and the Arizona senator then went on to win the Granite State primary by 18 percentage points.

Given that outcome and (to the extent anyone pays attention to this article) the results in table 3.11, it seems likely that other candidates will try to copy McCain's strategy in the future. Yet other campaigns may not be quite so fortunate. McCain could afford to ignore Iowa in 2000 because *no other candidate in the Republican nomination race was likely to derive much benefit from the caucuses.* Bush was such an overwhelming front-runner that the media were unlikely to make much of his victory there. More importantly, there was no second-tier candidate who could use a "better than expected" showing in Iowa to make himself the story of the week in New Hampshire, as Gary Hart had done in 1984. Steve Forbes, who actually did finish second, had so many obvious limitations that the media—and the voters—were unlikely to take him very seriously. And the other candidates—Alan Keyes, Gary Bauer, Orrin Hatch – seemed even less likely to catch fire. All of the candidates who might plausibly have used Iowa as a real source of momentum—Lamar Alexander, Pat Buchanan, Elizabeth Dole—had dropped out many months earlier. Absent such assurances, one suspects that most candidates in 2004 will take the safer route and mount serious campaigns in *both* Iowa and New Hampshire.

APPENDIX TO CHAPTER 3: NATIONAL NOMINATION
POLLS DURING THE INVISIBLE PRIMARY

Given the amount of attention in this chapter devoted to national nomination polls taken during the invisible primary, it is worth saying a few words about how such polls are conducted. Though the exact wording varies from year to year and organization to organization, the typical question on this subject asks respondents whom they would be most likely to support for their party's next presidential nomination or how they would vote today if their state were holding a presidential primary. In all of the questions analyzed here, *the pollster then provided respondents with a list of the major candidates running for that particular party's presidential nomination.*[31] For the first year or two after the preceding presidential election, it is pretty much up to the discretion of the pollster to determine who gets on this list: i.e., who is likely to become a presidential candidate. As a general matter, however, most pollsters try to be as inclusive as possible, with the result that some early polls will include fifteen or twenty names in the question. As the actual primary and caucus season gets closer, pollsters generally list only those candidates who have officially declared that they are running for president.[32] During the 2000 election cycle, for example, questions about the Democratic nomination race that were asked in 1997 and 1998 generally listed six or seven possible candidates, including Al Gore, Bill Bradley, Dick Gephardt, Jesse Jackson, John Kerry, Bob Kerrey, and (at times) Paul Wellstone. By April, 1999, however, all but two of these men had announced that they would not be running for president. As a result, from that point on, questions asked respondents whom they would choose between Gore and Bradley.

All of the polls shown in the next few pages and in tables 3.6–3.9 are *national* polls, but the responses of the entire national adult population are, in fact, rarely of interest. Survey questions of this type have two general uses: to predict who is going to be a party's next presidential nominee; and to assess how well the nomination process reflects and represents the preferences of the party rank-and-file.[33] For both purposes, it doesn't much matter what Democrats think about the Republican nomination race or vice versa. Hence, most survey organizations report results only for those respondents who identify with the party whose nomination race is at issue: i.e., questions about the Democratic race are asked only of Democratic identifiers; questions about Republican contests are asked only of Republican identifiers. As the primary season draws closer, some pollsters further limit the question to registered voters or those who say they are likely to vote in the presidential primaries.

The tables that follow show the complete Gallup Poll results for every contested nomination race between 1980 and 2000. For the earliest races in this period, Gallup was essentially the only organization that measured national nomination preferences on a regular basis. Though a number of other survey research firms now make frequent inquiries on this subject, using the Gallup data obviously makes it easier to compare results across election cycles. The Gallup Poll also has, I believe, a very admirable track record for carrying out its surveys in a careful and rigorous way and for making its results widely available to both scholars and the general public. In most cases, the survey results shown here are taken from various Gallup publications—in particular, the monthly *Gallup Report* and the yearly compilations of Gallup data published by Scholarly Resources. Where these results were not published in a form appropriate for my purposes or seemed to be in error, I have gone back to the raw data, which are archived at the Roper Center for Public Opinion Research at the University of Connecticut. In all of the following tables, an asterisk (*) indicates that a candidate received less than one-half of one percent of the vote; a dash (—) indicates that the candidate's name was not included in the list of candidates read to the recipient.

1980 REPUBLICAN NOMINATION RACE

Gallup: "Here is a list of people who have been mentioned as possible presidential candidates for the Republican party in 1980. Which one would you like to see nominated as the Republican candidate for president in 1980?" *Note:* Asked only of Republican identifiers.

	Aug. 19–22 1977	March 31 –April 3 1978	July 7–10 1978	Dec. 1–4 1978
Ronald Reagan	33	30	31	40
Gerald Ford	20	40	37	24
Howard Baker	8	11	9	9
John Connally	1	4	5	6
George Bush	1	—	*	1
Robert Dole	1	4	4	1
Elliot Richardson	1	4	3	1
James Thompson	1	—	2	3
Charles Percy	—	—	—	4
Philip Crane	—	—	—	1
John Anderson	—	—	—	1
Others	11	—	—	2
Undecided	23	7	7	7

With Ford's Name Included

	Feb. 2–5 1979	May 4–7 1979	June 22–25 1979	July 13–16 1979	Aug. 17–20 1979	Nov. 2–5 1979
Reagan	31	28	37	32	29	33
Ford	26	27	29	27	21	22
Baker	8	10	11	11	10	14
Connally	12	8	5	9	8	10

With Ford's Name Included (continued)

	Feb. 2–5 1979	May 4–7 1979	June 22–25 1979	July 13–16 1979	Aug. 17–20 1979	Nov. 2–5 1979
Bush	1	2	2	*	3	2
Dole	1	3	2	2	*	3
Crane	2	*	*	2	*	*
Anderson	2	*	*	3	*	*
Others	10	8	10	11	15	13
Undecided	7	14	5	3	14	3

	Nov. 16–19 1979	Dec. 7–10 1979	Jan. 4–7 1980
Reagan	40	40	33
Ford	24	18	27
Baker	11	9	9
Connally	8	10	9
Bush	5	7	9
Dole	3	4	*
Crane	1	*	*
Anderson	*	*	3
Others	4	6	na
Undecided	4	6	10

With the Ford Vote Redistributed

	Feb. 2–5 1979	May 4–7 1979	June 22–25 1979	July 13–16 1979	Aug. 17–20 1979	Nov. 2–5 1979
Reagan	43	41	49	41	47	41
Baker	9	13	15	16	11	18
Connally	16	10	11	14	11	13
Bush	2	*	2	*	*	2
Dole	3	4	2	6	3	3
Crane	2	*	*	2	*	*
Anderson	3	*	*	3	*	*
Others	12	na	16	15	na	15
Undecided	10	25	6	3	28	8

	Nov. 16–19 1979	Dec. 7–10 1979	Jan. 4–7 1980
Reagan	51	47	41
Baker	13	12	14

With the Ford Vote Redistributed (continued)

	Nov. *16–19* *1979*	*Dec.* *7–10* *1979*	*Jan.* *4–7* *1980*
Connally	10	12	13
Bush	7	8	9
Dole	4	6	*
Crane	1	*	*
Anderson	*	*	4
Others	6	6	na
Undecided	8	9	19

Note: For these surveys, Gallup redistributed the Ford vote based on the respondent's second choice.

Gallup: "Suppose the choice for President in the Republican convention in 1980 narrows down to Gerald Ford and Ronald Reagan. Which one would you prefer to have the Republican convention select?" *Note*: Asked only of Republican identifiers.

Sampling Date	*Ford*	*Reagan*	*Don't Know*
March 31–April 3, 1978	54	42	4
June 16–19	48	43	9
November 10–13	46	43	11
July 13–16, 1979	47	49	4
October 12–15	50	41	9

1980 DEMOCRATIC NOMINATION RACE

Gallup: "Here is a list of people who have been mentioned as possible presidential candidates for the Democratic party in 1980. Which one would you like to see nominated as the Democratic candidate for president in 1980?" *Note*: Asked only of Democratic identifiers.

	March 31 –Apr. 3 1978	*July 7–10 1978*	*Sept. 22–25 1978*	*June 1–4 1979*	*June 22–25 1979*	*July 13–15 1979*	*Nov. 16–19 1979*
Edward Kennedy	36	44	39	52	54	53	49
Jimmy Carter	29	20	34	17	22	21	33
Jerry Brown	12	11	8	8	9	8	6
Walter Mondale	8	5	4	3	3	5	2
Henry Jackson	5	4	3	4	*	3	2
Morris Udall	3	1	1	1	*	*	*
George McGovern	—	4	2	5	3	4	3
Pat Moynihan	—	1	1	*	*	2	1
Frank Church	—	1	1	2	*	2	1
Other/undecided	7	9	7	8	9	2	3

Gallup: "Suppose the choice for President in the Democratic convention in 1980 narrows down to Jimmy Carter and Edward Kennedy. Which one would you prefer to have the Democratic convention select?" *Note*: Asked only of Democratic identifiers.

Sampling Date	Carter	Kennedy	Don't Know
March 31–April 3, 1978	40	53	7
June 16–19	31	55	14
November 10–13	32	58	10
February 23–26, 1979	28	60	12
April 6–9	31	58	11
June 1–4	24	62	14
June 22–25	26	68	6
July 13–16	30	66	4
August 17–20	25	63	12
September 28–October 1	27	59	14
October 12–15	30	60	10
November 2–5	31	54	15
November 16–19	36	55	9
December 7–10	46	42	12
January 4–7, 1980	51	37	12

1984 DEMOCRATIC NOMINATION RACE

Gallup: "Which of these persons [a list of candidates was given to the respondent] would you like to see nominated as the Democratic Party's candidate for president in 1984?" *Note*: Asked only of Democratic identifiers.

	April 23–26 1982	July 30 –Aug. 2 1982
Edward Kennedy	45	43
Walter Mondale	12	13
Jimmy Carter	11	8
Jerry Brown	6	4
John Glenn	6	7
Alan Cranston	*	*
Gary Hart	*	*
Ernest Hollings	*	*
Reubin Askew	*	*
Others on list	na	6
None/undecided	na	19

	Dec. 10–13 1982	March 11–14 1983	Apr. 29 –May 2 1983	June 10–13 1983	July 22–25 1983	Sept. 9–12 1983	Oct. 7–10 1983
Mondale	32	32	29	41	41	34	40
Glenn	14	13	23	24	25	23	21
Cranston	2	3	3	8	7	5	6
Hart	2	2	4	3	4	3	3
Hollings	1	1	1	1	2	1	1
Askew	1	2	1	3	2	3	1
George McGovern	6	4	—	—	—	8	8
Jesse Jackson	—	—	—	—	—	8	10
Brown	5	6	—	—	—	—	—
Morris Udall	3	—	—	—	—	—	—
Jay Rockefeller	2	2	2	—	—	—	—
Bill Bradley	1	1	1	—	—	—	—
John Y. Brown	1	1	2	—	—	—	—
Pat Moynihan	1	2	1	—	—	—	—
Lloyd Bentsen	1	2	2	—	—	—	—
Other/none/undecided	26	28	31	20	19	15	10

	Oct. 21–24 1983	Nov. 18–21 1983	Dec. 9–12 1983	Jan. 13–16 1984	Jan. 27–30 1984	Feb. 10–13 1984
Mondale	34	47	40	47	47	49
Glenn	23	19	24	16	15	13
Cranston	3	3	3	4	3	3
Hart	1	2	3	3	2	3
Askew	2	3	1	1	2	2
Hollings	1	1	1	1	1	1
McGovern	7	7	8	4	7	5
Jackson	8	7	10	9	11	13
Other/none/undecided	21	11	11	15	12	11

1988 REPUBLICAN NOMINATION RACE

"Which ONE [of the persons on this list] would you like to see nominated as the Republican Party's candidate for president in 1988?" *Note*: Asked of Republicans and Republican-leaning independents.

	June 7–10 1985	Jan. 10–13 1986	April 11–14 1986	July 11–14 1986	Oct. 24–27 1986	Jan. 16–19 1987
George Bush	39	46	40	41	42	33
Howard Baker	13	7	8	7	6	6
Robert Dole	8	10	9	6	8	14
Jack Kemp	5	5	6	3	5	5

1988 REPUBLICAN NOMINATION RACE (continued)

	June 7–10 1985	Jan. 10–13 1986	April 11–14 1986	July 11–14 1986	Oct. 24–27 1986	Jan. 16–19 1987
Jeane Kirkpatrick	4	2	3	5	4	—
Thomas Kean	2	1	1	1	1	4
Jesse Helms	2	3	1	1	2	—
Richard Thornburgh	2	1	1	1	1	—
James Thompson	1	*	1	1	1	1
James Baker	1	1	*	*	1	1
Elizabeth Dole	1	1	*	*	1	—
Richard Lugar	1	1	2	1	2	—
Pete Domenici	1	1	*	*	*	—
Bill Brock	1	*	*	*	1	—
Newt Gingrich	*	*	*	—	—	—
Paul Laxalt	*	1	1	1	*	1
Lewis Lehrman	*	*	*	—	—	—
Robert Packwood	*	*	*	*	1	—
Alexander Haig	—	4	2	3	3	3
Pierre du Pont	—	1	*	*	1	1
Trent Lott	—	*	*	—	—	—
Donald Rumsfeld	—	*	*	*	*	1
Pat Robertson	—	—	4	6	6	5
William Armstrong	—	—	—	*	1	2
None/don't know	20	14	19	21	14	23

	April 10–13 1987	June 8–14 1987	July 10–13 1987	Aug. 24– Sept. 2 1987	Oct. 23–26 1987	Jan. 22–24 1988
Bush	34	39	40	40	47	45
Dole	18	21	18	19	22	30
Kemp	9	8	10	9	4	5
Haig	7	6	7	4	4	2
Robertson	4	5	5	8	7	8
Du Pont	2	2	3	2	1	2
Kean	2	—	—	—	—	—
Laxalt	1	2	1	—	—	—
Other/undecided	23	17	16	18	15	8

1988 DEMOCRATIC NOMINATION RACE

"Which ONE [of the persons on this list] would you like to see nominated as the Democratic Party's candidate for president in 1988?" *Note*: Asked of Democrats and Democratic-leaning independents.

	June 7–10 1985	Jan. 10–13 1986	April 11–14 1986	July 11–14 1986	Oct. 24–27 1986	Jan. 16–19 1987
Edward Kennedy	31	—	—	—	—	—
Gary Hart	16	29	24	20	17	32
Mario Cuomo	12	15	18	14	19	13
Jesse Jackson	7	9	10	12	9	14
Lee Iacocca	6	9	10	15	15	15
Geraldine Ferraro	6	—	—	—	—	—
Tom Bradley	3	4	4	3	3	—
Bill Bradley	2	4	3	3	2	4
Charles Robb	1	2	2	2	2	3
Dianne Feinstein	1	1	1	2	1	—
Dale Bumpers	1	*	1	*	1	2
Mark White	1	2	2	2	1	—
Bruce Babbitt	*	*	*	*	*	1
Joseph Biden	*	*	1	*	1	1
Sam Nunn	*	1	*	1	2	1
Jay Rockefeller	*	2	2	2	3	—
Patricia Schroeder	*	1	1	*	1	—
Tony Coelho	*	*	*	*	*	—
Richard Gephardt	—	1	*	1	1	*
Bill Clinton	—	—	—	*	*	—
Michael Dukakis	—	—	—	—	1	2
None/don't know	13	20	21	22	21	15

	April 10–13 1987	June 8–14 1987	July 10–13 1987	Aug. 24– Sept. 2 1987	Oct. 23–26 1987	Jan. 8–17 1988	Jan. 22–24 1988
Hart	46	—	—	—	—	25	23
Jackson	18	18	17	19	22	19	15
Bradley	7	—	—	—	—	—	—
Dukakis	4	11	13	13	14	10	16
Gephardt	3	7	3	6	5	4	9
Babbitt	2	2	2	2	1	2	4
Albert Gore	2	5	8	8	7	4	6
Biden	1	7	4	3	—	—	—
Paul Simon	—	7	7	7	8	8	9
Schroeder	—	—	—	6	—	—	—
Other/undecided	17	43	46	36	43	28	18

1992 Republican Nomination Race

Gallup: "Which one [of the persons on this list] would you like to see nominated as the Republican Party's candidate for president in 1992?" *Note*: Asked of Republicans and Republican-leaning independents.

	March 16–29 1990
George Bush	65
Robert Dole	7
Elizabeth Dole	4
Pierre du Pont	1
Alexander Haig	1
Jack Kemp	4
Jeane Kirkpatrick	1
Dan Quayle	5
Pat Robertson	2
None/don't know	9

Gallup: "Which of these three men would you most like to see nominated as the Republican Party's candidate for president in 1992?" *Note*: Asked of Republicans and Republican-leaning independents.

	Dec. 5–8 1991	Jan. 3–9 1992	Jan. 31 –Feb. 2 1992
George Bush	86	85	84
David Duke	6	3	4
Pat Buchanan	5	10	11
Don't know	3	2	1

1992 DEMOCRATIC NOMINATION RACE

Gallup: "Please tell me which one of these persons you would like to see nominated as the Democratic Party's candidate for president in 1992?" *Note*: Asked of Democrats and Democratic-leaning independents.

	March 16–29 1990	Feb. 14–17 1991	April 25–28 1991	Aug. 23–25 1991	Sept. 13–15 1991	Oct. 31 –Nov. 3 1991
Mario Cuomo	15	18	23	22	31	33
Jesse Jackson	14	12	14	18	14	—
Michael Dukakis	13	—	—	—	—	—
Lloyd Bentsen	9	6	9	12	—	—
George McGovern	—	9	8	—	—	—
Bill Bradley	4	4	—	—	—	—
Gary Hart	4	—	—	—	—	—
Richard Gephardt	3	8	11	—	—	—
Pat Schroeder	2	—	—	—	—	—
Sam Nunn	2	6	—	—	—	—
Chuck Robb	2	—	4	—	—	—
Al Gore	—	6	9	—	—	—

1992 DEMOCRATIC NOMINATION RACE (continued)

	March 16–29 1990	Feb. 14–17 1991	April 25–28 1991	Aug. 23–25 1991	Sept. 13–15 1991	Oct. 31 –Nov. 3 1991
Bill Clinton	—	2	1	5	3	6
Douglas Wilder	—	2	3	3	4	9
Bob Kerrey	1	1	—	—	4	8
Paul Tsongas	—	—	1	4	2	4
Jerry Brown	—	—	—	6	11	15
Tom Harkin	—	—	—	4	5	7
Other/none/don't know	32	26	17	26	26	18

	Sept. 13–15 1991[a]	Oct. 31 –Nov. 3 1991[a]	Jan. 3–9 1992	Jan. 31 –Feb. 2 1992
Brown	21	21	21	16
Wilder	10	12	9	—
Harkin	6	10	9	9
Clinton	6	9	17	42
Kerrey	5	10	11	10
Tsongas	5	7	6	9
Other/none/don't know	47	31	27	14

[a] In these surveys, respondents initially supporting Cuomo or Jackson were reassigned, based on their second choice.

1996 REPUBLICAN NOMINATION RACE

Gallup: "Next, I'm going to read a list of people who may be running in the Republican primary for president in 1996. After I read all the names, please tell me which of those candidates you would be most likely to support for the Republican nomination for president." *Note*: Asked of Republicans and Republican-leaning independents.

	March 28–30 1994	Feb. 3–5 1995	June 5–6 1995	Aug. 4–7 1995	Sept. 22–24 1995	Nov. 6–8 1995
Bob Dole	20	38	45	39	31	34
Colin Powell	13	—	—	—	31	33
Ross Perot	12	—	—	15	—	—
Dan Quayle	11	17	—	—	—	—
Jack Kemp	9	—	—	—	—	—
Newt Gingrich	—	7	9	—	—	—
Dick Cheney	7	—	—	—	—	—
James Baker	4	—	—	—	—	—
Bill Bennett	3	—	—	—	—	—
Phil Gramm	2	7	13	9	8	5

1996 REPUBLICAN NOMINATION RACE (continued)

	March 28–30 1994	Feb. 3–5 1995	June 5–6 1995	Aug. 4–7 1995	Sept. 22–24 1995	Nov. 6–8 1995
Pat Buchanan	1	2	6	7	7	4
Pete Wilson	1	5	5	3	3	—
Lamar Alexander	*	3	2	4	2	2
Carroll Campbell	1	—	—	—	—	—
Lynn Martin	*	—	—	—	—	—
Richard Lugar	—	2	2	2	1	1
Arlen Specter	—	2	4	3	1	3
William Weld	—	*	—	—	—	—
Bob Dornan	—	—	2	1	1	1
Alan Keyes	—	—	1	1	*	1
Steve Forbes	—	—	—	—	3	5
None/other/no opinion	16	17	11	16	12	11

* Less than 1 percent.

	April 5–6 1995	May 11–14 1995	June 5–6 1995[a]	July 7–9 1995	Aug. 4–7 1995[a]	Aug. 28–30 1995
Dole	46	51	51	49	46	45
Gramm	13	12	13	7	9	11
Buchanan	8	5	7	6	10	7
Alexander	3	3	2	4	4	4
Lugar	5	3	2	3	2	3
Wilson	6	7	6	8	4	10
Specter	2	3	4	3	3	2
Keyes	1	1	1	2	2	2
Dornan	2	2	2	1	1	1
No opinion	6	7	6	8	4	10

	Sept. 22–24 1995[a]	Nov. 6–8 1995[a]	Nov. 17–18 1995	Dec. 15–18 1995	Jan. 5–7 1996
Dole	46	46	45	49	47
Gramm	10	6	10	13	10
Buchanan	9	7	6	9	7
Alexander	2	2	4	1	2
Forbes	—	6	5	8	11
Lugar	2	2	2	3	5
Wilson	5	—	—	—	—
Specter	2	4	2	—	—
Keyes	1	1	1	2	2
Dornan	1	1	2	1	1
No opinion	22	25	23	13	15

[a] In these surveys, respondents initially supporting Gingrich, Perot, or Powell were reassigned, based on their second choice.

Republican Registered Voters Only

	Jan. 5–7 1996	Jan. 12–15 1996	Jan. 26–29 1996
Dole	49	55	47
Gramm	10	6	8
Buchanan	6	5	7
Alexander	1	3	3
Forbes	11	12	16
Lugar	6	2	3
Keyes	2	3	1
Dornan	1	*	1
No opinion	14	14	14

2000 REPUBLICAN NOMINATION RACE

Gallup: "Next, I'm going to read a list of people who may be running in the Republican primary for president in the year 2000. After I read all the names, please tell me which of those candidates you would be most likely to support for the Republican nomination for president." *Note*: Asked of Republicans and Republican-leaning independents.

	Apr. 11–13 1997	Sept. 6–7 1997	May 8–10 1998	Oct. 23–25 1998
Colin Powell	36	—	—	—
George W. Bush	14	21	30	39
Elizabeth Dole	7	—	14	17
Jack Kemp	14	15	9	—
Dan Quayle	11	10	9	12
Steve Forbes	6	9	7	7
Christy Whitman	4	9	—	—
Newt Gingrich	—	5	6	4
Fred Thompson	—	5	—	—
Pat Buchanan	—	4	3	—
John Ashcroft	—	3	*	4
Lamar Alexander	2	3	2	4
Bob Smith	—	2	—	—
John McCain	—	—	4	—
Gary Bauer	—	—	1	—
John Kasich	—	—	1	4
Other/none/don't know	8	14	14	9

	Jan. 8–10 1999	March 12–14 1999	April 13–14 1999	Apr. 30 –May 2 1999	May 23–24 1999	June 4–5 1999	June 25–27 1999
Bush	42	52	53	42	46	46	59
Dole	22	20	16	24	18	14	8
Quayle	6	9	7	6	7	9	6
McCain	8	3	5	4	6	5	5
Forbes	5	1	6	6	5	5	6
Buchanan	—	4	4	5	6	6	3
Kasich	2	3	2	1	2	1	3
Alexander	4	2	*	3	1	3	2
Bauer	2	1	2	3	2	1	2
Hatch	—	—	—	—	—	—	2
Smith	1	1	*	*	2	1	1
Other/none/don't know	8	4	5	5	5	9	3

	Aug. 16–18 1999	Sept. 10–14 1999	Oct. 8–10 1999	Oct. 21–24 1999	Nov. 4–7 1999	Nov. 18–21 1999
Bush	61	62	60	68	68	63
Dole	13	10	11	—	—	—
Quayle	6	5	—	—	—	—
McCain	5	5	8	11	12	16
Forbes	4	5	4	8	6	6
Buchanan	3	3	3	—	—	—
Bauer	2	2	3	1	2	4
Hatch	1	2	2	3	2	4
Keyes	1	1	3	2	2	1
Other/none/don't know	4	5	6	7	8	6

Republican Registered Voters Only

	Nov. 18–21 1999	Dec. 9–12 1999	Dec. 20–21 1999	Jan. 7–10 2000	Jan. 13–16 2000	Jan. 17–19 2000
Bush	63	64	60	63	61	63
McCain	16	18	17	18	22	19
Forbes	6	7	9	5	5	6
Bauer	3	2	2	1	2	2
Hatch	4	2	1	2	1	1
Keyes	2	4	4	2	3	1
Other/none/don't know	6	3	7	9	6	8

2000 DEMOCRATIC NOMINATION RACE

Gallup: "Next, I'm going to read you a list of people who may be running in the Democratic primary for president in the year 2000. After I read all the names, please tell me which of those candidates you would be most likely to support for the Democratic nomination for president." *Note:* Asked of Democrats and Democratic-leaning independents.

	Sept. 6–7 1997	*May* 8–10 1998	*Oct.* 23–25 1998	*Jan.* 8–10 1999	*March* 12–14 1999
Al Gore	47	51	41	47	58
Jesse Jackson	13	12	11	11	15
Bill Bradley	12	8	15	12	21
Dick Gephardt	6	7	14	13	—
John Kerry	5	2	4	5	—
Bob Kerrey	3	3	4	—	—
Paul Wellstone	—	1	1	1	—
Other/none/don't know	14	16	10	11	6

	Gore	*Bradley*	*Other/None/ Don't Know*
All Democrats			
April 13–14, 1999	54	34	12
April 30–May 2, 1999	66	23	11
May 23–24, 1999	59	30	11
June 4–5, 1999	63	28	9
June 25–27, 1999	64	28	8
August 16–18, 1999	58	31	11
September 10–14, 1999	63	30	7
October 8–10, 1999	51	39	10
October 21–24, 1999	57	32	11
November 4–7, 1999	58	33	9
November 18–21, 1999	54	35	11
Democratic Registered Voters			
November 18–21, 1999	56	34	10
December 9–12, 1999	54	39	7
December 20–21, 1999	52	38	10
January 7–10, 2000	59	30	11
January 13–16, 2000	59	30	11
January 17–19, 2000	60	27	13

NOTES

The author would like to thank Lois Timms Ferrara, Bryce Bassett, Robert Biersack, Stephen Ansolabehere, Tony Corrado, Randall Adkins, Gerry Pomper, and Amy Logan for their assistance with this chapter.

1. These figures come from Robert Biersack of the FEC, personal communication to the author, November 14, 2002. Actually, these numbers, large as they are, do not include

a number of people who made it onto the ballot in one or more states. When the latter are added in, the total count becomes 272 in 1992, 282 in 1996, and 253 in 2000.

2. The model is presented in William G. Mayer, "Forecasting Presidential Nominations," in *In Pursuit of the White House: How We Select Our Presidential Nominees*, ed. William G. Mayer (Chatham, N.J.: Chatham House, 1996), 44–71. An all-but-identical version of that article, however, was presented as a paper at the 1994 meeting of the Northeastern Political Science Association. In the last few years, several other scholars have developed models that use slightly different data and extend the model's reach in a number of ways, but are otherwise fully compatible with my own work. See, in particular, Randall E. Adkins and Andrew J. Dowdle, "Break Out the Mint Juleps? Is New Hampshire the 'Primary' Culprit Limiting Presidential Nomination Forecasts?" *American Politics Quarterly* 28 (April 2000): 251–69; and Wayne P. Steger, "Do Primary Voters Draw from a Stacked Deck? Presidential Nominations in an Era of Candidate-Centered Campaigns," *Presidential Studies Quarterly* 30 (December 2000): 727–53.

3. For an explanation as to why I limited the model to races occurring after 1976, see Mayer, "Forecasting Presidential Nominations," 60–63.

4. I use this formulation in order to make the fund-raising data as comparable as possible across elections. Simply using the raw, unadjusted amount of money collected by each candidate would create several problems. Most obviously, such figures would not take into account the effects of inflation. In addition, fund-raising totals are often affected by circumstances unique to each race. In 1992, for example, the fallout from the Persian Gulf War meant that most Democratic candidates did not enter the race until the *fall* of 1991, about six to nine months later than they probably would have under normal circumstances. See the data in Michael G. Hagen and William G. Mayer, "The Modern Politics of Presidential Selection: How Changing the Rules Really Did Change the Game," in *In Pursuit of the White House 2000: How We Select Our Presidential Nominees*, ed. William G. Mayer (New York: Chatham House, 2000), 21–25. As a result, Democratic presidential fund-raising in 1991 was, by historical standards, unusually modest. Expressing each candidate's fund-raising as a percentage of the leading money-raiser also incorporates the idea that the net effect of a candidate's spending in a competitive race is determined not only by what that one candidate spends, but also by what his or her opponents are spending.

5. As estimated here, this model almost certainly violates one of the standard regression assumptions, which requires the error terms to be uncorrelated across observations. That is to say, if the model underpredicts the vote for one candidate in a given race (say, Gary Hart in 1984), it will probably overpredict the vote for one or more other candidates in the same race (e.g., Mondale or Glenn). Unfortunately, in large, multi-candidate fields (which have tended to be the rule in most recent contested nomination races), it is impossible to specify in advance the correlation between the errors for any two candidates, and therefore difficult to invoke any of the standard remedies for this sort of problem (e.g., generalized least squares).

If the uncorrelated errors assumption has, indeed, been violated, the parameter estimates in table 3.3 will be unbiased, but inefficient. In other words, the estimated values of the coefficients will, over the long run, be equal to the true values, but the variances of these estimates will be larger than they would be if the assumption had not been violated. In particular, the standard errors in table 3.3 will likely be *under*estimated, and thus provide an inaccurate measure of the true confidence interval surrounding each coefficient.

In defense of my decision to continue using ordinary least squares to estimate this model, I would make two points. First, nothing of substance is really affected by reasonable assumptions about the true variance of the parameter estimates. Even if the real standard errors are three times the size of those listed in table 3.3, the first coefficient is still statistically significant and the second one still isn't. Second, after each of the last two elections, I have re-estimated the model in order to incorporate the results of the recently concluded nomination contests, which provides a kind of quasi-experimental test of the model's robustness. As can be seen in table 3.3, adding these additional races to the model's data base has very little effect on the coefficients.

6. Nothing in the model purports to explain why some people decide to run for president while others stay on the sidelines. Whether or not to seek the White House, particularly under present-day rules, has always seemed to me to be a very personal and highly idiosyncratic decision, that is not easy to explain (much less predict) on the basis of factors that can be specified in advance and observed by an outsider. To say the least, it is difficult to imagine a model that could have predicted that Jerry Brown, Pat Buchanan, Bob Smith, and Al Sharpton would all run for president, while Mario Cuomo, Jack Kemp, and Al Gore (in the 2004 election cycle) would decide not to.

7. By late-starting candidate, I mean, in this context, one who enters the race after the beginning of the caucus and primary season.

8. Henry E. Brady and Richard Johnston, "What's the Primary Message: Horse Race or Issue Journalism?" in *Media and Momentum: The New Hampshire Primary and Nomination Politics*, ed. Gary R. Orren and Nelson W. Polsby (Chatham, N.J.: Chatham House, 1987), 184.

9. Larry M. Bartels, *Presidential Primaries and the Dynamics of Public Choice* (Princeton, N.J.: Princeton University Press, 1988), 287.

10. James W. Ceaser, *Reforming the Reforms: A Critical Analysis of the Presidential Selection Process* (Cambridge, Mass.: Ballinger, 1982), 95. In the interests of full disclosure, I should point out that in my first academic article, published in 1987, I flirted with the same conclusion. See William G. Mayer, "The New Hampshire Primary: A Historical Overview," in *Media and Momentum: The New Hampshire Primary and Nomination Politics*, ed. Gary R. Orren and Nelson W. Polsby (Chatham, N.J.: Chatham House), 32–33.

11. I focus on these polls, rather than the candidates' fund-raising prowess, for two reasons. First, the results in table 3.3 clearly indicate that it is the candidates' standing in the polls rather than their fund-raising that has the greatest influence on nomination outcomes. Second, fund-raising data are not available until the candidates have set up their major campaign committees and filed the necessary papers with the FEC, which is generally not until the first or second quarter of the year before the election. By contrast, as the following analysis will show, polling data can generally be found from three or even four years prior to the actual election year.

12. My attempt to assemble a fairly complete collection of surveys on each of the ten nomination races considered here has been made dramatically easier by POLL, the remarkable on-line database of polling questions maintained by the Roper Center at the University of Connecticut.

13. On February 27, 1987, Baker agreed to become Ronald Reagan's chief of staff—and simultaneously announced that he would not be a candidate for the 1988 presidential nomination. Judging from the data in the appendix, even if Baker had made the race, he would have faced a distinctly uphill battle.

14. See *Gallup Opinion Index*, no. 168, July, 1979, 7; and no. 172, November, 1979, 6.

15. For an interesting argument along these lines, see Samuel L. Popkin, *The Reasoning Voter: Communication and Persuasion in Presidential Campaigns* (Chicago: University of Chicago Press, 1991), 138–40.

16. On the general way that presidential approval ratings go up during an international crisis, sometimes called the "rally-round-the-flag effect," see, among others, John E. Mueller, *War, Presidents, and Public Opinion* (New York: Wiley & Sons, 1973), chap. 9; Samuel Kernell, "Explaining Presidential Popularity," *American Political Science Review* 72 (June 1978): 506–522; and Richard A. Brody, *Assessing the President: The Media, Elite Opinion, and Public Support* (Stanford, Calif.: Stanford University Press, 1991), chap. 3.

17. There are fifteen Gallup Polls conducted between March 1978 and January 1980 that include both (a) the standard presidential approval rating question; and (b) a question asking Democrats whom they favored if the presidential nomination race came down to a choice between Carter and Kennedy. (Results for the latter question are shown in the appendix.) The correlation over time between the percentage approving of Carter's performance and the percentage favoring him over Kennedy is .84.

18. This point is worth more than passing notice, if only because so many Carter supporters would later blame their resounding loss in the 1980 general election on their bad luck in being unable to extricate the hostages—and on the fact that the first anniversary of the hostage seizure came on the same day as the election. This explanation ignores the fact that the U.S. economy was also in very bad shape that fall and that, had the hostages not been an issue, people might simply have voted their pocketbooks—which would probably also have resulted in Carter's defeat. More to the immediate point, blaming Carter's loss on events in Iran overlooks all the *benefits* that the president's campaign had received from the hostage crisis earlier in the year.

19. Though Clinton and many of his supporters have frequently complained about the way he was treated by the media, during the 1992 campaign Clinton received some of the most positive, even fawning coverage of any front-running candidate in recent history. As Margaret Carlson noted in *Time*, "The political press corps, which prides itself on how quickly it can knock the stuffing out of those who would run for President, has gone into a deep swoon over his [Clinton's] candidacy. . . . reporters seem entranced by Clinton's persona." *Time*, December 30, 1991, 19. For some examples, see Michael Kramer, "At Least Someone Has a Plan," *Time*, December 2, 1991, 20; and Joe Klein, "Bill Clinton: Who Is This Guy?" *New York*, January 20, 1992, 28–35.

20. That number dropped to five in late September, 1987, when Delaware Senator Joseph Biden withdrew from the race amid charges that he had plagiarized one of his best speech lines from a leader of the British Labour party and lied about several items in his personal history.

21. During 1987, the Dukakis campaign raised $10,371,000. The second most successful fund-raiser among the Democrats that year was Paul Simon, whose campaign raised $6,056,000.

22. This statement assumes, of course, that the early front-runner actually decides to run for president. As the preceding analysis makes clear, a number of early front-runners and near–front-runners took themselves out of the running when they decided not to become a candidate.

23. These prediction errors, however, need to be put in context. While the absolute

errors produced by most general election forecasting models are far smaller, the effective range of the variable being predicted in those models is also much narrower. The dependent variable for the equations in table 3.3, the percentage of the total primary vote won by each candidate, varies between 0.1 and 75.7. By contrast, the dependent variable in most general election models is the percentage of the two-party popular vote won by the candidate of the incumbent president's party. Over the thirteen elections between 1952 and 2000, this variable has never risen above 61.8 and never fallen below 44.6. Thus, a general election forecasting model that always predicted the incumbent party to win 53.2 percent of the vote would be virtually guaranteed never to be wrong by more than 8.6 percentage points. Viewed from this perspective, the failure of these models in 2000, when the *median* error was 4.7 percentage points, is even more remarkable.

24. Though the specification of the model that follows and the particular conclusions drawn from it are my own, the idea of adding Iowa and New Hampshire to the baseline model had not occurred to me until I read Adkins and Dowdle, "Break Out the Mint Juleps." I have also benefited from several subsequent conversations with one of the authors of that article.

25. My judgments over the next several paragraphs about which candidates gained or lost as a result of their showings in Iowa and New Hampshire are based partly on the data in table 3.10, partly on how these candidates fared in the next round of primaries. In Bradley's case, for example, he not only failed to make up any ground on Gore in the national polls, but also lost every one of the eleven primaries held on March 7 (the next day on which Democratic primaries took place) and then dropped out of the race entirely on March 9.

26. For Democrats in Iowa, there are generally two measures of how well each candidate did: the percentage of caucus attenders who preferred that candidate; and the percentage of "delegate equivalents" won by the candidate. I use the latter figures (the former are not available in some years). To measure the candidate's current standing in the national polls, I use, for Iowa, the data from the end of the invisible primary that are discussed in the second section of this article. For New Hampshire, I have, in almost every case, been able to find a national poll conducted between Iowa and New Hampshire that shows the state of the national race with Iowa taken into account. The lone exception is the 1996 Republican race, where I use an average of the pre-Iowa and post-New Hampshire figures.

27. I exclude the 1992 Republican nomination race for the simple but dispositive reason that the 1992 Iowa Republican caucuses did not take a poll of caucus attenders and there is thus no measure available of how well each candidate did in that event. For further details, see Hugh Winebrenner, *The Iowa Precinct Caucuses: The Making of a Media Event*, 2nd ed. (Ames: Iowa State University Press, 1998), 197–98. On the Democratic side, the 1992 Iowa caucuses were completely transformed by the fact that a favorite son, U.S. Senator Tom Harkin, was a presidential candidate. The result was that none of the other candidates waged an active campaign there, the media almost completely ignored the state, and Harkin wound up with 76.5 percent of the delegate equivalents. While I am loathe, in a model of this sort, to exclude a race or candidate simply because it is "exceptional," the 1992 results in Iowa are such an obvious outlier—*and were known to be that at the time*—that any attempt to include them in the model would probably distort the meaning and value of every other coefficient.

28. Some might add the case of Bill Clinton in 1992. But Clinton's well-publicized claim to be "the comeback kid" because he had finished second in New Hampshire seems, *at best*, to have prevented further damage to his campaign; it did not convert a loss into a victory. The evidence from table 3.10, in particular, shows that it was Paul Tsongas who received a huge boost from New Hampshire; the most that can be said of Clinton is that his standing in the national polls declined by only one percentage point.

29. Though table 3.12 shows poll standings only for the major candidates in each race, comparable figures are available for all the other candidates who were included in the original model.

30. Some might argue for creating two dummy variables to designate the winners of the Iowa caucuses, one for winners who were already the front-runner for their party's nomination (e.g., Dole in 1996, Bush and Gore in 2000), and a second for winners who were not the pre-race front-runner (e.g., Bush in 1980, Gephardt and Dole in 1988). But creating separate dummy variables for the two types of Iowa victors does not alter any of the conclusions drawn from table 3.13. The coefficients for *both* variables are small and statistically insignificant. Over the last two decades, neither front-runners nor non–front-runners seem to have derived much advantage in New Hampshire from winning in Iowa.

31. Pollsters sometimes ask open-ended questions on this topic, but generally just find that 60 to 70 percent of all respondents say they don't have an opinion.

32. An important exception was the 1980 Republican nomination race, in which Gerald Ford was included in the list of presidential candidates well into the election year, even though the former president had made no effort to organize an active campaign.

33. For the use of such polls to perform the latter function, see William H. Lucy, "Polls, Primaries, and Presidential Nominations," *Journal of Politics* 35 (November 1973): 830–48; and James R. Beniger, "Winning the Presidential Nomination: National Polls and State Primary Elections, 1936–1972," *Public Opinion Quarterly* 40 (Spring 1976): 22–38.

4

How Incumbent Presidents Run for Reelection

Kathryn Dunn Tenpas

In the presidential election of 1904, President Theodore Roosevelt refrained from campaigning since it was considered "undignified to campaign from the White House."[1] By 1916, this fear of losing one's dignity had apparently gone by the wayside, as Woodrow Wilson became the first sitting president to campaign for his own reelection. Since then, there has been no turning back. Today, the notion of presidents campaigning for reelection is commonplace. In fact, when presidents claim that they are avoiding the campaign trail in order to take care of government business, journalists and other observers generally scoff in disbelief.

In their quest for reelection, presidents have tremendous campaign assets: unrivaled name recognition, a coterie of strategists with the greatest incentive to see their candidate win, control of the national party organization, a national network of supporters (and the concomitant capacity to raise money), previous experience in running a national campaign, and ample "goodies" to dole out to key constituencies. What Theodore White said of Lyndon Johnson is, to a greater or lesser extent, true of all presidents:

> Lyndon Johnson was the Presidential Presence—and no challenger, at any time, can even approach the immense advantage that goes with being President. For, besides the majesty of the office, which cows the most hostile citizens to respect and attention, there are the facilities and the command that only a President can enjoy.[2]

Despite these advantages, the quest for reelection is by no means a simple undertaking. Former White House staff members profess that the campaign "overwhelms the White House" and "permeates everything."[3]

In 1992, President George H. W. Bush declared that he would "do what he had to do" to secure reelection.[4] But just what is it that presidents "have to do" to get reelected? Given the dual roles of president and candidate, what effect does the quest for reelection have on "business as usual" within the White House? How has the quest for reelection affected the institution of the presidency? During the late twentieth century, as we will see, presidents have gradually attempted to bring electoral expertise directly into the White House. Understanding the quest for reelection against this backdrop suggests that the simultaneous demands of governing and campaigning are a prominent feature of the modern presidency. Based on a study of eight presidential reelection campaigns (Eisenhower 1956, Johnson 1964, Nixon 1972, Ford 1976, Carter 1980, Reagan 1984, Bush 1992, and Clinton 1996), this chapter explains the mechanics of presidential reelection campaigns and assesses their impact on the institution of the presidency.[5]

FIRST STIRRINGS

When do incumbent presidents and their top advisors begin planning their reelection campaigns? The answer depends on what one means by the "campaign" or "campaign planning." On one side, there is the perspective of Harry Dent, a Nixon aide, who wrote, "The 1972 campaign for reelection of the president of the United States was underway from the time the Nixon team entered the White House in January 1969."[6] In a similar vein, when members of the Carter White House staff were asked when they began gearing up for reelection, they replied, "November 1976." The Carter staffers later admitted that, in the beginning, they were too caught up in the "daily grind" to think about such a distant event. However, they were aware that every task they performed was done, at least in part, to cast the president in the best light possible, and to some, this was equivalent to planning for 1980.

It is, then, often difficult to distinguish between campaign planning and performing a job that is inherently political. That said, at some point, the president and/or his advisors begin to hold meetings or perform concrete actions that are focused directly on the upcoming election. Such early efforts typically include strategic planning and the recruiting of campaign personnel. When does this sort of activity begin?

Table 4.1 provides three benchmarks to date the start of the reelection campaign for each of the last eight incumbent presidents who have run for reelection. The first of the three, which is based on presidential documents, personal interviews, and secondary sources, attempts to identify the date of the first major meeting(s) devoted specifically to the reelection campaign. As these data indicate, Presidents Nixon, Carter, and Clinton all began their reelection campaigns immediately after the midterm elections. Ronald Reagan's aides started laying the

Table 4.1 Three Indicators of When Presidents Begin Their Reelection Campaigns

Campaign	First Major Meeting Devoted to Reelection Planning	Filed Statement of Candidacy with FEC	Formal Announcement Date
Eisenhower 1956	Feb. 1955	—ᵃ	Feb. 1956
Johnson 1964	Dec. 1963	—ᵃ	None
Nixon 1972	Nov. 1970	—ᵃ	Jan. 1972
Ford 1976	May 1975	June 1975	July 1975
Carter 1980	Nov. 1978	March 1979	Dec. 1979
Reagan 1984	Jan. 1982	Oct. 1983	Jan. 1984
Bush 1992	Aug. 1991	Oct. 1991	Feb. 1992
Clinton 1996	Nov. 1994	April 1995	None

ᵃPrior to 1974, candidates were not required to file a statement of candidacy.

groundwork for his campaign quite early in the second year of his presidency; while Johnson, Ford, and Bush all began their campaign planning in the year before the election. Note, however, that the Johnson and Ford campaigns could not have started much sooner given the circumstances surrounding their ascent to the presidency.

Why the first Bush administration delayed its reelection planning so long remains a mystery. Given the fact that Bush possessed a seasoned group of political advisors as well as guidance from a number of veterans of Reagan's 1984 campaign, the Bush team should have been well positioned for 1992. Some observers have claimed that President Bush's personal uncertainty about seeking reelection was the principal source of delay, while others contend that the Gulf War, the absence of Democratic challengers, and his record-high approval ratings resulted in a dangerous sense of complacency.

A second way of identifying the formal start of an incumbent president's reelection campaign is to use the date on which the campaign filed a statement of candidacy with the Federal Election Commission (FEC). This statement, which is required by the Federal Election Campaign Act of 1974 (and is therefore not available for Eisenhower, Johnson, and Nixon), generally occurs when the campaign begins to raise money. As shown in table 4.1, presidents generally file their statement of candidacy several months after they actually begin their campaign planning. Nonetheless, this statement is the earliest publicly documented record of formal campaign activity.

A third set of dates for marking the start of the president's reelection campaign is the formal announcement speech, in which the president publicly declares his intention to run for another term. With the notable exception of President Ford, this speech occurred long after the presidents' operatives had begun their planning and strategizing—and far later than non-incumbent candidates generally declared their candidacies. Indeed, two of the presidents in table 4.1—Johnson and Clinton—never did make a formal declaration of candidacy.[7] Many presidents, it appears, are unwilling to jeopardize the many advantages of incumbency by appearing overly engaged in the campaign. Moreover, unlike the formal FEC filing that is required by law, there is no similar requirement that a president make a formal announcement of his candidacy.

THE ANATOMY OF A REELECTION CAMPAIGN: FROM PARTY TO WHITE HOUSE CONTROL

A systematic review of reelection campaigns from Eisenhower through Clinton reveals an important trend in the way these campaigns have been organized and controlled. When Eisenhower ran for reelection, his campaign was organized and directed by the national party organization. The 1964 Johnson campaign also assigned a major role to the national party, but experienced a substantially greater level of White House involvement. The remaining campaigns—Nixon 1972 through Clinton 1996—were plainly dominated by the White House, with the national party playing, at most, a distinctly subsidiary role.

The Republican National Committee was at the center of almost every aspect of Eisenhower's 1956 reelection campaign. RNC officials helped pressure the president to run for a second term, then approved plans for a late convention and, thus, a short general election campaign. As two scholars described the Eisenhower campaign:

> Leonard W. Hall of New York was chairman [of the RNC]. Below Hall several divisions were arranged. The Campaign Division, under the direction of Robert Humphreys, had responsibility for plans, programs, and the implementation of policy incidental to the campaign. The Executive Division, under the direction of Chauncy Robbins, a veteran national committee staff man, had charge of such matters as patronage and budget. . . . The organization of the Republican National Committee—which in 1956 was the campaign organization—was that simple.[8]

Though such an approach clearly suited a president with a widely known disdain for politics, Eisenhower's predecessor, Harry Truman, adopted a similar approach in 1948, delegating most of the operational responsibilities in his campaign—financing, research, publicity—to the Democratic National Committee, though maintaining an important strategic and advisory role for his White House aides.[9]

Though President Eisenhower was more than happy to rely on the RNC, Lyndon Johnson, the next president to run for reelection, was less willing to delegate campaign responsibilities. As Evans and Novak noted at the time:

> Johnson had not even named a campaign manager by the time the convention rolled around. . . . His campaign organization—disorganization was the better word—

defied schematic description. . . . He ended up with no manager at all, except Lyndon Johnson.[10]

According to some accounts, Johnson was not only inattentive to the needs of the party organization, but actually antagonistic to it. Nevertheless, the Democratic National Committee did play some role in the campaign, along with a number of holdovers from the Kennedy administration and some of Johnson's own advisors. The efforts of the various participants were by no means neatly partitioned. To the contrary, there was a high degree of overlap and sharing of resources, resulting in multiple points of contact with the president. This campaign organization, reminiscent of what Richard Neustadt once called the "radial style," suited Johnson's style as well as his penchant for intense personal involvement and supervision.

By 1972, Richard Nixon had cut all ties with the old Eisenhower, party-dominated campaign model. The Nixon reelection campaign was the first completely White House–directed campaign and the first to establish an independent campaign organization. According to one staff member, the Nixon high command never even considered running the campaign through the Republican National Committee.[11] Instead, as one political historian has noted, "The complete autonomy of the Committee for the Re-election of the President (CREEP) from the regular organization in the 1972 campaign was but the final stage of a long process of White House preemption of the national committee's political responsibilities."[12]

Partly as a response to the Watergate scandal, Gerald Ford, Nixon's successor, initially refused to establish an independent campaign organization. Ultimately, however, Ford had to follow Nixon's example. The absence of national campaign experience, the likelihood of a tough primary challenge from Ronald Reagan, and the need to comply with the new campaign finance laws all pushed the president in this direction. Every president since then has also adopted the Nixon model, creating a campaign structure that includes three major components—the White House, the national party organization, and an independent campaign organization—with the White House clearly in charge.

Since 1956, in short, there has been a substantial decline in the role of the national party organization in presidential reelection campaigns, along with an increased role for the White House and the emergence of independent campaign committees. There are two primary reasons for these developments: (1) procedural and legal changes in the presidential selection process; and (2) the expansion of the White House staff.

Perhaps the most salient procedural change affecting the role of the parties in the presidential nomination process was the series of electoral reforms that were adopted in the early 1970s, particularly those initiated by the McGovern-Fraser Commission, which resulted in a dramatic increase in the number of primaries and a concomitant decline in party-run caucuses. Since 1968, the presidential nomination process has essentially been taken out of the hands of party leaders and put in the control of ordinary voters. One symptom of the new system is that incumbents are more vulnerable to serious challenge. In the 1960s, a comprehensive study of the nomination process noted, "The tradition of renomination for a first-term incumbent is at present so firmly established that only the President, by declination or through his own mistakes, can prevent it from operating."[13] Twenty years later, presidential scholars Charles Euchner and John Anthony Maltese reached a strikingly different conclusion: "Despite the real advantages of incumbency for a presidential campaign, recent years have shown that renomination is not inevitable. Harry Truman, Lyndon Johnson, Gerald Ford, and Jimmy Carter all faced strong challenges when they sought a new four-year lease on the White House."[14]

In addition to the new delegate selection rules, in the wake of the Watergate scandals in the mid-1970s, Congress completely overhauled the federal campaign finance laws. The Federal Election Campaign Act of 1974 and its subsequent amendments have had a critical impact on campaign fund-raising, the role of political parties, and electoral strategy more broadly. (For a detailed discussion of the FECA, see chap. 2 in this volume.) After 1974, it would have been illegal for any president to raise campaign funds in the way that President Ford's predecessors had. In particular, the law required each candidate to designate a single campaign committee and then made it accountable for every dollar raised and spent on the campaign—a provision that, as we have seen, all but compelled Ford to establish an independent campaign organization even though he had initially hoped not to do so.

The central role of the White House in reelection politics is also due, in substantial part, to the expansion of the president's staff. There are a number of reasons for the growth of the White House staff: increased interest group activity and demands, an expanded U.S. role in international affairs, the growth of government, and the increased complexity of public policy. Another important reason is the ease with which presidents can expand their staff. As Terry Moe has pointed out, "Legislators do not care much about incremental changes in the institutional presidency unless their constituents are directly affected. There are no interest group 'fire alarms' to prod them into action, no clear electoral benefits to be gained from opposing the president. Meantime, presidents care intensely, and they dedicate their resources to getting what they want."[15]

INSTITUTIONALIZING POLITICS
WITHIN THE WHITE HOUSE

As the role of the national party has declined and that of the White House has increased, presidents have moved to bring electoral expertise directly into the White House. A crucial stage in this development was reached during the presidencies of Jimmy Carter and Ronald Reagan, with the establishment of a special office that was designed to deal with the earliest stages of reelection planning as well as other "political" tasks.[16] In the first two years of Carter's term, there was much criticism about the lack of political sensitivity in the White House; many observers characterized the administration as a "bunch of political novices." As a result, in 1978 Carter appointed his scheduling deputy, Tim Kraft, an Assistant to the President, with special responsibility for political affairs and personnel. Kraft's general mission was to sharpen political sensitivities within the executive branch, but along with Hamilton Jordan (who later became chief of staff), he also initiated the first efforts to plan the 1980 reelection campaign.

Though President Carter was the first president to designate a specific individual to fulfill these sorts of duties, it was not until the Reagan administration that this staff member was given a descriptive, formal title, Assistant to the President for Political Affairs, and a separate office, the Office of Political Affairs (OPA). Initially, the OPA was led by Lyn Nofziger, a longtime Reagan aide. When Nofziger resigned his position in early 1982 to return to California, he was succeeded by Ed Rollins, with Lee Atwater as his top assistant. Under Rollins, the OPA had a staff of about fifteen members. Like their counterparts in the Carter administration, Rollins and Atwater participated in the earliest planning for Reagan's reelection campaign. Eventually, in the spring of 1983, Rollins and the OPA staff left the White House and moved en masse to the Reagan/Bush campaign headquarters.[17]

In contrast to Carter and Reagan, George H. W. Bush tried to downplay the role of the Office of Political Affairs. In a sense, Bush attempted to create a structure similar to the one used by Eisenhower. The President appointed Lee Atwater, who had managed his 1988 campaign, as chairman of the Republican National Committee. Rather than building up the Office of Political Affairs and then designating a White House liaison to the RNC, Bush appointed a loyalist, known for his considerable strategic and political skills, to the RNC. How well this structure would have worked is difficult to say: In March 1990, Atwater collapsed while giving a speech and was diagnosed with a brain tumor, and played only a limited role in RNC affairs thereafter (he died in 1991). Clayton Yeutter, Atwater's successor as RNC chair, lacked his close, personal ties to the president, as well as Atwater's reputation as a savvy electoral strategist. Meanwhile, the OPA had three different directors, none of whom was very close to the president. The size of the office also declined. So while the White House had a central role in directing the Bush reelection campaign, the OPA did not have anything like the influence it had had in the two previous administrations.

After an inauspicious beginning, the Office of Political Affairs was both active and influential in the Clinton reelection campaign. While the first director of the OPA, Rahm Emanuel, had close ties to Clinton, he soon resigned from that post due to "personality conflicts" with a number of Democratic elected officials.[18] His successor, Joan Baggett, lacked Emanuel's access and influence and resigned shortly after the 1994 midterm elections. Thus, by the third year of President Clinton's first term, the OPA was already seeking its third director. That third appointment, however, worked out better. Douglas Sosnick was strongly supported by the president's chief electoral tactician and deputy White House chief of staff, Harold Ickes. In addition, Sosnick had served as an administrative assistant to Senator Christopher Dodd, the newly appointed chair of the Democratic National Committee. Sosnick thus possessed close ties to both senior White House staff members and the DNC. These connections enabled Sosnick to run an influential political operation from the White House. Unlike Rollins and Atwater in the Reagan administration, however, Sosnick remained in the White House rather than moving on to the Clinton campaign organization.

Two other offices in the White House have also assumed campaign-like responsibilities: the Office of Communications and the Office of Public Liaison. While not as involved in specifically campaign-related activities, both offices fulfill functions that are very similar to those of a presidential campaign. The Office of Communications hones the president's message and supervises press access to administration officials. During the Nixon administration, for example, "Communications Director [Herb] Klein was responsible for the larger coordination of news flow from the executive branch, for maintaining links with local editors, publishers, and broadcasters, and for scheduling interviews and television appearances by administration officials and other pro-administration spokespeople (such as members of Congress and party officials)."[19] Since this position is separate from the press office, the director has more time to formulate long-term communications strategies, while cultivating relationships with journalists at the state and local level. The Office of Public Liaison exists to gather support within the interest group community or, as one presidential scholar put it, "to lobby the lobbies."[20] Not only does this office reach out to such groups in the hopes of gaining support for the president's legislative agenda, but during an election year, the office may also be responsible for rounding up support among key voting blocs, such as labor, youth, or the elderly.

All three of these offices, then, represent an attempt by recent presidents to incorporate electoral expertise directly into the White House. Though these offices clearly facilitate reelection planning, they also reflect the broader theme of what has been called the "permanent campaign": "the remaking of government into an instrument designed to sustain an elected official's popularity."[21] The acquisition of campaign-related skills has been a paramount theme in the development of the White House over the past thirty years.

EARLY CAMPAIGN PLANNING:
WHO DOES IT AND WHAT THEY DO

Table 4.2, which is based on numerous interviews as well as a review of relevant documents and secondary sources, identifies the major players in early campaign

Table 4.2 Major Participants in Early Reelection Planning

President	Major Participants in Early Reelection Planning	Position or Title
Eisenhower	Sherman Adams	Chief of Staff
	Leonard Hall	Chair, Republican National Committee
Johnson	Marvin Watson	Special Assistant to the President
	Jack Valenti	Special Consultant to the President
	Bill Moyers	Special Assistant to the President
	Oliver Quayle	Presidential pollster
Nixon	H. R. Haldeman	Chief of Staff
	Jeb Stuart Magruder	Special Assistant to the President
	Hugh Sloan	Scheduling Aide
	Harry Fleming	Special Assistant to the President
	John Mitchell	Attorney General
	John Erlichman	Assistant to the President for Domestic Affairs
	Robert Finch	Counselor to the President
	Bryce Harlow	Counselor to the President
	Harry Dent	Special Counsel to the President
	Charles Colson	Special Counsel to the President
	Murray Chotiner	Special Counsel to the President
	Robert Teeter	Presidential pollster
Ford	Donald Rumsfeld	Chief of Staff
	Richard Cheney	Chief of Staff
	James Baker	Undersecretary of Commerce
	Robert Teeter	Presidential pollster
	Stuart Spencer	Political consultant
Carter	Hamilton Jordan	Chief of Staff
	Tim Kraft	Assistant to the President
	Jody Powell	Press Secretary
	Gerald Rafshoon	Assistant to the President for Communications
	Patrick Caddell	Presidential pollster
Reagan	James Baker	Chief of Staff
	Michael Deaver	Deputy Chief of Staff
	Richard Darman	Deputy to the Chief of Staff
	Ed Rollins	Assistant to the President for Political Affairs
	Lee Atwater	Deputy Assistant to the President for Political Affairs
	Stuart Spencer	Political consultant
	Richard Wirthlin	Presidential pollster

Table 4.2 (continued)

President	Major Participants in Early Reelection Planning	Position or Title
Bush	Samuel Skinner	Chief of Staff
	James Baker	Secretary of State
	Robert Mosbacher	Secretary of Commerce
	Fred Malek	Outside advisor
	Robert Teeter	Presidential pollster
	Fred Steeper	Presidential pollster
Clinton	Leon Panetta	Chief of Staff
		Advisor to the President for Policy and Strategy/Executive Assistant to the Chief of Staff for Policy
	George Stephanopoulos	Deputy Chief of Staff for Policy and Political Activity
	Harold Ickes	Director, Office of Political Affairs
	Douglas Sosnick	Political consultant
	Dick Morris	Presidential pollster
	Mark Penn	

Source: Job titles taken from *U.S. Government Organization Manual* (Washington, D.C.: Division of the Federal Register, various years) and contemporary news sources.

planning for each of the last eight incumbent presidents who have sought reelection. Though the composition of the White House reelection team varies across administrations, the central role of the chief of staff clearly emerges in seven of the eight administrations. The exception is President Johnson, who did not have a chief of staff. Johnson instead relied on a handful of senior aides, and among those, Marvin Watson may have been the equivalent of a chief of staff.

According to veteran presidential pollster Robert Teeter, "When you have an incumbent president, the chief of staff of the White House in some way has to be the linchpin of whatever is done in the campaign that involves the president."[22] Margaret Tutwiler, who held significant roles in both the 1984 and 1992 campaigns, was even more emphatic on this point:

> That particular election [1984], like this one [1992], was run out of the chief of staff's office at the White House. It happens to have been the same person in both instances, Jim Baker. Everybody else knew who had the final say and who ran the campaigns. Dick Cheney ran President Ford's campaign out of the chief of staff's office. You have to if you're a sitting president.[23]

Two trends in table 4.2 are worth noting. The first, which was discussed in the previous section, is the emergence of the Office of Political Affairs as a source of early campaign planning. In three of the last four presidential reelection campaigns (the exception was George H. W. Bush), the logistics of campaign planning were handled by members of the OPA. A second notable trend is the increasing involvement of outside advisors. Ever since President Nixon ran for reelection in 1972, presidents have turned to private-sector political consultants at a very early stage in their campaigns. In many cases, these "outsiders" are veteran campaign strategists who wield a great deal of influence, such as Stuart Spencer, Pat Caddell, Robert Teeter, and Dick Morris.[24] Though these individuals were not formal members of the White House staff, they have had access to the most senior staff members and often to the president himself.

In the earliest stages of a reelection campaign, the president and his advisors focus on two major activities: recruitment and strategic planning. Constructing a campaign team is perhaps the first and most important task. Those involved in recruitment generally look to three sources: White House staff members who are experienced campaigners, campaign veterans in the private sector who participated in the previous presidential campaign, and staff members from the party organization.

In terms of strategy formulation, campaign planners consider the president's record in the White House, the development of a future policy agenda, the interpretation of polling data, the assessment of possible opponents (in both the primaries and the general election), and the development of themes and messages. Citizens need to know why they should vote for the president, and to help them make this decision, most presidents feel they need to provide a blueprint for the future. The Clinton administration, for example, used election-year commencement addresses to outline his foreign, economic, and social policies, all in an effort "to answer critics who say he still has not painted a full vision for a second term."[25] Thus, in preparation for the election, the White House must not only carefully scrutinize its current record, but articulate an agenda for the next term. One especially important element of strategic planning is campaign fund-raising. While the president and his staff cannot legally conduct fund-raising efforts from the White House, they can strategize about how and when to begin this all-important effort.

As the president's campaign team begins to lay out its short- and long-run plans, perhaps the most significant immediate question they face is: Will the president be challenged within his own party? Under the current rules that govern the nomination process, as we have seen, presidents have a number of significant advantages over their potential challengers, but their renomination is not inevitable. A president who loses in the primaries and caucuses can no longer count on the "party establishment" to save him at the national convention. And even if the president does ultimately defeat his intraparty rival(s), the battle is likely to be messy, divisive, and expensive.[26] Of the last five incumbents who have sought another term in the White House, three faced significant opposition from within their own party: Gerald Ford, Jimmy Carter, and George Bush. While all three of these men were ultimately renominated, all were then defeated in the general election.

By contrast, a president who gets renominated without opposition can concentrate on his general election opponent and need not squander precious time and money on a preliminary battle with his own partisans. In a 1984 campaign memo, Lee Atwater provided this summary of the advantages that the Reagan campaign derived from its unobstructed path to renomination:

> This [the absence of a primary challenger] gives our campaign the opportunity to use our allotted $21.5 million—and these ten months—to build a strong organization. If we put the money into voter registration, local organizing, and some spot media, we can secure our electoral base earlier than any campaign in history.[27]

Presidents and their advisors therefore place great emphasis on trying to make sure that they are renominated without major opposition. In 1977, for example, the White House pushed the Winograd Commission, a Democratic party reform commission that had been set up to review the party's delegate selection rules, to adopt a set of "reforms" that were thought to help Carter in 1980 and discourage potential opponents.[28] In the 1996 election cycle, Bill Clinton found a more successful way to ward off Democratic challengers, by raising a record-setting war chest of $25.6 million (plus another $9 million in federal matching funds) during 1995.[29]

It is also worth noting that, of the three recent incumbents who have faced significant opposition from within their own party, all had committed various "crimes" against the dominant ideological wing of their party. Ford had chosen liberal Republican Nelson Rockefeller as his vice president and had continued the by-then controversial policy of detente with the Soviet Union; Carter had tried to scale back domestic spending and was perceived as not pushing very hard for a number of major items on the liberal wish-list. Bush's great flaw, in conservative eyes, was his decision to abandon his 1988 campaign promise not to increase taxes. (Each of these presidents had other weak spots as well, particularly the performance of the economy.) Undoubtedly, this has sent a signal to other incumbents that one way to avoid an intraparty challenge is to avoid antagonizing any of the major interests within their own party.

THE OTHER COMPONENTS: INDEPENDENT CAMPAIGN COMMITTEES AND THE NATIONAL PARTY ORGANIZATION

As noted earlier, every incumbent president since Richard Nixon eventually established a reelection campaign that consisted of three major components: the White House, the national party organization, and an independent campaign committee. Unlike the White House and the national party, the campaign organization has a short life span and a single function—to insure victory for the president. The independent campaign organization has emerged as a means for presidents to control and supervise the many activities of the presidential campaign that cannot legally be performed within the White House. Presidents and

White House staff members have also come to recognize the usefulness of having a campaign entity that, unlike the party, is solely responsible to the president and exclusively concerned with his reelection. As a result, each of the last six presidents has created his own campaign organization: CREEP, the President Ford Committee, the Carter/Mondale Presidential Committee, the Reagan/Bush '84 Campaign, the Bush/Quayle '92 Campaign, and the Clinton/Gore Campaign.

Initially, the president's campaign organization has only a small number of paid staff, many of whom have previously worked in the White House. Others come from the private sector, offering "outside the beltway" advice. Over time, this staff expands to include a larger number of supporters. Many of these participants campaigned for the president in the previous election; others are newcomers.

The structure of the campaign organization varies from president to president, but there is usually a single person who is designated the campaign manager and is in charge of day-to-day oversight of the campaign (for a list of presidential campaign managers, see table 4.3). These campaign managers are typically White House politicos-turned-campaigners with a wealth of experience and expertise. In addition to the campaign manager, there is often a campaign chairman, who is generally a more symbolic figure (again, see table 4.3). Other senior positions typically include deputy campaign manager, finance chair, public relations director (who is often in charge of direct mail, advertising, media, polling, and communications), research director, field coordinator, and special interests liaison.

The tasks of the campaign organization are substantial. According to a White House staff memorandum that was prepared during the Carter administration:

> Generally, the campaign committee must be responsible for media, overall strategy and resource allocation coordination (with the White House), a field organization (with regional political operation and desk system), polling, moving the candidate and surrogates (political advance and scheduling), plus necessary research, press, legal, accounting, and other related functions. The campaign committee should also have primary responsibility for voter contact and GOTV [get-out-the-vote] programs, although the costs and mechanics of this effort (e.g., list acquisition, phone bank and computer costs) may be shared with other entities.[30]

Given the high level of White House involvement, however, the campaign organization of an incumbent president does not take on the full range of responsibilities that fall to the campaign of a non-incumbent. Tasks such as security, scheduling, advance, speechwriting, and policy research are often shared with or handled entirely by the White House.

The final component in the president's campaign structure is the national party organization. As indicated earlier, it is much less influential than either the White House or the campaign organization, but it does perform a number of important functions for a president who is seeking reelection.

Table 4.3 Presidential Campaign Managers and Campaign Chairmen

A. Campaign Managers

Eisenhower	Leonard Hall, Chairman, Republican National Committee
Johnson	None (though Lawrence O'Brien and Kenneth O'Donnell played pivotal roles)
Nixon	John Mitchell, Attorney General (resigned July 1972)
	Clark MacGregor, Counsel to the President for Congressional Relations
Ford	Bo Callaway, Secretary of the Army (resigned March 1976)
	Rogers C. B. Morton, Secretary of Commerce (resigned August 1976)
	James Baker, Undersecretary of Commerce
Carter	Tim Kraft, Assistant to the President (resigned September 1980)
	Hamilton Jordan, Chief of Staff
Reagan	Ed Rollins, Assistant to the President for Political Affairs
Bush	Fred Malek, outsider advisor, held several major positions in the Nixon and Ford administrations
Clinton	Peter S. Knight, aide to Vice President Gore, veteran Washington lawyer and lobbyist

B. Campaign Chairmen

Nixon	Francis L. Dale, publisher, *Cincinnati Enquirer*
Carter	Robert S. Strauss, former chairman, Democratic National Committee, Special Trade Representative
Reagan	Paul Laxalt, U.S. Senator
Bush	Robert Mosbacher, Secretary of Commerce (resigned August 1992)
	Robert Teeter, pollster

Though many recent presidents have been accused of ignoring or marginalizing their own party, few have been shy about calling upon the party organization when it serves their own interest. The result is that the modern-day national party organization serves the president. It is, in truth, a veritable White House annex, staffed with presidential loyalists who are eager to see the president win reelection. The perspective from which the president and his top aides view the national party was nicely captured in a memo that Pat Caddell wrote to President-elect Carter in December, 1976: "It is clear that if the DNC is going to be 'Carterized' and made a political wing of the White House, that requires a chairman who is a loyalist and essentially a Carter insider." Not surprisingly, newly-elected presidents usually move early in their term to replace the existing chair of the national party with someone who has clearly demonstrated his personal loyalty to the new occupant of the White House.

The loyalties of the national party organization become particularly clear whenever the president faces opposition in his bid to be renominated. National party officials generally do not even claim to be neutral in such contests. In 1979, for example, DNC Chair John White openly told Senator Edward Kennedy, who was then contemplating a presidential bid, that he would be loyal to President Carter, just as the DNC chair during John Kennedy's administration would have been loyal to him.[31] In 1992, RNC Chair Rich Bond made no secret of the fact that he supported George Bush over Pat Buchanan. There is, it should be said, no rule that requires the party machinery to remain neutral when the president is faced with a challenge in the primaries. Nevertheless, candidates who challenge an incumbent president can generally be counted on to attack the party for its bias and partiality.

The national party helps the president's reelection effort in several ways, but most importantly in financial terms. During the early stages of a president's term, before the campaign committee has been established, the national party is responsible for paying many of the president's political expenses: campaign trips to assist state and congressional candidates; White House Christmas cards; presidential pens, cufflinks, or similar gifts to major contributors; hiring pollsters and other consultants to help advise the president.

The party organization, at both national and state levels, also carries on a variety of "party-building" activities that are designed to aid party candidates in general, such as voter registration drives, grassroots voter education efforts, and get-out-the-vote programs on election day. In recent years, this type of activity has mushroomed, as both parties have exploited loopholes in the campaign finance laws to run so-called generic or issue advertising, that promotes the party's presidential candidate and many of his favored issue positions, but does not explicitly urge the viewer to vote for that candidate. In addition, during the election year itself, the party can assume financial burdens for campaign-related activity if the nominee has reached the legal spending limits (see chapter 2).

Finally, it is the party organization that plays the lead role in organizing the national convention, including selecting the host city and then making arrangements for such matters as transportation, security, lodging, credentials, and media coverage. Since party conventions are thought to provide an important "bounce" in the polls to candidates as they enter the general election, responsibility for such a critical event is not trivial.

NO MORE BUSINESS AS USUAL

Given all the effort and attention that go into the campaign, it should come as no surprise that the quest for reelection has a profound impact on the institution of the presidency. For at least a year, and sometimes longer, the business of government must share the stage with the business of campaigning. A careful examination of the last eight presidential reelection campaigns suggests six major short-term effects that the campaign has on the presidency and the executive branch as a whole.

Staff Shuffling and Restructuring

One of the first things that changes when a president starts to run for a second term are the top personnel in the White House and the executive branch.[32] Actually, there are several different types of staffing changes that occur as a direct result of the reelection campaign. First, many presidential appointees leave the government to work for the campaign organization. In 1983, as we have seen, almost the entire Office of Political Affairs left the White House to set up the Reagan/Bush '84 Campaign. The exodus from the Nixon administration to the Committee to Re-Elect the President was even larger. By April of 1972, seventeen of twenty-two senior CREEP members came from the White House staff or administration. After the campaign was in full swing, two cabinet members, Attorney General John Mitchell and Commerce Secretary Maurice H. Stans, also joined the reelection campaign.

In other cases, presidents have felt it necessary to radically restructure their entire staff in order to remove unpopular or ineffective people, improve their own public image, or bring in new personnel who seemed better-suited to the tasks of an election year. In November of 1975, for example, President Ford asked for the resignations of Defense Secretary James R. Schlesinger and CIA Director William E. Colby; he also got Henry Kissinger to surrender one of the two key titles he held in the administration, as assistant to the president for national security affairs (Kissinger remained secretary of state). By most accounts, electoral motivations were at the root of the shake-up. Concerned about "public divisions" within the administration and the perception that he was being overshadowed by Kissinger, Ford sought to demonstrate that he was fully in command.[33] The shake-up also extended to the White House staff: Donald Rumsfeld, Ford's chief of staff, became the secretary of defense, while Dick Cheney took on the chief of staff's duties. At roughly the same time, Ford pressed Vice President Rockefeller to announce that he would not be a candidate for election to that office in 1976.

George H. W. Bush actually made several different attempts to restructure his top staff during the final year of his administration. In December, 1991, Bush secured the resignation of John Sununu, his chief of staff, who was disliked by many at the White House and who had become a political liability because of several ethical missteps. Sununu was replaced by Secretary of Transportation Samuel Skinner, who then conducted a wide-ranging overhaul of the White House staff structure. With the state of the economy emerging as a major campaign issue, which the administration was widely accused of ignoring, in late February, 1992, Skinner announced the creation of a Policy Coordinating Group, that was supposed to coordinate domestic social and economic policy, much as the National Security Council did in foreign affairs. Meanwhile, Bush appointed Clayton Yeutter, chairman of the Republican National Committee, as counselor to the president in charge of domestic policy. Yeutter's role, as one news account put it, was to "fill gaping holes in its [the administration's] policy and public relations operations for the reelection campaign."[34]

When this first attempt at restructuring the White House did not have its intended effect, in mid-August 1992, Bush tried something even more radical. With polls showing the president trailing Democratic presidential nominee Bill Clinton by 20–30 percentage points, Bush asked Skinner to step down and replaced him with Secretary of State James Baker, who was both a close friend of Bush's and a veteran of four previous presidential campaigns. The president's willingness to move a highly respected secretary of state to the White House in order to provide more hands-on assistance with the reelection campaign is striking testimony about how much the campaign comes to dominate everything else.

Beyond these sorts of highly-publicized incidents, a comprehensive study of White House staff turnover during the period between 1929 and 1997 found a marked increase in the rate of turnover over the last few decades, an increase that seems to be, in large part, a function of the changing nature of presidential campaigns. The transformation of presidential reelection campaigns from a party-based to a candidate-centered process means that the White House is largely responsible for managing the campaign. Hence, as the election draws near, presidents feel compelled to reorganize their advisory system in order to maximize the input of aides who are skilled in the arts of campaigning. The increasing rates of staff turnover are a reflection of the difficulty of melding governing and campaigning expertise into a single presidential staff.[35]

Substance and Amount of Staff Work

The president's reelection campaign also affects the substance and amount of work that White House staff members must accomplish during the final year of the term. This is perhaps pre-eminently true for the chief of staff, who must become the linchpin between the campaign and the White House and the president's chief political strategist, in addition to all his governmental responsibilities. But similar changes affect almost every corner of the institutional presidency. The press office, for example, must be prepared to respond and react to campaign events in addition to all its routine (and non-routine) dealings with the White House press corps. According to former presidential press secretary Marlin Fitzwater, "The workload multiplies by tenfold. . . . The dynamics of the press office changes in the sense that the press is the messenger of the opposition. It is an adversarial context—the margin of error gets much smaller."[36] Speechwriters and policy advisors are similarly pressed by the need to contribute to campaign stump speeches, policy addresses, and position papers.

Heightened Politicization

A third short-term effect of an incumbent's reelection campaign is the heightened politicization of the decision-making process. As one former member of

George H. W. Bush's staff noted, "Starting [in] the second half of '91, everything starts to take on a much more political tone."[37] A member of the Carter senior staff agreed: "During the campaign, things change dramatically because every political story has a reelection dimension and therefore everything you work on has that potential."[38] Of course, politics is never absent from the White House, but as one Bush official noted in March of 1992, "The domestic side of the White House and the political operation are really driving things in a way they never did before."[39]

One manifestation of this heightened politicization is the significant number of policy reversals that so often come in the fourth year of a president's term. George Bush the elder showed a particular inclination for this sort of behavior. In April, 1992, for example, Bush announced a freeze on the issuing of new federal regulations—even though in the previous three years he had signed several major pieces of legislation (such as the Clean Air Act and the Americans with Disabilities Act) that had generated vast new areas of regulation.[40] During Bush's first several years in office, he frequently defended the policies of John Frohnmeyer, whom he had appointed to head up the National Endowment for the Arts. When Pat Buchanan began to make an issue of the NEA, however, Bush responded by firing Frohnmeyer. In early September, 1992, the Bush administration announced a slew of additional policy reversals: the sale of combat jets to Taiwan and Saudi Arabia, support for modernizing the M1 tank and the Osprey V22 aircraft, the rebuilding of hurricane-damaged Homestead Air Force Base in Florida, additional disaster relief for farmers, and increased subsidies for wheat exports.[41]

Politicized decision-making can also come into play when presidents (or their appointees) award grants, contracts, and other government resources to electorally strategic states or key political allies. Consider two examples from the Carter years:

Thus, when the Small Business Administration decided, just before the Maine precinct caucuses and the New Hampshire primary, to designate five New England states an "economic dislocation area" because of the lack of snow this winter, enabling businesses to receive low-cost loans, . . . it was arranged that New Hampshire's governor, Hugh Gallen, make the announcement, and stories about it were in the papers while Vice President Mondale and Mrs. Carter were campaigning in the area.[42]

In the week before the Florida presidential-preference caucuses, for example, the administration announced a number of federally funded projects, including two in Miami, a new Job Corps center and a tourism project in the Cuban community.[43]

There are numerous examples from other administrations as well. President Clinton, having narrowly won California in 1992, devoted substantial attention to the Golden State. As the defense budget was scaled back during Clinton's first term, California alone was awarded 25–30 percent of all the money distributed under a technology reinvestment project.[44]

The doling out of government resources is, in many cases, a well-orchestrated effort. In 1984, for example, James Baker appointed Richard Darman to oversee efforts to bring government largesse to bear for the benefit of the campaign. As one account of the Reagan presidency noted, Darman "served as the conduit for programs and proposals that could be exploited for political gain. Whenever the campaign team saw the need for action by the administration, it was Darman who knew how to get the government machinery moving."[45] President George H. W. Bush formalized the process by creating a "funnel" system to coordinate the efforts of various departments and the White House to disburse government resources.[46]

Changes in Presidential Activity

Another noteworthy but unsurprising effect of a presidential reelection campaign is a change in the sorts of activities that presidents perform. Perhaps the most obvious reflection of this change is a sharp increase in the amount of presidential travel. Table 4.4 shows the number of trips each president being studied here took during each year of his first term.[47] As these data show, Presidents Ford, Carter, Reagan, Bush, and Clinton all traveled a lot more in their fourth year in office than they had in any of their first three. No such increase occurred for Eisenhower and Nixon, the former because of health problems, the latter because he seems to have made a deliberate decision to showcase himself as a statesman and activist president who had no time for ordinary, partisan politics.[48]

Other scholars, using slightly different data or counting procedures, have reached similar conclusions. Paul Brace and Barbara Hinckley, for example, found that, "Foreign trips [by the president] increase as election nears, most of them occurring in the spring of the reelection year, while domestic trips reach

Table 4.4 Presidential Political Travel, by Year of a President's Term

President	1st Year	2nd Year	3rd Year	4th Year
Eisenhower	21	29	24	25
Johnson	—[a]	—[a]	4[b]	144
Nixon	42	61	50	49
Ford	—[a]	53[b]	102	211
Carter	33	78	65	131
Bush	95	121	92	267
Clinton	96	145	111	235

[a] Did not serve as president that year.
[b] Served as president for only part of the year.
Sources: Compiled by the author from *Public Papers of the Presidency* (Washington, D.C.: U.S. Government Printing Office, 1953–1996).

their peak in the fall of the election year."[49] Similarly, King and Ragsdale show a dramatic rise in the number of "political appearances" for presidents who are seeking reelection.[50]

Cabinet Campaigning

It is not just the president who is distracted by the demands of the campaign. Many cabinet members are also asked to tend to campaign-related duties, such as making appearances around the country on behalf of the president. Cabinet members act as presidential surrogates, attacking the opposition and vigorously promoting and defending the administration, while allowing the president to stay "above the fray" and thus retain a presidential aura. In two off-the-record interviews, I learned that Jack Kemp, secretary of housing and urban development during the first Bush administration, spent up to one-third of his time (as of April, 1992) campaigning for President Bush's reelection. One White House staff member speculated that by the time of the general election, the portion of Kemp's time devoted to campaigning would increase to two-thirds. As the staff member put it, "When the general election season hits, cabinet business will be replaced with campaign business." Cabinet members are also asked to contribute information and ideas that can be used in election speeches, to publicize various administrative actions, or to allocate discretionary grants to strategically-located constituencies.

The Carter administration seems to have put special pressure on its top appointees to support the president's reelection bid. According to Joseph Califano, Carter's first secretary of health, education, and welfare:

> Each Cabinet officer would be asked to speak at least once a month for the White House, and . . . each should give a travel schedule to the White House so that political events could be worked in around departmental business. When a Cabinet officer was in a particular city on departmental business, he or she would stay a couple of hours and do an event to help raise money for the Carter campaign.[51]

In a January, 1980, memo to the president, Hamilton Jordan, Carter's chief of staff, made a number of more specific demands:

> We need three things from our Cabinet officers and from agency heads: (1) targeted calls to Iowans furnished by our Iowa campaign; (2) Cabinet members to mobilize their talented political appointees; and (3) Cabinet members and others to be creative in their efforts to influence the Iowa caucus.[52]

Not surprisingly, some cabinet members resisted such pressure, which resulted in stringent lectures by the president himself. In a memo to Carter about a forthcoming cabinet meeting, Jordan wrote:

The tone of the meeting should be straightforward and tough. The Cabinet generally regards the campaign as "somebody else's business," and you should let them know that we are in for the fight of our lives and without everyone helping, we will be in for a very bad time. You might brag a little on Bergland and Marshall who have really done yeoman's service over the past several months. They deserve some special praise.[53]

It is hardly surprising that presidents would ask their cabinet members to campaign on their behalf. Many cabinet members have strong regional ties or relations with important constituencies, and from an efficiency perspective, the reelection campaign can reach a lot more voters when cabinet appointees, and not just the president, are out crisscrossing the country.

Declining Policy Initiative

As presidents and their top advisors spend more time on campaigning and campaign strategy, that time must inevitably be taken from other things. One such thing is policy. There is strong evidence that one effect of a presidential reelection campaign is to drive down the administration's capacity to develop and push for new policy initiatives. As Marlin Fitzwater, press secretary to the first President Bush, noted:

It is very hard to govern and campaign at the same time. Everything changes. Nobody cares about anything except reelection. It is hard to focus on domestic issues. There are no new legislative programs. The initiative dries up after January [of the election year]. Policy analysts fall by the wayside. The White House focuses on those things they have to deal with—foreign policy and getting reelected. . . . Virtually nothing gets done.[54]

A top Reagan staff member concurred:

Policy in terms of making policy tends to atrophy towards the end of an administration. You can't create new policy in a short period of time especially when everything has more of a political appearance.[55]

One indicator of this decline in policy initiative is the number of presidential legislative proposals transmitted to Congress. As shown in table 4.5, for five of the last six presidents who sought reelection, there was a noticeable falloff in the number of such proposals between the third and fourth years of the president's term. Even the exception to this pattern is probably attributable to the pressures of the reelection campaign. By the end of his third year in the White House, George H. W. Bush was increasingly criticized for being too preoccupied with foreign policy and insufficiently concerned about the country's domestic ills. In an effort to rebut these attacks, as noted earlier, the White House created a new

Table 4.5 Legislative Proposals Transmitted to Congress by the President, by Year of a President's Term

President	1st Year	2nd Year	3rd Year	4th Year	Difference between 3rd and 4th Year
Johnson	—[a]	—[a]	0[b]	6	n.a.
Nixon	17	12	8	3	−5
Ford	—[a]	5[b]	10	6	−4
Carter	21	8	8	4	−4
Reagan	2	10	25	8	−17
Bush	10	6	6	22	+16
Clinton	9	4	8	3	−5

[a] Did not serve as president that year.

[b] Served as president for only part of the year. For 1974, number listed is the total number of legislative initiatives submitted by both Nixon and Ford.

Sources: Figures for Johnson, Nixon, Ford, and Carter are taken from Paul Light, *The President's Agenda* (Baltimore: Johns Hopkins University Press, 1991), 42. Light obtained his data from the Office of Legislative Reference in the Office of Management and Budget. For the Reagan, Bush, and Clinton presidencies, I have obtained comparable figures from the same source.

domestic policy coordinating group. Whatever that group's success in enacting legislation or solving problems, it clearly did produce a welter of new proposals during Bush's fourth year in office.

Another indicator of the same point is the number of executive orders a president issues, as shown in table 4.6. Of the seven recent presidents for whom meaningful data exist, six issued fewer orders during the fourth year of their term than they had in the third year. And again, the exception can readily be understood as simply a different type of response to election-year politics. In 1996, Bill Clin-

Table 4.6 Number of Executive Orders Issued, by Year of a President's Term

President	1st Year	2nd Year	3rd Year	4th Year	Difference between 3rd and 4th Year
Eisenhower	90	73	65	44	−21
Johnson	—[a]	—[a]	7[b]	56	n.a.
Nixon	61	72	63	55	−8
Ford	—[a]	29[b]	67	56	−11
Carter	83	78	77	73	−4
Reagan	76	63	57	41	−16
Bush	36	43	46	40	−6
Clinton	57	54	39	47	+8

[a] Did not serve as president that year.

[b] Served as president for only part of the year.

Sources: Lyn Ragsdale, *Vital Statistics on the Presidency* (Washington, D.C.: Congressional Quarterly Press, 1996), 342–43. Data for Clinton obtained from Congressional Research Service.

ton was anxious to show that he was still an active and industrious chief executive even though the Republicans had just won control of both houses of Congress. With little prospect of getting most of his legislative proposals enacted, "Clinton often issued executive orders on small-bore issues to show he was taking action rather than calling on Congress to do something."[56]

In short, the final year of a president's first term is typically a period when few if any new policy initiatives emerge. As Dick Cheney noted about his experience as Gerald Ford's chief of staff, "If you are in the middle of a tough, knock-down, drag-out campaign, it limits your ability to get things done. . . . The issue [the SALT treaty] sort of went on the back burner, so it didn't get mixed up in the campaign, but it [the campaign] did delay and defer policy."[57] Former chief of staff James Baker expressed a similar view: "Major initiatives tend to dwindle as you move into the reelection cycle. . . . You don't build a legacy in the final months of your term when you are running for reelection."[58]

CONCLUSION

For presidents who have served since the wholesale transformation of the presidential selection process in the early 1970s, running for reelection requires a delicate balancing act between the competing demands of campaigning and governing. This examination of presidential reelection campaigns suggests that this balancing act may be getting increasingly difficult. While the Nixon administration marks an important turning point in the evolution of incumbent reelection campaigns, the Clinton administration may signal a major acceleration of reelection activity. One Clinton innovation was the use of "issue advocacy" ads to pump up the president's popularity and discourage opposition from within his own party. But the record-setting amounts of money that Clinton raised to pay for these ads resulted in a surge of legal challenges and hefty legal bills for the Democratic National Committee.[59] Clinton also was the first president to use executive orders during the election year to showcase his attention to key issues. Campaign goodies disguised as policy, however, may ultimately trivialize the presidency, raising concerns that all manner of presidential actions are simply campaign tactics.

How many of these innovations will endure beyond the Clinton years is unclear. For example, the Bipartisan Campaign Reform Act of 2002—if the Supreme Court upholds it—will curb the worst abuses of sham issue ads. On the other hand, the first two years of George W. Bush's administration suggest that the frenzied pursuit of reelection is alive and well. In addition to the Office of Political Affairs, Bush created a second office within the White House—the Office of Strategic Initiatives, under the direction of Karl Rove, Bush's top political advisor—to keep watch over the president's electoral coalition.

In his first two years, President George W. Bush also shattered all previous records for the amount of money raised by a sitting president: more than $144 million, from 67 receptions in 34 states and the District of Columbia. Beyond fund-raising, "President Bush has harnessed the broad resources of the federal government to promote Republicans. . . . From housing grants in South Dakota and research contracts in Florida to Air Force One rides and photos in the White House driveway, Bush has made Republican success on November 5 [the day of the 2002 midterm elections] a government-wide project."[60] Not coincidentally, a disproportionate share of President Bush's midterm campaign travel took him to many of the states that he had narrowly won or lost in 2000, such as Pennsylvania, Iowa, Tennessee, and Florida.

However much attention the White House devotes to campaigning, the important tasks of governing cannot be neglected without dangerous electoral repercussions. In an era of international insecurity, economic uncertainty, and escalating deficit spending, the American electorate has a low level of tolerance for reelection shenanigans and overt politicking. Unless and until the rules of the game change, however, we will no doubt see future presidents slogging through the snow and sleet of Iowa and New Hampshire, overwhelmed by the twin tasks of governing and campaigning, and longing for the days of Teddy Roosevelt.

NOTES

The author wishes to acknowledge the helpful research assistance of Brookings Institution intern Courtney Hare; and of Chas Budnick and Elizabeth Redman, who helped prepare the data on political travel during the Clinton administration.

1. Gil Troy, *See How They Ran* (New York: Macmillan, 1991), 212.

2. Theodore H. White, *The Making of the President 1964* (New York: Atheneum, 1965), 354.

3. This chapter draws on over fifty interviews with former White House, party, and campaign staff that the author conducted. For further details, see Kathryn Dunn Tenpas, *Presidents as Candidates: Inside the White House for the Presidential Campaign* (New York: Garland, 1997), 173–76.

4. See Ann Devroy, "New Hampshire Awaits Latest Edition of Candidate Bush," *Washington Post*, January 15, 1992. The quotation is actually from an interview that Bush had with David Frost.

5. Though this chapter's principal focus is on the nomination phase of the president's campaign, the structural components of the reelection campaign, as well as its impact on White House operations, are features that remain well after the national conventions have come to an end.

6. Harry S. Dent, *The Prodigal South Returns to Power* (New York: Wiley and Sons, 1978), 229.

7. Nixon did not make an announcement *speech* but did reveal his intention to run for a second term in a set of letters that he wrote to the New Hampshire secretary of state and the chairman of a pro-Nixon group in New Hampshire that the White House then made public. See *New York Times*, January 8, 1972, 1.

8. Cornelius P. Cotter and Bernard C. Hennessy, *Politics without Power* (New York: Atherton, 1964), 126.

9. Clark Clifford oral history, cited in Bradley Patterson, *The Ring of Power* (New York: Basic Books, 1988), 233. See also David McCullough, *Truman* (New York: Simon and Schuster, 1992), 656–83.

10. Rowland Evans and Robert Novak, *Lyndon B. Johnson: The Exercise of Power* (New York: New American Library, 1966), 466.

11. Jeb Stuart Magruder, *An American Life* (New York: Atheneum, 1974), 155.

12. Sidney M. Milkis, *The President and the Parties* (New York: Oxford University Press, 1993), 364.

13. Paul T. David, Ralph M. Goldman, and Richard C. Bain, *The Politics of National Party Conventions*, rev. ed. (New York: University Press of America, 1964), 84.

14. Charles C. Euchner and John Anthony Maltese, "The Electoral Process," in *Congressional Quarterly's Guide to the Presidency*, ed. Michael Nelson (Washington, D.C.: Congressional Quarterly, 1989), 220.

15. Terry Moe, "The Presidency and the Bureaucracy: The Presidential Advantage," in *The Presidency and the Political System*, ed. Michael Nelson (Washington, D.C.: Congressional Quarterly, 1995), 425.

16. The following discussion draws on Kathryn Dunn Tenpas, "Institutionalized Politics: The White House Office of Political Affairs," *Presidential Studies Quarterly* 26 (Spring 1996): 511–22.

17. This approach also appears to be attractive to the current administration. In March 2003, Ken Mehlman, director of the OPA under George W. Bush, was designated his reelection campaign manager. See Mike Allen and Dan Balz, "Bush's '04 Campaign Quietly Being Planned," *Washington Post*, March 3, 2003, A1.

18. Richard Berke, "Clinton Moving to Avoid Losses in '94 Elections," *New York Times*, February 22, 1994, A1.

19. John Anthony Maltese, *Spin Control: The White House Office of Communications and the Management of Presidential News*, 2nd ed. (Chapel Hill: University of North Carolina Press, 1994), 28.

20. John Hart, *The Presidential Branch: From Washington to Clinton*, 2nd ed. (Chatham, N.J.: Chatham House, 1995), 127.

21. Sidney Blumenthal, *The Permanent Campaign* (New York: Simon and Schuster, 1982), 7. For a broader discussion of the permanent campaign, see Norman Ornstein and Thomas Mann, eds., *The Permanent Campaign and Its Future* (Washington, D.C.: American Enterprise Institute and Brookings Institution, 2000).

22. Teeter's comments appear in Jonathan Moore, ed., *Campaign for President: The Managers Look at '84* (Dover, Mass.: Auburn House, 1986), 103.

23. Interview with Margaret Tutwiler, May 24, 1994.

24. These services are not inexpensive. Expenditure reports filed by the political parties reveal that millions of dollars have been spent on presidential polling and political consulting. For detailed data on these expenditures across recent administrations, see Kathryn Dunn Tenpas, "The American Presidency: Surviving and Thriving amidst the Permanent Campaign," in *The Permanent Campaign and Its Future*, ed. Norman Ornstein and Thomas Mann (Washington, D.C.: American Enterprise Institute and Brookings Institution, 2000), 115. See also Kathryn Dunn Tenpas, "Words vs. Deeds: President George W. Bush and Polling," *Brookings Review*, Summer, 2003.

25. Alison Mitchell, "Behind the Cloak of Office, Clinton War Room Is in Gear," *New York Times*, May 7, 1996, C20.

26. For an assessment of the general argument that a divisive nomination contest hurts a party during the general election, see Lonna Rae Atkeson, "From the Primaries to the General Election: Does a Divisive Nomination Race Affect a Candidate's Fortunes in the Fall?" in *In Pursuit of the White House 2000: How We Choose Our Presidential Nominees*, ed. William G. Mayer (New York: Chatham House, 2000), 285–312.

27. As quoted in Peter Goldman and Tony Fuller, *The Quest for the Presidency 1984* (New York: Bantam, 1985), 386.

28. For further details, see James I. Lengle, "Democratic Party Reforms: The Past as Prologue to the 1988 Campaign," *Journal of Law and Politics* 4 (Fall 1987): 233–73.

29. See Anthony Corrado, "Financing the 1996 Elections," in *The Election of 1996: Reports and Interpretations*, ed. Gerald M. Pomper (Chatham, N.J.: Chatham House, 1997), 142–43.

30. "Coordination of General Election Planning," memorandum to Hamilton Jordan and Bob Strauss from Tim Kraft, May 24, 1980, Carter Presidential Library.

31. Interview with John White, August 13, 1991.

32. For a more detailed analysis of how a reelection campaign affects White House staffing and organization, see Kathryn Dunn Tenpas and Matthew J. Dickinson, "Governing, Campaigning, and Organizing the Presidency: An Electoral Connection?" *Political Science Quarterly* 112 (Spring 1997): 51–66.

33. Gerald R. Ford, *A Time to Heal* (New York: Harper and Row, 1979), 320.

34. Ann Devroy, "Yeutter Offered Top Bush Policy Post As White House Retools for Campaign," *Washington Post*, January 25, 1992, A10.

35. See Matthew J. Dickinson and Kathryn Dunn Tenpas, "Explaining Increasing Turnover Rates among Presidential Advisors, 1929–1997," *Journal of Politics* 64 (May 2002): 434–48.

36. Interview with Marlin Fitzwater, May 19, 1994.

37. Interview with Andrew Card, December 15, 1994.

38. Off-the-record interview.

39. Andrew Rosenthal, "White House Sees Trips As Way to Revive Bush," *New York Times*, March 27, 1992, A21.

40. See David E. Rosenbaum and Keith Schneider, "Bush Is Extending Regulation Freeze with a Fanfare," *New York Times*, April 29, 1992, A22.

41. See "Bush Backs Sale of 150 F-16s to Taiwanese," *International Herald Tribune*, September 3, 1992, 1; John Lancaster, "From National Security, An Advantage for Bush," *International Herald Tribune*, September 4, 1992, 1; Jurek Martin, "White House Defends Bush Largesse," *Financial Times*, September 4, 1992, 18; and Kevin Brown, "Australia Angry at U.S. Subsidized Wheat Plans," *Financial Times*, September 4, 1992, 4.

42. Elizabeth Drew, "A Reporter at Large," *New Yorker*, April 14, 1980, 126.

43. Herbert Alexander, *Financing the 1980 Election* (Lexington, Mass.: D.C. Heath, 1983), 219.

44. Burt Solomon, "Clinton: California on His Mind," *National Journal*, January 20, 1996, 134.

45. Bob Schieffer and Gary Paul Gates, *The Acting President* (New York: E.P. Dutton, 1989), 183.

46. See Robert Pear, "White House 'Funnel' Gets Help for States with Primaries Nearing," *New York Times*, March 10, 1992.

47. Presidential travel is defined here as any travel outside of Washington, D.C. in which the president made formal remarks (which then become part of the *Public Papers of the President*, on which this count is based). One exception to this definition is travel to presidential vacation locations such as Camp David, San Clemente, Vail, Plains, and Kennebunkport, which I have omitted from the totals. I have borrowed (and modified) this approach from William Lammers. See Lammers, "Presidential Attention-Focusing Activities," in *The President and the American Public*, ed. Doris Graber (Philadelphia: Institute for the Study of Human Issues, 1982).

48. For a similar conclusion, see Lammers, "Presidential Attention-Focusing Activities," 162.

49. Paul Brace and Barbara Hinckley, *Follow the Leader* (New York: Basic Books, 1992), 54.

50. See Gary King and Lyn Ragsdale, *The Elusive Executive* (Washington, D.C.: CQ Press, 1988), 274.

51. Joseph A. Califano, *Governing America* (New York: Simon and Schuster, 1981), 420.

52. Memo from Hamilton Jordan to President Carter, Re: Iowa, January 12, 1980, Carter Presidential Library.

53. Memo from Hamilton Jordan to President Carter, Re: Cabinet Meeting Tonight, November 5, 1979, Carter Presidential Library.

54. Interview with Marlin Fitzwater, May 19, 1994.

55. Off-the-record interview.

56. Mike Allen, "With Adoption Push, Bush Adopts a Clinton Tactic," *Washington Post*, July 24, 2002.

57. As quoted in Samuel Kernell and Samuel L. Popkin, eds., *Chief of Staff* (Berkeley: University of California Press, 1986), 101–102.

58. Remarks by James Baker made at the Washington Forum on the Role of the White House Chief of Staff, June 15, 2000. Quotes are taken from section 3. Video available at http://www.rice.edu/projects/baker/resource/paevents/whcos/whchiefs.html.

59. Clinton's fund-raising in 1995 set a record at the time. In the 2000 election cycle, three different candidates—Gore, Bradley, and Bush—all exceeded Clinton's pre-election year total.

60. Mike Allen, "Bush Enlists Government in GOP Campaign," *Washington Post*, October 22, 2002, A8.

5

From Resistance to Adaptation
Organized Labor Reacts to a Changing Nominating Process

Taylor E. Dark III

The so-called McGovern commission was supposed to produce the most democratic convention in the history of the parties. . . . Oh, 300 labor delegates managed to get there, but only one was allowed to address the delegates. [Instead,] we listened for three days to the speakers who were approved to speak by the powers-that-be at that convention. We listened to the gay-lib people—you know, the people who want to legalize marriage between boys and boys and legalize marriage between girls and girls. . . . We heard from the abortionists, and we heard from the people who look like Jacks, acted like Jills, and had the odor of johns about them.

—George Meany, AFL-CIO President, speaking in the
aftermath of the 1972 Democratic National Convention[1]

We must dominate this convention—with our spirit, with our signs, with our presence and participation in the convention hall. You, my brothers and sisters, are the largest delegation of down-home, uptown, grassroots, kick-ass union leaders in the history of the Democratic National Convention.

—John J. Sweeney, AFL-CIO President, addressing a meeting of union
delegates to the 2000 Democratic National Convention[2]

These two quotations—one a bitter denunciation of the Democratic party for allegedly excluding unions from the party's procedures for choosing a presidential candidate, the other a triumphal assertion of labor's continuing power and relevance at the last nominating convention of the twentieth century—illustrate the dramatic twists and turns in the history of labor unions in the Democratic party. Ever since the emergence of powerful industrial unions during the Great Depression, organized labor has been the single most important mass-membership interest group in the Democratic coalition. Dependent on the federal government for the effective enforcement of labor laws, and with an abiding interest in a vast range of public policy issues, the labor movement has been deeply concerned to have a friend in the White House (in some instances, the very survival of particular union organizations has depended on it). To secure an allied executive, unions have not only helped Democratic presidential candidates in the general election, but have gone a step further, becoming intimately involved in the party's initial choice of a presidential nominee. It is this effort to determine the party's nominee, and what it teaches us about the nature of the current nominating process and the role of interest groups within it, that will be my concern in this chapter.[3]

Political scientists have long recognized the role of institutional rules and procedures in altering political behavior, an insight well-summarized in the oft-quoted maxim: "When you change the rules, you change the game."[4] Nowhere is the point better confirmed than in the case of organized labor's evolving role in the presidential nominating process. The rules of this process underwent major reform in the early 1970s, forcing labor unions to significantly adjust the ways in which they sought to influence presidential nominations. After a period of resistance, including a failed effort by some leaders to roll back reform entirely, the unions spent the early 1980s adapting to the logic of the new system and learning how to manipulate it to their own advantage. In the nominating contests since that time, labor has been a crucial player, effectively promoting its favored candidates and often undermining those it opposes. In order to achieve this influence, however, the labor movement first had to undergo a wrenching set of internal changes, democratizing and opening up its own endorsement procedures and creating new methods to consult and mobilize the union rank-and-file. Without many noticing it, party reform thus catalyzed a process of labor reform, issuing in a new distribution of power within the contemporary union movement. This, too, counts as one of many unintended consequences of party reform.

THE RISE OF A NATIONAL LABOR MOVEMENT

An understanding of the current nature of the labor/Democrat relationship requires some brief consideration of the historical origins of organized labor and the factors which have driven it so deeply toward political activism. Labor unions have always been interested in politics, if for no other reason than the need to prevent local, state, or federal governments from stepping in to repress their efforts to form effective workplace organizations. While other issues have always been on their agenda, the basic task of organizational survival has necessarily been paramount. A defense of the right to organize was, therefore, the main political goal endorsed by the fledgling craft unions that joined together in 1886 to form the American Federation of Labor (AFL). The unions of skilled workers in the AFL, typically employed in the construction (or "building") trades or in small-scale craft production, succeeded in forming robust but small organizations that managed to survive despite their lack of a secure place in the nation's legal order. These unions did not aspire to represent all the workers in a specific firm or industry but instead concentrated only on those who possessed a particular skill (such as carpenters, plumbers, bakers, tailors, and so on) regardless of employer. The typical form of organization for a craft union was a "local" based on a geographic area, and within that area its members could be found in many different enterprises.

Even in the best of times, the hostility of the federal judiciary to union activity always reminded unionists that a friend in the White House, willing to use his power to appoint liberal judges and to sign the occasional pro-union piece of legislation, could make a major difference for the future of their organizations. It was this reasoning that in 1908 led the AFL, then representing nearly three million union members, to endorse the election of Democratic presidential nominee William Jennings Bryan—an act that marks the definitive entry of labor unions into presidential politics. While the AFL would also work for the election of Woodrow Wilson in 1912, and gain some influence within his administration, the national shift toward conservatism following World War I drove labor away from both major parties, and in 1924 the federation went so far as to endorse a third party presidential candidate (the Progressive nominee, Sen. Robert LaFollette of Wisconsin). Thus, on the eve of the Great Depression, the AFL remained wedded to the idea of non-partisanship—the belief that labor should never make a serious and long-term commitment to any political party. With this approach prevailing, an intervention in the Democratic party's procedures for nominating presidential candidates remained virtually unthinkable.

All this was to change with the formation of the Congress of Industrial Organizations in 1935. For decades, the AFL had refused to organize the millions of unskilled workers, often African-Americans and immigrants from eastern and southern Europe, who had been drawn into such growing mass production industries as automobiles, rubber, steel, and electrical goods. Craft unionists saw these underprivileged, uneducated, and socially "inferior" masses as poor material with which to build strong and sustainable unions. Efforts to organize such workers in the past had always failed, AFL leaders argued, and they would do so this time also. Other union leaders, however, saw it differently. A few unions in the AFL, such as the mineworkers and textile workers, had always had a semi-industrial character, and they argued that the growing workforce was ripe for a new kind of organization: "industrial" unionism, in which workers of all skills and job types were brought together in a single organization based on the employer or industry in which they labored. Advocates of this brand of unionism were strengthened in 1935 when a Democratic Congress passed and President Franklin Roosevelt signed into law the National Labor Relations Act, a statute that created powerful new protections for workers seeking to achieve union representation. With this legal framework in place, the mineworkers and other unions could be restrained no longer: they broke off from the AFL and established a second, rival federation called the Congress of Industrial Organizations (CIO). The first task of the new organization was to launch a huge drive to organize mass production workers, an initiative that turned out to be spectacularly successful, resulting in millions of new union members in the space of only a few years and the creation of such powerful organizations as the United Auto Workers and United Steelworkers. The CIO's successes, along with the changes in labor law, also stimulated growth in the old AFL unions, so that by the end of the 1930s the nation had a much more powerful, albeit divided, labor movement, and one much more closely aligned with the national Democratic party.

By the early 1950s it was clear that both the CIO and the AFL were here to stay, with the CIO claiming a membership (in its affiliated unions) of some 6,000,000 workers, and the AFL achieving even greater success with more than 9,000,000 members. By 1952, total union representation in the workforce had risen to nearly 33 percent, a stunning increase over the 13 percent that unions had possessed at the start of the Depression.[5] With the successful unionization of formerly intractable workers and industries, and increasing overlap between the craft and industrial models of organization, the historic clash between the two labor federations began to soften. Thus, in the more placid setting of mid-century America, the two federations were finally able to set aside their differences, officially merging in 1955. Unable to agree on a new name, union officials simply christened the resulting body the AFL-CIO. With this development, the basic organizational structure of American unionism as we know it today was in place.

ORGANIZATIONAL STRUCTURE AND THE QUEST FOR LABOR UNITY

The foundational principle of the AFL-CIO is that workers will be organized into separate nationwide (or international) unions that have exclusive responsibility for the major functions of new organizing, collective bargaining, and contract administration. These unions are the sovereign entities of the labor movement. They are the only bodies that individual workers can directly join, and they are capable of performing most of their functions quite well without the assistance of the labor federation (indeed, some have never joined it, or have chosen to exit when they have concluded that affiliation was no longer helpful). Most unions do find affiliation worthwhile, however, for the AFL-CIO plays a helpful role in resolving jurisdictional disputes (i.e., conflicts over which unions get to organize which workers), in providing assistance to unions engaged in new organizing drives or embroiled in expensive strikes, and in planning and coordinating an overall political strategy. To carry out these tasks, the top officials of the federation—a president, vice president, secretary-treasurer, and a 54-member executive council—are elected for four-year terms at a national convention composed of delegates from the affiliated unions and local and state AFL-CIO bodies. Each national union in the federation (there were a total of 66 in 2002) provides a portion of its members' dues monies to the national headquarters, and with 13 million members in affiliated unions, the AFL-CIO can tap impressive financial resources. However, as with all federations, the use of these resources is deeply constrained by the need to hold together an organization that depends entirely on the voluntary affiliation of its members.

The decentralized structure of the labor movement ensures that the various national unions can, if they so desire, pursue a thoroughly independent path in electoral politics, even endorsing competing candidates and adopting divergent political demands. Cooperation has to be negotiated, not dictated. In the case of presidential nominating politics, this organizational structure allows three possibilities:

1. A **united front** in which the AFL-CIO throws its own organizational weight and that of each affiliated union behind a single candidate, ideally one selected well before the delegate selection process has commenced
2. A **free-for-all** in which the federation stands aside and lets each national union decide on its own which candidate (if any) to endorse, and when
3. An agreement for **collective neutrality**, in which the federation secures the agreement of all affiliated unions to endorse no candidate at all in the nominating process.

Each one of these options has been used over the last several decades and, as we shall see, each carries with it a distinctive array of costs and benefits (see table 5.1).

In the case of the free-for-all strategy, an obvious problem is that it may encourage a descent into fratricidal conflict as unions align behind competing and often antagonistic candidates. Although a more restrained and hospitable electoral competition is also possible, there is no question that a strategy that encourages unions to line up publicly behind different candidates is not conducive to labor unity. A united front, in contrast, would seem to offer organized labor the most effective form of influence. But this strategy, too, has its problems, the most intractable of which is that achieving unity behind a single candidate can be quite difficult. The labor movement is always torn by differing economic, cultural, and ideological commitments. Public employee unions have different interests than private sector unions, and the goals of private sector unions often reflect the competing industries and companies in which their members are employed. While many unions seek to restrict foreign competition, for example, others may find it unobjectionable or even desirable. With millions of workers in AFL-CIO unions, all the usual American conflicts over religion, guns, abortion, race, ethnicity, and gender come into play when unions make political endorsements. Some unions (especially those in the building trades) have a pre-

Table 5.1 Union Strategies in the Reformed Nominating Process

	Strategy		
	United Front	*Collective Neutrality*	*Free-for-All*
Years of Utilization	1984 1996 2000	1988	1972 1976 1980 1992
Key Feature	Federation-level endorsement of single candidate	Federation-led agreement for all unions to remain neutral	Federation stands aside as individual unions make their own endorsement choices
Benefits	Labor unity enhanced; labor can control outcome; winner will have ties to federation, not just national unions; demonstration effect to other politicians	Union rivalries reduced; labor makes fewer enemies; saves energies for the general election	Each union has autonomy; victor is likely to have close ties to one or more unions; presence at the convention assured
Costs	Labor is made a target of criticism; difficult to achieve unity in absence of a clear front-runner; labor may get blame for general election defeat	Each union is more likely to be split internally; labor loses all direct control over selection of nominee; does not enhance labor reputation as a power-broker	Bitter inter-union rivalries are possible; may allow a disliked candidate to slip through; winner may be beholden to only narrow section of labor movement

dominantly white male membership, with conservative cultural preferences and a willingness to consider the endorsement of Republican candidates. Other unions, especially those in the service sector or representing public employees, may have a large female or minority membership with very different cultural and political proclivities. The involvement of labor in a wide range of foreign policy issues only adds another wild card to the mix. Thus, just as the national parties find it hard to aggregate the diverse interests of American society, so too does the comparably diverse union movement find it difficult to come up with common political positions.

The story of labor's involvement in nominating politics is, therefore, as much one of managing internal discord as it is a tale of pressuring politicians or mobilizing voters. The way in which labor resolves conflict and attempts to reach unity will be determined not only by its internal procedures, but also by the rules of the nominating process, which dictate whether labor's influence will be exercised publicly or behind closed doors, across many states or in a single convention hall. To understand how changes in the rules have impacted union strategy, we must return once more to the postwar period and the moment of labor's full acceptance into the counsels of the national Democratic party.

LABOR'S INCLUSION IN THE PRE-REFORM PRESIDENTIAL NOMINATING PROCESS

The dramatic increase in the size, scope, and power of labor unionism in the 1930s and 1940s did not go unnoticed by Democratic party politicians, who eagerly sought union votes, money, and organizational resources as they engaged in fierce electoral competition with their Republican adversaries. The acquisition of these resources, however, required the nomination of Democratic candidates for office who could generate enthusiastic union support. At the presidential level, therefore, it became increasingly important to ensure that the Democratic nominee was someone acceptable to labor leaders and their members. One obvious and easy way to do this was for party leaders to consult with union officials prior to the selection of presidential and vice presidential nominees. For their part, union leaders were eager to make their views known and to squelch the candidacies of those they considered unreliable or unelectable.

The character of the mid-century presidential nominating process made the exercise of union influence fairly straightforward, requiring mainly that union leaders clearly express their preferences to the party leaders who ultimately controlled the nomination. Prior to the reforms of the 1970s, each state party was free to adopt its own procedures for selecting delegates to the national convention, with the national party providing virtually no supervision or regulation. Left to do as they pleased, state parties usually set up procedures that allowed party leaders to effectively control the selection of delegates and the subsequent behavior of those delegates at the national convention. The most popular arrangement was to organize a series of local meetings or "caucuses" in which party members would elect delegates to district or state conventions that would in turn elect delegates to the national convention. While in theory open to widespread participation, the "caucus-convention" system in practice produced delegations that were frequently controlled by one or a small number of individuals (often a governor or other high-level elected official). Even in the minority of states that adopted some kind of primary, where ordinary Democratic voters could register their preferences, party leaders were willing and able to use a variety of techniques to ensure that the actual delegation at the convention remained under their personal control. At the national convention, therefore, most of the power was concentrated among the leaders of the state delegations, who could then negotiate among themselves over the issue of which candidate would best serve the party's interests in the general election. The essence of convention decision-making was captured in journalist Theodore White's comment that the convention was "a universe in itself, a nucleus of thirty or forty tough-minded power brokers, making decisions behind closed doors."[6]

Insider bargaining of this kind was something with which union leaders were quite comfortable—they were, after all, "tough-minded power brokers" in their own right, professional bargainers who made deals with both employers and other union leaders on a daily basis. Lane Kirkland, AFL-CIO president from 1979 to 1995, described why the system was, from his perspective, decidedly advantageous for labor. There was a "tacit, invisible but real arrangement," he argued, in which "the party leaders knew that, in the general election, they needed labor to draw some of the water and hew some of the wood. The leaders of the party wanted to win. They wouldn't nominate anyone who was too offensive to the trade union movement."[7] This arrangement "was a collective bargaining relationship, in effect: the key people involved in the process would discuss with us the acceptability of various candidates. A relative handful of people exercised a profound influence on the process."[8] While union leaders could not always ensure the nomination of their first choice, Kirkland acknowledged, they knew that party leaders would listen to their concerns, anticipate their reactions, and avoid choosing a candidate they actively disliked. Because of this, union influence was mainly exercised behind the scenes, either in negotiations with party leaders before the convention or in the intense interactions at the convention itself. The union leaders with the most influence in this system were those who made the greatest effort to be heard, and these were typically the representatives of the larger unions that cared most deeply about national political outcomes. The president of the AFL-CIO, in contrast, would frequently play a secondary role, secure in the knowledge that whatever choice the convention made would already have incorporated the preferences of the most important union leaders.

A distinctive feature of this arrangement was that the scale of union involvement was generally kept well hidden from both the general public and the union membership. Even as union leaders actively pushed their favored candidates, they were careful to issue denials that they were playing any role at all in the party's internal deliberations. In the midst of the 1960 Democratic nominating contest, for example, United Auto Workers President Walter Reuther would publicly proclaim that "the UAW has not—nor will we—endorse a candidate for the presidential nomination of any party. This is properly the responsibility of the delegates who make up the conventions of both parties."[9] Yet, at almost the same time, the *Washington Post* was reporting that at the Democratic convention Reuther had "played the key role for the Kennedy forces. Although technically neutral, he quietly quarterbacked a campaign for Kennedy in his hotel suite. The Michigan delegation delivered 42 votes to Kennedy, which helped put him over the top."[10] As this episode suggests, in the old nominating system the leaders of the national unions could operate behind a facade of formal neutrality, enjoying a remarkable degree of autonomy from their own membership and even secondary leaders within their own organization; the power and autonomy of the AFL-CIO president, should he choose to exercise it, was equally privileged. This kind of informal and unpublicized influence rarely required the mobilization of even a portion of the rank-and-file membership, nor did it require the expenditure of a large quantity of union financial and organizational resources. This was truly influence on the cheap.

There was, however, a danger in this system that only a severe political crisis would make evident. What would happen if large numbers of Democratic party voters—including rank-and-file union members and lower-level union activists—began to develop strong preferences about the selection of the party nominee that were divergent from those of the union leadership? Would those preferences be taken into account? And if they were not, what would be the consequences? In the hothouse conditions of the late 1960s, it was precisely this possibility that would soon be realized, with momentous consequences for both organized labor and the rules of American politics.

1968: THE LAST HURRAH OF A "BOSSED" CONVENTION

The old system of elite brokerage would finally be destroyed as a result of the profoundly disruptive forces unleashed in the presidential nominating process of 1968. The most important stimulant to change was, of course, the Vietnam War, which had produced a fierce movement in opposition by the beginning of 1968. The raging energy of the movement was channeled into support for the candidacy of Minnesota Senator Eugene McCarthy, who launched a challenge to President Lyndon Johnson for the Democratic nomination. When McCarthy did unexpectedly well in the March 12 New Hampshire primary, suggesting that Johnson might actually be vulnerable, Senator Robert Kennedy also threw his hat in the ring. Then, just two weeks later, on March 31, an embattled President Johnson surprised everyone by withdrawing from the race altogether. With only the two insurgents—Kennedy and McCarthy—left as announced candidates, the more "establishment" forces in the party, including most of organized labor, now found themselves without a candidate of their own. Deeply satisfied with the policies of Lyndon Johnson, most union leaders wanted to see the selection of an electable Democratic nominee who would defend the prevailing liberal order in Washington: neither Kennedy nor McCarthy—each unpredictable and provocative in his own way—seemed likely to fit the bill.

At this point, the leadership of the labor federation decided to act. AFL-CIO President George Meany, a powerful and even domineering figure who led the federation from 1955 to 1979, moved quickly to encourage Vice President Humphrey, a loyal friend of labor and a favorite of other party leaders, to announce his own candidacy for the nomination. As Meany later boasted: "Lane [Kirkland] and I went over to see Hubert Humphrey and got him to agree he would run."[11] Meany also issued an AFL-CIO press release stating: "We . . . strongly urge that Vice President Hubert Humphrey declare himself now as a candidate for the presidency."[12] Although the use of "we" implied an official organizational commitment, Meany's announcement was not in any way the product of formal procedures or deliberation within the federation. Meany chose to endorse Humphrey and to actively oppose the antiwar candidacies of Senators Kennedy and McCarthy, well before the electability of any of these candidates or their appeal to union members had been properly tested in caucuses or primaries.

The danger here for Meany was that he could be getting out ahead of not only union members, but also of other union leaders, who were slowly growing skeptical about the seemingly endless involvement in Vietnam. As the *Washington Post*'s David Broder observed, "Never before has the national labor federation become so openly involved at so early a stage in the fight for the Democratic presidential nomination."[13] At a time of great controversy, Meany was now leading the federation into a very public endorsement of a candidate who may well have been the second-choice of a large number of unionists. Moreover, Meany's own personal role was easily eclipsing that of the individual national union presidents who had in previous nominating contests typically been the main voice of labor. While Meany's reputation as the "unchallenged strong man of American labor" (as one journalist put it) was no doubt enhanced, the AFL-CIO leader was coming perilously close to overstepping his role as the leader of a *federation* of formally equal sovereigns.[14]

Despite such risks, Meany and the AFL-CIO went about promoting the vice president's nomination the old-fashioned way, pulling strings behind the scenes in elite party circles around the country. Entering the race on April 27, Humphrey chose not to enter a single primary, instead working with labor to secure the support of the party leaders who actually controlled the delegate votes at the convention. AFL-CIO Secretary-Treasurer Lane Kirkland described the federation's role: "I was involved with others in putting together a committee—a labor committee—for Hubert Humphrey. . . . Labor was instrumental in rounding up the delegate votes to get him nominated. We didn't do that by participating in primary elections. . . . But in the non-primary states, we rounded up most of the votes."[15] Humphrey himself credited labor with doing critical work for his campaign, and Theodore White concluded that the AFL-CIO delivered the delegations of Pennsylvania, Maryland, Michigan, and Ohio—accomplishments that made it unlikely that anyone could have defeated Humphrey at the August convention.[16] As it turned out, the assassination of Robert Kennedy on June 5 (the very night of his victory in the California primary) made Humphrey's nomination a virtual certainty.

When the delegates finally met in Chicago, labor officials continued to smooth the way for the vice president; the *Wall Street Journal* reported: "Mr. Humphrey has no more important ally at this convention than labor. . . . The unions are the Vice President's bedrock of support."[17] Working closely with the Humphrey campaign, the AFL-CIO's political director used union delegates, spread across forty-four state delegations, to gather political intelligence and help control the unruly convention floor. Blocked by organized labor and the rest of the party establishment, the antiwar forces led by Eugene McCarthy failed to significantly shift the foreign policy commitments of the Democratic party, just as Meany and top AFL-CIO officials had hoped. The voice of opposition to the war would ultimately find greater expression in the streets of Chicago, where outraged protestors clashed with local police (themselves employees of the powerful Democratic machine controlled by Mayor Richard J. Daley). The hapless Hubert Humphrey would pay the cost for this debacle, as it no doubt helped Richard Nixon to eke out his victory over the vice president in the November election.

In so effectively containing the antiwar insurgency, however, the federation and its traditional party allies had perhaps succeeded too well. With Robert Kennedy dead and Eugene McCarthy pushed to the margins, the antiwar forces felt they now had little voice in the affairs of the national Democratic party. In response, they raised numerous complaints about delegate selection procedures around the country, which they characterized as controlled by unelected party officials and as totally inaccessible to ordinary Democratic voters. In Pennsylvania, for example, McCarthy won the primary by a wide margin, but under the state party's rules was entitled to only a small fraction of the actual delegates, the vast majority going instead to Vice President Humphrey. Repeated episodes of this nature, inevitable under party rules that gave more weight to the views of elected party leaders than those of primary voters, were seen as fundamentally unfair by the "disenfranchised" supporters of the "New Politics." In response to these complaints, and in the hope of securing party unity for the general election, the convention agreed to establish a new party committee to study delegate selection procedures and suggest improvements: the age of party reform was about to begin.

PARTY REFORM AND THE NEW LOGIC OF PRESIDENTIAL SELECTION

While the antiwar forces of 1968 were snubbed by labor and the party establishment, they soon had a taste of revenge when they gained a commanding influence over the party's new Commission on Party Structure and Delegate Selection (also known as the McGovern-Fraser Commission after its first chair, Sen.

George McGovern, and his eventual successor, Rep. Don Fraser). The commission's report, issued in 1970, proposed that each state party follow a set of "guidelines" for delegate selection prepared by the national party. States that did not follow these rules would not have their delegations accepted at the national convention. Starting in 1972, the national party agreed, delegates would have to be chosen either through primary elections or at caucuses that were publicly announced and open to all party members who wished to participate. The old procedures that had made it easy for state party leaders to control the delegate selection process from the top down were now officially proscribed. In response to the new rules, states opened up previously closed convention systems or, in many cases, simply switched to primaries, which were easier to understand and unambiguously met the demands of reform. The ensuing increase in the number of primaries, from 17 in 1968 to 23 in 1972 and then to 29 in 1976, meant that the nominating process moved from a system where primaries played only a limited role—mainly serving as a test of a candidate's popularity and campaigning skills—to one where they were of crucial importance in allocating delegate votes at the national convention. The task for candidates also changed: instead of obtaining the support of key party leaders, the goal was to mobilize lots of supporters to attend caucuses or to vote in primary elections. The valued skills were now public campaigning and mass mobilization, not elite bargaining and personal persuasion. Without much fanfare, the incentives of the nominating system for both candidates and interest groups had been thoroughly transformed.

The adoption of these procedures meant that the old system of convention-based elite brokerage could no longer function as it had previously, and that labor would eventually be forced to adjust its strategy. If union leaders hoped to exercise power within the new system, they would have to systematically influence outcomes in caucuses and primaries, either by sending their own members to the polls or by altering the preferences of other constituencies. While the allocation of union financial and organizational resources would undoubtedly be helpful, the most fundamental need of candidates was for the support of groups that could bring out their members to vote in a predictable fashion. One consequence was that if the union membership was significantly divided or even opposed to the leadership's choice, this fact would now have immediate political effects: the members could support a different candidate in primaries or caucuses. In addition, the candidates themselves could make appeals directly to union members in their capacity as primary voters, thus bypassing those union leaders who would otherwise be accepted as the sole brokers for labor's electoral and organizational resources; inevitably, the autonomy of union officials was reduced.

Having utilized the old system so effectively in 1968, the AFL-CIO leadership saw virtually nothing of value in any of the reform initiatives. As far as President Meany and his allies were concerned, the established procedures had done a fine job of selecting electable and friendly presidential nominees—there was no need to change them! But in an astonishing case of political misjudgment, the AFL-

CIO encouraged its representative on the McGovern-Fraser Commission to boy-cott its meetings altogether rather than make a principled defense of the existing system. The decision proved to be a major miscalculation, as the commission eventually issued a report calling for the dismantling of the old procedures. AFL-CIO operatives did recognize the dangers in the reform effort, but assumed they would be able to block any inimical changes at a later stage. To their surprise, however, they were soon outmaneuvered in party councils, and the reforms were quickly adopted nationally and implemented at the state level. In what one scholar has called a "quiet revolution," the old and easy ways of elite negotiation were now rendered inoperable.[18]

While the AFL-CIO's opposition to reform was intense and bitter, a number of labor unions concluded that party reform—and the more open nominating procedures that it would create—could ultimately have beneficial consequences for both the Democratic party and organized labor. The political director of the United Auto Workers (UAW), for example, actually served on the McGovern-Fraser Commission, and local UAW members testified in favor of reform at com-mission hearings around the country. The UAW was joined in this support by the Communications Workers of America, the International Association of Machinists, and the American Federation of State, County and Municipal Employees (AFSCME)—three large and very powerful organizations. The pro-reform unions, composed mainly of industrial workers or service and public sec-tor employees, had a strong commitment to the advancement of liberal policies at the national level, including civil rights, labor law reform, and the expansion of the welfare state in all its forms. They were sympathetic to reform because they believed that institutional renovation could help channel the energy of the new protest movements directly into the party, expanding the ranks of its sup-porters and encouraging the unity of the Democratic coalition. Reforms could also improve the quality of representation for individual union members, who might find direct participation in party affairs much easier than ever before.

President Meany and his allies had different interests, and a correspondingly different vision of the most appropriate political strategy. Meany's strongest base of support was among the building trades unions (Meany himself had begun his career as a member of the plumbers' union), organizations that traced their lin-eage back to the conservative craft unions that had originally founded the AFL in the 1880s. These unions were mainly focused on local politics, for policies decided at this level—zoning laws, the distribution of city contracts, licensing and apprenticeship statutes, police behavior during strikes, etc.—had the most impact on their immediate well-being. The first impulse of these unions was to ally with Democratic "machine" politicians in the big cities who could fulfill union demands at the local level. They had little interest in the plans for broad social reform, welfare state expansion, and economic regulation that were advanced by the industrial and public employee unions. Beyond these economic concerns, the construction unions were composed of workers who were likely to be culturally conservative and disdainful of the movements of the 1960s that challenged existing attitudes toward sexuality, race, and patriotism: they had nothing but contempt for the protestors who had rallied outside the Chicago convention. Although Meany was considerably more liberal than most building trades leaders when it came to issues of economic policy, he shared their resentment of those forces that now threatened the political arrangements that, in his view, had served the working man quite well. Thus, by 1970 the labor movement was increasingly divided about how to respond to the new social movements in the Democratic party and the institutional reforms they so assiduously pursued.

1972–1980: LABOR DISUNITY AND FRAGMENTATION

The political conflicts of the 1960s that fractured the Democratic party were, by the early 1970s, also dividing the labor movement itself, as unionists found themselves increasingly torn over how to respond to the Vietnam War, political reform, and cultural change. The extent to which the labor movement, like so many institutions in American society at this time, was internally conflicted would only become clear in its response to the Democratic party's selection of South Dakota Senator George McGovern as its presidential nominee in 1972. McGovern, who had briefly served as chair of the Democrats' party reform commission, stunned most observers by winning the Democratic party presidential nomination against the wishes of most of the party leaders and interest group leaders who, in earlier years, would have been able to block his bid and install their own choice. Mobilizing the same political forces that had been excluded four years before—opponents of the war in Vietnam, youthful liberal activists, reformers of all stripes—McGovern was able to obtain the nomination by appealing to party voters in primaries and in the newly open and more participatory caucuses. Delegates selected in this manner arrived at the convention already pledged to McGovern, rather than remaining open to persuasion as events at the convention unfolded. In achieving this victory, McGovern had effectively bypassed not only the party establishment but the labor movement as well, and he now had no real political debts to these ancient forces. By winning the nomination in a new way, McGovern had demonstrated unequivocally that the amended rules of the system had fundamentally changed presidential politics.

McGovern was able to achieve his victory partially because of the unwillingness of both the AFL-CIO and the national unions to devote substantial resources to mobilizing their own membership and other voters in support of an alternative candidate. As the 1972 contest began, the field included several politicians who had established long records of productive cooperation with the labor leadership. Former Vice President Humphrey, now serving as a senator from his home state of Minnesota, was again a contender, as were Senators Henry "Scoop" Jackson from Washington and Edmund Muskie of Maine. Any one of the three would have been preferred by most labor leaders over McGovern, who was widely seen as too liberal and incapable of uniting the party effectively for the general election. But the federation's top officials were still entranced by the logic of the old power broker role that they had been playing for decades. Rather than quickly adapt to the demands of the new system by investing serious quantities of money, time, and effort into organizing union voters to turn out in caucuses or primaries, union leaders instead relied on personal contacts with state party leaders and the mere announcement of their preferences. Needless to say, these techniques would have little real impact on a race where voter mobilization was key. Like the party "regulars" who watched in dismay as McGovern accumulated more and more delegates, the AFL-CIO and national union leadership simply failed to adjust. In the aftermath, the *Wall Street Journal* quoted a Democratic political operative who concluded: "Labor let a bunch of long hairs and college kids beat them. . . . The new rules ruined the unions—absolutely ruined them."[19] While the assessment was overdrawn, the fact remained: for the first time in many decades, labor had lost most of its influence over the Democratic nominating process.

The selection of McGovern was achieved, then, with almost no support from individual labor unions and against the strong preferences of the AFL-CIO leadership, which tried whatever maneuvers it could to block McGovern at the convention (all to no avail). This hostility was so great that George Meany chose soon after the convention to encourage the entire labor movement to stay neutral in the upcoming general election contest between McGovern and incumbent President Richard Nixon. Under great pressure from Meany, the AFL-CIO Executive Council chose to do the virtually unthinkable, and voted (by 27 to 3) to remain officially neutral in the general election contest. In justifying the decision, Meany accused McGovern of being weak on national security, unreliable in his political commitments, and disrespectful of the union leadership. He also criticized McGovern for being too close to the social movements of the 1960s, whose cultural innovations on issues of drugs, sexuality, and patriotism were deeply offensive to Meany's conservative cultural sensibilities. But another, and perhaps more important, reason for Meany's hostility went unmentioned: the unique route that McGovern took to the nomination itself. AFSCME President Jerry Wurf would make the point clearly in 1972: "The Executive Council vote had more to do with how McGovern won the nomination than with his record before or during the campaign. . . . The real concern was participation and access, the AFL-CIO's vested interests which ignored the rich opportunities for workers and their unions in the more open, 'new' party."[20] A McGovern operative had reached a similar conclusion earlier in the campaign: "The one thing the AFL-CIO can't forgive McGovern for is the one thing he can't do anything about: if he's nominated, he won't owe them anything."[21]

Indeed, Meany and his aides clearly felt that the party needed to be punished for the "crime" of party reform. Neutrality would teach the Democratic party a lesson for not having properly consulted the labor leadership, they suggested, and force party leaders to initiate a rollback of the reforms and the reinclusion of labor on the old terms. The AFL-CIO's political director angrily lashed out at party leaders who aligned with McGovern: "You so-called responsible leaders of this party seem to think the kids and the kooks and the Bella Abzugs can win you some elections. Well, we're going to let them try to do it for you this year."[22] The problem with this strategy, however, was that teaching "party elites" a "lesson" would be of little consequence when the elites themselves had lost much of their control over the rules of the nominating process. The relatively easy passage and implementation of party reform prior to the 1972 convention suggested that the capacity of party leaders to return to the old system was highly circumscribed; a strategy that assumed they would do so in order to please organized labor always contained a strong element of wishful thinking.

Not only was the decision to remain neutral based on erroneous strategic premises, it was also reckless in its disregard for the views of union leaders and members who intended to support McGovern regardless of the Executive Council's decision. The lopsided vote for neutrality in the council made it appear that Meany had brought the entire labor leadership along behind him, but in truth the decision was widely unpopular. In keeping with the "federal" principles underlying the entire structure of the AFL-CIO, the neutrality policy was officially binding only on the federation itself and its local and state branches, and did not preclude independent action in support of McGovern by the affiliated national unions. In this context, dissatisfaction and anger with the neutrality decision soon spawned a separate campaign on McGovern's behalf by more than forty national unions, mainly from industrial and public employee backgrounds, and representing nearly half the union members in the AFL-CIO. These unions had traditionally been among the most politically active in the labor movement, regularly providing large amounts of money, staff, and volunteers to campaigns. As their anger with Meany's decision grew, several of them—including such powerhouses as the Communication Workers, Machinists, and AFSCME—took the extreme step of cutting off their financial support to the AFL-CIO's main political arm, the Committee on Political Education (COPE). Joseph Beirne, president of the Communication Workers, summarized the complaints of the dissident union leaders about the system of political brokerage that had developed under Meany's leadership:

> I withdrew from COPE because it was out of touch with what was happening in the political process—with the reforms which I think were a natural evolution in the Democratic Party, and with McGovern who was the candidate who had done the most for the working man. COPE must be changed. We who contribute to it have no control over it or participation in its policy decisions. The COPE leaders live in the dreams of the past, where they wheeled and dealed in politics. The Executive Council of the AFL-CIO should be reformed, too. All we do there is endorse candi-

dates and nothing else. Our union now feels we can make our own political decisions and spend our money more fruitfully by going it alone.[23]

The logic of reform, it seems, can be catching. As Beirne's lament reveals, it was not just long-haired antiwar protestors who were fed up with the old nominating process and the unaccountable role that party elites, including the AFL-CIO president, increasingly played within it. Major parts of the union leadership itself were also deeply dissatisfied, outraged at the AFL-CIO leadership's lack of accountability to the rest of the labor movement and the autocratic character of its maneuvers in party politics. The dissident unions thus chose to enlarge their own political machinery, allotting more money and personnel to this function than ever before; the result was a greatly expanded capacity to follow their own path in party politics. The significance of this new independence would be on full display in 1974, when the Democratic party held a special mid-term convention to approve a new national charter and consider other party business. The old-guard AFL-CIO leadership under Meany's command arrived at the party gathering determined to roll back the McGovern-Fraser reforms, but had their plans dashed when the liberal unions spoke out forcefully against their proposed changes and chose to ally with the forces defending the new nominating system.[24] As this episode confirmed, the consequence of Meany's effort to maintain a system of elite brokerage was a backlash within the labor movement that only weakened his power further. From this point on, if the labor movement was to endorse a single candidate in the presidential primaries, it would have to do so on the basis of a genuine *consensus* among union leaders, not the peremptory declarations of the federation president. As with the bossed conventions themselves, the days of a boss-run labor movement were now over.

With both power and capabilities now more widely dispersed within the labor movement, unity around a single candidate would prove highly difficult in 1976 and even in 1980, when incumbent Democratic president Jimmy Carter was running for reelection. A key feature of the new nominating process was that effectiveness within it required the early and *public* endorsement of candidates, followed up by major expenditures of time, money, and effort to mobilize union members and others to the polls. This was problematic for union leaders in that it forced them to pick and choose among a field of candidates that, ideally, would include many friends of organized labor. The public nature of these endorsements could not only alienate important politicians with whom one would have to bargain in the future, but it also encouraged conflict and even bitterness among labor unions aligned behind different candidates. But unless the unions could all agree on a single candidate early in the process (a united front strategy), or agree to endorse no one (collective neutrality), they would inevitably be left with a free-for-all in which egos would be bruised and competitive instincts unpleasantly aroused.

These considerations all came to the fore as unions debated what to do in the

1976 presidential nominating competition. The union leaders who had chosen to spurn the AFL-CIO's demand for neutrality in 1972 and to mobilize separately on behalf of McGovern discovered that they had enjoyed the experience of running their own political operation. Determined to avoid a repeat of the 1972 debacle, they now decided to enter the primaries and caucuses in a major way. A coalition of nine of these unions, now calling themselves the "Labor Coalition Clearinghouse," was established before the election season in order to coordinate involvement in the upcoming nominating campaign. While they hoped to make a unified endorsement of a single candidate, this plan was dashed when confronted with the unusually large field (including five U.S. senators, five governors, and one member of the House of Representatives) drawn out by the prospect of an especially good year for the Democrats in the aftermath of the Watergate scandal. Unable to agree on a first choice, the coalition defaulted back to a free-for-all strategy, united only by a strong commitment to make their presence known in the caucuses and primaries. At a minimum, the coalition unions hoped to guarantee a large union presence at the convention and good ties with whomever emerged as the nominee.

Several unions were attracted to a little-known southern governor, Jimmy Carter of Georgia. The influential leader of the UAW, Leonard Woodcock, saw Carter as a candidate capable of both winning the South for the Democrats and effectively blocking the presidential aspirations of Alabama Governor George C. Wallace. Woodcock's support was crucial in the Iowa caucuses, where autoworker activists and members showed up in large numbers, helping Carter win an important early victory. In the Florida primary, Woodcock also personally campaigned for Carter and strongly urged the state's large community of UAW retirees to support Carter's bid for the nomination. For his part, Carter consulted closely with UAW officials in the development of his position on national health insurance and several other policy issues. The public employees' union, AFSCME, also made an early endorsement of Carter, and mobilized volunteers in the crucial Florida primary. The support of these two powerful unions, as well as that of local unions in many other states, meant that Carter had established a solid linkage with at least part of the labor movement well before he actually won the nomination.

His ties with the AFL-CIO leadership, however, were to form much later, and in less auspicious circumstances. President George Meany announced early on that the federation would remain neutral in the nominating competition. "The biggest reason for staying out of the primaries is that you're forced to pick and choose among your many friends if you don't," said his political director.[25] Despite such proclamations, the AFL-CIO leadership and the building trades unions were soon making a major effort to help their own favored candidate, Washington Senator Henry "Scoop" Jackson. The senator was an attractive choice because of his virulent anti-communism, strong support for liberal social programs and economic policies, and, not least of all, his outspoken opposition to the party's reform wing. But the old-guard politicos in the AFL-CIO had still not really learned the lessons of the new nominating system. Their efforts to promote Jackson in primaries in Massachusetts, Pennsylvania, and New York all foundered when the federation leadership abjectly failed to orchestrate a sufficient mobilization of union voters. After this ill-conceived intervention, the AFL-CIO would lose all influence in the nominating struggle in 1976, and would only come to endorse Carter after he had officially won the nomination and was preparing for the general election contest.

The record in 1976 was, in summary, one of only partial adjustment to the new system. While the Labor Coalition Clearinghouse unions had not been able to maximize their influence through a united front, their free-for-all strategy did allow good ties with the eventual nominee, a significant role in some primaries, and a notable union presence at the convention. Moreover, the Coalition unions had learned more about how to work through the reformed system and, by successfully mobilizing their members, had enhanced their reputation and credibility among Democratic politicians. In contrast, the AFL-CIO as a distinct organization was still "out of it": unable to forcefully intervene in primaries and caucuses (partially because it lacked its own distinct membership base) and left in a basically marginal role until the general election rolled around. One consequence of this pattern of union involvement was revealed in Carter's allegiances once ensconced in Washington: for most of his presidency he would be more closely aligned with a few leaders of various national unions (such as those of teachers, public employees, and auto workers) than he was with the top leaders of the federation. This estrangement from a major part of the labor movement (exacerbated, to be sure, by labor's own robust internal divisions) was a significant factor in diminishing the quality of his relationship with the labor movement as a whole, and was clearly a contributory factor to the larger problems of his presidency.[26]

The 1980 election brought forth yet more evidence that the unions were having great difficulty in forging a coordinated strategy in presidential nominating politics. While one might have expected that the renomination of a sitting president would have united both party and union elites in near-unanimity, Carter's difficult record as president ensured a great deal of labor dissatisfaction. Angry at Carter for failing to deliver labor law reform or more liberal social and economic policies, many unions were drawn to the candidacy of Massachusetts Senator Edward M. Kennedy, who hoped to displace the president as the Democratic nominee. Among the unions that formally endorsed Kennedy were such powerful organizations as AFSCME, the International Association of Machinists (then led by a fiery self-declared socialist), the Service Employees International Union, and the American Federation of Teachers. Despite these and other union endorsements, Kennedy ultimately failed to secure the sweeping support within labor that he needed; with the movement deeply split, the efforts of the pro-Kennedy unions could not overcome the inherent liabilities of their candidate and the impressive strengths of an incumbent president. As it turned out, Kennedy's failed campaign, in which so many unions played a major role, mainly had the effect of weakening Carter further as he faced the potent (and exceptionally conservative) challenge posed by Ronald Reagan.

After Carter's decisive defeat in the general election, the labor leadership could look back and assess the three nominating contests that had now taken place under the new rules. In 1972, the party had nominated an unelectable candidate with a bad relationship with large parts of the labor movement. In 1976, most of the movement ended up sitting on the sidelines as the party chose an outsider who had little natural affinity with the labor leadership. This candidate won the general election, but then proceeded to govern in a manner that unionists found frustrating and unimpressive. In 1980, the labor movement split right down the middle over Senator Kennedy's candidacy, and was neither strong enough to displace President Carter nor united enough to squash the Kennedy challenge in the first place. The question this history posed was obvious: Could there be a better way for unions to operate in the nominating system? Was there a way for labor to coordinate and plan union interventions so that a mainstream, pro-labor, and electorally effective candidate could prevail?

1984: LABOR MANIPULATES THE REFORMED SYSTEM

The development of a new strategy for labor in presidential nominating politics was enhanced by the resignation in 1979 of the old war-horse George Meany, whose obstreperous character had often stood in the way of both compromise and innovation, and his replacement as AFL-CIO president by the less colorful but far more conciliatory figure of Lane Kirkland, a longtime official in the federation with deep experience in national politics. Long a witness to labor's difficulties in navigating the reformed system, Kirkland was as intent as anyone on coming up with a better strategy for both the federation and its affiliated unions. At his direction, the AFL-CIO began to gingerly pursue the possibility of securing some modest changes in the rules of the current nominating process. Although the AFL-CIO and party establishment had long recognized that a full rollback of the reforms was impossible, changing political currents suggested that the adjustment of a few key elements was no longer a pipe dream. It was this hope that animated union involvement in the Hunt Commission—a new Democratic party commission (formally known as the Commission on Presidential Nomination) that was set up to take yet another look at party rules and the delegate selection process.

Chaired by Gov. James B. Hunt, Jr., of North Carolina, the commission succeeded in winning approval for a set of incremental changes, beginning in 1984, that were intended to increase the power of party "regulars" and to advantage mainstream candidates. With UAW President Douglas Fraser serving as one of two vice-chairs, and 15 of the 70 members associated with organized labor, the views of union leaders were well-represented in the commission's deliberations—a marked change from the situation in the previous decade, when the AFL-CIO had effectively boycotted such forums.[27] The re-engagement of the labor establishment with the reform process would bear fruit in two areas of change. First, about 14 percent of the convention delegates would now be composed of a new class of unpledged "super-delegates," mainly party officials and elected officeholders, who would, it was widely believed, help nominate a more electable, traditional Democrat. Second, an effort was made to help front-running candidates by relaxing the system of proportional representation that in previous years had allowed candidates with little support to go on accumulating delegates long after it was clear they had no chance of actually winning the nomination. To rectify this problem, the commission voted to prevent candidates that received less than 20 percent of the vote in a particular state or congressional district from receiving any delegate representation at all from those locales—a change that made continued campaigning a rather quixotic enterprise. At the same time, the commission made it easier for states to use a variety of procedures to award extra delegates to the candidate who came in first among Democratic voters. While small in scale, these changes were lauded by union leaders who desperately wanted to see the party unite early in the nominating process around an electable candidate with mainstream political affiliations.

But Lane Kirkland had a far more ambitious plan up his sleeves than a mere tweaking of party rules. The idea had long been floated in both union and academic circles that the new nominating system might actually *enhance* union power if the labor movement were to unify around a single candidate and then mobilize on his or her behalf even a fraction of its vast 13-million membership. It was this argument that led Kirkland and others to begin considering an official AFL-CIO endorsement of a candidate for the Democratic nomination (something that had never been done before, notwithstanding George Meany's informal role in promoting Hubert Humphrey in 1968). Kirkland argued that the involvement of unions in primaries had revealed "a pattern that . . . was damaging to the internal solidarity of the trade union movement. With a premium on early and active participation in support of a prospective candidate, different parts of the trade union movement went for various candidates without consultation among themselves . . . So you had the development of factionalism, with unions competing with and vilifying each other."[28] The obvious solution was for the federation to forge an agreement—a united front—in support of a single candidate. This initiative would simultaneously improve labor unity and enhance union power over the final outcome. Kirkland observed: "If we are not in it, if we wait until the convention is over, then we are stuck with other people's choices one more time. Why should we be stuck with other people's choices—particularly if it coughs up candidates who are not saleable?"[29]

With such calculations in mind, the Executive Council in 1982 approved a plan for a unified federation endorsement in the 1984 nominating campaign. A key component of the plan was a provision that no candidate would be endorsed unless he attained the support of unions representing at least two-thirds of the total AFL-CIO rank-and-file membership—a stipulation that made an endorsement more difficult but ensured that the labor movement would go into the process with a high level of unity. Faced with this requirement, the first challenge for union leaders was to somehow converge on one candidate among a large field of announced aspirants for the nomination. The possible choices for labor included former Florida Governor Reuben Askew, Senators Alan Cranston, John Glenn, Gary Hart, and Ernest Hollings, former Vice President Walter Mondale, the Reverend Jesse Jackson, and, rather improbably, former presidential nominee George McGovern. Several of these politicians had long and impressive records of support for traditional labor issues. As fortune would have it, however, the implementation of the plan was eased by the fact that the clear front-runner for the Democratic nomination, Walter Mondale, was also a longtime friend of the labor movement. Mondale was pro-labor, an experienced campaigner, and favored by many party officials, Democratic officeholders, and liberal interest groups. Moreover, union leaders reported that their own internal surveys and straw poll meetings showed strong membership support for Mondale over such rivals as Senators Glenn and Hart. While it was possible that Mondale could win the nomination even without an AFL-CIO endorsement, union leaders were not in a mood to leave anything to chance: on October 1, 1983, the representatives of AFL-CIO's affiliated unions voted by an overwhelming majority to give Mondale their support.

As both union leaders and Mondale operatives were well aware, there were three distinct perils inherent in the federation's move. First, it was likely that Mondale would be publicly tagged as the "big labor" candidate and possibly suffer corresponding electoral damage. For their part, Mondale's advisers dismissed these concerns, arguing that since Mondale would be characterized as an errand boy for the unions even without the endorsement, it made sense to seek and accept the benefits that it would bring. Second, an endorsement of a single candidate meant that other candidates would have little reason to avoid attacks on the AFL-CIO itself. This problem was manifested shortly after the endorsement decision was announced, when Senators Hart and Glenn as well as Rev. Jesse Jackson attacked the AFL-CIO endorsement as an undemocratic decision by union "bosses."[30] Third, and most pressing, there was the risk that the AFL-CIO and its affiliated unions would fail to deliver the promised resources. As one union leader noted: "If we are, in fact, a paper tiger, we certainly are going to be making that clear."[31]

Despite these challenges, the labor movement proved by most measures quite capable of providing highly beneficial assistance to its chosen candidate. Most important, labor protected its choice from some very serious electoral competition. Senator Gary Hart did surprisingly well in early primaries, winning a surprise victory in New Hampshire and suddenly threatening to steal the nomination away from the presumptive front-runner. It was organized labor that became the crucial force in derailing Hart's campaign in the later primaries, as well as in squelching the aspirations of Jesse Jackson. Two academic observers noted: "Labor's endorsement of and activities on behalf of Mondale were an influential—and probably essential—factor in his nomination. Mondale won seven of the 10 states with the largest blocks of AFL-CIO affiliated unionists, including New York, Pennsylvania, Illinois, Michigan, and New Jersey."[32] Even in the South, where unions have historically been weak and small, union support proved surprisingly useful, as unionized public employees (especially school teachers) emerged as a large percentage of voters in Democratic primaries. In Alabama, for example, a state with a unionization rate of only 15 percent, nearly 30 percent of the Democratic primary voters were from union households.[33] Labor union financial assistance was also an important part of these electoral successes (though determining the exact amount spent by the unions is always difficult). While a total of $3.1 million in pro-Mondale expenditures by labor unions was officially declared, unofficial estimates placed the total monetary value of union activity in the nominating contest at well over 10 million dollars.[34] Bolstered by this robust support, Mondale succeeded in dispensing with his challengers, notwithstanding a few perilous moments on the campaign trail.

The successful installation of Mondale as the Democratic nominee proved that it was possible for organized labor to effectively utilize primaries and caucuses, thus confirming the argument that the liberal unions and other party reformers had made over a decade earlier (but which had long been resisted by the AFL-CIO establishment and its conservative allies). While critics have since argued that the unified early endorsement was foolhardy, both because it made labor itself a lightning rod for criticism and because it facilitated the nomination of a candidate who went down to a crushing defeat in November, union leaders themselves saw the endorsement as a definite success. Mondale did secure the nomination, after all, and was clearly in debt to the AFL-CIO for his victory. Moreover, labor had shown that it could defend its candidate against powerful rivals and proven this to future Democratic hopefuls: Would any be so foolish as to spurn or ignore labor demands in the future? Most important, the labor movement had avoided the fragmentation and factionalism that had been the dominant tendency in the "wild nominations" of the previous decade.[35] Lane Kirkland observed: "Our motive in taking the new approach was designed as much to find a way to maintain trade union solidarity as it was to support any particular candidate. Because this was our major motive, we were wholly successful. We supplanted factionalism and division in the unions with a high degree of solidarity."[36]

1988: AN EXPERIMENT WITH
COLLECTIVE NEUTRALITY

Given its positive evaluation of the 1984 experience, the AFL-CIO leadership gave serious consideration to orchestrating a repeat of the strategy in 1988. It soon became apparent, however, that achieving unity would be impossible in the absence of a candidate who stood out as either a uniquely close friend of labor or an especially electable one. At the beginning of the 1988 race, eight candidates were available to choose from: Massachusetts Governor Michael Dukakis, Arizona Governor Bruce Babbit, Rev. Jesse Jackson, Rep. Richard Gephardt, and Senators Gary Hart, Albert Gore, Jr., Paul Simon, and Joseph Biden. Although Hart remained anathema to most union leaders for his attacks on the AFL-CIO in 1984, most of the other candidates had their share of supporters within the labor movement. Internal polling and other forms of consultation undertaken by the AFL-CIO and the national unions suggested that the membership was itself widely dispersed in its preferences.

This dispersion of support meant that unions might end up in a mutually antagonistic free-for-all, much as they had in the contests from 1972 to 1980. In order to avoid this outcome, federation unions reached agreement prior to the 1988 campaign on a pledge that neither the AFL-CIO nor the national unions would endorse candidates or wage campaigns for them unless there was an official federation endorsement. The national unions would, however, be encouraged to have their members and leaders serve as convention delegates for the candidates of their choice. Union strategists hoped that this arrangement would lead to a significant labor presence in each candidate's delegation to the convention, yet do so without precipitating the division of the national unions into competing and hostile camps. In this respect, at least, the plan was successful. With only a few exceptions, the national union headquarters all remained formally and substantively neutral in the nominating process. A spokesman for Lane Kirkland expressed satisfaction at the outcome: "We're so proud of ourselves for staying out together, for not gutting each other as we did in the Carter-Kennedy fight of 1980."[37]

The costs of this approach, however, soon became apparent. While an agreement to avoid official union endorsements at the national level did prevent the mutual "gutting" feared by union leaders, the result of this policy was to disperse union support even more widely as activists *within the same union* ended up behind competing candidates. In the Iowa caucuses, for example, the leaders of the state branch of the United Auto Workers issued a "recommendation" that members vote for Rep. Gephardt, whose strong stance on trade issues made him a particularly attractive candidate for those employed in the manufacturing sector. Yet in the absence of an official endorsement of Gephardt, local UAW leaders were still expected to offer assistance to members who sought to become delegates for other candidates. One such leader commented: "This puts me in an awkward position: I'm for Gephardt, but I have to train Jackson people how to participate in the caucus if they ask. Instead of hammering away for one guy, we're going every which way." Naturally, such fragmentation did little to increase the bargaining power of the labor leadership at the national level. A top AFL-CIO official observed: "When you have a concentrated effort behind a single candidate, your effort generates more influence. This time we have a lot of activity, but not that concentrated influence."[38]

Notwithstanding this overall pattern, at least one union found a way of evading federation policy and arriving at the equivalent of a national endorsement. The national headquarters of AFSCME chose to encourage and coordinate the activity of its locals in support of Michael Dukakis's nomination, thereby creating a de facto national endorsement by the union. In crucial primary states, AFSCME locals rented office space to the Dukakis campaign and provided telephones and volunteers. For the Iowa caucuses, the state AFSCME assigned six full-time workers to help expand turnout through phone banks and mass mailings. Because of such efforts, some observers within the labor movement expected that AFSCME would have special access to a Dukakis administration—a result decidedly at odds with the goals that had led to the neutrality policy in the first place.

Despite the general pattern of dispersed support, union involvement did result in a very large number of union member delegates—approximately 1,000 out of a total of 4,161. This figure was, however, rather misleading. In the reformed nominating system, a large union presence at the convention provides notable bragging rights and can be of relevance when it comes to the writing of the party platform, but in truth the actual identity of the delegates is of little importance: they might as well be robots for all the autonomy they are actually allowed in convention decision-making. The sizable union presence at the convention could not disguise the fact that in the absence of a clear front-runner in party circles, the labor movement had found it impossible to unify in support of a single choice. Looking on the bright side, the Dukakis campaign's labor liaison would argue: "In 1984, we exhausted people financially and psychologically in the primaries. This time they haven't spent their resources and they are ready to go."[39] But while labor may have been energized for the fall campaign, with the nomination of Michael Dukakis the union movement was saddled with a Democratic candidate who simply did not generate much enthusiasm among union leaders, activists, and members (or, it would turn out, the general public). The policy of collective neutrality had prevented the outbreak of bitter warfare between the national union headquarters, but in the end labor was, as Kirkland had put it six years before, still "stuck with other people's choices."

1992: THE UNIONS CONVERGE ON CLINTON

After the defeat of the Democratic nominee in 1988, unionists were more intent than ever to see the party nominate a viable candidate in 1992. The initial field was composed of Arkansas Governor Bill Clinton, former California Governor Jerry Brown, Senators Bob Kerrey and Tom Harkin, and former Senator Paul Tsongas. With no obvious front-runner, and several candidates with good ties to labor, the usual problem of dispersed preferences within the labor movement was confronted once more. Under these circumstances, the AFL-CIO Executive Council voted to abstain from an early endorsement, and to instead let each national union make its own choice: essentially the "free-for-all" strategy that had been labor's de facto option in 1972, 1976, and 1980. While this decision allowed a large number of union members to eventually be elected as delegates to the national convention, it also opened the door to a thorough (and all too familiar) fragmentation of labor's bargaining capacity.

The candidate that initially attracted the most union backing was Senator Harkin. With his traditional New Deal message, criticisms of free trade, and advocacy of strong pro-union changes in the labor law, Harkin was supported by many industrial unions threatened by changing economic circumstances. Most unions, however, adopted a "wait and see" attitude: if Harkin did well, surviving into the later primaries held in major industrial states, they might deploy more resources on his behalf—but they were not prepared to sink vast resources into a ship that might never get out of port. As one union leader put it: "If the Democrats are going to have a chance, a candidate has to show signs of starting fire before we get behind that candidate."[40] The wisdom of such reticence was confirmed when Harkin performed poorly in New Hampshire and subsequent primaries. By mid-March, the senator had withdrawn from the race altogether.

Even before Harkin's withdrawal, however, several important unions had lined up behind Bill Clinton. The public employees in AFSCME and the American Federation of Teachers (AFT) offered endorsements in January 1992, as did the Hotel and Restaurant Employees and the Retail, Wholesale, and Department Store Union. AFSCME's support was especially important, as the massive union had more than a million members and immense financial and organizational resources. Since the mid-1970s, the union had emerged as one of the most effective forces in nominating politics, with a membership highly motivated by the close relationship between the size of its pay check and the fiscal health of the public sector. The comments of an AFSCME official reveal the political calculations motivating their decision to endorse Clinton: "We believe that we need to be about winning in 1992. . . . If we went for Harkin we probably could get 90 percent of our agenda. If we went for Clinton we probably could get 85 percent of our agenda. But it's Clinton who, in my opinion, can get us to the White House."[41] The National Education Association (NEA) also endorsed Clinton early, joining with the AFT in citing Clinton's electability and his opposition to tuition tax credits for private schools. Ironically, despite his self-identification as a "new" Democrat, Clinton thus found himself aligned with large public sector unions with a strong vested interest in big government. Meanwhile, the more conservative building trades unions sat out the nominating process altogether.

As the primary season progressed, Clinton increasingly benefited from labor support. In the important New York primary on April 7, Clinton's success was attributed in large part to the mobilization of public employees by AFSCME, the NEA, and the AFT, and the activity among private sector workers by the International Ladies' Garment Workers Union and the Hotel and Restaurant Employees.[42] As Clinton went on to additional primary victories, his candidacy gained the endorsement of yet other labor organizations, including the UAW, the Service Employees International Union, and the Mineworkers. In this series of sequential endorsements, the national unions acted strategically and in conjunction with other elite actors (such as fund-raisers and elected officeholders) to unify the party around a candidate they saw as the most likely nominee, even if he had not been, for some, their first choice. At the same time, the unions were intent on blocking the candidacy of Sen. Tsongas, who had angered them by publicly opposing labor law reform proposals that had previously been backed by the vast majority of Democrats in Congress. As Clinton gained increasing support from both national unions and primary voters, the AFL-CIO also joined the bandwagon, announcing in mid-April that it would endorse the governor officially at a May 5 Executive Council meeting, some two months before the Democratic convention. While this endorsement came late, after Clinton was the all-but-certain nominee, it would nonetheless help in the process of closing ranks behind the party's new standard bearer.

In comparison to other years, then, the 1992 campaign was unusual in that labor did converge on a single candidate, but only after that candidate had been tested in the primaries and shown to be an effective campaigner. In 1984, labor had made a collective endorsement very early, while in other years the AFL-CIO had made no official endorsement in the nominating contest at all. The 1992 contest added a twist in that the AFL-CIO did make a united endorsement well before the convention, but only after the primaries had revealed the presumptive nominee. With the success of Clinton in the general election and his renomination and reelection in 1996, unions could feel confident that their most difficult days in the Democratic nominating process were now over. In 1992, the unions had converged on a single choice before it was too late, avoided deep or bitter conflicts, and helped secure the nomination of a capable and generally labor-sympathetic candidate. When the unified party sailed to victory in November, unionists felt that their role in the "new" Democratic party was about as secure as could be hoped for in a time of declining union membership and widespread conservative sentiment. Four years later, union leaders would be sufficiently satisfied with Clinton's tenure, despite continuing disagreements on trade issues, to make an official federation endorsement of his renomination and actively discourage any primary challenges from the party's more liberal constituencies.

2000: A UNITED FRONT ONCE MORE

Much as in 1984, the 2000 nomination provides a vivid example of the labor leadership acting in conjunction with other party leaders to promote a quick resolution to the nominating contest in support of the larger goal of triumph in the general election. While Al Gore had made new friends in the labor movement as vice president, he had never been a traditional labor favorite, and his support for the Clinton administration's free trade policies severely disappointed several important union leaders. In addition, other potential candidates, such as House Minority Leader Dick Gephardt, Senators Paul Wellstone, Bob Kerrey, and John Kerry, and former Senator Bill Bradley, all had labor records that were as good as or better than Gore's. Despite these reasons for doubting Gore, from the very beginning of the pre-primary maneuvering in late 1998 the AFL-CIO leadership did nothing to recruit possible rivals to the vice president. When one liberal contender—Senator Bradley—did have the temerity to throw his hat in the ring, the labor establishment did almost everything in its power to ruin his candidacy. For union leaders, the most important thing was for a Democrat to retain the White House. If this meant supporting a candidate with a disappointing record on trade issues, but who could unite the party and campaign well in the general election, then so be it. With a vast array of day-to-day interests to protect, purism was not a luxury that most union officials could afford.

Determined to bolster the early front-runner, the new AFL-CIO president, John Sweeney (elected in 1995), was resolute in his support for Gore from early 1999 onwards, and he was seconded in this support by such powerful unions as AFSCME and the Communication Workers of America.[43] Sweeney and labor's top political operatives argued strongly for an early AFL-CIO endorsement of Gore, which they argued would allow the vice president to tap the massive resources of the labor movement when they mattered most. Gore was the right choice, in their view, because he was the most likely candidate to secure the support of other key party elites and mass constituencies, and thus the most likely to emerge as the victor even without labor's endorsement. If labor could move this process along more quickly and gain credit with the eventual nominee for doing so, this was all to the good, for internal party conflict only increased the likelihood of a general election defeat. Finally, there was every reason to believe that an experienced campaigner like Gore would be an effective candidate in the general election.[44]

From the standpoint of union leaders, moreover, Gore had demonstrated that he was a reliable politician with a sincere respect for the labor movement. As vice president he had made it a point to be accessible to union leaders and had insisted that they be included in relevant deliberations in the executive branch. For the status- and protocol-conscious union leaders, this commitment alone was important and reassuring, but Gore was equally diligent in calling for enhanced legal protections of the right to organize. He strongly opposed GOP efforts to limit union political spending and enact anti-union changes in existing labor law, and he spoke in favor of the controversial Clinton-appointed National Labor Relations Board and such longtime labor favorites as Medicare and the Occupational Safety and Health Administration. In this respect, at least, Gore's credentials as a pro-labor Democrat were about as good as those of any other Democratic presidential nominee in the postwar period.[45]

Not all union leaders, however, were willing to overlook Gore's drawbacks. The biggest single cause of dissatisfaction was Gore's commitment to continuing the free trade policies of the Clinton administration. Powerful unions such as the Autoworkers, Steelworkers, Machinists, and Teamsters found Gore's trade policy detrimental to their members and tantamount to a betrayal of union interests. These concerns were, however, of far lesser importance to the growing public and service sector unions, as well as to those unions in the private sector that did not feel negatively impacted by import penetration. A second complaint was much more unnerving to other union leaders: this was the claim that Gore was simply not a very popular candidate and was unlikely to appeal to the crucial swing voters in the general election. With Texas Governor George W. Bush, the likely Republican nominee, way ahead in the polls in late 1999, and increasing signs that restive Democratic primary voters might bolt to Bradley in Iowa, New Hampshire, and elsewhere, a number of union leaders were reconsidering the wisdom of any early endorsement at all.

These concerns all came to a head as the AFL-CIO convention prepared to meet in Los Angeles in October 1999. The plan had always been to make an endorsement at this meeting, but now the convention was taking place at the very moment that Gore's candidacy was threatened by the rising popularity of Bradley. In this context, a decision even to delay the endorsement would be seen by the media and other party elites as a sign that Al Gore was in serious trouble. Conversely, a decision to endorse Gore would be seen as a strong vote of confidence and an indication that his standing with the core constituencies of the party remained strong. Gore simply had to win this AFL-CIO vote or face the danger that support for his candidacy might suddenly and thoroughly unravel.

It was, finally, John Sweeney who made the difference for the Gore campaign. Sweeney insisted that Al Gore had been there for labor over the past eight years, and that it was now time to repay him for his loyalty. A protracted nominating contest could only hurt the party in the general election, Sweeney maintained, and Bill Bradley was, in any case, no better than Gore when it came to trade issues. The AFL-CIO leader thus went all-out in support of the vice president, pressuring affiliated unions to support him in the days and hours preceding the convention. In making such an active and open commitment to Gore, Sweeney put his own reputation, and that of the federation, on the line. By making the issue one of personal loyalty and the federation's prestige, he made it all the more difficult for most union leaders to vote against an endorsement. Sweeney got the federation to this point, however, only through a long process of internal consultation and persuasion—a far cry from George Meany's issuance of a peremptory press release to announce his endorsement of Hubert Humphrey in 1968.

On October 12, 1999, the AFL-CIO convention endorsed Gore with little open dissension, and Sweeney triumphantly introduced the vice president to the assembled delegates. In his acceptance speech, Gore expressed his support for union organization in terms that were unequivocal: "I believe that the right to organize is a basic American right that should never be stopped, never be blocked, and never be taken away. Let me tell you, that right needs to be strengthened today."[46] He also promised that as president he would veto all anti-union legislation and stand firmly against any Republican efforts to "take back the country to an anti-union, anti-worker past." With such words, Gore had strayed far from his previous "New Democrat" emphasis on markets and choice as the main vehicles for social progress—a leftward tilt that he would continue in the general election and in his criticisms of the Bush presidency after January 2001.

Gore's rhetorical adjustments would be well worth it, however, as the AFL-CIO's large apparatus of money, staff, and volunteers was now swung into action to ensure Gore victories in the crucial early caucuses and primaries. For the Iowa caucuses, the AFL-CIO and other national unions sent 35 full-time organizers to the state, and made at least 30,000 phone calls to union members. The AFL-CIO worked with the Iowa State Education Association to send four separate mailings, one of which included a five-minute video promoting Gore's candidacy, to 25,000 union households. A group of political scientists studying the caucuses reported that, "The AFL-CIO and affiliated unions actually brought a tractor-trailer to Iowa City and parked it outside the Gore headquarters just off Interstate 80. Inside the trailer was a 'war room,' with computer systems, telephones, and a sophisticated phone banking plan."[47] But the most important factor was simply labor's ability to bring out volunteers and members willing to attend the caucuses for a few hours on a cold winter's night; Bradley's amateurish (albeit well-funded) campaign would pose no challenge to this kind of operation. The results were clear on caucus night, when Gore beat Bradley 63 percent to 35 percent and union caucus attendees comprised an impressive 33 percent of the turnout (in a state where only 14 percent of the workforce was unionized). Among union participants, Gore received a landslide 69 percent of the vote to Bradley's paltry 24 percent, while non-union attendees gave Gore a more restrained 57 percent to Bradley's 35 percent.

Labor was also an important force in New Hampshire, despite the low union density in the state. Union volunteers made more than 5,000 house visits and hand-delivered videos extolling Gore's "longtime support for working families." Labor's grassroots effort generated seven contacts for each union household, union leaders claimed, and was followed up in the days before the election by multiple telephone calls and yet more outreach in the form of get-out-the-vote drives. On Election Day, members of union households constituted 24 percent of the turnout (more than twice their 10.5 percent rate of representation in the state's workforce) and cast their vote 62 percent to 37 percent for Gore—crucial help in securing Gore's narrow 50 percent to 46 percent victory over Bradley.[48] With these defeats, Bradley's campaign was effectively over, and he was soon forced to withdraw. The capacity of unions to ensure that their members constituted a major fraction of the turnout in both Iowa and New Hampshire, despite a record of declining union density in both states and the nation at large, undoubtedly contributed much to the collapse of the senator's candidacy.

With Gore's successful nomination, the integration of organized labor into the national Democratic party reached a new highpoint. At the August convention, labor delegates numbered 1,500 (out of 4,368 total delegates) and were the largest single-interest-group bloc without question. President Sweeney, AFL-CIO Vice President Richard Trumka, and AFSCME President Gerald McEntee all spoke from the convention podium—a marked departure from the more discreet and behind-the-scenes role of the 1960s and earlier. And in successfully engineering the endorsement, Sweeney established himself as the unrivaled broker for the political resources of the labor movement—a fact which did not go unnoticed by Democratic politicians as they contemplated future presidential bids. The second use of a united front strategy had thus paid off in labor unity, great union influence in the nominating process, and a near-victory in the general election. With the peculiarities of Florida to blame for the general election result, there was every reason to believe that federation leaders would pursue the united front strategy again should the opportunity arise.

LOOKING TO 2004: UNITED FRONT
OR FREE-FOR-ALL?

As we approach the 2004 race, there is one prediction that can be made with certainty: organized labor will be desperate to win (i.e., elect a Democratic president), both because of the dispiriting reality of unified Republican party government at the national level following the 2002 congressional elections and because of the still-bitter feelings left by the electoral debacle in Florida that allowed George W. Bush to ascend to the presidency. In the general election we are sure to see a mobilization of union resources to rival or exceed any ever witnessed before. In the nominating process, however, the nature and magnitude of union involvement is harder to foresee. On the minds of many observers in early 2003 was this question: Will the resources of the labor movement be concentrated behind a single candidate for the nomination, as in 1984 and 2000, or will labor adopt the less challenging free-for-all or collective neutrality strategies?

In previous elections, a united front strategy was adopted only if two things were true:

1. There was a clear front-runner for the Democratic nomination as measured in some combination of opinion polls, fund-raising, and public and private endorsements.
2. The front-runner was friendly to the labor movement and trusted by its leaders.

This confluence of conditions is not commonly found in contested nominations, however, which explains the rarity of the united front option. And it is no coincidence that the two contested nominations where labor was able to use the united front strategy were races featuring *a sitting or very recent vice president.* The high status and visibility provided by the vice presidency goes far to establish a candidate as a front-runner, and provides a natural coordination point for party elites (of which labor is one) who seek common agreement on a single electable candidate as early as possible in the race. In 2000, Gore had this unique status, and used it to rally the early support of labor and other key party elites (such as fundraisers, elected officials, and interest groups). With the withdrawal of Gore in late 2002, no obvious front-runner was apparent in early 2003, and it seemed quite possible that none would emerge until much later in the year, if at all.

The most likely scenario, therefore, was a return to the somewhat tarnished free-for-all strategy used so often in the past. By the end of 2002, it was clear that the emerging field would include several candidates with a legitimate claim on labor's loyalty. Such early entrants as former House Minority Leader Dick Gephardt, Senators John Kerry, Joseph Lieberman, and John Edwards, and Governor Howard Dean of Vermont were all known figures with good to very good records on labor issues. While Gephardt had the longest and best ties with the union movement, especially with the industrial unions whose cause of "fair trade" he so strongly championed, as of January 2003 union political operatives were openly speculating that it would be very difficult for him to ever gain the two-thirds support needed for a unified federation endorsement.[49] As in previous years, a key concern for union leaders was electability. With one failed bid for the Democratic nomination behind him, and a mixed record in orchestrating Democratic efforts to retake the House of Representatives, Gephardt generated fears that he might turn out to be the Mondale of 2004: a labor favorite destined for a humiliating defeat. This anxiety, and the evident acceptability of most of the other candidates by labor's usual criteria, made it unlikely that union leaders would agree on a single choice for the nomination. Under these circumstances, and barring the emergence of a clear front-runner in 2003, the 2004 contest was shaping up to look much like 1992. In that year, a few powerful unions made early endorsements, but many others kept their powder dry, watched and waited as candidates competed in the early contests, and then closed ranks to help the emerging victor wrap things up and get ready for the general election.

Assuming that the individual unions will be in play, their endorsements will be among those most prized in the 2004 election. The unique value of union backing is best understood by considering a recent observation by a team of political scientists studying the effects of the party reforms adopted in the 1970s. By encouraging the proliferation of primaries, the authors note, the reforms meant that "seeking a presidential nomination required an active campaign in every state in the nation, often at the level of counties or congressional districts. This is a vast, vast undertaking. No presidential candidate has the staff, financial resources, or know-how to conduct what are, in effect, hundreds of campaigns all around the country."[50] While it is true that candidates may not have the resources, unions frequently do. A notable example is AFSCME, which ran the country's fourth largest political action committee (PAC) in the 1999–2000 election season and in 2003 had more than 1.3 million members.[51] Composed of well-motivated public employees located in virtually every state, the union was by any measure a highly desirable ally. It had, after all, made early endorsements (either officially or unofficially) of Carter in 1976, Dukakis in 1988, and Clinton in 1992, a track record that would certainly catch the eye of any serious Democratic hopeful. In addition, many other unions also have massive PACs and very impressive political operations. In the crucial state of Iowa, the United Auto Workers are especially influential, with a well-earned reputation for recruiting members for campaign rallies and mobilizing them to come out on a cold January night for the state's legendary caucuses. Only a profoundly foolish (or exceptionally cavalier) candidate would not want the support of these organizations, or, at a minimum, to secure their neutrality (a reality that, for example, went far to explain the pro-labor voting record of North Carolina Senator John Edwards, notwithstanding the conservative sentiments prevailing in his home state).[52]

Although labor may not adopt a united front strategy in 2004, it will still have the same deep interest in seeing the nomination wrapped up early once an acceptable candidate starts to emerge from the pack. Union leaders desire this for the same reason that elected officeholders and other party officials do: because they believe that ending the race soon, and converging upon a single favored candidate, is the best means for prevailing in the general election.[53] In this respect, at least, union leaders can be usefully thought of as actually being *part* of the party, not an "outside" interest trying to move "into" it. This partisan mentality, and the pragmatism and long-term perspective that it fosters, goes far to explain union behavior in the nominating process. In 1992, for example, most unions closed ranks expeditiously for Bill Clinton once he had demonstrated electability in the primaries, swiftly putting aside any lingering doubts about his labor record as governor of Arkansas. The analysis here predicts that unions will act the same way if given the opportunity in 2004, as long as the emerging front-runner is receptive to their institutional and policy interests. Given the undeniable capacity of unions to alter outcomes in caucuses and primaries, their endorsement decisions will provide a leading and perhaps definitive indicator of which candidate for the Democratic nomination is likely to prevail.

CONCLUSION

In the aftermath of the campaigns of 1972 and 1976, in which candidates with ambiguous ties to the labor movement were able to grasp the Democratic nomination, some authors concluded that the new primary-oriented nominating system had inherent disadvantages for organized labor.[54] The argument was that since "white-collar" Democrats were more likely to participate in caucuses and primaries than "blue-collar" Democrats, these venues would have an innate white-collar bias that would hurt traditional Democratic candidates concerned with economic issues and help those committed to "post-materialist" values like environmentalism, feminism, homosexual rights, and so on. In short, labor would get stuck with strange outsiders unsympathetic to the concerns of ordinary working people. While persuasive at first, experience has shown this analysis to seriously underestimate the capacity of unions to become "passionate factions" in their own right, mobilizing their members effectively to participate in Democratic nominating procedures. Once the unions demonstrated this capacity (with the result eventually being the "largest delegation of down-home, uptown, grassroots, kick-ass union leaders in the history of the Democratic National Convention," as John Sweeney pungently put it), the old charges of innate white-collar bias had to be amended. In truth, there were few real barriers to unions playing a major role in the reformed nominating process once they understood the logic of the new system and knew how to adapt to it. As early as 1984 this had become clear, and unions have only been refining their strategies and tactics since then (as the smooth exercise of union power in 2000 effectively demonstrated).

This is not to say, however, that the current structure of the nominating system is necessarily ideal for the exercise of union power. The need to make formal endorsements requires that labor publicly choose among friendly candidates, a practice that can create hurt feelings (or worse) and unavoidably stimulates divisions within the labor movement. Such public endorsements can also allow labor's antagonists—both inside and outside of the party—to make union involvement itself the issue, as happened in 1984 (although not in 2000, when Bill Bradley chose not to castigate the AFL-CIO as a "special interest" in the way Gary Hart had some sixteen years earlier). With its cozier and more insulated settings for elite bargaining, the old system usually avoided these problems, and labor certainly had less to fear about a completely disconnected outsider worming his way directly into the party nomination. In practice, though, the current system has itself become rather unreceptive to wild outsiders, and the candidates selected since 1980 seem to be just the kind of established, mainstream figures that any reasonable nominating system would have produced. Accordingly, unions have made their peace with the current system, and no longer constitute a major constituency in support of a further bout of reform (or counter-reform, as the case may be). Indeed, with the rise to power of a new generation of union leaders with no experience at all with the old nominating process, proposals for a return to a more deliberative, elite-oriented system may increasingly fall on deaf ears.

The lasting impact of party reform on interest groups, then, is not its consequences for some putative white-collar/blue-collar power balance, but rather its consequences on the requirements that all groups must meet to exercise effective influence. Groups that can provide money, organizational heft, and, most important, the participation of their members in the caucuses and primaries, are the groups that will have an impact on the final outcome. The irony is that while this aspect of the system helps unions in one sense (since they are usually effective in getting their members to participate), it also poses new constraints on union leader decision-making. With the proliferation of primaries, it was no longer enough for union leaders to simply declare that their members wanted a certain candidate to be the Democratic nominee; they now had to *prove it* by getting those members to participate in the process on the candidate's behalf. In bringing this change, party reform had yet one more consequence: it created an additional democratic check on the leadership of organized labor (and, in fact, on all interest group leaders who claim to speak on behalf of a mass membership). In a political system based upon the idea of multiple checks upon established power, the reformed system can be considered, at least in this respect, more democratic than that which went before it. But however evaluated, this consequence of party reform, as well as all the others, needs to be added to the scales as we attempt to weigh the pros and cons of the current system for selecting our presidential candidates.

NOTES

1. Meany is quoted in Archie Robinson, *George Meany and His Times* (New York: Simon and Schuster, 1981), 322–323.

2. Sweeney is quoted in Robert Zausner, "Democrats Proudly Wear the Union Label," *Philadelphia Inquirer*, August 16, 2000, A1.

3. In lieu of a massive proliferation of footnotes about party reform, labor history, and presidential politics, the reader seeking further background and documentation in support of the claims in this chapter should consult Taylor E. Dark, *The Unions and the Democrats: An Enduring Alliance*, updated edition (Ithaca: Cornell University Press, 2001).

4. Perhaps the first use of this maxim with respect to the nominating process can be found in William Cavala, "Changing the Rules Changes the Game: Party Reform and the 1972 California Delegation to the Democratic National Convention," *American Political Science Review* 68 (March 1974): 27–42; a more recent example is Michael G. Hagen and William G. Mayer, "The Modern Politics of Presidential Selection: How Changing the Rules Really Did Change the Game," in *In Pursuit of the White House 2000: How We Choose Our Presidential Nominees*, ed. William G. Mayer (Chatham, NJ: Chatham House, 2000), 1–55.

5. Figures on union membership for the entire twentieth century can be found in Barry T. Hirsch and David A. Macpherson, *Union Membership and Earnings Data Book: Compilation from the Current Population Survey* (Washington, D.C.: Bureau of National Affairs, 2000).

6. Theodore H. White, *The Making of the President 1972* (New York: Atheneum, 1973), 236.

7. Lane Kirkland to International Union Presidents et al., memo, November 12, 1982, "Politics and Labor" file, AFL-CIO Library, Washington, D.C.

8. Lane Kirkland, "Politics and Labor After 1980," *AFL-CIO Federationist*, January 1981, 20.

9. Reuther is quoted in Frank Cormier and William J. Eaton, *Reuther* (Englewood Cliffs, NJ: Prentice Hall, 1970), 369.

10. William J. Eaton, "Labor Hails Kennedy Victory," *Washington Post*, July 15, 1960.

11. Meany is quoted in Robinson, *George Meany*, 276.

12. AFL-CIO Press Release, April 3, 1968, AFL-CIO Library, Washington, D.C.

13. David Broder, "COPE Director Al Barkan Flexing Labor's Big Muscle," *Washington Post*, May 7, 1968.

14. See Joseph Goulden, *Meany: The Unchallenged Strong Man of American Labor* (New York: Atheneum, 1972).

15. Memo, Lane Kirkland to International Union Presidents.

16. Theodore H. White, *The Making of the President 1968* (New York: Atheneum, 1969), 336; for Humphrey's views, see Hubert H. Humphrey, *The Education of a Public Man* (Garden City, N.Y.: Doubleday, 1976), 368.

17. James P. Gannon, "Unions Strive Mightily to Win the Nomination for the Vice-President," *Wall Street Journal*, August 26, 1968.

18. Byron E. Shafer, *Quiet Revolution: The Struggle for the Democratic Party and the Shaping of Post-Reform Politics* (New York: Russell Sage, 1983).

19. Norman Miller, "Democratic Reforms: They Work," *Wall Street Journal*, May 16, 1972.

20. Jerry Wurf, "What Labor Has Against McGovern," *New Republic*, August 5 and 12, 1972.

21. Quoted in Norman Miller, "As Convention Opening Nears, All-Out Warfare Threatens to Rip Party," *Wall Street Journal*, July 5, 1972.

22. Quoted in William J. Crotty, *Decision for the Democrats: Reforming the Party Structure* (Baltimore: Johns Hopkins University Press, 1978), 111. Abzug was an outspoken feminist and liberal congresswoman from New York City.

23. Beirne is quoted in Stephen Schlesinger, *The New Reformers: Forces for Change in American Politics* (Boston: Houghton Mifflin, 1975), 95.

24. See Denis G. Sullivan, Jeffrey L. Pressman, and F. Christopher Arterton, *Explorations in Convention Decision Making: The Democratic Party in the 1970s* (San Francisco: W. H. Freeman, 1976), 74.

25. Quoted in James Singer, "Election Victories Mean Labor Can Come in from the Cold," *Congressional Quarterly Weekly Report*, November 20, 1976.

26. See Taylor E. Dark, "Organized Labor and the Carter Administration: The Origins of Conflict," in *The Presidency and Domestic Policies of Jimmy Carter*, ed. Herbert Rosenbaum and Alexej Ugrinsky (Westport, CT: Greenwood Press, 1994).

27. David Price, *Bringing Back the Parties* (Washington, D.C.: Congressional Quarterly, 1984), 160. Price, who served on the staff of the Hunt Commission, provides a comprehensive description of its activities and recommendations.

28. Kirkland is quoted in Joseph Clark, "Labor Remains in Politics," *Dissent* 32 (Spring 1985).

29. Kirkland is quoted in Martin Schram, "The Man Who Would Be Kingmaker: 'Boss' Kirkland and the AFL-CIO's Gamble on Electing the Next President," *Washington Post*, December 15, 1982.

30. See Howell Raines, "Jackson Assails Labor's Support for Mondale as Move by 'Bosses'," *New York Times*, November 28, 1983.

31. Quoted in Robert S. Greenberger, "Labor & Democrats: Can the Marriage Be Saved?" *Wall Street Journal*, August 25, 1982.

32. Herbert Alexander and Brian Haggerty, *Financing the 1984 Election* (Lexington, MA: D. C. Heath, 1987), 183.

33. Jack W. Germond and Jules Witcover, "Labor Unmoved by Kirk's No-Endorsement Plea," *National Journal*, March 30, 1985; A. H. Raskin, "Labor: A Movement in Search of a Mission," in *Unions in Transition: Entering the Second Century*, ed. Seymour Martin Lipset (San Francisco: Institute for Contemporary Studies, 1986), 30; CBS/*New York Times* exit polls; and Barry T. Hirsch, David A. Macpherson, and Wayne G. Vroman, "Estimates of Union Density by State," *Monthly Labor Review* 124 (July 2001). "Union households" refers to those households where at least one person is a member of a labor union.

34. Alexander and Haggerty, *Financing the 1984 Election*, 181.

35. This term is drawn from Marty Cohen, David Karol, Hans Noel, and John Zaller, "Beating Reform: The Resurgence of Parties in Presidential Nominations," paper presented at the American Political Science Association meeting, San Francisco, September 2001.

36. Lane Kirkland, speech, December 5, 1984, AFL-CIO Library, Washington, D.C.

37. Quoted in David Broder, "Renaissance of Labor's Power," *Washington Post*, August 19, 1988.

38. Both officials are quoted in David Shribman, "Divided and Dispirited as Iowa Caucuses Near, Organized Labor Just Isn't Organized Politically," *Wall Street Journal*, January 19, 1988.

39. Quoted in Broder, "Renaissance of Labor's Power."

40. Quoted in Richard L. Berke, "Unions, Changing Strategy, Try Local Approach on Candidate," *New York Times*, January 14, 1992.

41. Quoted in Berke, "Unions, Changing Strategy."

42. See Sam Roberts, "Brown and Clinton Trade Blows in New York Contest," *New York Times*, March 26, 1992; and Todd S. Purdum, "Union Members Do Footwork of Candidates," *New York Times*, April 4, 1992.

43. For the story of Sweeney's rise to the AFL-CIO presidency, see Taylor E. Dark, "Debating Decline: The 1995 Battle for the AFL-CIO Presidency," *Labor History* 40 (August 1999).

44. This description of labor's motivations is based on an interview with Steve Rosenthal, AFL-CIO Political Director, on Sept. 1, 2000, at AFL-CIO headquarters in Washington, D.C.

45. For comparisons of the view of the candidates over the twentieth century, see Dark, *The Unions and the Democrats,* and the detailed findings in John Gerring, *Party Ideologies in America, 1828–1996* (Cambridge: Cambridge University Press, 1998), esp. chaps. 6 and 7.

46. Remarks of Al Gore at the 23rd Constitutional Convention of the AFL-CIO, October 13, 1999.

47. David Magleby, ed., *Getting Inside the Outside Campaign: Issue Advocacy in the 2000 Presidential Primaries* (Center for the Study of Elections and Democracy, Brigham Young University, 2000), 4.

48. Mike Hall, "Mobilizing for Labor 2000," *America@Work,* April 2000; union density figures in this and the previous paragraph are drawn from Hirsch, Macpherson, and Vroman, "Estimates of Union Density by State."

49. See comments by Steven Rosenthal in Katharine Q. Seelye, "Veteran Lawmaker is Restyling Himself as Can-Do Candidate," *New York Times,* January 6, 2003.

50. Cohen, Karol, Noel, and Zaller, "Beating Reform: The Resurgence of Parties in Presidential Nominations,"15.

51. For the size of AFSCME's PAC in comparison to others, see the Web site of the Center for Responsive Politics: <http://www.opensecrets.org/pacs/index.asp>.

52. Edwards scored a remarkable (for a southern senator) 94 percent "correct" record on AFL-CIO key votes; see David M. Shribman, "Democrats' Daring: To Dream of McCain," *Boston Globe,* May 7, 2002, A3.

53. They may not be *correct* in this reasoning, but this is a proposition that few party or union leaders care to test; for further discussion, see Lonna Rae Atkeson, "From the Primaries to the General Election: Does a Divisive Nomination Race Affect a Candidate's Fortunes in the Fall?" in *In Pursuit of the White House 2000: How We Choose Our Presidential Nominees,* ed. William G. Mayer (New York: Chatham House, 2000), 285–312.

54. See Thomas Edsall, *The New Politics of Inequality* (New York: W. W. Norton, 1984), 52–56; James I. Lengle, *Representation and Presidential Primaries: The Democratic Party in the Post-Reform Era* (Westport, CT: Greenwood, 1981); and Shafer, *Quiet Revolution.*

6

The Net and the Nomination

Michael Cornfield and Jonah Seiger

Spring, 2003
TO: All Candidates for the Democratic Nomination for President, 2004
RE: How to Use the Internet in Your Campaign

With more than 55 percent of Americans now using the Internet regularly, and nearly 70 percent with ready access, there is little question that your campaign must have a comprehensive strategy for harnessing this powerful medium.[1] The Internet can host everything from a face-to-face conversation to a global television broadcast, and do it on the cheap. It also does a few things better than any other medium, including reaching people while they are at work and adjusting fund-raising appeals and field organization instructions for maximum effect. Those of you who use the Internet regularly already appreciate its communicative versatility, workplace penetration, and optimization powers. Those of you who don't should acknowledge that nearly two hundred million U.S. users cannot be wrong . . . or ignored as potential supporters.

The authors of this memo have been employed in online politics since 1994, as paid observer and practitioner, respectively.[2] In the pages that follow, we describe what we have seen in online politics, and what we think it suggests for Net campaigning in the race for the 2004 Democratic presidential nomination. Some of our comments apply to all candidates; some depend on whether the candidate is an underdog or überdog (front-runner).

The fundamental lesson we offer is that getting the political utmost out of the Internet requires that strategy dictate the use of the technology. Computers can automate many processes, but do not be seduced (or intimidated) by "Nomination 1.0" political software packages. Loading a suite of online campaigning tools onto your hard drive will empower you to do a great many things. But which should you do, and when? The help icon on your screen won't answer those recurring questions. Neither will a customer support line. You need a campaign plan predicated on a realistic assessment of your political strengths and weaknesses and a shrewd reading of the nomination calendar.

As you prepare your overall campaign strategy for winning the nomination, five tasks will stand out. We list them here together with the "old media" channels traditionally relied upon to accomplish them:

- Recruiting Delegates (personal networking)
- Raising Money (personal networking)
- Projecting a Distinct Appeal (mass media image-making, elite media issue position-taking, press relations)
- Monitoring Public Opinion (polling, focus groups, dial response)
- Excelling at Key Moments, such as debates and early primaries (internal communications and all of the above)

With the Internet, these activities may be supplemented, accelerated, multiplied, integrated, and fine-tuned. The better the campaign plan—that is, the degree to which the campaign has and continues to take into consideration its unique goals, resources, and situational standing—the better the Internet can be used. This is true of all media, of course. But smart planning and dedicated execution pay off especially well on the Internet. Its huge capacity to store and circulate messages will be a boon or a bear depending on how well the campaign sets up its databases and communication channels.

The calendar is also a key consideration in developing your Internet strategy. Months before any actual votes are cast, the so-called invisible primary begins. In this long period, opinion leaders in and around the news media shape public perceptions of the nomination race on the basis of what they see and think about your interactions with delegates, donors, and party officials. We argue that the advent of the Internet has transformed this period, by making much of what was invisible, visible.

Next come Iowa and New Hampshire, the first official votes. History teaches that a good showing in these early contests greatly benefits a candidate in subsequent primaries. We contend that the Internet can be a crucial force multiplier here, expanding the amplitude of the proverbial post-election day "bounce" in public standing by swelling the campaign's volunteer ranks and funding coffers as if by magic. But there is little actual magic involved; instead, proper preparation of your online operation does the trick. We think online advertising and micro-targeting of campaign messages will help.

A wave of primaries, many in large states, follows quickly, indeed with record compression in 2004. Campaigns must accelerate, proliferate, and indeed transform their efforts, from retail to wholesale style, in this phase of the calendar. We discuss how a campaign can, in Net jargon, take maximum advantage of the Internet's "scalability," to win as many of these fast-breaking and widespread delegates as possible.

Then begins the long slog to the summer convention. Given that the nomination could be sewn up as early as mid-February, 2004, it is likely that this period will be extraordinarily long compared to past years. Sustaining interest and raising money will be the main concerns during these months. This will be especially challenging as the competitive frame of reference shifts from an intra-party contest to one in which the nominee presumptive is seen in comparison to an incumbent president. We suggest how the Internet can help the campaign make the challenger a viable contender and build both public and partisan interest in the campaign as it heads toward the convention.

We conclude with a few observations about television, the dominant medium in presidential politics for a generation or two. We think that the political power of television is waning. The Internet is not a replacement for television, but it can be, in the hands of an innovative candidate, a substantial, and perhaps decisive, supplement.

PRELIMINARIES

Before jumping into strategies and tactics for effectively leveraging the Internet as part of your campaign for the nomination, it is useful to lay out some basics about the medium as a political tool.

Unlimited Consideration, Direct Response

The Internet is a global, decentralized medium of interconnected networks. Unlike television and radio, it contains few if any points of centralized control. Every individual on the Internet has the capacity to communicate with literally every other user.

The most visible element of the Internet is the World Wide Web. Anyone can establish a Web site, and, once created, a Web site is immediately available to everyone with access to the Internet. Web sites range from extremely sophisticated, multi-layered, interactive destinations containing glossy images, searchable databases, and video-on-demand, to simple skin-and-bones text-only sites. Experience has shown that fancy sites don't necessarily captivate political viewers. What matters is how compelling the site content is, and how well it fits into the larger context of whatever else the public happens to be thinking about at the time.

E-mail is less visible but more pervasive than the Web. To date, it has proven to be the "killer-application" of this new medium for politics. E-mail is a low-cost and easy way for a campaign to communicate with individuals, groups, and the world at large. E-mail messages can contain text, video, sound, graphics, and interactive forms (such as those which accept contributions and ship them directly to the campaign). When combined with a sophisticated database, e-mail can be used to generate messages specifically tailored to segments of a campaign's audience: by geographic location, demographic category, issue preferences, any other criteria in the database, and any combination of the above.

Everything on the Web and, with the right set-up, all of one's pending and preserved e-mail are available to each person at all hours of the day. This ready access to archives has helped make the Internet extremely popular for research. That, in turn, makes the Internet a great medium to reach the managerial and professional stratum of the workforce. More than fifty million Americans regularly log on to the Net while at work.[3] They take multiple breaks during their day to check e-mail and surf the Web. It is the easiest (and least detectable) work break available. One does not have to swivel the chair, let alone rise from it, to switch from work to another online pursuit.

This ordinary circumstance creates an extraordinary opportunity. As figure 6.1 documents, it opens up new bands of the day to the campaigner, beyond the off-hours in which television, surface mail, and telemarketing reach people, and the commuting hours when radio holds sway. No other medium reaches into the workplace (or, to be more precise, the work and study hours) as thoroughly or conveniently.

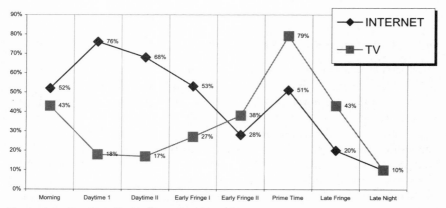

Figure 6.1   Total Media Audience by Time of Day

Source: The Media Consumption Study, Online Publishers Association and NIBQ, Nov 2001

The Internet is best understood, in comparison with other media, as a locus that uniquely combines unlimited consideration and direct response. As with print and digital disks (CDs, DVDs), voters can see what they please and take as long as they want to look at it. But online content adds a third dimension of consumer choice: through hyperlinks, voters can switch to related messages with a swiftness and precision unmatched in print and digital repositories (i.e. libraries and archives). To be sure, it is often quite difficult to get voters to look at something they have not chosen to see, especially through the Web. The Internet is not a great attention-grabbing medium, and strategies should acknowledge that. Retaining attention can also be a challenge; the related message an individual voter wants to see may well exist off the campaign Web site. However, to the extent a campaign has a voter's attention, the medium imposes no time or size limits on the message to which that voter can be exposed.[4]

Meanwhile, for voters sufficiently motivated by a campaign message, the Internet facilitates a number of ways they can get directly involved—again, without so much as turning their chairs. They can send money, right to the campaign. They can spread the word, right to the people they want. And they can, under some current legal arrangements, register to vote with the proper authorities. (They cannot, as yet, vote online, and that is probably a good thing today. Unlimited time with a ballot and related materials would be a plus. But there are serious privacy, security, and fraud problems entailed with the construction of an online voting system.)

Web Sites and E-mail Lists

We can now present the basics of a Net politics strategy. First, your campaign should seek to promote your Web site through the attention-getting media: yard signs, bumper stickers, business cards, direct mail, personal appearances, and advertisements. Wherever the name of your campaign is depicted or uttered, the URL (Web address) of your Web site should not be far behind. Second, your campaign Web site should be viewed as a destination to steer interested voters. It is where people can find out more about your candidate, compare and contrast your record with that of your opponent(s), watch a video, volunteer, and make a contribution to your campaign. Above all, you should use your campaign Web site to obtain the e-mail addresses of visitors to your site. Once you have that address, you have permission to contact people through e-mail whenever you need their attention and support. Third, your list of e-mail addresses is a cornerstone of your online campaign: an economical and powerful means of mobilizing volunteers and increasing their ranks.

There are a variety of ways to obtain e-mail addresses. Collecting e-mail addresses while promoting your Web site can be very effective. Direct mail appeals should include reply cards which encourage supporters to supply an e-mail address. Volunteers should work the crowds at events to obtain addresses from attendees. Your campaign Web site should invite visitors to sign up for a newsletter for more information. GOP 2000 presidential hopeful Steve Forbes dispatched a team with a digital camera to events to take snapshots of the candidate with supporters. The photos were e-mailed after the event—a clever incentive to build the Forbes list.

We have found that people will provide an e-mail address to a campaign as long as they feel they will get something useful in return (newsletter updates, a campaign keepsake, a chance to win a prize), and as long as the terms under which the e-mail address will be used (and shared) are clearly disclosed. Internet users resent unsolicited e-mail, or "spam." As long as your campaign does not send messages to people without their permission and promises never to release the e-mail addresses it obtains to anyone else, you will probably stay clear of trouble. We don't yet have good data on the extent and intensity of popular aversion to spam, particularly in the context of politics as opposed to business. The definition of what constitutes legitimate "permission" remains fuzzy. But it only takes one angry spam recipient to set off a chain reaction that could block your access to lots of people (Internet service providers take spam complaints quite seriously) and bring a torrent of bad publicity and return e-mail to your campaign.

Of course, you will be using your Web site and e-mail communication not just to recruit and mobilize volunteers, but to raise money as well. One major asset the Internet brings to campaigns is the ability to process contributions quickly and easily. Online forms can enable the campaign to automatically ensure that contributions meet many Federal Election Commission (FEC) requirements. Credit card transactions can be cleared immediately online, putting the money directly into your campaign's bank account. Furthermore, once your campaign has installed an online contribution system, it can dovetail with your e-mail outreach and your Web site promotion, such that the marginal cost of raising money will fall toward zero. Each piece of surface mail, each new fund-raising event, and even each new phone call your campaign places to a donor exacts a discrete cost (your candidate's time on the phone being a scarce resource). For the time being, the Internet cannot match these traditional methods in the raw dollar amounts they will raise. But in terms of "cost per acquisition," that is, the average number of pennies the campaign must spend to get a donor dollar, the Internet is the most efficient way to raise money.

Make the Web the Hub of Your Entire Campaign

If you use the Internet as we have sketched it so far, that will put you in the middle of the pack for 2004 in terms of sophistication. Approximately three-quarters of the major-party candidates for House and Senate in 2002 had campaign Web sites; of those, over half provided visitors with the opportunity to donate money and subscribe to an e-newsletter (i.e., join a volunteer list).[5] There are still a few basic steps rarely taken by political candidates, such as posting excerpts from speeches, which could bring you additional distinction and, if well-deployed, an electoral advantage. However, the next frontier for online campaigning will be reached when someone makes the Web the hub of the entire campaign.

There are two aspects to putting the Web at the center of a campaign. The first concerns the "back-end," that is, the use of computers within the campaign organization. As you well know, your campaign's database of contacts is the foundation for all your efforts. For example, a great deal of campaigning consists of keeping in touch with a variety of people. Much of that work is done on the phone, which is why "the Rolodex" has become the symbol of a personal network, as in, "She has a great Rolodex." But a Rolodex page cannot contain as much information as a Web page, it can get defaced or misplaced, it does not lend itself to cross-referencing and analysis based on cross-referencing, and it cannot dial calls. A Web-situated database can do all this. Other databases can work similar wonders for other aspects of your campaign. Connecting and aligning databases yield that often ballyhooed, if rarely seen, effect known as synergy. Thus, a Web-centered campaign is one that enters as much information as is practical and prudent (beware accidental releases!) into databases, and integrates those databases.

When combined with a program that solicits and integrates feedback—that is, evaluative reactions from those who receive your messages—database analysis enables a campaign to communicate with people in an iteratively effective way: better each time the virtual file card is refreshed. This, in a word, is cybernetics, the origin of the ubiquitous cyber- prefix.

Through cybernetics, Net content can be dynamically tailored to suit the stated preferences and collected characteristics of individual visitors. In the commercial world, this concept is known as CRM ("Customer Relationship Management"). We think rewards await the first candidate to substitute "Constituent" for "Customer," making the requisite adjustments for the political world. To launch such a CRM system, your Web site should be built to enable visitors to register and personalize the contents of the site according to their information characteristics and preferences. You can then customize message content and delivery to individuals, while compiling aggregate data on what sorts of people are visiting your site, when, in search of what. For example, if the candidate will be appearing at an event in Des Moines, a CRM-equipped campaign can alert Web site visitors who live and work there. If the event is built around the candidate receiving an endorsement from the Chamber of Commerce, another alert can go to Web site visitors interested in business issues. The alerts can be sent by e-mail or any medium the visitor prefers. Similar communications can be sent after the event.

During the 2000 and 2002 campaigns we began to see database integration and cybernetic communication on a rudimentary level.[6] As you prepare for the 2004 challenge, you should consider going further.

The second aspect of making the Web the hub of your campaign concerns its visibility and embeddedness in the World Wide Web, of which your Web site is but a minuscule part. The online equivalent of getting your name out there can pivot on more than just your name. The more you link with other sites, the more key words you list for indexing purposes with search engines; the more you conceive of your Web site and Net operation as part of an organic whole, the more traffic will come your way. No campaign should depend on people taking the initiative to give their time and money, but since the structure of the Internet makes it phenomenally easy for individuals to do just that—checking out your Web site at 3:30 A.M. five months before the primary, because they just saw your name in connection with a favorite cause or group—the next generation online campaign will systematically clear and mark virtual paths to its doors.

This two-faceted hub concept may be difficult for non-users to assimilate. Understanding the Internet is comparable to a paradigm shift. The people in all walks of life who "get it" strew links into their e-mails and Web pages. They track down and ship out information online during phone conversations, to illustrate a point or fulfill a request. Most fundamentally, they look for database and network solutions to communication problems (e.g., "our message is not being heard"; "we can't get in front of this story"; "our candidate is not spending enough time with the right people.")

A Net-oriented mind-set is a new thing, but it happens to coincide with the basic approach of coalitional politics: to get something done, reach out to those with similar and shared interests. The everyday significance of that congruence is still lost on most campaigns, which regard the Internet as an afterthought, if at all. It may still be an afterthought in most campaigns for the 2004 nomination. But sooner or later, campaigns will route all of their internal and external communications through a computer program. Such packages are already on the market, and we reiterate that they are no substitute for strategy. But they are great tools to have. They link a campaign's communications to archived data, the Internet, and a console (instrument panel) that enables those with access to it to make smart, rapid, and systematic adjustments.

Net Campaigning in a Nutshell

Web site design, promotion, and content all matter, but messages and lists are the primary goods to manage in online campaigning. Messages don't come out as finished productions, as in the old media; instead, a message gets released and then altered progressively on the basis of its reception, as registered in the feedback to the campaign and the campaign's monitoring of the Web. Lists are similarly dynamic entities requiring constant attention; they should be subdivided, recombined, and protected against abuse. But even if you do not want to embrace online campaigning fully, there are benefits to Net use. That basic lesson you don't need to get, as a mentality. You can simply learn it from history.

THREE LESSONS FROM 2000

In making recommendations, we obviously want to draw on the record of success and failure. The record, alas, is abbreviated, consisting of just four campaign cycles (1996, 1998, 2000, 2002). With the technology and the online population changing markedly even in this short time period, the last two cycles—with broadband applications available and a population consisting of more than just high-tech pioneers—are really the only ones with relevant examples, and of course only 2000 contains examples from presidential primaries. One of the hardest things to do in attempting to learn from the early days of using a new technology is to distinguish between what worked once and what will work again. Over the long run, repeated successes by many identify the latter; but we are in the short run, looking for an edge, and so we must guess in order to have a good shot at becoming the very repeat success that will confirm an application for future campaigners. With this *caveat*, we offer three exemplary stories from the 2000 election cycle.

GWBush.com

The lesson of story number one is that there is no percentage in attempting to stifle online detractors of your campaign. In April, 1999, the George W. Bush campaign sent a cease-and-desist letter to the creators of a parody site at www. GWBush.com. Zack Exley, the chief parodist, had copied aspects of the official campaign site, at www.georgewbush.com—an extremely easy thing to do with computer software—and he responded to the letter by revising the look but not the attitude. Indeed, they stepped up their criticism. On May 3, 1999, the Bush campaign filed a complaint with the Federal Election Commission, petitioning the agency to enforce regulations applicable to political action committees. (The FEC would reject the complaint in April, 2000.) Calling upon the government brought the parody site more traffic and news coverage than it could have ever garnered on its own. Then the candidate compounded the tactical error. On May 22, 1999, in responding to a reporter's question about the site, Bush slammed its creators as "garbage" and said "there ought to be limits to freedom." Traffic zoomed at GWBush.com. The parodists began to sell T-shirts with the "limits to freedom" line. As of March, 2003, GWBush.com was still operating.

The explanation for the continued relevance of this tale is that the decentralized, "open" architecture of the Internet alters the calculus of going after critics in the critics' favor. Had the parody aired on television, the Bush campaign could have placed a few phone calls to network executives and commercial sponsors and accomplished its goal. During the 1960s, for example, "The Smothers Brothers Comedy Hour" was forced to tone down its political criticism. But Web site operators are not licensed by the government. Some care not a whit about making money in the course of airing their views. The Bush campaign would have handled the online gadfly better by remaining silent. Then, GWBush.com would have faded under the remorseless tide of information and information purveyors that the Net has brought into computer terminals everywhere.

McCain and the Internet

The lesson of story number two is: be ready for a magic moment. We derive the term "magic moment" from "defining event," as coined by Lee Atwater, Bush Sr. operative *extraordinaire*. Atwater told 1988 presidential campaign chroniclers Jack W. Germond and Jules Witcover that:

> In presidential politics, each candidate ends up having two or three defining events, events that are so big that they actually transcend the political echo chambers universe . . . and actually melt down to the public. [T]he next day after any defining event, if you go to any bar in America, or ride in any taxi, or go to a laundromat or the YMCA, and stand around for a few moments, that's the event people are going to be talking about.[7]

Atwater was describing the impact of a live in-studio interview of George Bush on the *CBS Evening News* in which Bush and anchorman Dan Rather got angry with each other. The dust-up took its place in presidential campaign lore, not just because it was unexpected and out-of-the-ordinary behavior by political insiders, but also because it stimulated a publicly registered response by members of the general populace, who flooded the proverbial and actual switchboards at CBS and the Bush campaign. The public reaction sealed the status of the event as a turning point for narrative accounts of the 1988 campaign. With Bush, Atwater, and other campaign spokespersons leading the way, the "Bush-Rather debate," as the incident became titled, served the vice president's candidacy by developing into a shorthand reference to the perception that Bush was not a wimp, as he had been derogated in public, but a tough guy fully capable of filling the job of commander-in-chief.

The Internet transforms the action-reaction dynamic of defining events. Web servers can be flooded as readily as telephone switchboards, but if an organization is prepared for a surge of traffic to arrive at some point during the campaign, it can put it to work, not only to redefine public perceptions, but to raise money, recruit volunteers, and otherwise multiply the impact of the event. This was demonstrated when the John McCain campaign won the 2000 New Hampshire primary.

The magic moment for the McCain campaign arrived when the Arizona Senator defeated George W. Bush by 18 percentage points in the New Hampshire primary, on February 1, 2000. As word of McCain's victory spread, money started gushing into the campaign Web coffers at a rate of $30,000 an hour—this according to the campaign, which cleverly fed the news media with e-mail bulletins on the phenomenon, which then reported it, which then generated more donations. After four days, the total topped $2 million, a rate of almost $21,000 an hour. In all, the McCain campaign said it raised $6.4 million through the Internet, representing 27 percent of its entire fund-raising take.[8] Since much of this money came in amounts less than $250 (the average was $112, according to the campaign), McCain reaped an additional $4 million in matching funds from the federal government. The McCain campaign also enjoyed a huge influx of volunteers. Its e-mail list rocketed from 60,000 to 142,000. As a result, it became easier for the campaign to advance and populate candidate appearances. (This utility of e-mail was first demonstrated by the 1998 Jesse Ventura campaign for governor of Minnesota.)

The McCain campaign had just about spent all of its money by the day of the New Hampshire primary. The online contributions, processed swiftly by the banks and government, came to the rescue. Together with the publicity and volunteers, the money enabled the campaign to convert its "momentum," a political asset akin to a mandate in that it exists primarily in rhetoric, into more concrete political resources. Over the next few weeks, the McCain campaign won primaries in Michigan and Arizona. This may well not have occurred (especially in Michigan, Arizona being the senator's home state) had the McCain campaign not explored and embraced online campaigning during the previous year.

A year of Net work preceded the magic moment. Senator McCain and his communications chief Dan Schnur were willing to experiment with the Internet. Two McCain aides, Max Fose and Wes Gullett, devoted six weeks to planning, one month to programming, and then four to six hours a day to maintaining the online operation. Each day, Fose walked around campaign headquarters collecting information for the site. After he showed McCain how much their Web site traffic rose after the candidate gave out its address on CNN's "Larry King Live" on October 13, 1999, the senator made such an invitation a standard feature of his stump speech. Visitors to the site would see underscored calls to action: *send money so we can purchase air time for this ad* (attached as an audio file); *view the list of more than $13 billion in wasteful and low-priority congressional pork-barrel spending items; e-mail headquarters with your opinions of the new site navigation tools.*

The two-way communication paid a big dividend for the first time in December 1999, when the campaign realized it needed help procuring signatures to get on the ballot for the Republican primary in Virginia. The campaign augmented its Web site appeal for help with an online advertising buy that attracted just under one hundred volunteers, and made the deadline. The next month, the campaign asked for volunteers to make ten phone calls to registered Independents and Republicans in New Hampshire. Eleven hundred people enlisted within six hours. After a week, 8,000 calls had been completed and tabulated; the Interactive Phone Bank had been invented. Cost of volunteer transportation, office rental, phone equipment, line leasing, supervisors, and donuts: zero. Value to grassroots politics: priceless.

The magic moment actually began when the polls in New Hampshire opened, not when the result first became apparent. New Hampshire (like Minnesota, Jesse Ventura's state) permits same-day registration for voting. More than 38,000 Granite Staters took advantage of that option on the day of the 2000 primary. There is no telling how many of them voted for McCain, but chances are that quite a few did. There is also no telling how many McCain voters were moved to show up and register by an online message or a personally delivered turnout message logistically facilitated by the Net, but again, chances are that quite a few were.[9]

The McCain for President online operation did not cease when the campaign ended. It turned into StraightTalkAmerica.com, a Web platform for grassroots support of campaign finance reform and candidates for office whom McCain had endorsed.

The magic moment phenomenon turns out to be a specialized version of a general phenomenon. While your online operation should be ready for positive news about your campaign, it should also be ready for negative news (see "Scaling Up for Super Tuesday," ahead). And you should be alert to news about the nation and world which could stimulate the formation of an online ad hoc interest group. That is the third lesson of the early years of online campaigning, illustrated by the story of MoveOn.org.

MoveOn.org

In September, 1998, Wes Boyd and Joan Blades, a Berkeley, California couple who had recently sold their successful screen-saver business, created an online petition to express frustration with the impeachment of President Clinton. They were not famous. They held no executive positions with any corporate, labor, governmental, or political organization. They spent no money on marketing or publicity. But the message embodied in the original title of their Web site, "Censure and Move On," resonated with individuals who, while not forgiving of the president's moral transgressions, nevertheless recoiled at the Republican response to those sins.

More than 100,000 people signed the petition the first week. By the midterm election, 300,000 had signed. The day before the House voted on impeachment (December 18, 1998), the count stood at 450,000. Each signature came with contact information. Boyd and Blades began to collect pledges of money and volunteer time to defeat those who voted to impeach. In early February, 1999,

MoveOn.org announced that it had collected $13.4 million and 750,000 hours in pledges.

Pledges are symbolic; the couple wanted something more concrete. They selected about a dozen congressional races for 2000 in which a challenger stood a good chance of unseating a pro-impeachment incumbent. The Web site was revised so that visitors could read up on the challengers and electronically donate money to any or all of them. By election day 2000, MoveOn.org had bundled and distributed more than $2.1 million to its candidates. One of them, Jean Elliott Brown of Florida, had been moved to run by her experiences as a volunteer for MoveOn. Another, Adam Schiff in California, received more money from MoveOn than any other contributor. Schiff defeated House impeachment manager James Rogan.

MoveOn.org used the Internet to generate political power out of a shared emotional reaction to the news. It shared that power with its supporters to a remarkable degree, turning the form of the Political Action Committee (PAC) on its head into a Citizen Action Portal. After the impeachment story ended, MoveOn could have disbanded; instead, it has continued to try and ride the opinion waves that news leaves in its wake. Its membership list remains in the hundreds of thousands. In the summer of 2001, during the California energy crisis, Boyd invited MoveOn members to meetings where he distributed long-lasting light bulbs, attempting to create a physical correlate to his virtual political community. The couple also opened a Washington, D.C., office. In October, 2002, MoveOn distributed $1 million it had collected in 48 hours to "heroes" running for federal office who opposed war with Iraq. On February 26, 2003, MoveOn coordinated a "Virtual March on Washington" which jammed Senate and White House switchboards with an estimated one million phone calls and faxes as a demonstration of opposition to such a war. MoveOn's membership on that date topped 850,000.

There are variations on the MoveOn approach to organizing grassroots power through the Internet. William Greene's "60-Second Activist Club" sends one e-mail a day to conservatives, who read an outline of an issue position and then click to register their opinion with government decision-makers. The point, for presidential candidates, is that these instant influence mechanisms are now present in the political environment. The long-term success of parties and interest groups in electoral campaigns still depends on traditional methods of organization: bureaucracy, membership fees, lobbying, and well-publicized victories or defeats to foster an image of potency. The success of candidates depends on their own strategy and management. But the Internet allows individuals to summon quick strikes through key strokes, coalescing support off the news.

THE INVISIBLE PRIMARY, REVEALED

For a quarter of a century, political insiders have adopted the coinage and argument of Arthur Hadley, and referred to the period between the last presidential election day and the first statewide vote as "the invisible primary."[10] During these years, candidates mix with donors, party faithful, and political journalists, striving to make the idea of their candidacy plausible (underdogs) or inevitable (überdogs). Much of this mixing occurs behind closed doors. Still, it is our contention that the Internet has made enough of the candidates' actions and insiders' conversations about those actions public as to render this process of angling for advantage *visible*.

For one thing, the aspect of the process which contributed most to its invisibility was its location. Much of the invisible primary occurred outside the media/ politics centers of New York City and Washington, D.C. What candidates did at dinners and meetings, even in Iowa and New Hampshire, could not be covered thoroughly and distributed everywhere through the old media. C-SPAN came closest, but it allocated only a few hours per week to campaign politics, much less the race for the presidency. Now, however, thanks to the digital grid, Podunk is inside the Beltway. *The Hotline,* in its twenties the granddaddy of political insider news briefing services, has since January 21, 2001, posted a running tally of which states have been visited by the president, vice president, and twelve possible Democratic candidates.

A second way that the Net has stripped the cloak of invisibility away from the long interim period concerns campaign finance disclosure. The existence of the Net, combined with the popularity of money-in-politics as an insider topic, has led to the inflation of the significance of filing deadlines. On June 30, 1999, candidates for president filed disclosure reports with the Federal Election Commission; two weeks later, they sent the FEC the names of donors to their campaigns. Candidates have been doing this since the 1970s. But this time, the compliance procedure became a campaign event. Candidates sent out last-minute fund-raising appeals, telling supporters that they needed to make a good public impression. Indeed, the news media accorded the filing information the "horse-race journalism" treatment. They ran stories about who was ahead of and behind the others, and of expectations, in dollars collected. And so it appeared to all the political world in the summer of 1999 that George W. Bush, on the strength of his record-setting $37 million take, possessed an insurmountable lead in the race for the Republican nomination. Shortly after the FEC numbers surfaced, Congressman John Kasich dropped out of the race. Another Republican at the back of the pack, former Tennessee governor and cabinet secretary Lamar Alexander, said, "Something is wrong when the system doesn't permit an articulate, thoughtful man of John Kasich's stature to even get to the starting line of the presidential race: the Iowa caucuses."

What was wrong? The starting line had changed. In July of 1999, Bush won what constituted a "money primary." Simultaneously, the image of Vice President Al Gore as the probable Democratic nominee flickered and wobbled when challenger Bill Bradley, the former New Jersey senator, posted $11 million in contributions to Gore's $18 million. Gore had been expected to have a much bigger lead, and so he effectively lost a money primary. The money primary exists thanks to the Internet, which makes it possible to collect and circulate financial disclosure data in a matter of days. Turning the FEC filings into an event meets the strategic need of überdogs to brandish a huge advantage and of underdogs to demonstrate that they have more strength than anticipated. It also meets the need of the campaign community to have fresh evidence to talk and write about. For the 2004 election cycle, the opportunity for a money primary has been increased by the passage of the Bipartisan Campaign Reform Act (BCRA) of 2002. BCRA requires the FEC to provide Internet access to financial records within 48 hours of receipt. A money primary can now occur soon after presidential campaign committees report: every three months in 2003 and monthly in 2004.

Changes in the tracking of advertising provide a third reason to revamp the concept of the invisible primary. The Internet, in combination with satellite-television technology, makes advertising buys virtually transparent. The Campaign Media Analysis Group, a Virginia-based consulting firm, has since 1996 tracked paid advertising as it appears in the nation's top 100 media markets on six broadcast networks and twenty-six national cable networks. Hours after an ad appears, clients receive via e-mail data on its contents, cost, placement, and type of viewing audience.[11] Ad buys are windows into strategy. Molding the issue environment through early television advertising was a key to Dick Morris's strategy to reelect Bill Clinton in 1995. Morris wrote about it as a secret weapon, but that can no longer be the case.[12] In 2003 and 2004, everyone will be on the lookout for ad buys.

Fourth, and most fundamentally, because the Net is an archive as well as a medium of communication, it has boosted both the number of people who conduct research into the existing and likely field of candidates and the audience for the findings of those people. Those findings can be voluminous. Often, however, an incident or remark speaks volumes. Such a "telling detail" reverberates through the ranks of political insiders, whose numbers the Net has enlarged and entwined more closely, and functions much like a magic moment on a smaller scale.

A telling detail could be a gaffe at one of those previously obscure candidate appearances. It might be uncovered from the financial disclosure or advertising buy data. Or it might be dredged up from the candidate's pre-political or private life: the younger the candidate, the greater the percentage of his or her days that have been lived in an era of posted and post-able artifacts. Whatever its nature, whereas twenty years ago the telling detail may well have been reported by the press, today insiders can hear of it, see it, and forward it to others without any news media involvement. As fast as the online news media work today, "word of mouse" sometimes moves even faster and indeed provides leads for the campaign press.

In sum, we no longer have an invisible primary. We have a virtual primary period, a long, long season of winnowing highlighted by the "money primaries" that quickly follow the filing deadlines. During this run-up to the Iowa caucuses and New Hampshire primary, slated for late January, 2004, you should be courting the same key people you did before, but with the awareness that the Net should be an instrument of that courtship and will be a light upon it no matter what you do.

WHAT TO DO DURING THE
VIRTUAL PRIMARY PERIOD

On Wednesday, November 6, 2002, presidential campaigns kicked into a higher gear. Those eyeing the nomination began to remind the previous day's winners that they had raised money and made appearances for them. Political consultants and staffers appended their victories to their resumés. Researchers pored over the election and exit poll results, hunting for patterns that could be interpreted as omens. And the new campaign finance rules went into effect.

You will devote much of this fourteen-month period to working the continental foyer to the grand ballroom that is Iowa and New Hampshire. Thanks to the oddity of the process, you will shake hands, pat backs, wave, point, laugh, and otherwise work this anteroom for much longer than you will appear in the main hall. As you do, make sure that one of your assistants collects e-mail addresses, and that you invite people to visit you online. By now, your campaign should have a proxy Web presence: a leadership PAC; a volunteer/fan site; and at the very least, a well-indexed page where the people you encounter, along with those who want to meet you, can sign up for news at such time as you are ready to make it.

As you circulate, your efforts should focus on three key groups: virtual delegates, opinion leaders, and financial donors. Remember that circulation in the digital age depends on a timely combination of e-mail, telephone, and face-to-face contact, a fusion of high-tech and high-touch. Between October 1999 and March 2000, the dozen top Democratic and Republican primary candidates sent 336 e-mail messages to their public lists (the ones signed onto by researchers at the George Washington University Graduate School of Political Management [GSPM]). All the candidates put a great deal of emphasis on reinforcing their overall campaign themes, raising money, and recruiting volunteers. They also used e-mail to draw attention to media coverage, influence online polls, and encourage supporters to spread the word about the campaign.

This time, the bar is higher. Your campaign will need to generate more messages: direct and third-party, online and offline, specialized and general. It will also have to pay closer attention to the messages it receives in return.

Virtual Delegates

Party leaders, county coordinators, and local activists sympathetic to your candidacy constitute the pool of virtual delegates. A few may become actual delegates on your slate, and to the convention. During the virtual primary period, they play a role analogous to convention delegates, working on your behalf and being seen doing so. These early supporters will expect personal attention from your campaign team and reward that by giving their personal attention to others, widening the pool for you. They can augment your field operations in New Hampshire and Iowa, and enable the campaign to recruit a virtual field operation in later primary states that can be ramped up quickly if success is achieved in the early votes. Thus, even if they do not actually become delegates, the pool of virtual delegates is invaluable to your campaign.

Communicating with these people boils down to favor requests. E-mail is a wonderful channel for talk about small tasks: "Could you . . . ?" "Sure." "Great, here are the details." "Done." "Thanks, now could you . . . ?" After a few rounds, the subject line can suffice as message, with the details in an attachment and the body of the message devoted to funny asides, birthday greetings, and other intimacies. It pained George W. Bush, a devotee of this craft, when he had to cease his e-mail correspondence three days before his inauguration, because as president it would be subject to open record requests.[13] For underdogs, who have a harder time identifying support and forming bonds, resorting to e-mail for this type of communication confers another benefit: the database of favor requests can help the campaign ascertain the key characteristics of its nascent base and track how firm and extensive it is becoming.

At the same time, any e-mail activity is most useful when it is part of a larger and coordinated message strategy. You can reward your most faithful supporters by giving them back an advance look at a poll or ad. Plus, you often want to know what they think. You don't want them to be surprised or feel betrayed.

Where e-mail schmoozing gets tricky, as the president's experience suggests, is in maintaining security and privacy. You can't enforce a hierarchical command structure that well in this medium, which seems to rotate vertical lines to the horizontal and expand them in every direction. For example, field organizers in New Hampshire and Iowa should have direct access to the growing online database of supporters. Supporters should be contacted regularly with specific actions they can take, with the goal of recruiting additional supporters. But some people will leave the campaign, and they cannot be permitted to take data with them. In 2001, a Virginia candidate for local office contacted supporters of Bill Bradley without authorization, an embarrassment to the Bradley image mitigated by the fact that Bradley was no longer a candidate.

Opinion Leaders and the News Media

An opinion leader is anyone whose views of the world command a following. Although the Internet technically gives everyone with access to it a shot at playing this role, in presidential politics, chances are the key opinion leaders who are *not* virtual delegates will come from the news media. We have already discussed how delegate types can spread the word for you, as part of a favor-giving circle. There are other methods to engage the news media.

Some news media voices have the Net as their central platform: *The Drudge Report*; *Slate* and *Salon*; state- and city-oriented political sites such as *Rough and Tumble* and *Gotham Gazette*; and the national political e-newsletters *The Hotline*, *The Note*, and *Washington Wrap*. *The Note*, ABCNews.com's weekday newsletter, entitles its section on the 2004 presidential race "The Invisible Primary." We think it is being too modest in retaining that heading. You must take care to look good in *The Note* and its online competitors.

Other media voices have incorporated the Net into their portfolio of outlets; for example, the august media bigfoot David Broder, in addition to his newspaper columns and reports and his weekend political talk show appearances, now tapes Web video stand-ups and participates in Q & A sessions on the Washingtonpost.com site. Then there are the political bloggers (short for web-logger), online diarists with columnar orientations such as Rich Galen, Andrew Sullivan, and Joshua Micah Marshall.

The big change involving the Internet and media politics has less to do with who the key opinion leaders are than with what their opinions are likely to be about. There has been a significant increase in the number and range of available sources for opinion-relevant information. There is, additionally, a greater incentive to draw from this cyber-well because the opinion leaders/media stars must file more frequently. Consequently, the roster of story topics on the mythical agenda that the media do so much to set has been greatly expanded. It is easier to get a fresh take, a blurb about a new group, etc., onto the digital agenda, where insiders will see it. However, it is harder to stay visible there for long and to break through to the crowded and diffused mass media agenda.

Regarding campaign political coverage, there is much, much more about money thanks to online media. One Web site, the Center for Responsive Politics's Opensecrets.org, ought to be book-marked on every press secretary's computer. This site makes it easy for campaign correspondents to file a money-in-politics inflected report at will. The stories they will file are just as easy to anticipate. You know the horse-race will be written about at each "turn" of the track, that is, the financial filing report deadlines will be covered as "money primaries" that indicate who is ahead and by how much. You know that as soon as a company becomes big news in the business section, reporters for the politics page will type the company's name—and the name of the industry sector to which it belongs—into one of Opensecrets.org's Web site boxes to see if your name pops up. You know that when President Bush announces a new policy, casts a veto, or makes another big decision, the same thing will occur. Be ready with material to give your side of the inevitable story.

For example, Opensecrets does not supply human interest details on contributors, so have donors ready to talk with the press about why they have given money to your candidate. For a second example, political money numbers don't put themselves in perspective, and it's up to you to provide the media with comparative and benchmark figures that can help its audiences understand a $1,000 or $100,000 donation in a rational context. Citizens should know how much donor X contributed to candidate Y this year. But they should also know how much will probably be spent in that race overall; how political spending on advertising compares with commercial and even governmental advertising; and how much a 30-second spot costs.

A viable strategy for dealing with media opinion leaders begins with a media e-mail list. Gore 2000 had a password-protected area of its campaign Web site available to press only, which enabled the campaign to track coverage. Smart campaign researchers will feed the cyber-beast (via proper channels) with news releases that feature statements, votes, and other data about the candidate's consistency and opponents' inconsistencies, which the reporters can check for themselves via links. On the same logic, the media production team should contribute previews of ads they want to publicize, either to expose an opponent's tactic or to brag about one's own. The campaign can also look better by advising the press about the satellite sites you launch (Web sites that sport flashy names, contain a few pages, and link to your campaign site), and the refurbishings (or "re-launches") of your main site. Web site watches comparable to the "truth boxes" that evaluate television ads are not around yet, but 2004 may be the year they debut somewhere. Even if they don't, media opinion leaders will rely on their readings of your Web site to inform their assessments of your campaign's organization and intelligence.

Donors

There is no substitute for high-touch, high-dollar fundraising events and contacts. We do not expect that the Internet is in any way capable of rivaling these traditional forms of fundraising in 2004. However, the Net can be very effective for enabling a flow of slow, steady low-dollar contributions from supporters. And, as we have seen with McCain and MoveOn, it can not only keep up with the speed of donations inspired by a news event, it can also keep score for publicity purposes.

One false assumption about the Web is that donors are more likely to make a contribution online because the process is so simple. Of 181 House candidates in 2000 who conducted online fundraising, only one in five combined a Web page "contribute" button or downloadable form with an "ask": a direct request for money.[14] This was analogous to sending a piece of direct mail containing a reply form but no letter or brochure. To be sure, a Web page appeal cannot be targeted well. But why not a general request? And why not a general request from the candidate in a video? And why not e-mail appeals with links to the Web page?

To be effective, your online solicitation should give the donor something in exchange for the money. This means an immediate online thank-you and one or more of the following: a souvenir item from the online campaign "store," access to a special newsletter or event, a personal phone call or surface letter from a campaign principal. Donors contacted offline should be encouraged to give online, so that the money can be turned around more quickly and efficiently, and so that the donors may be recontacted through e-mail.

Sidebar: The Impact of BCRA

The Bipartisan Campaign Reform Act of 2002 (BCRA), which took effect on November 6, 2002, will enhance the value of online fundraising to a considerable, if at this writing incalculable, degree. The Act bans soft-money–funded television and radio ads by candidates, political parties, and outside groups 30 days before a primary and 60 days before a general election. This provision faces a serious constitutional challenge. However, if the U.S. Supreme Court upholds the restrictions, the Internet will suddenly be the only nationwide medium available to soft-money campaigners during the critical run-ups to election days. That would greatly boost the salience of online ads, which link to online solicitations.

Some parts of the BCRA will withstand constitutional muster. Campaign finance experts will find ways of getting around the new restrictions. Even so, the BCRA will put a premium on raising hard dollars. In the perception of the news media and a significant portion of the electorate, this hard money will be "clean money." Candidates will want to show off large numbers of low-dollar donors willing to give $2,000 or less per candidate per cycle. That goes double for candidates who opt out of the public financing system. Thus, a big opportunity opens up for candidates (and specialists) skilled at using the Internet to locate and tap these donors.

IOWA AND NEW HAMPSHIRE

As 2004 opens, your strategy and tactics will undoubtedly be influenced by your standing relative to your competitors. You know that a magic moment will be awarded to whoever most exceeds the expectations shaped by the scientifically conducted and publicly distributed polls.[15] It is likely that only one Democrat will be anointed as the "gaining underdog" after each of the early plebiscites. The concomitant momentum boost may not be enough to catch the front-runner, but it will surely put the leader to a "test" of organization and cool in news media narratives. The two or three candidates with a legitimate shot at the nomination after Iowa and New Hampshire (and, perhaps, South Carolina) will be subjected to an intense ritual of political scrutiny. This is "Survivor" for keeps.

The Internet can help your campaign make the most of a momentum boost and/or character test. You should optimistically assume that you will undergo the public hazing ritual which early success at the polls brings. As those first wintry votes approach, you should lay plans to step up your online advertising and the micro-targeting on which it and some of your e-mailing efforts rely.

Online Advertising: Don't Be Put Off

With limited exceptions, presidential contenders in 2000 did not make use of online advertising. Most of the political community has been similarly averse to banner ads, pop-ups, sponsored Web content, and the like. Even as their Web sites have grown in sophistication and size and their e-mail has swelled, today's candidates, advocacy groups, and parties continue to regard online advertising as a sporadic indulgence. We think that 2004 presents a compelling opportunity to test some of the underlying assumptions about the effectiveness and value of online advertising. The costs are low and the benefits are concrete.

For all its woes, online advertising already represents at least 5 percent of all advertising spending in the United States, equal to expenditures for local radio (see table 6.1). How much benefit these outlays brought to those who purchased the ads is at once startlingly clear and frustratingly opaque. Clear, because the success of an online ad in luring a viewer to click through to a Web site can be measured with a fast precision unavailable in any other medium. Opaque, because the ad industry and political community have yet to agree on what constitutes success. For instance, online advertisers can know within hours of posting an ad the percentage of its viewers who have "clicked through" to the sponsor's Web site. But is one percent a good click-through rate for a campaign? Or 5 percent? Click-throughs measure direct response. So do "conversions," the percentage of click-throughs which lead to a requested action being taken, such as subscribing to a campaign e-newsletter or making a donation. Again, what is the benchmark to hope for, and look for?

Table 6.1 Distribution of Advertising Spending by Medium in 2002

Advertising Medium	% of Total Spending in 2002
Local Newspapers	17
Network Television	17
Spot Television	10
Cable Television	9
Internet	5
Local Radio	5
Outdoor Ads	2.5
Other*	34.5

Source: From November 18, 2002, news release data about advertising spending during the first three quarters of 2002 compiled by CMR.com/TNS Media Intelligence (www.cmr.com).
*Other includes magazines, national radio, and Spanish language media.

Regardless of how many people click through and convert, an online ad might help "brand" the campaign, raising its viewers' awareness of your name and basic message. Some argue that Net users possess tunnel vision, that they ignore everything other than what they are searching for, and therefore that online advertising has no branding value, and should instead be used mainly to recruit and mobilize supporters. Others maintain that the right number of online ads in the right locations at the right times can lift brand awareness within a population. If the latter proves to be correct in 2004, then the Internet might not be as poor an attention-grabbing medium as it has been to date. Becoming the campaigner who overturned that conventional wisdom could enhance your campaign immeasurably.

In the final analysis, this debate over the proper use of online advertising should not matter to you, because online ads cost so little that you can afford to experiment. In the fall of 2002, the authors of this article made inquiries to major online properties that reach Democratic voters in Iowa. For a modest outlay of $250,000, it is possible for a campaign to obtain as many as 2.1 million impressions per week during the months of December 2003 and January 2004. (An "impression" is an exposure to one person.) There were 538,000 registered Democrats in Iowa as of January 1, 2003.[16] So online advertising is a bet worth taking—all the more so because, in addition to whatever recruiting and branding benefits come the campaign's way, the news media will cover the foray as a novelty. Favorable coverage is especially likely from news media outlets with their own online ventures, because they want to nourish the online advertising industry.

Micro-targeting and Viral Distribution of Messages

Taking a systematic and sustained approach to online advertising will carry your campaign into a degree of targeting which goes beyond that associated with cable, radio, magazines, and surface mail. The Internet permits micro-targeting: sending ads not just to Web pages that will be seen by people who fit certain demographic, geographic, and political categories, but to people who have demonstrated their receptiveness to previous ads by clicking through them. The template for a second, micro-targeted ad thanks individuals by name for responding to the first ad, and nudges them along toward becoming delegates, volunteers, donors, and voters.

It may be that the added complexity of micro-targeting has daunted some campaigns in the past from committing to online advertising. Again, we say, the cost is so low you cannot lose by trying, so long as you keep track of what you are doing. As it is, you should already be engaged in monitoring your e-mail operation. In the weeks leading up to the first primary vote, you should subdivide your e-mail lists by precincts and issue focus and send targeted messages to these sub-lists. For example, if you surmise that a pocket of registered voters in one precinct would be more likely to turn out for you if they knew the gun control position of one of your opponents, then highlight that difference in a message sent only to those voters. Another population segment might be motivated by the knowledge that the candidate will make an appearance in their town on a particular day. You should also be increasing the frequency of messages sent to your campaign's e-mail lists: providing the latest information about the race, talking points on key issues, and plans and incentives for supporters to help to turn out the vote.

In addition, you should promote e-mail communication in and around your campaign. If your campaign has been endorsed by a local civic group, ask its leaders to send an e-mail to its own list, complete with a link to your Web site. Encourage individual supporters to send informal messages of support to their friends and co-workers. Voters are often more willing to listen to the endorsement of a trusted friend than the campaign itself. Through your Web site, you can provide "action kits" to interested supporters that include draft messages and instructions on how to distribute them. (The Bill Bradley campaign did this quite well in 1999 and 2000.) "Forward this page to a friend" features allow you to monitor the personal messages you are encouraging. Such "viral" campaigning can have a major impact.

Online advertising, micro-targeting, viral messaging, e-mail schmoozing, and Web site recruiting will create a network of communications lines that converge on your campaign. This network will experience a surge of volume when your magic moment arrives. It is up to you to convert this higher volume into an expansion of the network, as incarnated in your campaign lists. You should be ready to devote a special section of your Web site to commemorating the moment. (You might also consider setting up a special Web site, separate from your official campaign site, but that can complicate things unduly for both your staff and interested visitors.) Be ready to adapt your contribution page and fund-raising appeals, as well as your volunteer recruitment efforts and press outreach. And don't forget to have a plan in place to ramp up your Web servers to handle the increase in traffic.

SCALING UP FOR SUPER TUESDAY

Instant expansion is a phenomenon most online operations are learning to plan for, but the need is especially acute for presidential campaigns. Having emerged successfully from the first wave of votes, your campaign will now need to morph from a two- or three-state operation to one with ground forces in dozens of states. Your campaign's Internet efforts will play a critical role in "scaling up" for Super Tuesday. Anyone can perform the technical feat of converting from one-to-one to one-to-many communication (e.g., hit "Reply All" instead of

"Reply"). For scalability to serve a purpose, however, you need a strategy and the right talent and commitment to execute it.

The compressed time period in which you must campaign for the second wave of votes (basically, the month of February, 2004) assures a multiplication of contexts that first-time visitors will bring to your online campaign. You should be ready to greet newcomers with a variety of versions of your message, that is, with content custom-made for people living in new states, people previously committed to another candidate, and people who have just caught wind of your name through general interest media. For example, a prominent Republican consultant builds pages into campaign Web sites aimed at "Undecided Voters"; they tend to feature contrast charts. If you have devised and pursued a thorough online campaign strategy to date, some of this material will be ready to upload. Your communications staff should be prepared and primed to churn out the rest of it.

Content on Tap

You will want to strike a fresh pose in the wake of New Hampshire and Iowa, if for no other reason than press narratives will impose one on you anyway. Having content in reserve will enhance your capacity to argue that you (as rising underdog) are not just a sectional or single-issue candidate, or that you (as current überdog) have more going for you, and more facets of your character, than previously thought. So you should be ready with new issue positions, "chapters" of your autobiography, endorsements, and features for your Web site. For example, you might choose this phase of the campaign to unveil an array of candidate-to-camera videos; the ones that work can become the basis for a series. Alternately, you can trot out a clever interactive game on your Web site. Whatever you debut, remember that millions of Americans are now trying to imagine you as a worthy opponent for the president and, indeed, as president. Meet them more than halfway, and use the Internet to help burnish your image.

Of course, now that the field has narrowed, you will also want to draw upon your opposition research and attempt to revise your opponent's image. Going negative has been a staple of online campaigning since the prehistoric year of 1994, when an entity known as "De-Foley-ate Congress," or DF8, relied on e-mail and Usenet news groups to drum up opposition to House Speaker Thomas Foley (who lost).[17] A separate Web site, sponsored by a coalition of friends, makes a good platform from which to mount such an attack. A site constructed by an amateur enthusiast (as with Zack Exley and GWBush.com) serves you even better, because of its populist authenticity. If an attack is working, the isolated traffic will let you know. If it isn't, you can disassociate from it at low cost to your own image, as depicted on your own campaign Web site. You may also opt to launch an attack site under your campaign's name. This is a perfectly justified move if you are the underdog, and it may serve your campaign even if you are the favorite and the move gets widely interpreted as a sign of desperation. Wherever you locate the attack, keep in mind that humor works better online than unadulterated outrage (of the sort common to direct mail). Your research and sense of the current situation will help you decide on the proper tone.

The same dynamic that suggests the efficacy of going negative simultaneously warns you to expect attacks on you to intensify and proliferate in this period. The Internet will help you with damage control. A good news media list and a reputation for quick link-laden responses will help you quash rumors, correct flawed facts, and, in the worst case, get beyond embarrassments—ideally, in the very same news cycle in which potentially damaging information breaks. In 1998, the campaign network known as the JesseNet effectively doused the incendiary rumor that candidate Ventura favored legalizing prostitution in Minnesota. In his 2000 run for the presidency, John McCain was accused of writing a letter to a regulatory agency on behalf of a contributor. The accusation, if true, would have undermined McCain's position as an opponent of special interest politics. As a response, the McCain campaign argued that the senator routinely wrote letters on behalf of many constituents. The campaign posted more than one hundred letters as proof. The scandalous charge evaporated.

The Vote-Trading Gambit

As one candidate approaches the threshold of delegates needed to sew up the nomination, the possibility exists for a coalition to try and stop that from happening by setting up a vote-trading operation. In this scenario, supporters of other candidates (principally the underdogs, but also, perhaps, one or more also-rans) would come together in emulation of a technique first demonstrated in October, 2000. A vote-trading movement might come about as the result of a deal among candidates. But, as Moveon.org demonstrated, the Internet can be a hothouse for grassroots movements without any campaign's involvement.

Vote-trading was invented by political activists concerned that Ralph Nader's candidacy would keep Al Gore from winning the presidency. Web sites emerged that facilitated the voluntary pairing of Nader supporters in states where the polls showed a close race between Bush and Gore, on the one hand, and Gore supporters where the race was not close, on the other hand. Individuals from each category would make contact and agree to vote for the other's favorite, such that Gore would win in the close states, while Nader would amass more than 5 percent of the national vote and thereby qualify the Green party for federal funding in 2004. By one careful calculation, 16,024 online swaps were consummated, including 1,412 in Florida.[18]

The Nader-Gore vote-trading initiatives were stymied by legal actions and threats, largely from Republican Secretaries of State. That response attests to the potential power of the technique. Nothing yet seen in the short history of online electoral politics empowers individual voters as much as a vote-trading movement. It is perfectly legal and eminently moral, so long as citizens entering such a pact cast their own votes, under no coercion, and with no material or statutory benefit. Likewise, the Web site operators must only inform the public about the possibility of pairing, and neither bundle nor broker votes.

"Stop[front-runner's name].com" would be an initiative in "strategic voting and basic political speech," to quote Amy Morris, a Californian who co-founded votetrader.org in 2000.[19] Every Democratic candidate for the 2004 nomination should be aware of vote-trading. An independently organized "stop the front-runner" movement would be the best scenario underdogs could want; they would benefit without being susceptible to accusations of manipulating the nomination process.

TO THE CONVENTION AND BEYOND

Because of the compressed primary schedule, it is likely that the race for the nomination will be over by early March 2004, with five long months until the convention starts. When coupled with the GOP's inherent advantage of incumbency, the Democratic nominee presumptive will have a significant challenge sustaining interest and momentum behind his campaign.

Over this long slog, the Democratic nominee should seek to enroll the party faithful in a "virtual campaign committee." The price of membership would be an e-mail address and proof of registration to vote in November, 2004. The reward would be access to participate (everyone could view the proceedings) in an online forum where party activists can propose, discuss, and vote on slogans, platform planks, advertisements, vice-presidential nominees, and other items traditionally associated with a national political convention and the general election campaign to follow. It should be stated up front that the virtual campaign committee is strictly an advisory body, which actual party leaders will consult but not regard as binding.

By this time, the candidate should have an online diary. It will be of particular interest when the nominee presumptive travels abroad to establish foreign policy-making credibility. It will also be useful to smooth over factional rifts, online publicity for a faction being an inexpensive yet surprisingly effective compensation for losing a platform battle.

Staff Turnover and Database Security

By now you should have quite a campaign network: 500,000 Americans at least, we believe.[20] Across the nation (and to a limited degree, around the world), you are converting the curious into supporters, supporters into givers, givers into volunteers, and volunteers into staffers. The challenges of security and privacy now acquire extra urgency. Breaches are more likely to occur and will cost more to repair. There is no purely technological fix, but there are basic technological steps to take early in the campaign and review at regular intervals, such as the use of passwords and encryption. More important, you should backstop the technology with rules and responsibilities about data spelled out for each concentric band of your network. Volunteers should sign virtual contracts much as staffers sign actual contracts; although no money changes hands with volunteers, they can get you into trouble, as well as into office. As underdogs turn into also-rans, it is important for both their future and the immediate future of the nominee presumptive to have campaign policies in place to prevent list theft. Spell out what staff can and cannot take away from the campaign before the scramble for new positions begins.

The Convention News Hole

The hype bubble for online politics popped during the 2000 Republican and Democratic conventions. Dozens of online news mediators, including some dot-com start-ups, counted on the 2000 conventions as an opportunity to build loyal traffic. But "Internet Alley" and "Internet Avenue," as the online media areas of the convention press tents became known, respectively, turned out to resemble Potemkin villages more than corridors of power. For this the online entrepreneurs had themselves to blame, but only in part. The presidential nominees and their parties abetted the collapse through their neglect of the Net. No speaker at either convention invited the television audience to visit a political Web site. The only time George W. Bush referred to the Internet during his acceptance speech was to jibe at his opponent for being the reputed "father" of the medium. The line got a huge laugh, yet there was no online follow-through. And Gore did not attempt to refute or otherwise turn the tables on the assault. As a result, the mediators struggled to fill the enlarged news hole for the conventions.

The fate of online media is, of course, not your concern. But the 2000 nominees and parties missed a great opportunity. Historically, political campaigns have used new media to surprise and out-maneuver the opposition.[21] In 1952, for example, the Eisenhower campaign relied on television to win a crucial confrontation at the Republican convention. The Internet is no longer a new medium, strictly speaking, and confrontations seem to have been eliminated from conventions. But they still afford the presidential nominee and the party a great deal of news media coverage. The public still pays attention to them. Your campaign should incorporate the Internet into its publicity plans for the convention.

THE INTERNET AND THE REIGN OF TELEVISION

Your traditional media strategists will undoubtedly encourage your campaign to allocate significant resources to television advertising. The more you allocate, the more they make. While television spots and made-for-television events should certainly be a part of your communications plan, there is growing evidence from recent election cycles that the political power of traditional television is steadily diminishing. Cable channels, video-cassettes, and now DVDs have eroded the broadcast audience considerably. Just as presidents no longer command a huge audience for prime-time addresses, presidential nominees must also work over-time to get millions to see them speak.[22]

Television audiences may also be less influenced by political advertisements. They are exposed to them in droves at peak moments of a campaign. The ads lack the polish and pizzazz of corporate spots. So viewers press their mute and channel-change buttons, literally and figuratively, and they don't get the mes-sage. During the 2002 election cycle, both the Republican and Democratic parties were beginning to express concern about the diminishing impact of television. To quote then House Minority Leader Richard Gephardt (D-MO):

> We are moving into a new world, and I think the traditional model that we have gone on for 30 years, jamming millions of dollars into a television set and hope you drive enough folks to the polls on Election Day, is a passing method.[23]

One instructive example of the use of the Web as an alternative to TV advertis-ing was the Democratic National Committee's use of animated video to inject the debate over social security "privatization" into the campaign discourse during October of 2002. They created a short animated cartoon, posted it on the DNC Web site, and e-mailed it to their list of supporters and the media. The cartoon was controversial: it included an image of President Bush pushing a blue-haired senior in a wheelchair down a graph depicting the plummeting stock market, and within a few days had generated a great deal of media attention for the issue. It was also successful, attracting capital buzz for a week, and tens of thousands of new names to the DNC e-mail list. The RNC responded in kind, with a car-toon in which President Bush, dressed in a Superman costume, rescued the woman. Whereupon the DNC released a sequel, in which she berated the presi-dent over prescription drugs. Evidently, cartoons grab attention from the online public, many of whom are at work or study and are thus receptive to a break.

We do not know whether the much-vaunted "convergence" of media will take place in the machinery and the business. Indeed, we confess to not being sure whether convergence means cross-media promotion, all-purpose media receiv-ers, media industry consolidation, media content homogenization, or all of the above. But, as Walter Lippmann famously taught, important public messages have always converged in people's heads, and the Internet is now a significant part of the media mix delivering those messages.[24] At this stage of the Internet's development, we believe that the people are ahead of the politicians in going back and forth regularly and even seamlessly among media. Take the lead among your peers and catch up to the people. The Internet does not level the playing field among campaigns. Nor does it remove the access and exposure gates con-trolled by media conglomerates. But for those campaigns that start smart and stay with it, online campaigning can smooth bumps along the trail—providing extra amounts of money, credibility, and turnout when and where they are needed.

NOTES

1. For the latest data on Internet usage, see "The Big Picture" section at *www.cyberat las.com*, the annual reports produced by UCLA at *www.ccp.ucla.edu*, and the periodic reports at *www.pewinternet.org*.

2. The authors would like to thank Douglas Bailey, Mark Halperin, Michael McCurry, Dan Schnur, and Greg Simon for speaking with us at length about this subject.

3. U.S. Department of Commerce, National Telecommunications and Information Administration, "A Nation Online: How Americans Are Expanding Their Use of the Internet," February 2002, 45.

4. There are, however, speed limits constraining voter access to online campaign materials, especially for the majority today who connect to the Internet through their tele phone lines.

5. For final percentage figures not available at this writing, see *www.politicalweb.info*.

6. For an example involving fundraising letters sent out by an environmental group, see Roger Stone, "Case Studies: Using the Internet to Build Citizen Armies," *Campaigns & Elections*, April, 2001, 44–50.

7. Jack W. Germond and Jules Witcover, *Whose Broad Stripes and Bright Stars? The Trivial Pursuit of the Presidency 1988* (New York: Warner, 1989), 125.

8. These contribution figures were publicly challenged. Critics contended the McCain campaign padded its online take by directing donors contacted through other media to the Internet. The controversy is mooted on two grounds: first, even if one cuts the McCain figure in half, it is still a record; second, the contributions did not have to be solicited and collected solely through the Internet to qualify the phenomenon as an object lesson in how to use the medium.

9. For a good account of how the Internet can be used to get out the vote, see Nicho las Thompson, "Machined Politics," *Washington Monthly*, May 2002.

10. Arthur T. Hadley, *The Invisible Primary* (Englewood Cliffs, NJ: Prentice Hall, 1976). For a summary and reassessment of Hadley's argument, see Emmett H. Buell, Jr., "The Invisible Primary," in *In Pursuit of the White House: How We Choose Our Presiden tial Nominees*, ed. William G. Mayer (Chatham, NJ: Chatham House, 1996), 1–43.

11. *www.politicsontv.com*.

12. Dick Morris, *Behind the Oval Office: Getting Reelected Against All Odds* (Los Angeles: Renaissance Books, 1999), chap. 8.

13. Richard L. Berke, "The Last (E-Mail) Goodbye, From 'gwb' to His 42 Buddies," *New York Times*, March 17, 2001.

14. Ryan Thornburg, "Digital Donors: How Campaigns Are Using the Internet to Raise Money and How It's Affecting Democracy," Democracy Online Project Occasional Paper #1, November 2001, *www.ipdi.org*.

15. People like to take and see the instant results of phone-in and online polls, but no one regards the results as accurate barometers of public opinion. The participants are

self-selected, and therefore unrepresentative of an electoral population. Legitimate online polling is in its infancy.

16. Iowa Secretary of State Web site, *www.sos.state.ia.us*. The capacity and propriety of online media to place ads before residents of a specific geographic locality, and better yet, before those residents who are registered and even likely voters in a primary or caucus, is a matter of continuing dispute. Reviewing this dispute is beyond the scope of this chapter. Suffice it to say that this kind of online targeting lags the capacity of direct mail today, but that it is improving quickly.

17. Chris Casey, *The Hill on the Net* (Boston: AP Professional, 1996), 221.

18. Steve Davis, Larry Elin, and Grant Reeher, *Click On Democracy* (Boulder, CO: Westview Press, 2002), 122.

19. Davis, Elin, and Reeher, *Click On Democracy*, 139.

20. In the 2002 South Korean presidential election, the upset winner, Roh Moo-hyun, received 500,000 visitors a day to his campaign Web site. Over 180,000 donated money to his campaign, mostly through Internet-based campaign groups. About 25 million South Koreans regularly use the Internet, as compared with 116 million Americans, according to the Pew Internet & American Life Project. Multiplying Roh's numbers by 5 (assuming 125 million Americans online regularly by 2004) yields higher target numbers than the 500,000 we have conservatively designated here for a Democratic nominee presumptive. For more on the South Korean election, see Geoffrey York, "In South Korea, It's the Mouse that Roars," *Toronto Globe & Mail*, *www.globetechnology.com*, December 30, 2002.

21. Zachary Karabell, "The Rise and Fall of the Televised Political Convention," Joan Shorenstein Center on the Press, Politics, and Public Policy, Kennedy School of Government, Harvard University, October, 1998. Discussion Paper D-33.

22. Samuel Kernell and Matthew A. Baum, "Has Cable Ended the Golden Age of Presidential Television?" *American Political Science Review*, 93 (March 1999): 99–114.

23. Adam Nagourney, "TV's Tight Grip on Campaigns is Weakening," *New York Times*, September 5, 2002.

24. Walter Lippmann, *Public Opinion* (New York: Harcourt Brace, 1922), chap. 1.

7

Only a Lunatic Would Do This Kind of Work

A Journalist's Perspective on the Perspective of Journalists

David M. Shribman

The production of the first draft of history sometimes is not a pretty thing to watch. For generations the first draft of the history of presidential elections has been produced on laps—first, of course, on yellow legal pads, then on portable typewriters and, finally, on laptops. This is not contemplative work performed in tucked away study carrels or quiet office suites. It is produced against the soundtrack of an orator droning from the stump, or amid the street noise of a bus traveling through a crowded urban corridor, or while airplane engines roar and flight attendants pass with food trays. No Haydn symphonies play in the background. No reference books are employed, no graduate student researchers are deployed. No lengthy teas are taken in the library lounge, either. This first draft of history is produced on the run—written in haste and, as the old chestnut goes, repented in leisure.

Political journalism, much revered among its practitioners and much reviled among scholars, is an art form that is meant to be ephemeral. It is written by men and women in a hurry, working under impossibly trying conditions, and it is meant to be read by men and women in a hurry, reading under impossibly trying conditions; sometimes it is skimmed by well-meaning people hanging onto a subway strap but not hanging onto every word and not even gleaning the meaning. It captures today's thoughts and, in its most ambitious form, occasionally sketches them in context. It gives the who, the what, the where, and the when and then, not satisfied with polishing off four out of five, it goes on and attempts the why, almost always bungling it. The miracle, as Doctor Johnson, himself a promiscuous perpetrator of journalistic sins, might say, is not that it is done well but that it is done at all.

This art form, if the phrase be permitted, is occasionally fun to write and less often fun to read. It is often indispensable to insiders and inconsequential to others. It is indecipherable to many. It is difficult to produce and easy to ridicule. It is intertwined with the important questions of the day, and its importance has often faded by nighttime. It is produced for the literate class but its quality almost never approaches literature.

But no one argues that it is unimportant. The founders conceived of a political system based on the considered views of an informed citizenry. The modern American system is a republican form of government with a democratic foundation; the notion that voters should be informed about their choices is implicit in our politics, and in an era of mass culture and mass media the opportunities to be informed are nearly without limit. Even so, the elected class and those who vote for its members depend on an unelected class of journalists for the information they need. It is a formula for tension among competing interests and for resentments among all the principals. It is also a formula for a fascinating struggle played out, as all American civic dramas are, in public.

H. L. Mencken, the great student of American culture and the great sociologist of the American journalist, once wrote that Washington reporters were "unable to distinguish men of sense and dignity from mountebanks," adding: "They come in as newspapermen, trained to get the news and eager to print it; they end as tin-horn statesmen, full of dark secrets and unable to write the truth if they tried."[1] Things have improved, if perhaps only marginally, since then. Most political reporters have college degrees. A few read books, some of them produced by college professors. By and large they can name, in correct chronological order, all of the American presidents since Franklin Delano Roosevelt. But as a class they have only the most tentative grasp of economics; they know the difference between an appropriations bill and an authorization bill, to be sure, but not between monetary policy and fiscal policy. (They take refuge in the fact that John Kennedy did not either. He was told to remember that the word "monetary" and the name of the chairman of the Federal Reserve Bank, William McChesney Martin, both began with "m.") Many of them feel that the Tariff of Abominations is the last one they were forced to cover on Capitol Hill. Their acquaintance with science is fleeting, based mainly on what they remember from the space program and what they saw at the Three Mile Island hearings. They are experts in American aviation, as long as the subject is the nuances of the hub-and-spoke system, a topic they have mastered with great fluency and great enthusiasm; when it comes to ailerons, however, they are completely flustered. They have been to more state fairs than the average American, but fewer PTA meetings. They have seen the inside of American Legion halls from coast to coast but probably haven't spent much time in uniform themselves. They have eaten more meals in buses than most Americans, but during campaign season they are less likely than the average American to be carrying their car keys.

They think they have a broad outlook but they think narrowly. They believe it is common knowledge that the second congressional district in Oregon borders Washington, and it is a matter of orthodoxy among them that everybody knows that South Dakota has only one member of Congress. They think that the people they stop at a shopping center care as much about the election that is approaching as their editors do. They labor under the conviction that theirs is the most important, most selfless, most vital work performed by anyone in the nation. They believe it is possible they are wrong about some things, but they think that the matters they are wrong about are little things, like how many votes Eugene V. Debs got in 1912 or how many ballots it took the Democrats to nominate John W. Davis in 1924.

In an age of doubt, they believe. They believe in the virtue of free exchange of information and ideas. They believe in the virtue of newspapers. (They are less sure about cable television.) They believe in their right to ask candidates their views on all manner of subjects. They believe in their right to ask candidates whether they think their poll ratings are so low that they ought to drop out of the race. They believe that political candidates will actually tell them the truth, even when the question is about whether they think their poll ratings are so low that they ought to drop out of the race. They believe that politicians should respect their deadlines. They believe that politics is important.

They pride themselves on not being innocent, and yet they may be the last innocents. They believe that everyone should vote. They believe that politics— elective politics, the kind they like to cover from buses and airplanes and, best of all, from the seat beside the candidate in a private automobile too small to accommodate a correspondent from a competing outlet—is the best way to address a nation's problems or to gauge a nation's priorities. They think, as Richard Harding Davis wrote in 1891, that "the sun rises only that men may have light by which to read" the morning paper.[2]

They are cynics but they are idealists. They know the system's limits but they believe in the system's sense of justice. They believe that the virtuous are rewarded and the evil are punished. (They believe the resignation of Richard M. Nixon in 1974 proved this.) They believe that there is nothing wrong with the country that honest politicians, high voter turnout, gavel-to-gavel television coverage of political conventions, immediate disclosure of campaign contributions, and a decent hotel room at the end of a long campaign day won't cure. They especially hope that that hotel gives frequent-guest points.

They have an ethos. They believe in inquiry. They believe in the value of the pointed question. They believe in catching their prey in an unscripted moment, or in a lie. They believe in asking impertinent questions of their social betters. They believe small deviations from a candidate's basic stump speech have grave implications. They believe they are independent thinkers, even though their work is filtered through several layers of editors who adjust their language, trim their excesses, and assure their copy conforms with the version produced by the wire services.

Theirs is hard work but it is meant to be read easily. They endure physical strains, mostly exhaustion, but they have an inexhaustible enthusiasm for the story. They believe that exhaustive coverage is the very best coverage. They believe, in fact, in the broader definition of coverage—that there should be nothing about politics that should remain uncovered. In non-election years they are far less orthodox about that doctrine; the thought of blanket coverage of Washington's regulatory agencies, where real political dramas of a different sort are played out day by day, often without press witness, fills them with a primeval fear. There is no meeting of a regional governors association that is too obscure for them to attend. There is no meeting of the Securities and Exchange Commission that is important enough for them. They know how members of the Republican National Committee are chosen but they are less sure about how the members of the Federal Highway Commission are chosen. They attach great meaning to the selection of the honorary chairman of the Democratic National Convention but are not sure how long the chairman of the Federal Aviation Administration serves.

They believe their jobs confer upon them immense social status. They believe that at their college reunions their classmates who head billion-dollar mutual funds or played in the World Series or Super Bowl would gladly swap lives with them for the chance to go to the Iowa Straw Poll, where a meaningless event has been infused with great meaning. Their editors tell them, and they believe, that they are the people's representatives, travelling to remote country crossroads so they can tell the rest of the country what America is like. They count the number of states they have visited and every one of them knows the exact number. (Hawaii, Alaska, and North Dakota are among the most coveted. The prominence of an early-winter primary and bitterly contested Senate races in the state have removed much of the appeal of South Dakota.) They believe that they can better understand America, and thus American politics, by travelling, and thus they attach special importance to the dateline, the capitalized first word of a news story that identifies where the piece was produced.

Behind all of their bravado, however, political reporters have a deep sense of insecurity. In some of them it is actually a sense of inferiority. They know that, unlike doctors, dentists, and lawyers, they are required to have no formal training. There is no licensing authority, no qualifying boards. They like to think of themselves as professionals but in truth their profession is more of a craft. They learn on the run, not in laboratories or libraries. They learn by making mistakes, which is a humbling experience, particularly because a 1,000-word story has 1,000 opportunities for mistakes. They know that the very serious preparation required by chemists and geneticists has no analogue in journalism. They are more like blacksmiths than biochemists.

These insecurities are particularly pronounced in their relationships with political scientists and, to a lesser extent, historians. On the surface, they are all practitioners of the same arts—education, research, the examination of political life. But the assumptions they bring to bear on the subject, the preparations required to be in the professions, the work habits, the time constraints, and the working conditions could not be more different. They read different materials, spend their leisure hours differently, have different professional norms.

And yet their work is complementary. Political scientists depend enormously on the work of political journalists, a notion that is held particularly strongly by political journalists—who sometimes note with quiet humor that most of what the political scientists they encounter say about contemporary politics is directly traceable to daily newspapers, public television, magazines, and political journals.

Political journalists, for their part, lean heavily on the work of political scientists. They depend on their polling data, their perceptions, and their perspectives. In the past generation, when increasing numbers of college-educated correspondents began covering politics, political coverage has become more academic. Many of the correspondents and columnists themselves hold degrees in government or political science and at the very least are conversant in the language of political science, familiar with the literature of political science, and comfortable in conversation with political scientists. As a result, many correspondents have been holding the equivalent of telephonic brown-bag lunches with political scientists at colleges and universities around the nation, exchanging ideas, perspective, information, and gossip.

One of the tangible results of this discourse is the increasingly frequent use of professors in political stories. These professors often are quoted as informed observers and analysts. In many cases they play the role of impartial arbiters in stories, giving a detached and reliable view or perspective. Political journalists are far more willing to quote a professor with a partisan outlook than they are to quote a partisan giving the very same perspective; from the journalist's point of view, the professor's perspective is somehow less contaminated than the partisan's. In addition, political journalists turn to political scientists for the equivalent of a hasty seminar on a complicated subject; a reporter travelling to Tennessee to cover a governor's race of which he has no prior knowledge will often call a professor in the state to get a quick "fill." Some of the information imparted in that conversation will form the background of the story, some of it will be inserted in the story, and some of it will appear as a quotation. It is in all senses an honest exchange—professors and the public relations specialists at their universities will be pleased that they are cited as experts in the public prints and the political journalist will have reputable commentary inside his story.

There is another, important role that remarks from political scientists play in political journalism. One of the bedrock principles of journalism is that news stories should be "straight"—i.e., that they should not lean to one side ideologically or in a partisan manner. Often a political journalist will want to impart an idea that the normal strictures of objective journalism make it impossible to convey—the notion, for example, that one candidate's campaign is sputtering hopelessly, or that another candidate's views are out of synch with his constituents'. These are points that are almost impossible to make within the normal confines of orthodox journalism. But a journalist can lean on a so-called expert, particularly one whose credentials include tenure in a reputable college or university, to make the very same point. In that case, the journalist merely quotes *someone else* making the very point his editors or his sense of journalistic convention prohibit him from making. This phenomenon underscores one of the critical but often unrecognized characteristics of modern journalism: the importance of the political journalist's decision to include one idea, or to exclude another, from a story.

Political scientists and political journalists do share one thing in common—a respect for a body of literature that can be described as a "canon." These are different canons, to be sure. The one revered by journalists is, not surprisingly, produced mainly by journalists. But an observer of American political journalism can better understand the genre if he understands what journalists know and revere. Even if all political journalists have not read all of these volumes, they have been taught, or reprimanded, or mentored by journalists who have. The ideas in these books are embedded in the consciousness of every political journalist. They are as much a part of his tools as his notebook, his computer, and, of course, his cell phone.

The first entry in this canon is Theodore H. White's *The Making of the President 1960*. For political reporters, it is the equivalent of *Beowulf*, the *Chancon de Roland*, *The Canterbury Tales*, *King Lear*, and the King James Version of the Bible—combined. Much imitated and much derided, it nonetheless survives, for conventional political correspondents at least, as the founding document of their craft. Its attributes are compelling: The writing is crisp and intimate, the descriptions are detailed and telling, the range is wide and inclusive. Many aspects of the book seem treacly at the distance of four decades, but the access to John F. Kennedy and Richard M. Nixon that White had and the scenes he painted still provoke awe among even the most seasoned professionals.

White's book created a new genre, the campaign book—one which was exhausted with astonishing speed, all but disappearing a quarter-century later. But it also created a new style of political reporting. Its emphasis on the small observation, on the daily details of campaign life, continue to this day; hardly a newsmagazine story on a presidential campaign begins without a paragraph describing the candidate at work at his trade, either reaching for the outstretched arms of eager campaign supporters or huddling over a cheeseburger with worried aides or relaxing on the campaign plane. Indeed, the scores of stories each campaign cycle that begin with a candidate leaning back in the seat of his charter jetliner is a measure of the impact White had on the political correspondents who followed him. At the heart of this technique was the notion that great truths about a candidate could be found by examining not only how his mind worked, not only how his campaign style worked, not only how his campaign staff worked, but also how the mechanics of his campaign worked. The logic is tenuous, but the dramatic appeal is undeniable.

Critics later chided White for his chumminess with the candidates he covered—for the breezy familiarity he had with them. His campaign book is full of asides about remarks the candidate made in private, about how things affected the candidate, and together these made for what, years later, would seem a cloying identification with the candidate—or, more broadly, a sympathy with the governing or the political class. White is vulnerable to such a critique. But the brilliance of his book was not how he handled a form that was well-established but, instead, how he established a form that had barely existed before.

Despite the critiques, there remains great appeal, at least to the political correspondent, for what White invented in 1959 and 1960. There breathes few of that band who have not tried, consciously or not, to write a paragraph like this one, which is actually only the sixth paragraph of the book:

> He was tense, it seemed, as he voted, thronged and jostled by the same adhesive train of reporters who had followed him, thronging and jostling, for three months across the country; only now his wife was with him in the press, and he was uncomfortable at how the pushing might affect her, she being eight months pregnant. He let himself be focused as he came from the booth, and then the last cavalcade began, in familiar campaign order—photographers' car first, candidate's car second (the top of the convertible shut, for he did not want his wife to catch cold), security car next, three press buses following. It moved swiftly out of the West End, down through the grimy blight of Scollay Square, under the tunnel to East Boston and the airport. This had been his first political conquest—the Eleventh Congressional District of Massachusetts, immigrants' land, full of Irish, Italians, Jews, some Negroes, few Yankees.[3]

This description of Senator Kennedy's trip from the voting booth in the third precinct, sixth ward, of Boston, to Logan Airport on Election Day 1960 is in some ways the apotheosis of the genre. It shows familiarity, intimacy, and history, all in four sentences that, by the modest standards of journalism, approach the lyrical. And this paragraph hints at White's greatest asset as a student of American politics, his knowledge of the country, its byways, its folklore. Only a page earlier he had imparted the knowledge that "America is Republican until five or six in the evening," adding: "It is in the last few hours of the day that working people and their families vote, on their way home from work or after supper; it is then, at evening, that America goes Democratic if it goes Democratic at all."[4]

And there is mystery: "All of this is invisible, for it is the essence of the act [of voting] that as it happens it is a mystery in which millions of people each fit one fragment of a total secret together, none of them knowing the shape of the whole."[5]

But most of all there is deep familiarity with the territory, with that word taking on multiple meanings: the land, of course, but the people, too. White understood the power of people, the power of demographics, in a democratic country, and so he studied, with ruthless attention to detail, the demographic patterns that make a nation. It was a happy accident of history that a compelling presidential race, matching two young men who were alike in promise and experience, each with Naval service in his background, came at the time of one of the nation's decennial censuses. White saw the trends the census unearthed, the slow death, for example, of the cities—all but one of the 15 biggest cities lost population between 1950 and 1960, a trend that would continue and would shape elections far beyond 1960—and stitched these trends, seamlessly, into his narrative. He told of the rise of the suburbs, the drive to develop the open lands and the farmlands, the relentless change in employment patterns (only 822,000 men worked on the railroads in 1960, down from 1,464,000 at the end of World War II), the rise in the use of oil and gas and the decline in the use of coal. "From the figures of the census, as from a crossroads, a dozen highways of analysis led forth," he wrote. And so he talked about credit, and mortgages, and the eternal American struggle between public and private enterprise, and the growth in professional and clerical employment and the decline in industrial employment, even the decline in the kinds of apples available to the American consumer. All this to him was politics, and to the modern political correspondent that constitutes a remarkable birthright. All of American life, from 1960 onward, was political. All of American life was fodder for the political correspondent.[6]

The effect of the White book on political correspondents cannot be overemphasized. Suddenly news stories were full of insider stuff—so much so that these details (what the candidate wore off camera, whether there was cantaloupe or honeydew on the fruit plate) became standard, almost clichés.

Newsmagazine editors began to refer to them as "nuts on the fruitcake," and ordered their correspondents to search them out. Indeed, some presidential campaigns—Walter F. Mondale's, for example, in 1984, and George W. Bush's, in 2000—put aside time late in each week to brief *Time* and *Newsweek* correspondents on just such items; the practice has carried over to the Bush administration, which on Fridays briefs newsmagazine correspondents in sessions that both sides call "feedings." The White book also led to increased attention to "roar of the greasepaint, smell of the crowd" coverage, in which political writers described what it was like to stand in the Quad Cities and see the candidate's rally, and to a new emphasis on what correspondents call "process" stories.

These process stories have become a mainstay of political coverage. They examine how, for example, convention delegate slates are chosen, or how convention delegates, once elected, are wooed by various campaigns. (One classic of the genre explored how the Michael S. Dukakis campaign in 1988 discovered that a critical delegate liked ceramic dogs. The campaign tailored its appeal to this delegate through the ceramic-dog connection.) These process stories reach their high point every four years with the selection of a running-mate, as campaigns now traditionally give briefings on how the nominee chooses his vice-presidential candidate. The level of detail sometimes is astonishing. In 1984, for example, the Mondale campaign secretly flew Representative Geraldine R. Ferraro of New York to the candidate's Minnesota home. The chronology of the vice-presidential selection process that the Mondale campaign provided included how one of the Mondale children noticed that a blonde woman was sleeping in one of the bedrooms of their home. This phenomenon isn't confined to campaigns. In the summer of 2001, the George W. Bush administration provided extensive details on how the president reached his stem-cell research decision; the briefing included which books Bush had read and which experts he consulted. All that is the legacy of Theodore H. White.

The bookend to the White volume might be Hunter S. Thompson's *Fear and Loathing on the Campaign Trail.* The Thompson book, perhaps the high point of "gonzo journalism," portrayed the presidential election in all its insanity, in all its frenzy, in all its dehumanizing and preposterous excess. That, of course, was its appeal, even to mainstream journalists who couldn't have persuaded their editors to print even a single paragraph of reportage in the Thompson style even if they were capable of producing one. But Thompson also expresses the political reporters' frustration:

> It never occurred to me that anything could be worse than getting stuck on another Nixon campaign, so it came as a definite shock to find that hanging around Florida with Ed Muskie was even duller and more depressing than travelling with Evil Dick himself.[7]

Or:

> Only a lunatic would do this kind of work: twenty-three primaries in five months; stone drunk from dawn till dusk and huge seed-blisters all over my head. Where is the meaning?[8]

Thompson had his own writing style and his own lifestyle; his colleagues on the campaign plane were more likely to repair to drink than to drugs, despite Thompson's assertions to the contrary. But the point stands. During every campaign every sane person has this epiphany: Only a lunatic would do this kind of work. (The only thing worse than covering an election, the political reporter concludes, is not covering an election, which is why there is so much recidivism.)

The place of *Fear and Loathing* in the journalists' pantheon illuminates another aspect of the political reporter's character—his knowledge that, for all the earnestness he brings to bear on his written product or his television spot, the process of electing a president is itself a portrait in absurdity. Presidential elections begin, for example, in two of the least representative states in the nation, Iowa and New Hampshire, each with a population of less than 3 percent African-Americans. In some of the states, including Iowa, the convention delegates are selected not by voters in the privacy of curtained-off booths but by caucus goers who are even less representative than primary voters and whose actions are vulnerable to the group dynamics and peer pressure inherent in any open, social gathering. Then the convention delegates meet at a national convention where their actions are not bound by law and where little of consequence has happened on the floor since 1952. Finally, the general election campaign begins but, in theory, the candidate with the most votes doesn't necessarily win. In 2000, that theory became reality, to the immense discomfort of the George W. Bush campaign, to the immense distress of the Albert Gore Jr. campaign, and to the immense embarrassment of anyone trying to export the American system to developing nations abroad.

The Thompson book also underlines another aspect of modern political correspondence, the tendency of journalists to become marinated in the meaningless blather of the conventions of politics. These conventions include rhetorical offensives known popularly as "spin"; the overly cautious language of candidates whose thoughts and words are controlled by overly cautious handlers; the mind-numbing repetitiveness of the ordinary campaign day; and the effort to make a process that has become a mass-marketing exercise look and feel like a mom-and-pop retail operation. Campaigns were always manipulative; the whole point of them is to persuade people to perform something they might not otherwise be disposed to do. But in recent years, the level of manipulation has grown substantially while the entire process has become laced with cynicism. In late 1987, for example, while working as a *Wall Street Journal* political correspondent, I visited a tiny community north of Concord, New Hampshire, which is the customary demarcation point for the end of urban and suburban New Hampshire and the beginning of the state's more remote areas. In the course of speaking with a state senator about the approaching New Hampshire primary I overheard the sound of children shouting playfully. To a native New England ear that meant one thing. "Is that the sound of kids skating on a pond?" I asked. The senator answered: "You want kids skating on a pond? We can do that."

Such exchanges only reinforce the political reporter's notion that, as some correspondents say, the entire process "isn't on the level." In many ways it is not. But political correspondents bear some measure of the blame. They perpetuate stereotypes that conform to their own romantic views of the story they are covering, writing, for example, of the public's rabid interest in the political process when reports prepared by the Committee for the Study of the American Electorate show a steep and alarming drop in voter participation. In this regard, most political journalists have sinned. They have written of communities seething with political passion, of huge masses of voters who immerse themselves in political literature, of spontaneous coffee shop debates about taxation or war. By and large this phenomenon does not exist.

A third element of the political canon is Timothy Crouse's *The Boys on the Bus: Riding with the Campaign Press Corps*, which reporters like in part because it is about them. In truth, the Crouse book elevated reporters from mere spectators in the political drama to full participants. In that regard, Crouse merely acknowledged the obvious, though he did so with style and depth. But he also helped contribute to the new image of news reporters—an image that would only be burnished by the Watergate scandal, which elevated news reporters into modern-day crusaders for all that is right and pure, or at least that is the way reporters see it. In any case, in the Crouse book the beat reporters who once were nearly anonymous became well-known figures, transforming R. W. Apple of the *New York Times* and David S. Broder of the *Washington Post* into near celebrities. Both, of course, are giants of our trade. But neither thought of himself as a "personality"—just as a reporter.

And yet Crouse didn't only feast on the heavy-hitters from the big eastern papers. A onetime reporter, he knew where power in the press lies:

> If you live in New York or Los Angeles, you have probably never heard of Walter Mears and Carl Leubsdorf, who were covering McGovern for the Associated Press, or Steve Gerstel, who covered him for United Press International. But if your home is Sheboygan or Aspen, and you read the local papers, they are probably the only political journalists you know. . . .
>
> So the wire services are influential beyond calculation. Even at the best newspapers, the editor always gauges his own reporters' stories against the expectations that the wire stories have aroused. The only trouble is that wire stories are usually bland, dry, and overly cautious. There is an inverse proportion between the number of persons a reporter reaches and the amount he can say. The larger the audience, the more inoffensive and inconclusive the article must be.[9]

Wire-service news reporting has changed considerably since then; Mears and the reporters who followed him, including David Espo, John King, and Ron Fournier, themselves helped change that perception. But the larger point stands: In the first draft of history, the wire service reporters draft the first draft.

Crouse understood, too, the limits of the genre. In his book, he quotes a young assistant to Jack Anderson named Brit Hume, who would later win celebrity as a gritty ABC News White House reporter and now as managing editor and chief Washington correspondent of Fox News:

"Those guys on the plane," said Hume, "claim that they're trying to be objective. They shouldn't try to be objective, they should try to be honest. And they're *not* being honest. Their so-called objectivity is just a guise for superficiality. They report what one candidate said, then they go and report what the other candidate said with equal credibility. They never get around to finding out if the guy is telling the truth. They just pass the speeches along without trying to confirm the substance of what the candidates are saying. What they pass off as objectivity is just a mindless kind of neutrality."[10]

That, too, would be addressed, though only partially, by the next generation of journalists, a generation that grew up reading the Crouse book.

But one element still has not been fully addressed. Crouse called his book *The Boys on the Bus*, and in 1972 virtually all of the riders on the bus were boys. They were also white. Some strides have been made, with women playing more prominent roles in campaign coverage. The *Washington Post, New York Times*, and Associated Press, among others, assigned women as their principal reporters on the Gore campaign in 2000, for example. But there is still room for progress. The boys on the bus should be a literary metaphor, not an accurate description.

These are not the only books in the canon. The veteran reporters Jack W. Germond and Jules Witcover wrote several volumes about presidential elections. Tom Rosensteil's *Strange Bedfellows*, written after the 1992 election and concentrating on the interplay between television and presidential elections, is regarded as a classic. So, too, is Richard Ben Cramer's monumental *What It Takes: The Way to the White House*, which was published in 1992 but which dealt with many of the principal figures in the 1988 campaign. The latest entries into the pantheon are Roger Simon's *Showtime*, about the 1996 election, and Frank Bruni's *Ambling Into History: The Unlikely Odyssey of George W. Bush*. In many ways these volumes reflect political correspondents' views of the process they cover. The cover of the accounts of the 1960 and 1964 elections, White's *Making of the President*, featured the seal of the president of the United States. The most memorable account of the next election was *The Selling of the President 1968*, by Joe McGinnis. On its cover was a pack of cigarettes with Richard M. Nixon's face. Later books by Germond and Witcover had titles such as *Wake Us When It's Over* and *Blue Smoke and Mirrors*. And, of course, the big book from the 1996 election was called *Showtime*. From *The Making of the President* to *Showtime* in one generation—the titles themselves are a portrait in the decline of politics.

Part of the decline of politics is the decline in the public's view of many of the principals in politics. This includes politicians themselves, to be sure, but it also includes the writers who report on politics. This has led to several widely held views about how political reporters approach their jobs, the most harmful of which is that political journalists are biased.

This is a conviction that is deeply held by many who watch the press cover elections. It is a view that countless studies have sought to examine. It is a view that many journalists contest—and the fact that they do so is sometimes cited as evidence itself of journalists' blindness to reality. This is an argument as old as the hills, unlikely to be settled anytime soon. For the purposes of this chapter, let it be said that the charge of bias is apt—but not in the way most critics make it.

Journalists indeed do have a strong bias, but that bias is more a bias toward change than it is a bias toward either of the political parties or toward the right or the left. The entire premise of journalism is change; journalists chronicle how the world is different today from the way it was yesterday. In years of Democratic rule, that bias often takes the form of a subtle preference for Republican gains. In years of Republican rule, that bias often takes the form of a subtle preference for Democratic gains. In this regard, the elections of 1992 and 1994 were the fulfillment of journalists' subconscious dreams; after a dozen years of Republican rule in the White House, a Democrat, Bill Clinton, was elected president, and after forty years of Democratic rule in the House, a new group of Republicans, led by the insurgent Newt Gingrich, was in power. This was inconvenient, to be sure—journalists suddenly found that their Rolodexes of important sources were worthless—but it was exciting as well. This bias toward change doesn't grow only out of the journalistic desire for something new. It also grows out of journalists' inclination to be distrustful of established authority, which is itself a bias.

There is no proof either way in this longstanding dispute. But this theory of bias—that journalists prefer change more than they prefer the ideology of either party—is buttressed by the impatience that presidents of both parties have with reporters. Presidents Bill Clinton and George W. Bush may agree on very little, but they share a deep distrust of the press.

Political journalists are more vulnerable to the notion that they are inclined to fit much of what they see on the campaign trail into a narrative they have established in their minds beforehand. This critique has bipartisan support. In the 2000 election, the supporters of Al Gore believed that reporters approached the campaign with the fixed idea that the former vice president was prone to exaggeration. Similarly, George W. Bush's supporters were convinced that reporters believed he was uninformed and careless with language. As a result, according to this argument, every time Gore committed even a meaningless exaggeration, members of the travelling press jumped all over it as evidence of their theory. The pattern worked the same way with Bush; whenever he bungled a sentence of his syntax, reporters seized on the episode as evidence of his intellectual shallowness.

Journalists are also vulnerable to charges that they are captives of their sources and of their relationships in the political establishment. This argument holds that political journalists are in too cozy a dance with politicians, that they socialize with them too intimately, that they identify with their interests too closely. Indeed, sometimes there is an unmistakable sense of we're-all-in-this-together among politicians and the journalists who cover them. This sense is reinforced not only on the campaign trail, where as travelling companions they are thrust together in work and social settings—and often in settings where it is impossible to distinguish between the two. It is reinforced, too, in Washington, where correspondents encounter politicians at receptions, neighborhood parties, and formal dinners. Sometimes the contact is unavoidable; journalists find themselves interacting with politicians, consultants, and staff members in civic activities, in the PTA, or in places of worship. It is not unusual for a correspondent to run into a politician in line at the supermarket or on the shuttle to New York or Boston.

There are no formal rules for handling these situations, for life on the road and in the capital is full of chance encounters. Not long ago, for example, a reporter discovered that one of the people for whom her daughter was babysitting was a professional contact of hers; the babysitting arrangement was made by the daughter without knowledge of the interaction of her parent and her employer. Similarly, some journalists in their role as parents would casually encounter Vice President Gore at school events. These episodes do not necessarily mean that any inappropriate conversations or arrangements ensued; they only serve to indicate that, in the small world of the political establishment, complete isolation is sometimes not possible. One guideline, however, might be applied with success: In these encounters, journalists should be polite but businesslike—friendly, in short, but not friends with politicians.

A more serious problem might be the notion that political journalists and politicians share many of the same assumptions about life. They do read the same materials, see the same polls, talk with the same people, travel to the same places. They identify, moreover, with some of the same values and inclinations—big ones (like the importance of politics in the life of the nation) and little ones (like an obsession with the intricacies of public opinion research or the utility of negative campaign advertising). In short, they share the same view of the world and they share the same shorthand.

The careful journalist takes knowledge from these shared views but resists identifying with the interests of a politician or of the political class as a whole. This requires enormous discipline and vigilance. But the journalist who succeeds in achieving this can remain an outsider even while understanding the mind of the insider. That is the ultimate challenge of political reporting today.

So what are we to make of the modern journalist in the modern age?

That he or she must navigate a difficult passage, between the knowledge of the insider and the outlook of the outsider. That he must be vigilant against bias even in its most subtle form, the bias toward change that is embedded in the business of journalism itself. That the zeal of the journalist—to know, to understand, to ferret out, to write—is at once the cause of admiration within his profession and suspicion outside of it. That the work of the journalist is hard but exhilarating, that it offers an intoxicating sense of variety and a mind-numbing repetitiveness, that it is critical to the operation of democratic rule but that it is open to the criticism that is inherent in any democratic society. That the modern journalist examines the story of our time, but sometimes operates in a world whose language and assumptions are part of a small elite. That, above all, the political journalist practices an imperfect art chronicling the work of imperfect people in an imperfect system.

NOTES

1. H. L. Mencken, *A Gang of Pecksniffs,* (New York: Knopf, 1975), 135–136.

2. Richard Harding Davis, "The Reporter Who Made Himself King," *Encyclopedia of the Self* (2002), *www.selfknowledge.com/rking10.htm.*

3. Theodore H. White, *The Making of the President 1960* (New York: Atheneum, 1961), 4.

4. White, *The Making of the President 1960,* 3.

5. White, *The Making of the President 1960,* 3.

6. White, *The Making of the President 1960,* 218.

7. Hunter S. Thompson, *Fear and Loathing: On the Campaign Trail '72* (New York: Popular Library, 1973), 116.

8. Thompson, *Fear and Loathing,* 186.

9. Timothy Crouse, *The Boys on the Bus: Riding with the Campaign Press Corps* (New York: Random House, 1973), 19.

10. Crouse, *The Boys on the Bus,* 305.

8

The Perils of Polling in New Hampshire

Andrew E. Smith

The consensus of ten pre-election polls taken during the final days of the 2000 New Hampshire presidential primary campaign was that both John McCain and Al Gore would win comfortably over their main rivals, George W. Bush and Bill Bradley. The estimates for McCain's margin over Bush averaged 8 percentage points, and ranged from 12 percentage points (Gallup, Zogby) to a tie (ARG). Gore's predicted margin of victory also averaged 8 percentage points and ranged from 1 percentage point (UMass-Boston) to 17 percentage points (Quinnipiac).

But on election day, the pollsters took it on the chin. Both McCain and Gore won, but as shown in table 8.1, none of the ten major media polls came close to estimating correctly the magnitude of McCain's 18-percentage-point victory over Bush, and few predicted that the race between Gore and Bradley would be so close: In the end, the vice president beat the former New Jersey senator by just 4 percentage points. *None* of the polls predicted both races with a high degree of accuracy.

Although the polls did not perform well in 2000 when there were two competitive primaries, they had done a remarkably good job in predicting the 1996 Republican primary (Bill Clinton ran unopposed on the Democratic side that year). Most polls showed a very close race between Bob Dole and Pat Buchanan and, indeed, Buchanan pulled out a narrow 27 percent to 26 percent victory.

Predicting elections is perhaps the only time that survey researchers are judged against a clear, real world standard: how close their predictions come to the actual vote. If a polling organization claims that 60 percent of Americans support the president's economic policies or that 45 percent favor tax cuts, there is no obvious way to prove that these assertions are off the mark. But when a poll

Table 8.1 How Pollsters Fared in Predicting the 2000 New Hampshire Primary

	Actual Results Feb. 1	American Research Group Jan. 29–31	Boston Globe/WBZ by KRC Jan. 29–30	Boston Herald/WCVB by RKM Jan. 30–31	CBS Jan. 26–30	CNN/USA Today/Gallup Jan. 30–31	UMass Jan. 29–30	WMUR Fox/UNH Jan. 28–31	WNDS by Franklin Pierce Jan. 27–30	Quinnipiac College Jan. 27–30	Zogby/Reuters/WHDH-TV Jan. 30–31
REPUBLICANS											
McCain	48.5	36	38	40	39	44	37	41	40	39	44
Bush	30.4	36	34	29	35	32	28	34	29	29	32
Forbes	12.7	16	13	11	10	13	15	13	15	12	14
Keyes	6.4	5	5	10	6	7	7	8	5	10	9
Bauer	0.7	1	3	1	1	1	1	0	1	1	1
Other/Undecided	1.4	5	7	9	9	12	12	4	9	10	0
McCain Lead over Bush	18.1	0	4	11	4	12	9	7	11	10	12
DEMOCRATS											
Gore	49.7	51	48	48	55	54	45	49	47	53	56
Bradley	45.6	45	42	43	39	42	44	46	41	36	44
Other/Undecided	4.7	4	10	9	6	4	11	5	11	11	0
Gore Lead over Bradley	4.1	6	6	5	16	12	1	3	6	17	12
Total Error[a]		20	16	8	26	14	12	12	9	21	14

Source: Compiled by David W. Moore and cited with permission.

[a]Total error is the sum of the differences between a poll's predicted gap between the top two candidates and the actual gap in the vote between the top two candidates.

taken just before an election says that candidate Smith is solidly ahead of candidate Jones, every pollster knows that the events of the next few days may show that prediction to be either right on the mark or disastrously, embarrassingly wrong. Accurately predicting elections can put a polling organization on the map (as happened to Zogby in the 1996 presidential election), while inaccurate polling can literally bankrupt a company (as happened to the *Literary Digest* after they wrongly predicted that Alf Landon would easily defeat Franklin Roosevelt in the 1936 election). When election polls are not accurate, pollsters therefore spend considerable effort trying to determine where they went wrong, so that they can improve their methods for future elections.

What made the 2000 New Hampshire presidential primary so difficult for pollsters? This chapter will attempt to answer that question in the context of a larger analysis of how pre-election polls are conducted and how they should be evaluated. I begin therefore with a brief overview of pre-election surveys. Next, I will look at a number of factors that make polling in New Hampshire particularly problematic. These include legal issues concerning the universe of eligible voters, recent demographic changes in the state, and certain methodological problems that, while common to almost all pre-election polling, operate with special force in New Hampshire. All of which will, I hope, provide readers with a better background for evaluating polls in the 2004 campaign.

A PRIMER ON PRE-ELECTION POLLING

Before discussing the particular problems of polling in New Hampshire, it may be helpful to present a brief look at how pre-election polls in general are conducted. What follows is not a step-by-step, "how to" guide, but is simply designed to familiarize the reader with the basic concepts and terms involved in polling.[1] Since almost all contemporary pre-election polls are conducted by telephone, this discussion is confined to that method of data collection.[2]

Sampling

The most difficult problem in conducting a pre-election poll is to determine who is actually going to vote, a process generally known as identifying the electorate. A pollster's approach to this question will determine the sampling methodology he or she chooses to employ—a decision that can have a significant impact on a poll's accuracy. To put it simply, when predicting elections, pollsters are not interested in interviewing *all* adults in a state or even all registered voters. For predictive purposes, pollsters are only interested in interviewing *likely voters*: those people who have a high probability of voting. Any pre-election poll conducted among a population other than likely voters deserves to be treated with a great deal of skepticism.

There are a variety of ways that pollsters use to identify likely voters. Some pollsters make an assumption that the people who are most likely to vote in an upcoming election are those who have voted in past elections. All states keep public records of those who are registered to vote and whether or not they have actually voted in past elections. These records are purchased by companies that construct databases of voters which they then sell to candidates, political parties, interest groups, and polling organizations. The databases typically contain the names and addresses of voters, their voting districts (town, ward, or precinct), and which past elections they have voted in. Computers are then used to match voters with telephone numbers to construct the final lists.[3] In the particular type of situation we are concerned with in this chapter, what matters, of course, is not whether a given person votes in general, but whether they vote in primary elections. Hence, voter lists are often screened for *previous primary voters* (PPV), the assumption being that the people who have voted in primaries in other years are most likely to vote in the current primary.

The biggest advantage to using voter lists of the type just described is that they reduce the costs of conducting a poll. Since every name on the list is qualified for inclusion in the poll, interviewers need not waste time contacting a respondent and beginning the interview, only to find out that the person is not an eligible or likely voter. Being able to ask for a respondent by name also reduces the number of refusals.

But there is a major drawback to using registered voter lists, especially PPV lists: they systematically exclude a high percentage of the people who could vote in an election. Since it typically takes six months to compile a voter list, people who have recently moved into the area or who have just recently registered to vote are excluded. Anyone with an unlisted telephone number is also left off the list. Finally, in states that permit election-day registration (a point I discuss in greater detail below), potential voters who are not registered but who intend to register and vote on election day will be excluded. The net result of all this is that more than half of the potential electorate may be systematically left out of the sample.

The main alternative to voter lists is *random digit dialing* (RDD). In an RDD survey, a random sample is drawn from all residential telephone numbers in a geographic area.[4] When a household is called, the interviewer asks to speak to a randomly selected adult within the household and only this person can be interviewed. Once the desired respondent has been contacted, a series of screening questions are then asked about such matters as the respondent's interest in the current campaign, how often he or she has voted in past elections, and whether he or she intends to vote in the current election, in order to determine how likely it is that the respondent will vote.[5]

The major advantage of RDD sampling is that it greatly reduces the number of potential voters who are left out of the sample. The only voters who are excluded are those who do not have telephones at all or who are for some reason unavailable during the interviewing period (for example, those who are on vacation or away on business). The major disadvantage of RDD polls is the cost, typically more than twice as high as polls using voter lists. In the 2000 New Hampshire presidential primary, only 43 percent of the voting age population actually voted. This means that more than half of the people contacted in an RDD pre-election poll will probably not be included in the final sample, resulting in greatly increased interviewing costs.

Which sampling method works better? In theory, surveys using RDD samples are clearly preferable, since surveys that rely on voter lists exclude such a large segment of the potential electorate. Certainly they are preferred by academic pollsters. Perhaps the better question is: In a world where polling is expensive and many campaigns and media outlets are seeking to hold down costs, how much of a "penalty" does one pay for using the less expensive list-based sampling method? Unfortunately, little systematic research has been done on this question—in part, because many pollsters do not release the methodological details of their surveys.

At a minimum, one can say that using voter lists as a means for drawing samples is a risky proposition, since the samples that result may differ from the actual voting population in a variety of significant ways. For a campaign that is desperately short of money but feels it needs some guidance in devising its pre-election strategy, that risk may, in the end, be worth taking. It is, however, considerably more difficult to provide a compelling justification as to why a media poll would use a list-based sampling procedure. Media organizations have a responsibility to the larger public, and should be extremely wary of sponsoring a poll that may provide quite misleading information about the state of a contested election campaign.

Contacting Respondents

Another source of variation in pre-election polling methodology is how much effort a pollster is willing to expend in trying to contact a particular respondent or household. Some pollsters, in order to reduce costs, will call a selected telephone number two or three times and, if no one answers or the selected respondent is not available, will then discard that number and call another. This may save money, but systematically excludes those voters who are most difficult to reach, who often differ in important ways from voters who are more easy to contact. Better quality polls typically make five to ten callbacks before discarding a number.

Even after a respondent has been contacted, the survey is not necessarily completed. Sometimes, respondents are too busy to complete the survey when they are first contacted. Most organizations will try to set up an appointment with these respondents to call them back at a more convenient time. Some pollsters, however, will simply discard that respondent and call the next number on the

list. Other respondents will hang up on the interviewer, refusing to be interviewed at all. Ideally, a pollster will call back these refusals and try again to get
them to participate in the survey, a process known as refusal conversion. Since
this process is expensive and time-consuming, however, many polling firms do
not do refusal conversions. The effort a pollster puts into completing interviews
with sampled respondents has a significant effect on the survey's response rate
and may lead to higher quality data.

Asking the Questions

Several types of questions are asked in pre-election polls, including screening
questions, favorability ratings, trial-heat questions, and demographics. Screening
questions, as we have seen, are used to determine how likely it is that a particular
respondent will vote and thus "screen out" those who are not likely to participate
in the upcoming election. Favorability ratings, as their name implies, ask respondents whether they have a generally favorable or unfavorable opinion of each
candidate. Such questions are used to judge how well candidates are known and
how voters feel about them, and are very useful in understanding why a candidate is winning or losing. Demographic questions record information about the
age, race, gender, education, and so forth of each respondent; they are used both
to assess how well each candidate is running within particular subgroups of the
electorate and to evaluate the quality and accuracy of the sample.

The questions that receive the most attention in pre-election polls, however,
are the so-called *trial-heat questions*, which ask respondents whom they are going
to vote for. This type of question can be worded in a number of different ways,
but most read something like this trial-heat question from the WMUR/Fox News
tracking poll conducted during the 2000 New Hampshire primary campaign:

> Currently, Al Gore and Bill Bradley are on the Democratic primary ballot. If you
> were voting in the 2000 New Hampshire Democratic primary today, would you vote
> for Al Gore or Bill Bradley?

It is, by now, pretty common knowledge that even fairly subtle changes in
question wording can have a dramatic impact on the answers that are recorded
in a poll and thus on the perceived state of public opinion. Less often appreciated
is the fact, amply documented in a considerable body of research, that responses
can also be affected by the *order* in which questions are asked within a survey as
well as by the order in which responses are presented in an individual question.[6]
In order to minimize these sorts of effects, pollsters often randomize the names
of the candidates. For the Gore-Bradley race in 2000, for example, half of the
sample would be asked if they would vote for "Al Gore or Bill Bradley," while
the other half would be asked if they would vote for "Bill Bradley or Al Gore".
Pollsters also try to mimic the election ballot as closely as possible—so if there

are multiple races in a single election (which is not the case in the New Hampshire presidential primary), they will be asked about in the poll in the same order in which they appear on the ballot.

Weighting the Data

After the interviewing has been completed, the data are typically weighted to adjust for known differences in demographic characteristics between the sample and the target population. For example, women are significantly more likely than men to answer telephone surveys. Women also frequently vote for different candidates than men do. In general elections, for example, women have in recent years been more likely to vote for Democrats. Therefore, a careful pollster will account for this systematic bias by adjusting the sample so that the proportions of men and women reflect census figures. Other demographic variables that are commonly used in weighting adjustments are age, race, level of education, and the part of a state or region of the country in which a respondent lives.

The other type of weighting that is frequently employed is a likely voter weight. As was noted earlier, identifying the likely electorate is one of the most important things a pollster can do to ensure accurate predictions. While screening questions help exclude people who have essentially no chance of voting, many pollsters further tighten their forecasts by weighting the remaining respondents according to how likely it is that they will vote. The precise way that these turnout weights are constructed varies from organization to organization, and are sometimes among the more carefully guarded secrets of the profession.

Timing

It is very rare that support for the various candidates will remain constant throughout the course of an entire election campaign. More typically, the number who prefer each candidate will wax and wane as election day draws nearer. When polling was in its infancy, polls were often completed weeks before election day, sometimes with disastrous consequences for the pollster. In the 1948 presidential contest, to take a particularly celebrated example, the Gallup organization stopped polling four weeks before the election, thus making it impossible for them to catch the late swing toward Harry Truman. By most accounts, this was one of the principal reasons that Gallup (along with other pollsters) predicted that Thomas Dewey would handily beat Truman, a forecast that is still regarded as one of the greatest debacles in the history of polling.

In light of this, pollsters try to continue interviewing as close as possible to the election. In a 1988 analysis of pre-election polls, Irving Crespi concluded that the two most important factors in explaining the accuracy of pre-election polling predictions were the identification of the likely electorate and how close a poll was conducted to election day.[7] As computer software and hardware have improved, pollsters now routinely interview up through the day before the election. Polls that continue interviewing until the eve of the election are generally more accurate than those that are completed even a few days earlier.

While many pre-election polls are one-time surveys of the electorate, in recent years *tracking polls* have become increasingly common. A tracking poll is an ongoing pre-election poll that typically lasts for one or two weeks before an election. In a tracking poll, the pollster generally calculates a daily result based on a "rolling sample" of likely voters, so that they can better understand the dynamic qualities of the race—which candidates are gaining and which are losing ground. Tracking polls are not necessarily more accurate than one-time or cross-sectional surveys, but they do enable election observers to get a better sense of how things are changing as election day approaches.

Rolling samples usually consist of the results from three or four consecutive days worth of interviews. For example, to determine the state of the race for a Tuesday night newscast or a Wednesday morning newspaper, a pollster using a three-day rolling sample would base his estimate on interviews conducted on Sunday, Monday, and Tuesday. For Thursday morning's release, the interviews from Sunday would be dropped out of the rolling sample and interviews from Wednesday would be added in. This process continues throughout the period of the tracking poll.

Allocation of Undecided Voters

Despite the best efforts of pollsters to write clear questions and interview right up until election day, a small percentage of the likely voters in their polls will still be undecided as to who they will vote for. How a pollster handles these undecideds can significantly impact the accuracy of a poll.

Pollsters have developed several models for allocating undecided voters. Perhaps the simplest method is to assume that the undecided vote will split in the same proportion as those voters who have already decided. Table 8.2 shows a hypothetical pre-election poll for an election in which candidate John Doe, the incumbent, is running against a challenger named Jane Jones. Column A shows the initial poll results: Doe has 46 percent, Jones 39 percent, and 15 percent are undecided. Using a proportional allocation strategy, the more relevant statistic is that Doe has 54.1 percent *of the decided vote* and Jones has 45.9 percent—which is how the election will turn out if the undecided voters split in the same proportion (see column B).

An alternative model for allocating undecideds is based on the theory that in races in which one of the candidates is an incumbent, the election is essentially a referendum on that incumbent, the key question for the voters being, do they want to keep him or not. Since most voters already know the incumbent, any voter who is still undecided in the closing days of the campaign is really leaning against the incumbent. Panagakis, in an analysis of 155 pre-election polls con-

Table 8.2 Models for Allocating Undecided Survey Respondents in a Hypothetical Election

	A	B	C	D
	No Allocation	*Proportional*	*Incumbent Rule—A*	*Incumbent Rule—B*
John Doe (inc.)[a]	46%	54.1%	46%	51%
Jane Jones	39	45.9	54	49
Undecided	15			
Doe's margin	+7.0	+8.2	−8	+2

[a] Indicates he is the incumbent.
Note: Undecided vote was allocated as follows:
A. Undecideds not allocated.
B. Undecideds allocated in the same proportion as decideds.
C. All undecideds allocated to the challenger.
D. Two-thirds of the undecideds allocated to the challenger and one-third to the incumbent.

ducted by his own firm and other organizations, found that 82 percent of the time, the challenger got most of the undecided vote. The incumbent, by contrast, won a majority of the undecided vote in just 12 percent of the cases studied (in the other 6 percent, the undecideds split evenly).[8] Based on these findings, Panagakis proposed the "incumbent rule," which holds that in any race with an incumbent, most of the undecideds will go to the challenger. For the hypothetical election discussed earlier, column C shows the extreme case where the challenger gets the entire undecided vote, resulting in an 8-percentage-point win for Jones. If Jones were to get two-thirds of the undecided vote, as shown in column D, the prediction is for a statistical dead heat, with the incumbent Doe holding a narrow 51 percent to 49 percent lead.

A final strategy, of course, is not to allocate the undecideds at all: to report that Doe has 46 percent and Jones 39 percent, with 15 percent still undecided. The problem with this method is that it still contains an implicit prediction: Doe, the poll says, is clearly ahead (assuming the difference between the candidates exceeds the margin of sampling error). But if the incumbent rule is accurate and Doe is the incumbent, this may provide a quite inaccurate indication of the real state of the race.

As this example illustrates, how undecideds are allocated can significantly impact both the magnitude and direction of election predictions. Although more research needs to be done, indications are that some version of the incumbent rule is the best way of handling undecideds when an incumbent is running—which, however, has generally not been the case in recent presidential nomination races. (Two of the last three incumbent presidents who have sought renomination have not had a single major opponent from within their own party.) When there is no incumbent in the race, pollsters have less information they can use in allocating the undecideds. In these cases, proportional allocation is often employed.

POLLING IN NEW HAMPSHIRE

With that as background, let us now examine the specific problems involved in conducting polls in New Hampshire, how pollsters have tried to cope with these problems, and how they may have impacted predictions in the 2000 New Hampshire primary.

Undeclared Voters

Changes in New Hampshire's voting laws that were enacted during the 1990s have made the pollsters' task of identifying likely voters substantially more difficult. Perhaps the most important of these was a technical change in the provisions concerning party registration.

When New Hampshire citizens register to vote, they can choose to register as a member of one of the major parties (Democrats and Republicans) or they can register as "undeclared." While a registered Republican or Democrat can vote only in his or her own party's primary, an undeclared voter can vote in the primary of either major party, simply by asking for that party's ballot on election day. Once they have voted in a party primary, however, undeclared voters lose that status—at least temporarily—and are classified as a member of whichever party's primary they just voted in.[9]

All this has been true for a number of years. Up through 1992, however, a person who had just voted in a party primary and wished to change his or her registration back to undeclared had to make a separate trip to the local town hall. In 1993, this was changed: Voters are now allowed to fill out a form at the polling place, immediately after voting, that returns them to undeclared status. Partly as a result of this new procedure, the percentage of undeclared voters has risen steadily from 23 percent in 1992 to 31 percent in 1996 and then to 38 percent in 2000 (see figure 8.1). As of 2002 (the most recent figures available for this book), 37 percent of all registered voters in New Hampshire were registered as Republicans, 37 percent were undeclared, and 26 percent were registered Democrats.

Being registered as an undeclared voter has several advantages. Some voters no doubt value the sense that they are independents, who "vote for the candidate, not the party." Maintaining the appearance of non-partisanship may be particularly important for government employees and members of the press. Not being registered as a Democrat or Republican also keeps voters off the parties' mailing lists.

But the greatest advantage of being undeclared is that it allows voters to vote in either party's primary. This is particularly important in a state like New Hampshire, where the presidential primary commands such extraordinary national attention that it has become a hallowed part of the state's political identity. Turnout in the New Hampshire presidential primary tends to be far higher than in most other states. Voters *want* to vote—but just as important, they want

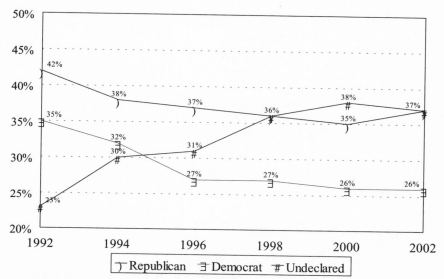

Figure 8.1   Voter Registration in New Hampshire

Source: New Hampshire Secretary of State.

to vote in a race that *matters*. In 1984 and 1996—and most likely in 2004—only one party had a competitive primary. Registered Republicans in 1984 and registered Democrats in 1996 had little to get excited about. Since undeclared voters can vote in either primary, they are almost always assured of being able to vote in a meaningful race.

Whatever advantages undeclared status holds for the voters, it unquestionably makes life a lot more difficult for pollsters. As the number of undeclared voters increases, it becomes substantially more difficult to determine the makeup of each primary's electorate. Not only do voters have the choice of whether or not to vote, a significant portion of them—more than a third—also have the choice of *which* primary to vote in.

In both 2000 primaries, as shown in table 8.3, the differences between undeclared voters and party registrants were quite stark. On the Republican side, according to the VNS exit polls, John McCain scored an overwhelming victory among undeclared voters, winning 61 percent to just 19 percent for George Bush. McCain also defeated Bush among registered Republicans, but by the much narrower margin of 44 percent to 36 percent. In the Democratic primary, Bill Bradley actually beat Al Gore among undeclared voters, 57 percent to 42 percent. Fortunately for Gore, he defeated Bradley among registered Democrats by an almost identical margin, 58 percent to 42 percent.

The outcomes of both primaries, then, were determined in part by the deci-

Andrew E. Smith

Table 8.3 Vote in the 2000 New Hampshire Primaries by Party Registration

A. Republican Primary

	Registered Republicans	Undeclared
John McCain	44	61
George Bush	36	19

B. Democratic Primary

	Registered Democrats	Undeclared
Al Gore	58	42
Bill Bradley	42	57

Note: Totals may not sum to 100 percent because of votes for other candidates.
Source: VNS Exit Poll.

sions that undeclared voters made about which party's primary to participate in. Had more undeclared voters decided to vote in the Democratic primary, Bradley would probably have beaten Gore. Had there been a sharp drop in the number of undeclareds who requested a Republican ballot, McCain would still have won, but by a considerably smaller margin.

When the voting intentions of undeclared voters as a whole are examined (see table 8.4), they seem to have moved toward John McCain during the final days of the campaign. McCain's strategy of appealing to undeclared voters worked, and their support helps explain the size of McCain's win. But the fact that the undeclared swing to McCain came so late in the campaign made it difficult for pollsters to detect the shift. Because most tracking polls use a three- or four-day rolling sample (Gallup shifted to a two-day rolling sample over the final week-

Table 8.4 Candidates Supported by Undeclared Voters Who Are Likely to Vote, during the Final Twelve Days before the New Hampshire Primary (Three-Day Averages)

	Jan. 20–22	Jan. 23–25	Jan. 26–28	Jan. 29–31
John McCain (R)	29%	30	30	37
George Bush (R)	14	18	13	13
Al Gore (D)	21	16	21	19
Bill Bradley (D)	19	21	18	15
Other candidates	12	11	16	13
Undecided	5	4	2	3
(N)	(164)	(239)	(179)	(218)

Source: WMUR/FOX News 2000 New Hampshire Primary Poll, conducted by the University of New Hampshire Survey Center.

end), late trends can be difficult to distinguish from the sorts of day-to-day fluctuations that occur because of sampling error. In the end, 61 percent of undeclared voters voted in the Republican primary; and those that did, as we have seen, supported McCain over Bush by a three-to-one margin.

Demographic Change

New Hampshire has seen fairly dramatic demographic change over the past decade, particularly when compared to the other states in New England. Between 1990 and 2000, the population of New Hampshire grew by 11.4 percent, compared to just 5.4 percent for the New England region as a whole.

Most of the in-migrants since the end of the last recession (i.e, since 1992) have come from other New England states, particularly Massachusetts.[10] When compared to those adults who had lived in New Hampshire since before 1990, the new arrivals were younger (median age 38 versus 46 for other adult residents) and better educated (51 percent of new arrivals reported having a college degree versus only 40 percent for other adults). Many came to New Hampshire because of the growth in the state's high-tech sector, its natural environment, and its low tax rates—almost half as low, on a per capita basis, as neighboring Massachusetts and Vermont. These new residents have helped change the character of New Hampshire. The Granite State now has the sixth highest per capita income in the United States ($23,844), up from eleventh in 1990 and twentieth place in 1969.

What impact have these demographic changes had on New Hampshire politics? The evidence is mixed. On many important political characteristics, recent arrivals are not much different from longer-term residents of the state. The two groups are approximately the same in their party identification, the amount of attention they paid to the 2000 presidential primary, and their reported likelihood of voting in the primary.

At a minimum, however, the new arrivals add one more layer of "mystery" to the attempt to predict New Hampshire voting patterns. Unlike those who have lived in the state for a decade or two, recent in-migrants have little in the way of past history to help us determine whether and how they will vote in the future. (We could, of course, ask them about what they did in the last primary held in their previous place of residence, but it is unclear that the way a person voted in Massachusetts or New York provides much guidance about how they will behave in the strikingly atypical circumstances of a New Hampshire presidential primary.) Recent arrivals are also more likely than long-term residents to register as undeclared (45 percent of recent in-migrants are undeclared, versus 39 percent of those who have been in the state since 1990) and thus can participate in either party's primary.

Election-Day Registration

Another wrinkle in New Hampshire's election law that can confound unwary pollsters is election-day voter registration. In most states, a voter who wishes to cast a ballot in a particular election must register several weeks or months prior to election day. While this was once the case in New Hampshire as well, in 1994, in response to national "motor voter" legislation, the state legislature significantly relaxed the restrictions on voter eligibility. As a result, prospective voters need only present themselves at their polling place on election day and declare that they are residents of that town or ward, and they are then allowed to register and vote. The percentage of voters who registered at the polls has varied from 4.0 percent in the 1994 general election to 12.3 percent in the 2000 general election. In presidential primaries, the "walk-up vote" was 8.7 percent in 1996 and 9.8 percent in 2000 (see table 8.5).

Not taking proper account of the walk-up vote can significantly affect the accuracy of pre-election polls. A common screening question in pre-election polls is to ask if the respondent is registered to vote. If the respondent says he is not, the call is typically terminated. While such a procedure is unexceptionable in most states, in New Hampshire failing to interview the unregistered in a pre-election poll means that 8–10 percent of the electorate are systematically excluded from the sample. According to exit polls, in the 2000 primary walk-up voters behaved much like undeclared voters, participating disproportionately in the Republican primary and voting for John McCain.

Fluctuating Turnout

Most models that are used to identify the likely electorate require the pollster to make a reasonably good estimate of total turnout. In national presidential elections, this is rarely a problem, since turnout tends to fluctuate within fairly narrow limits. Over the last three decades, turnout in presidential elections, measured as a percentage of voting age population, has never risen above 55 percent and never fallen below 49 percent. In New Hampshire, by contrast, the election laws discussed earlier, along with the vagaries of primary competition, has produced a situation in which turnout has varied significantly over the past several elections, in ways that are difficult to predict.

In 1988, total turnout in both party primaries combined was only 48 percent,

Table 8.5 Proportion of New Hampshire Voters Who Registered to Vote on Election Day, 1994–2000

	General Election	*Presidential Primary*
1994	4.0%	—
1996	8.1	8.7
1998	5.0	—
2000	12.3	9.8

Source: New Hampshire Secretary of State.

despite the fact that there were competitive primaries among both Republicans and Democrats. In 1992, turnout increased to 62 percent, probably because of uneasiness about the economy and dissatisfaction with President Bush. Turnout dropped to 43 percent in 1996, as the Democratic primary was uncontested that year. The 2000 election, by contrast, had all the makings of a high turnout affair: competitive races in both parties, attractive candidates, lots of spending, and good weather. Despite these factors, turnout was only 50.5 percent. With turnout varying so widely—and unpredictably—identifying the likely electorate becomes all the more difficult.

Non-Response Rates

A poorly kept secret in survey research is that response rates—the percentage of respondents contacted that yield a completed interview—have been declining over the past several decades.[11] While the magnitude of the problem varies with the interviewing method and how much effort the survey organization is willing to expend in converting refusals or contacting respondents who are initially unavailable, in telephone surveys response rates of 20 percent or less are not uncommon.

Response rates have been declining for a number of reasons. One important part of the explanation, it seems clear, is that the public's tolerance for unsolicited telephone calls has worn increasingly thin. When political polls, marketing research, and telemarketing are added together, there has been a huge increase in the number of such calls that Americans receive. Partly to combat these unwanted calls, several technologies have been introduced and made inexpensively available to consumers, such as answering machines, caller ID, and call blocking, all of which make it that much more difficult for pollsters to reach the households in their sample.

While declining response rates are a problem for pollsters generally, there is some reason to think that they may pose a special challenge in New Hampshire. Long known as a place that sees a lot more of the presidential candidates than any other state and receives a disproportionate amount of press coverage, over the last several election cycles New Hampshire has also emerged as perhaps the most over-surveyed state in America. The amount of polling that was done in New Hampshire during the final weeks before the 2000 presidential primary was truly extraordinary.[12] As we have already seen (in table 8.1), there were ten distinct survey organizations that conducted pre-election polls on a regular basis for various media outlets.[13] Six of these were tracking polls, that interviewed an average of 325 people per night. Of the five major presidential candidates (Bush, McCain, Forbes, Gore, and Bradley), all did regular polling—and four of the five had tracking polls. Add in the number of surveys sponsored by interest groups or by academic organizations that were not designed for immediate release to the media, and a conservative estimate is that 50,000 completed interviews were conducted with New Hampshire residents during the final two weeks before the primary (January 18–31), with perhaps another 15,000 occurring during the first half of January.

From the perspective of the harried household, it is important to stress that these last two figures are estimates of the number of *completed* interviews. When one takes account of all the calls that only reached an answering machine or were screened out by a caller ID system, and all the contacts that did not yield a valid interview (because the person refused to talk or said he had no intention of voting), a good rule of thumb is that it generally takes five phone calls to produce a single completed interview. So pollsters probably called 325,000 New Hampshire households during the month before the primary.[14]

What makes these figures particularly noteworthy is that they are based on what is, in polling terms, an unusually small universe. There is also a lot of polling done in the United States during the final days before a presidential general election—but in that case, pollsters are attempting to predict the voting behavior of a potential electorate that consists of about 200 million voters, about 100 million of whom will actually cast a ballot. In New Hampshire, by contrast, the total voting age population in 2000 was just 911,000; and of those, just 392,000 voted in both primaries combined. To make 325,000 calls and complete 65,000 interviews in a target population of 400,000 is the polling equivalent of saturation bombing.

How much effect did all these unsolicited calls have on response rates in New Hampshire? The evidence is mixed. Several of the pollsters listed in table 8.1 actually commented on how *easy* it was to poll in the Granite State. New Hampshire voters, they argued, were politically very engaged and understood that they had a special role in the presidential nomination process. Hence, they were more willing to talk with pollsters than residents of, say, New York or Connecticut. John Zogby, for example, said that response rates in New Hampshire were "extremely good." Lou DiNatale of the UMass poll called New Hampshire "the least poll-resistant place I've ever seen."

On the other hand, polls conducted by the University of New Hampshire Survey Center suggest that the percentage of households who avoid being interviewed, by refusing to complete the survey, not answering their telephone, or letting calls go through to their answering machine, is 10 to 15 percentage points higher in polls conducted immediately before the primary than in polls conducted at other times of the year.

Almost all of those involved in survey research agree that declining response rates are, at a minimum, a cause for concern.[15] Many media commentators have gone a lot farther, claiming that with response rates so low, pollsters can no longer hear the "silent majority" that refuses to speak with survey interviewers.[16] To this point, however, there is no persuasive evidence that declining response rates have had a noticeable effect on the accuracy of pre-election polls. Despite a small number of races in which the polls were seriously in error, several comprehensive reviews of recent election polls have found most pre-election polls to be quite accurate. In 2000, for example, the National Council of Public Polls examined the performance of national surveys of the Bush-Gore contest and concluded, "The accuracy of the election projections based on the pre-election polls of 2000 was surpassed only by the polls of 1976 and 1960." An examination of 79 state-level polls of the same election found that 85 percent correctly forecast which candidate would carry the state, with an average error margin of just 1.9 percentage points.[17] Similarly, in 2002, a review of 159 polls of gubernatorial and U.S. senate races reported in the media found that 87 percent predicted the correct winner, with an average error of 2.4 percentage points. Indeed, in 84 percent of these polls, the difference between the final poll and the actual results was less than the theoretical margin of error.[18]

SOME ADVICE FOR POLLSTERS AND POLL CONSUMERS

Pre-election polling has been conducted in the United States since the 1930s and pollsters have been continually adjusting and improving their methods. In general, pre-election polls have become more accurate, both nationwide and within individual states. But there are lessons that pollsters can take from this analysis of polling in the New Hampshire primary that apply not only to New Hampshire but to other elections as well.

The first suggestion is that pollsters need to be fully aware of the election laws of the state in which they are polling and make sure that their polls are designed to accommodate any peculiarities in the law. In New Hampshire, this means asking follow-up questions to respondents who say they are not registered to vote to determine the likelihood that they will register at the polls on election day, and probing undeclared voters to find out which primary they intend to vote in.

Second, it is critical that pollsters understand historical patterns in turnout. In New Hampshire, it is much easier to identify likely voters in a particular party's primary when that party is the only one that has a competitive race (as in 1996) than when both parties have contested primaries, since in the former case it is much easier to figure out where undeclared voters will go. Looking ahead to 2004, it appears that there will not be much competition between the parties for undeclared voters, since President Bush will probably not be challenged in his quest for renomination. (Some caution is in order, however: Through most of 1991, it was widely assumed that George H. W. Bush would have no opposition in the 1992 Republican primaries.)

Third, pollsters should not use samples based on registered voter lists. Polls that use voter lists are less expensive than random digit dialing polls, but list-based samples can systematically exclude a quite large proportion of the eligible electorate.

For poll consumers—the press, political scientists, and voters—it is important to recognize that all polls are *not* created equal. A number of clues are available that reveal important information about the quality of a poll. These include: the type of sampling procedure used (look for RDD); when the poll was conducted (the closer to the election, the better); who was interviewed (look for polls of likely voters); the response rate of the survey (the higher, the better); and how accurate the organization has been in the past. Unfortunately, this information is not usually published in the newspaper or shown on television. More and more organizations, however, do make this information available on their Web sites. A few minutes spent researching the polls may be well worth the effort.

NOTES

1. For a fuller description of the concepts and issues discussed here, see Herbert Asher, *Polling and the Public: What Every Citizen Should Know*, 5th ed. (Washington, D.C.: CQ Press, 2001); Irving Crespi, *Pre-election Polling: Sources of Accuracy and Error* (New York: Russell Sage Foundation, 1988); and Michael W. Traugott and Paul J. Lavrakas, *The Voter's Guide to Election Polls*, 2nd ed. (New York: Chatham House, 2000). Traugott and Lavrakas provide a useful glossary of terms for beginning students.

2. For an interesting examination of the possibility of doing pre-election surveys by mail, see Penny S. Visser, Jon A. Krosnick, Jesse Marquette, and Michael Curtin, "Mail Surveys for Election Forecasting? An Evaluation of the *Columbus Dispatch* Poll," *Public Opinion Quarterly* 60 (Summer 1996): 181–227.

3. There are a huge number of companies that provide registered voter lists for campaign consultants, pollsters, market researchers, and others. Most can be located by searching on the Web.

4. There are many companies that provide RDD samples for survey researchers. Two of the best known are Survey Sampling of Fairfax, Virginia, and Marketing Systems Group, located in Washington, Pennsylvania. For a more detailed description of how an RDD sample is drawn and the benefits and drawbacks of this type of sampling, see William R. Klecka and Alfred J. Tuchfarber, "Random Digit Dialing: A Comparison to Personal Surveys," *Public Opinion Quarterly* 42 (Spring 1978): 105–114.

5. The precise method of identifying likely voters in RDD samples varies among polling organizations. For a good description of several of the methods used, see Eric Rademacher, "The Path to Accurate Pre-election Forecasts: An Analysis of the Impact of Data Adjustment Techniques on Pre-election Projection Estimates" (Ph.D. dissertation, University of Cincinnati, 2002).

6. For a comprehensive review of this and other polling effects, see Howard Schuman and Stanley Presser, *Questions and Answers in Attitude Surveys: Experiments on Question Form, Wording, and Context* (New York: Academic Press, 1981).

7. See Crespi, *Pre-election Polling*, chap. 9.

8. See Nick Panagakis, "Incumbent Races: Closer than They Appear," *The Polling Report*, February 27, 1989. Many of the apparent exceptions are easily explicable within the framework of Panagakis's theory. As he notes, "Many challengers who did not get a majority of undecideds were recent or current holders of an office equal to the one they

were seeking. Voters were equally or more familiar with the challenger's past performance in a similar office, so the challenger assumed incumbent characteristics. Other exceptions include well-known challengers or short-term incumbents."

9. That is to say, requesting a given party's ballot in a primary election is treated as a declaration of party affiliation.

10. In the *NH 2000 Survey*, conducted by the University of New Hampshire Survey Center in July 2000, 33 percent of New Hampshire adults reported that they were born in New Hampshire, 27 percent in Massachusetts, 13 percent in another New England State, 12 percent in a mid-Atlantic state, and 28 percent in some other state or another country.

11. The literature on this topic is quite large. For two good reviews of the evidence, see Robert M. Groves and Mick P. Couper, *Nonresponse in Household Interview Surveys* (New York: John Wiley, 1998), 156–72; and Edith de Leeuw and Wim de Heer, "Trends in Household Survey Nonresponse: A Longitudinal and International Comparison," in *Survey Nonresponse*, ed. Robert M. Groves, Don A. Dillman, John L. Eltinge, and Roderick J. A. Little (New York: John Wiley, 2002), 41–54.

12. The following estimate was put together by the author and William G. Mayer.

13. Actually, there were eleven, if one includes three surveys that Dartmouth College conducted for the Associated Press. The Dartmouth surveys are not included in table 8.1 because the last of them took place between January 23 and 26, and thus is not strictly comparable with the ten listed in the table, all of which continued to poll until the Sunday or Monday before the election.

14. As the preceding discussion should indicate, this number includes only calls that were made for the purpose of conducting a legitimate survey interview. It does not include all the calls the campaigns may have made to help persuade voters (including so-called push polls), to invite them to attend a local event, or to urge them to turn out on election day.

15. See, for example, Norman M. Bradburn's presidential address to the American Association for Public Opinion Research, published as "A Response to the Nonresponse Problem," *Public Opinion Quarterly* 56 (Fall 1992): 391–397.

16. See, for example, Arianna Huffington, "Pollsters can't hear silent majority," *San Diego Union-Tribune*, November 15, 2002, B-9.

17. Both studies are discussed in Eric W. Rademacher and Andrew E. Smith, "Poll Call," *The Public Perspective*, March/April, 2001, 36–37.

18. See National Council of Public Polls, "National Council on Public Polls Polling Review Board Analysis of the 2002 Election Polls," press release, December 20, 2002. This release may be accessed at the Council's website: www.ncpp.org.

9

The Emerging International Trend toward Open Presidential Primaries

The American Presidential Nomination Process in Comparative Perspective

James A. McCann

One of the most distinctive features of American politics is the process through which presidential candidates are selected. To secure a nomination with a major party, individuals seeking the White House must compete for support in a long series of state contests. The rules of engagement vary somewhat from place to place. Some states allow any registered voter to take part; others require participants to declare a partisan affiliation in advance. A trait common to all contests, however, is an emphasis on active citizen involvement. No candidate can make it to the top of the ticket without first mobilizing scores of people into the cause, nearly all of whom hold no formal positions within the party and pay no dues.[1] The belief that fair-minded voters at the grassroots are best suited, and perhaps even morally obliged, to choose nominees is deeply rooted in American political culture. "What we need now," declared a Progressive Era writer at the turn of the twentieth century, "is not merely a sincere and accurate expression of opinion, but an opportunity to nominate and to vote effectively for anyone whom we desire . . . While much still remains undone, much may well be expected from the rapidly growing body of primary reformers."[2]

The voters turning out for primary elections and local caucuses often face a dizzying array of choices, especially in the early contests. This is because Democratic and Republican leaders exercise little formal control over who may run for president.[3] Vice presidents, members of Congress, governors, religious evangelists, social movement activists, television personalities—all are welcome to campaign within the party. With millions of citizens holding the power to choose a standard bearer, the potential for polarizing and unpredictable conflict is great.

For decades, political scientists have puzzled over whether the divisions that are created or deepened by contentious battles over candidate selection make parties less cohesive and weaker during the general election. So far, the evidence in this literature has been mixed. Some studies suggest that bitterness at the nomination stage can be long lasting and cause voters to disengage from the party if their preferred candidate does not win. In Andrew Hacker's words, "The party whose candidate is obliged to fight a hard primary campaign has an important strike against it upon entering the general election."[4] Others find that a party can do much to repair the damage from a bruising nomination fight by waging an effective campaign during the general election.[5]

Outside of the United States, more than thirty nations can be classified as "presidentialist" democracies where chief executives are elected separately from representatives in the legislature and serve a fixed term of office.[6] Coming up with effective procedures for choosing nominees in these countries is as critical and challenging a task as in the United States. Nowhere do we encounter an extensively regulated system of primary elections, local caucuses, and nominating conventions that is directly comparable to the American model. Most contenders are chosen through elite bargaining. A good example of this is the French system. To get their names on the presidential voting ballot, candidates in France must be sponsored by at least five hundred elected officials spread out across the country.[7] In 1995, some forty thousand leaders, most of whom were mayors, had the right to sponsor a candidate. Under the French constitution, if no contestant receives more than 50 percent of the vote, there is a run-off between the two top finishers. Since 1965, when the French began choosing the president through a direct vote, every election has gone into a second round.[8]

While the U.S. model with all its intricacies stands as one of a kind, a number of parties around the world have begun to experiment with open presidential primaries where aspiring nominees are free to appeal directly to citizens both inside and outside the party. These elections often resemble American contests, complete with live televised debates, prodigious fundraising, attack ads, photo-ops, horserace-style news coverage, and the involvement of hundreds of thousands, if not millions, of citizens. To date, little has been written about this curious trend.[9]

In the next section, I describe several of these primary contests. Following this, I consider how the adoption of presidential primaries may affect party organizations and competition during the general election and beyond. I will focus most keenly on one case in particular, the open primary held in 1999 by Mexico's Institutional Revolutionary Party. Eight months after staging this primary, the party unexpectedly lost the presidency. Some commentators have argued that internal fighting at the nomination stage was partly responsible for this defeat. If true, this experience would serve as a cautionary lesson for democratic reformers across the globe. To assess this claim, I make use of several large-scale public opinion surveys conducted in Mexico during the primary and general election campaign. The empirical findings indicate that the primary did indeed shape the citizen's beliefs and actions long after nomination decisions were reached, though not in the ways that critics have suggested.

PRIMARIAS, ESIVAALIT, PREDVARITELNI IZBORI . . . AN OVERVIEW OF RECENT OPEN PRESIDENTIAL PRIMARIES OUTSIDE OF THE UNITED STATES

For all their potential divisiveness and unpredictability, primary elections offer many potential benefits for a party. In an age of rampant worldwide cynicism about "politics as usual," a presidential primary can bestow upon a party, its leaders, and its nominee an aura of trust and legitimacy, especially if rival contenders for the presidency have been chosen in private smoke-filled rooms.[10] Primaries might further serve to bond participants more closely to the party.[11] This could be particularly important in newer democracies where parties have not yet cultivated a reliable mass following. Still another possible advantage of primaries is that the candidates who emerge may be more politically viable. The traits that could make party leaders competitive in an American-style open primary—e.g., moderate stands on policy issues, a TV-friendly manner, the ability to organize a national campaign—no doubt give them an edge in the general election.

Among party elites themselves, primary elections could also help settle potentially vexing problems of organizational coordination and maintenance. As John Aldrich writes, parties in a democracy are obliged to come up with reasonable strategies for regulating competition for a scarce and valuable commodity, nominations for high office. "For elective office seekers, regulating conflict over who holds those offices is clearly of major concern. It is ever present. And it is not just a problem of access to government offices but is also a problem internal to each party as soon as the party becomes an important gateway to office."[12] Nomination via backroom bargaining may be effective if a party has ample consolation prizes to award ambitious office seekers who do not make the cut. Promises of future cabinet or diplomatic appointments, for example, may suffice. If the party has no such benefits to bestow, or if the different blocs making up the party do not trust each other enough to accept such deals, conflict over candidate selection could wreck the organization. Letting "the people" decide nominations in an open primary might well be the only method acceptable to all factions.

Table 9.1 lists six "first ever" open presidential primaries that took place during the 1990s. Each of these contests represented a significant departure from traditional nomination procedures.[13]

Table 9.1 A Sampling of Recent "First Ever" Open Presidential Primaries

Country	Year	Party	Number of Participants	Turnout/ Voting Age Population (%)	Primary Winner's Name	Winner's Vote Share in the Primary (%)	Did Nominee Win/Lose the General Election?
Argentina	1998	Alliance Coalition	2,000,000	8	Fernando de la Rua	63	Win
Bulgaria	1996	Union of Democratic Forces	858,560	13	Petar Stoyanov	66	Win
Chile	1999	Concertación Coalition	1,380,000	14	Ricardo Lagos	71	Win
Finland	1993	Social Democrats	135,000	3	Martti Ahtisaari	61	Win
Mexico	1999	Institutional Revolutionary	9,720,000	16	Francisco Labastida	55	Lose
Uruguay	1999	Colorado	455,699	20	Jorge Batlle	55	Win
		National	361,182	16	Luis Alberto Lacalle	48	Lose
		Progressive–Broad Front	362,683	16	Tabaré Vázquez	82	Lose

Note: Turnout rates in all cases but Bulgaria and Uruguay are approximations. The number of participants in the Institutional Revolutionary Party primary has been disputed; the figure given here is what the party reported.

Argentina[14]

In November of 1998, a fledgling political coalition known simply as the "Alliance" conducted a primary to pick its presidential nominee. This coalition, formed only one year earlier, was a fusion of two major political forces in Argentina, the Radical Party, which had held the presidency between 1983 and 1989, and the Solidarity Front, an emerging center-left political movement.

A desire to win elections was the principal driving force binding the Alliance coalition together. The dominant party at the time was the Judicialist (Peronist) Party. The Solidarity Front was an offshoot of the Judicialists, more a breakaway faction of disgruntled leaders than a political party in its own right. The Radical Party was much more deeply rooted in Argentine politics, but it had suffered several recent setbacks. President Raúl Alfonsín, a Radical, was unable to deal with a massive economic crisis in the late 1980s and ended up leaving office in disgrace in 1989. In the 1995 presidential election, the Radicals came in a distant third, far behind the Judicialist Party. At that point, one message seemed clear: a union between the Solidarity Front and the Radical Party was the only way to defeat the Judicialists. A national primary offered a means to decide on a single candidate. It could also, Alliance leaders reasoned, help extend the fledgling coalition's reach and solidify its mass base.

The two contestants who competed in this primary had very different backgrounds in politics and clashed over policy. The front-runner was Fernando de la Rua, a moderate who believed in laissez faire economics and had served as a Radical Party member in the federal congress for over twenty years. De la Rua's opponent was Graciela Fernandez Meijide, an affiliate of the Solidarity Front who came to electoral politics late in life. Once a professor of French, Fernandez Meijide became politically active after Argentine security forces abducted her son in 1976. When democracy returned to Argentina in 1985, Fernandez Meijide led a commission to investigate violations of human rights. In 1993, she successfully ran for the Argentine congress. In her campaign, Fernandez Meijide emphasized social justice issues and expressed doubts about the benefits of free trade.

Presidential primaries had been conducted in earlier Argentine elections, but the Alliance contest was by far the most open.[15] All citizens except members of other parties were eligible to take part. The Judicialist Party did not hold a primary election that year. Instead, party leaders picked the nominee, with the incumbent president Carlos Menem having the greatest say. On the day of the Alliance primary, approximately two million people turned out, which was 8 percent of the adult population.[16] (In comparison, 18 percent of all eligible voters took part in American primaries in 2000.[17]) By nearly a two-to-one ratio, Argentine primary voters preferred de la Rua. His opponent conceded defeat and pledged to work for the Alliance during the general election campaign. Fernandez Meijide did not, however, run as the coalition's vice-presidential nominee, in spite of an earlier agreement that whoever came in second would fill this position. The following year, Fernando de la Rua was again successful. In the general election, he decisively beat the Judicialist candidate by a 10-percentage-point margin.

Bulgaria[18]

The 1996 presidential primary in Bulgaria functioned in a similar way to solidify an emerging political alliance. After being in the socialist camp for decades, Bulgarians turned against the country's communist regime in 1989. The first direct presidential election was held three years later. The winner, Zhelyu Zhelev, came from the Union of Democratic Forces (UDF), a loose and diverse coalition of over a dozen small western-leaning parties and interest groups.

As the next presidential election approached four years later, Zhelev announced that he intended to stand for reelection. Unfortunately for him, he had lost the confidence of many in the UDF. Fearing that the president might run as an independent against any other UDF nominee and thereby split the pro-western vote, UDF leaders along with several outside groups engineered an open primary to choose a single candidate five months before the general election. President Zhelev initially resisted this proposal, but eventually he agreed to respect the results and step aside if beaten. The main party in opposition to the UDF, the Socialists, did not stage its own primary that year.

On the day of the primary election, nearly 860,000 voters turned out, which represented 13 percent of the entire electorate. Coalition leaders saw this as a sign that the primary worked, inasmuch as open and competitive elections of any sort were still a new phenomenon in Bulgaria. (When UDF officials first discussed the possibility of holding a primary, naysayers predicted that few citizens would wish to participate.) Zhelev lost the primary by nearly 30 percentage points to Petar Stoyanov, a relative newcomer to politics who had the support of most UDF officials. True to his word, the incumbent president accepted defeat. Stoyanov then proceeded to beat the Socialist candidate in the general election.

The Bulgarian primary stands apart from the other cases in table 9.1 in the degree to which Americans were actively involved in the process. When it looked as if internal squabbles over candidate selection were going to tear the UDF apart, which would have given the presidency to the Bulgarian Socialist Party, the Washington-based International Republican Institute (IRI) sent a team of advisers to Bulgaria to consult with coalition leaders.[19] In December of 1995, the president of the IRI brought up the possibility of holding an open primary. Over the next three months, Americans affiliated with the Institute and the UDF worked out a blueprint for the nomination. The IRI sponsored an opinion poll to gauge the public's likely reaction to such an event. Most Bulgarians, the IRI found, expressed great support for this idea. This reassured Bulgarian reformers and helped bring apprehensive factions within the UDF coalition to the negotiating table. In the final stages of planning, the IRI helped draft the pledge President

Zhelev and Petar Stoyanov took to abide by the results. It also secured funding (approximately $700,000—$750,000) to cover administrative costs.

Chile[20]

In the late 1980s, Chileans likewise turned back to democratic governance after a long period of authoritarian rule under Augusto Pinochet. The most significant political force to emerge during the transition to democracy was the *Concertación de Partidos para la Democracia* (Coalition of Parties for Democracy). Sixteen parties made up this bloc, with the centrist Christian Democratic Party (PDC) taking on the central leadership role. In the first presidential election after Pinochet, the coalition's nominee, Patricio Aylwin, won the presidency. Four years later, another candidate from the PDC camp, Eduardo Frei, became president.

With the next presidential election on the horizon in 1999, the smaller leftist parties in *Concertación* pushed to have one of their own nominated as the standard bearer. When no backroom deal was offered, these members persuaded the other parts of the coalition to conduct an open primary, a first for Chileans. The competition in this campaign was fierce and bruising. By a decisive margin—71 percent, with nearly 1.4 million voters going to the polls—the left's candidate Ricardo Lagos won the match. *Concertación*'s main opponent in the general election, the rightist bloc "Alliance for Chile," did not stage a primary. Its leaders nominated Joaquín Lavín, the mayor of an affluent suburb of Santiago, through in-house negotiations.

In the aftermath of the primary, news reports described many Christian Democrats as being deeply disillusioned and ready to leave the coalition. For his part, Lagos' rival in the primary, Andreas Zaldívar of the PDC, stopped his campaign for the presidency when the results were in. Declaring that the open nomination contest was "fair, honest, and transparent," Zaldívar pledged loyalty to the coalition and Ricardo Lagos. Several months later, Lagos kept *Concertación* in power for a third term by narrowly defeating Joaquín Lavín in the general election.

Finland[21]

In comparison to Argentina, Chile, and Bulgaria, Finland's party system and democratic political institutions are much more firmly established. Over the last decade, however, the route to the Finnish presidency has changed considerably. Finland, like many European nations, has traditionally functioned as a "consensual democracy," where different political actors work out key decisions through collegial give and take.[22] Between 1919, when Finland became an independent republic, and the late 1980s, this norm governed presidential selection. When voters went to the polls, they did not cast a ballot directly for president, but only for a delegate to attend an Electoral College, much as in the United States. In fact, in formal terms there were no "candidates" for the Finnish presidency, only candidates to serve in this college. Nevertheless, in practice Finland's many parties announced their presidential candidates before the election so citizens would know how a delegate would vote if sent to the Electoral College. Typically there was very little conflict within the parties over the naming of presidential candidates. Parties would simply close ranks around an experienced leader who expressed interest in becoming president. After a general election, if no candidate received a majority of votes in the Electoral College, delegates engaged in old-fashioned horse-trading, and additional ballots were taken. If by the third round there was still no majority favorite for president, the Finnish parliament had the power to select the chief executive.

The electoral system went through a major overhaul following the 1988 election. In future contests, presidents would be chosen by direct vote. The parliament passed this reform in response to criticism that traditional methods of presidential selection suffered from "oligarchic tendencies." Five years later, three of Finland's political parties—the Social Democrats, the Center (Agrarian) Party, and the Conservatives—held primaries to choose candidates for the 1994 presidential election. For the Social Democrats, this was an open primary. In total, the party managed to bring in over one hundred thousand Finns. Many of these participants were new to the party. In Helsinki, for example, nonmembers outnumbered dues-paying members by nearly two-to-one.

The winner of the contest was Martti Ahtisaari, a career diplomat who had never been seen as someone who was particularly "political." He garnered nearly twice as much support as his rival, Kalevi Sorsa, a veteran parliamentary and party figure. This tally surprised many Finnish pundits, since leading Social Democrats had endorsed Sorsa. In the general election six months later, Ahtisaari was again victorious. At this stage, the candidate's status as an outsider was undoubtedly an asset. Finland's economy was in the doldrums and Finns were ready for a change.

Mexico[23]

Few nomination reforms have been as sweeping as Mexico's. From the 1920s until 2000, one party controlled the executive branch, the Institutional Revolutionary Party (PRI). Throughout much of the period, the PRI's rule went completely unchallenged. What little opposition existed was often propped up and controlled by the ruling party itself. Until recently, commentators did not generally refer to Mexico as a democracy, though to call the regime a dictatorship would not have been right either.[24] At the center of the political system stood the president, who enjoyed nearly absolute power, but would leave politics after a single six-year term. The principle of "no reelection" was part of the settlement worked out at the end of the Mexican revolution; it remains a pillar of Mexican politics today.

As one might expect in such a system, the selection of presidential candidates through much of the twentieth century was left in the hands of the incumbent president. The process of nomination would begin informally and privately. In the latter half of a president's administration, PRI leaders would forward the names of potential successors (called "precandidates"). The president would weigh these options and confer with leaders of the different sectors making up the party (labor unions, peasants, business interests). Once the president announced his decision, the party's governing council ratified the choice. *Priísta* leaders across Mexico then would step up to praise the nominee, and grassroots organizing on his behalf would commence.

In their day, these procedures ran like clockwork. Campaigns were generally free of violence, and the military did not interfere in presidential transitions. The same could not be said of many other Latin American nations since the 1920s. PRI leaders broke with this precedent, however, by agreeing to hold an open national primary on November 7, 1999, to choose a contender for the July 2, 2000, presidential election. The major impetus behind this reform was the growing demand for more democracy and accountability in Mexico. A Gallup poll taken in 1988 shows how little support there was for the traditional system. When asked whether they would like to see the ruling party choose its nominee through the usual method of presidential prerogative, through a convention of party leaders, or through a primary, Mexicans overwhelmingly rejected the status quo. Their responses appear in table 9.2. Six out of ten wanted the party to hold a primary, while only 4 percent were content to leave candidate designation up to the president. Even individuals who had voted for the PRI in the previous presidential election and planned to do so again wished to have a more open process.[25]

Calls for democracy became louder throughout the 1990s. Parties opposed to the PRI made substantial gains in state-level elections by channeling discontent

Table 9.2 Public Attitudes toward the Candidate Selection Process: Mexico, 1988

How would you like the Institutional Revolutionary Party to choose its presidential candidate?

	Full Sample	Regular Party Supporters
Leave it to the president	4%	4%
National assembly of party leaders from across the country	24%	26%
Primary election	60%	61%
Not sure	12%	8%
Total	100%	99%

Note: Respondents who reported voting for the Institutional Revolutionary Party in the previous presidential election and planned to do so again were designated "regular party supporters" (N = 735).
Source: IMOP (Gallup) survey of 2,960 randomly selected Mexican citizens in May of 1988.

over the 1994 peso devaluation crisis, political scandals, and social unrest. In 1997, the PRI lost control of the federal congress for the first time in its history, and President Ernesto Zedillo of the PRI struggled to make policy under American-style divided government. Opening up the candidate selection process was one way to respond to critics, given that the two leading opposition contenders for the presidency, Vicente Fox of the National Action Party and Cuauhtémoc Cárdenas of the Party of the Democratic Revolution, were not chosen through competitive primary elections of their own.

To be listed on the primary ballot, "precandidates" needed to take a leave of absence from any political post they currently held and obtain signatures of support from various sectors or councils of the party. Four nationally known PRI leaders entered the presidential race. The front-runner was Francisco Labastida, the minister of the interior under Zedillo. The president and most of the party leadership backed Labastida, but he faced a significant challenger, Roberto Madrazo, the powerful governor of the southern state of Tabasco.[26] Madrazo ran a center-left campaign rich in populist themes and was able to amass a huge war chest. More importantly in this new electoral environment, the challenger had a knack for television.

As is often the case in a competitive race, the tone of the campaign became increasingly shrill. According to the PRI's ground rules, nomination seekers were to refrain from voicing "criticisms that could dishonor or discredit any other 'precandidate,' as well as party leaders and bodies responsible for conducting the primary."[27] In practice, this regulation was unrealistic and unenforceable. In his speeches and in a nationally televised live debate, Madrazo labeled Labastida a failure and liar. "The official candidate [Labastida] just wants to continue the same failed policies we have now. And that's logical, because he supports everything you and I want to change," the Tabasco governor charged.[28]

Francisco Labastida withstood this barrage, fought back in kind, and went on to win the primary with 55 percent of the vote.[29] Going into the primary, many officials in the PRI worried that Roberto Madrazo might defect from the party and run an insurgent presidential campaign if he were not given the nomination. When these results came in, Madrazo opted instead to be a "team player" and endorsed his rival.[30] Labastida was not so fortunate eight months later. On July 2, 2000, he became the first *priísta* nominee ever to lose a presidential election. Vicente Fox beat Labastida by a margin of 6 points (43 to 37 percent, with Cuauhtémoc Cárdenas getting 17 percent), and the PRI conceded defeat. In the Mexican context, this event was as significant as the fall of the Berlin Wall for Eastern Europeans.

Uruguay[31]

Out of the six countries in table 9.1, only Uruguay has a system of presidential primaries mandated by law.[32] Traditionally, the rules for choosing presidents in

Uruguay blended candidate nomination and general election. Under this design, which was known as the *double simultaneous vote,* each party could field several contenders for the presidency. On the day of the election, Uruguayans would pick a single candidate from the full range of choices. The contestant who garnered the most support, *within the party that received the greatest number of votes,* became president. Over the years this method had allowed Uruguay's major political parties, the National Party and the Colorado Party, to avoid damaging internal splits. Candidates with very different views and backgrounds were free to run for president under a common party label, with "the people" eventually determining the outcome.

While nominally fair and democratic, the method of double simultaneous voting could easily contradict the principle of majority (or plurality) rule. It also made the connections between mass preferences and candidate selection murky. A party could win the presidency if it had two or more contenders with just "medium-sized" followings appearing on the voting ballot; parties that had just one strong standard bearer were at a disadvantage. Analysts point to the Uruguayan presidential race of 1971 to illustrate this pitfall. That year, one of the Colorado Party candidates became president after receiving approximately 380,000 votes. The front-runner from the National Party managed to get over 60,000 more votes than this, but the aggregate tally for his party fell below the Colorado total.

In March of 1996, the Uruguayan parliament approved a constitutional amendment to change the electoral system. Under this reform, each party would be required to select a single nominee via an open primary six months in advance of the general election. To obtain the nomination, a candidate would need to win the party primary with a majority, or receive at least 40 percent of the vote with no other challenger coming within 10 points. If no candidate did this well, a national party convention would be called to choose a standard bearer. In the general election, similar procedures were proposed. Any candidate receiving a majority would become the next president. If none of the contestants made it past the 50 percent mark, a candidate who garnered as little as 40 percent would be declared the winner as long as each opponent fell at least 10 percent below this margin. If this condition did not hold, the two top candidates would compete in a run-off election. Uruguayans approved of these changes to the constitution in a popular referendum, and the parties held their first open primaries in 1999.

Candidates in the Colorado and National parties clashed both in terms of ideology and personality. The nomination contest was particularly intense in the National Party. In this race, the two leading contenders voiced profound differences over social and economic policies. The eventual nominee, former Uruguayan President Luis Alberto Lacalle, favored expanding the economy through increasing "free trade," while his principal opponent was committed to preserving a larger state sector and providing a stronger safety net for the poor. Jorge Batlle of the Colorado Party, a senator and a member of one of the most politically connected families in Uruguay, did somewhat better in his primary race; he garnered 55 percent of the vote, as opposed to 48 percent for Lacalle. Yet internal party divisions were amply on display in this case too. Indeed, incumbent president Julio Maria Sanguinetti, who was from the Colorado Party, had endorsed Batlle's opponent in the primary.

The third major bloc in the Uruguayan election was a coalition of two center-left organizations, the Progressive Alliance and the Broad Front. The winner of this joint primary, Tabaré Vázquez, received 82 percent of the vote. This makes it appear that the internal contest was more harmonious. In fact, as Roberto Espíndola writes, the coalition was deeply divided after the primary.[33] A telling indicator of this conflict was the decision of Vázquez not to choose the second-place finisher as his vice-presidential candidate, as had been expected. Vázquez continued to do well in the general election, garnering a plurality of the vote. This was not enough to win a victory outright. In the run-off election, the conservative Lacalle was dropped from consideration because he placed third. He and many other National Party leaders threw their support at this stage behind the more moderate of the two remaining candidates, Jorge Batlle. The Colorado Party nominee apparently profited from this. At the second round, Batlle beat Vázquez 54 to 46 percent.

ASSESSING THE MOVE TOWARD
MORE OPEN NOMINATIONS

Americans are generally satisfied with the way democracy works in the United States, even if they have mixed feelings about the candidates running for office.[34] If asked, most citizens would likely agree that the American way of selecting candidates is a model that other nations should be encouraged to emulate.[35] The veteran political consultant Dick Morris, who has worked with many clients overseas, captured this sentiment in a comment to a newspaper reporter. "In the cold war, the CIA was all over the world teaching armies how to fight and intelligence services how to spy. Now, instead of teaching dictators how to be dictators, we're teaching people how to win elections. That's a positive thing."[36]

The electoral process is, of course, a central part of any democracy. If our standard for judging nomination procedures is whether they produce competitive candidates for the general election, the track record in table 9.1 looks promising. In five countries, only one major party held an open presidential primary; in four of these cases (Argentina, Bulgaria, Chile, and Finland) that party was ultimately victorious. For Argentines, this meant that a different partisan coalition took charge of the executive branch. On the whole, Andrew Hacker's conjecture about the debilitating effect of contested primaries—that they represent "an important strike" against candidates in general elections—does not gain much support internationally.

A more difficult matter to consider is whether primary elections are good for political parties and coalition building.[37] Representation would be difficult if not impossible without reasonably coherent and consolidated political parties. Nomination seekers single-mindedly pursuing their personal ambitions in an open primary may jeopardize the integrity of the party. In one of the first comparative works on nomination procedures, Austin Ranney stressed over twenty years ago that political parties in presidentialist democracies tend to be pushed back into the periphery. As presidential contenders emerge, "party organizations are less important, and candidate-centered organizations are much more important. The selection of controversial candidates by the victory of one faction over another is more likely to result in open party splits and secessional candidates."[38] The staging of primary contests where party members and nonmembers alike can take part might well exacerbate this inherent tendency. Candidates aspiring to the presidency may win a primary election with the assistance of political strategists such as Dick Morris. Yet in the process, many voters, including traditional supporters of the party, could become alienated if they back a losing contestant. In all of the cases in table 9.1, party leaders expressed grave concerns about fragmentation at the grassroots because of this.[39]

In the United States, some researchers argue that fears of partisan breakdown are overstated. Animosities that look severe when candidates vie for a position on the ticket may be forgotten after the summer nominating conventions. This is because the great majority of voters in the United States possess reliable psychological connections to one of the major parties.[40] Many also take strong and consistent stands on liberal or conservative policy issues. The party standard bearer can do much to fix any damage from a nomination fight by appealing to these dispositions. The dominance of the American two-party system makes this repair job all the easier. Most voters who were thwarted in a primary or local nominating caucus would have little choice other than to accept their party's duly selected candidate. In all likelihood, the opposing party nominee would be less desirable still. If three or more viable presidential contenders were in the field, the party might find it much more difficult to bring these individuals back to the fold.

In our international cases, were similar dynamics at work after the primaries? A plausible argument can be made for this, in that voters taking part in the nomination were unambiguously acting as *partisans* involved in a most important task—even if many had considered themselves independents, outsiders, or neophytes. Such an experience could have instilled a deeper sense of partisanship among participants and left them well primed to support the party in the general election, no matter which candidate was selected. This is certainly what party reformers intended.

On the other hand, it may not be wise to generalize from the American case. In several of the countries in table 9.1, voters in the general election had more than two viable candidates from which to choose.[41] Participants in the primary who were not successful in getting their preferred candidate on the ballot might have found an attractive substitute in another party.

More importantly, in countries facing monumental political and economic transformations, the very meaning of partisanship could be in flux. Presidential candidates nominated by a party experiencing unprecedented internal turmoil (e.g., Mexico's PRI) or a political coalition a decade or less old (e.g., Chile's *Concertación*, Bulgaria's UDF, Argentina's Alliance) could find it far more difficult to heal the wounds from a divisive primary through an appeal to partisan solidarity. A more likely scenario, perhaps, is that after landing a place on the ticket by running a highly personalized campaign, a nominee would continue in this "candidate-centered" vein during the general election. In this case, many voters who opposed the candidate in the primary might be all too ready to vote against him once again. This would not necessarily be bad for the candidate if an equal or greater number of citizens could be rounded up before election day. From the standpoint of the party, however, such behavior could prove corrosive over the long run, for the organization would be left with a less stable, more candidate-oriented mass base.

Public opinion data could clarify the relationship between citizen nomination preferences and choices in the general election, as it has in the United States. To my knowledge, only in the Mexican case are adequate survey data available to study the effects of the open primary.[42] Consequently, we turn once more to the PRI primary held in November of 1999.

Defenders of American-style presidential primary elections abroad would have their hardest challenge in Mexico. As noted above, the confrontation between Francisco Labastida and Roberto Madrazo was extremely harsh, with each candidate attacking the other's policy stands and fitness to govern. Labastida's subsequent poor showing in the general election is the only case in table 9.1 where an incumbent party lost control of the executive branch following an open primary. In an interview several months after this defeat, Labastida lamented the sparring that took place at the start of his campaign. He further warned party leaders against staging such contests in the future. "If the party's internal elections are not conducted with a great deal of skill, intelligence [and] judgment, and if the consequences are not properly gauged, fractures are provoked like the one we [the PRI] are still dragging behind us."[43] Are these remarks justified? Did the rancorous internal debate contribute to the defeat of the Mexican ruling party?

Public Evaluations of the Primary and the PRI

Party officials hoped that the open primary would generate a great deal of public attention and underscore their argument that the PRI-dominated political system was now fully democratic. President Zedillo promised repeatedly not to become involved in candidate selection. Many in the ruling party did nonetheless signal that Francisco Labastida was the preferred choice. These signals were described in news accounts, and Labastida became widely known as the "official candidate." As mentioned earlier, presidential elections in Mexico for much of the twentieth century were not truly competitive. The main purpose for holding them was to demonstrate support for the ruling party and its governing regime. Given this past, many citizens were understandably suspicious about the PRI's commitment to democratic reform. Could the primary be just an elaborate hoax? Was the president pulling the strings, as always?

As shown in table 9.3, approximately half of the respondents in a national survey conducted two weeks before the primary were suspicious. Forty-one percent felt that there had not been true competition for the nomination. Fifty-one percent agreed with the statement, "The primary election appears to be democratic, but in reality the president is the one naming the candidate." One out of three respondents expressed skepticism in both survey items. Only 22 percent of the sample thought that competition was fair and the president was keeping out of the process.

We also find little change in the public's evaluation of Mexico's political system after the primary (top of table 9.4). Before the November 7, 1999, contest, only 43 percent of the respondents believed that there was "a lot" or "some" democracy in the country. Slightly more (46 percent) saw "little" or "no" democracy. Reactions to a similar survey item three months after the primary were nearly identical: 41 percent called the Mexican political system democratic, while 47 percent stated that it was not yet a democracy. Critics of the PRI regime were evidently unmoved by the party's brush with internal democracy.

Nor was the PRI able to attract a significantly larger following after its presi-

Table 9.3 Mexican Citizens Evaluate the Primary Election in the Institutional Revolutionary Party (PRI)

Thinking about the PRI's process of presidential candidate selection, which statement comes closest to your views?

The process has been impartial with true competition	38%
The process has favored one candidate, and there has not been true competition	41%

With which one of the following statements about the upcoming primary do you most agree?

The primary election is truly a democratic way of selecting the presidential candidate.	30%
The primary election appears to be democratic, but in reality the president is the one naming the candidate	51%

Note: To simplify the presentation, "not sure" percentages are left off.
Source: Reforma/El Norte/Mural poll in late October of 1999 (approximately two weeks before the primary); N = 2,531 randomly selected Mexican citizens.

Table 9.4 Beliefs about Mexico's Democracy and Party Identification: Pre- and Post-Primary Comparisons (%)

	October, 1999	February, 2000
How much democracy would you say there is in the country?		
A lot	16	
Some	27	
Only a little	34	
None	12	
Not sure	11	
Do you consider Mexico these days to be a democracy or not?		
Yes, the country is democratic		41
No, it is not a democracy		47
Not sure		12
With which party do you sympathize?		
Institutional Revolutionary Party (PRI)	34	37
One of the other political parties	22	31
None/Not sure	44	33

Note: The PRI presidential primary was held on November 7, 1999.
Source: *Reforma/El Norte/Mural* poll (N = 2,531); first wave of the Mexico 2000 Panel Survey (N = 2,355).

dential primary. In the pre-primary survey, one third of the sample sympathized with the party. Only 22 percent identified with one of the opposition parties, and the rest, a rather large bloc, were independent or not sure how to respond. Come February of 2000, with the general election campaign growing more salient, the number in the "none/not sure" category shrank to 33 percent. At this juncture, the PRI still had the lion's share of mass identifiers (37 percent), but opposition forces clearly were gaining strength.

The Impact of Nomination Choices on General Election Behavior

As a device to raise the party's sagging profile and legitimacy, the PRI primary failed. If we turn specifically to the respondents' voting preferences in the general election, is there any evidence to suggest that mobilization efforts at the nomination stage further split the party, leaving it in bad shape for the July contest? In the poll conducted in October of 1999, individuals stated whether they planned to vote in the primary or not. In table 9.5, we find that among likely participants, just half said that they would back the party no matter what in the general election. Nearly a quarter of these likely voters planned to defect if their preferred

Table 9.5 Signs of Schisms within the Institutional Revolutionary Party (PRI) on the Eve of Its Presidential Primary (%)

	Likely Primary Voters	PRI Members
If your preferred candidate for the presidency does not win, what will you do?		
Vote for the PRI candidate no matter what	52	67
Vote for the candidate of another party	22	11
Abstain from voting	6	9
Not sure	20	27

Note: "Likely primary voters" are respondents who were registered to vote and stated that they "definitely" planned to take part; $N = 1,121$. For self-described party members, $N = 94$.
Source: Reforma/El Norte/Mural poll taken approximately two weeks before the primary.

candidate were not nominated. Even among self-described PRI members (approximately 4 percent of the sample), the chance of defection was fairly high. Only 67 percent of the *priístas* pledged unconditional support. On the face of it, it appears that the candidate-centered campaign for the Mexican presidency had the potential to tear the mass foundation of the party apart.

Were these participants sincere in their threat to flee? Regression analysis provides a means to address this question. In the February 2000 poll, survey participants were asked about their preferences for president. They also reported how they had voted in two previous national elections, the midterm congressional races of 1997 and the 1994 presidential contest.[44] By regressing preferences in the 2000 presidential election (coded 1 if the survey participant preferred Francisco Labastida and 0 otherwise) on decisions made in 1994 and 1997, we establish a baseline forecast of support for the ruling party candidate at the start of his general election campaign. This can be thought of as the vote share that any PRI nominee might have expected given the party's recent showings. We can examine how mobilization over candidate selection affected this expectation by adding two more predictors to the model: a vote for Labastida in the November primary; and a vote for one of his nomination rivals (each coded 1 or 0 as well). These effects are calculated via logistic regression. The results from this analysis appear in table 9.6, first two columns.[45] As noted in this table, the model also includes a number of demographic and socioeconomic control variables. Studies of public opinion in Mexico have found that older people, women, individuals living in rural areas, the less educated, and union members tend to back the PRI in national elections.[46] Labastida, the so-called official candidate, drew disproportionately from these groups in the primary. When modeling the effects of participation in the primary, it is important to factor in such traits. To simplify the presentation, however, the results for these control variables are not shown.

In February of 2000, 41 percent of the sample favored Labastida for president. This support was heavily dependent on voting choices in 1994 and 1997; both coefficients are highly significant. The figures in the second column, labeled

Table 9.6 The Impact of Primary-Stage Choice on Support for Francisco Labastida, the PRI Presidential Nominee, in February and during the July 2, 2000, General Election

	February, 2000		July 2, 2000	
	b	Exp(b)	b	Exp(b)
Nomination-Stage Choice				
Voted for Labastida in the November primary	1.19	3.29**	1.18	3.25**
Voted for another nomination candidate	−.17	.84	.58	1.78*
Choices in Previous National Elections				
Voted for the PRI presidential candidate in 1994	1.43	4.18**	.97	2.65**
Voted for the PRI congressional candidate in 1997	1.10	3.00**	.69	1.99**
N	1,641		898	

Note: These effects were estimated via logistic regression. The dependent variable took on a value of 1 for individuals reporting support for Francisco Labastida in the general election, and 0 otherwise. Independent variables were also scored on a 0 or 1 scale. "Exp" refers to the exponentiation function. (Regression coefficients transformed by exponentiation indicate how the odds of preferring Labastida were affected on average as the independent variable moved from 0 to 1.) * = $p < .05$; ** = $p < .01$. When calculating these effects, the respondent's place of residence, gender, age, level of formal schooling, and connection to a labor union were controlled; to simplify the presentation, these additional coefficients are not shown. Pseudo-R^2 = .35 in the first regression model and .36 in the second.

Source: First and fourth waves of the Mexico 2000 Panel Survey.

exp(b), indicate how the odds of preferring the *priísta* were affected on average by the independent variables. We see that individuals who had voted for the PRI in the previous presidential election were over four times more likely than other respondents to prefer its nominee; moreover, those who supported PRI congressional candidates in 1997 were three times more likely to back Labastida. Against this backdrop, the effect of the nomination contest also stands out mightily. The odds of preferring Labastida were 3.29 times higher for respondents who had turned out for him three months earlier in the primary. For this bloc, mobilization in November boosted support for the PRI well beyond its 1994 and 1997 levels.

This would have been welcome news for party leaders who knew they were taking a chance in staging a primary. More importantly, those who supported another nomination seeker evidently *were not* ready to abandon ship. The negative sign for the coefficient for this group suggests some possibility of defection, but the effect is small and statistically insignificant.[47]

Survey respondents were contacted again immediately following the July 2 presidential election. At this time, only 32 percent reported marking a ballot for Labastida, a margin that is in keeping with the official tally. While Labastida was not able to win the necessary plurality of votes, he at least managed to pull those who had originally opposed his nomination back toward the party (third and fourth columns, table 9.6). Respondents who voted for Roberto Madrazo or another of Labastida's rivals were nearly twice as likely as those who abstained from the primary to turn out for the PRI in the general election. The divisive internal contest over candidate selection appears to have left participants well disposed to heed the nominee's later call for support. For their part, primary voters who were with Labastida from the start continued to stand by him even as he lost ground. They too were apparently quite responsive to his campaign appeals.

The path diagrams in figure 9.1 show this process of general election mobilization and persuasion in finer detail. The two dependent variables are summary evaluations of the PRI nominee, based on an eleven-point "feeling thermometer" scale ranging from "very negative" to "very positive," and a four-point scale measuring the degree of identification with the party. Attitudes measured at the end of the campaign were regressed on survey responses from February, preferences in the primary, and the other control variables from table 9.6. In each case, attitudes toward Labastida and the PRI changed markedly over the course of the campaign. The standardized coefficients linking February and July responses are only .23 for the feeling thermometer scores and .48 for party identification.[48] We find here that nomination choices can be linked to this change. By the end of the campaign, Mexican citizens who turned out for the primary, regardless of whether they backed the winner or a loser, had become more positive toward Labastida and closer to the PRI. In each case, these effects are statistically significant.[49]

Was the primary similarly useful in shaping activism for the PRI? Political parties, if they are to prosper, must have the wherewithal to attract committed followers willing to do the hard work of politics—attending meetings and rallies, canvassing neighborhoods, raising funds, and the like. Mexico's ruling party had a long history of recruiting troops through a vast network of social groups, economic organizations, and governmental offices. Promises of career advancement and other forms of patronage served as the major incentives for participation. By the 1990s, these traditional methods for incorporating members into the organization had seriously worn down. Old networks of "patrons" and "clients" were simply disappearing. In this changing environment, the primary could have served as an important new recruitment device for the party. Citizens taking part in as critical a decision as presidential candidate selection might have been more readily inducted into PRI affairs as the organization jumped into action in May and June of 2000. The attitude changes described in figure 9.1 lend a rationale for this effect: individuals who feel more favorable toward the nominee and identify more strongly with the PRI should, all things equal, be more inclined to work for the party.

In the surveys collected over the course of the general election, individuals stated whether they had recently attended a local meeting on behalf of one of the parties. In the homestretch of the campaign, 7 percent of the respondents reported attending PRI functions, a small but politically important minority. What was the relationship between the primary and this activist bloc? The regres-

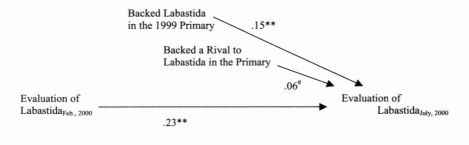

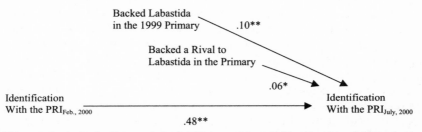

Figure 9.1 Attitude Change over the Course of the Mexican Presidential Campaign: Path Models for Party Identification and Evaluations of Francisco Labastida, the PRI Nominee

Note: These coefficients are standardized OLS slopes. The same controls from table 9.6 were in place here. # = $p < .10$; * = $p < .05$; ** = $p < .01$. Party identification was measured on a four-point scale (4 = strongly identify with the PRI, 3 = weakly identify, 2 = lean towards the PRI, 1 = does not identify with the party). Evaluations of Labastida were based on eleven-point "feeling thermometers" scores.
Source: Mexico 2000 Panel Survey (N = 1,178 in the first model and 985 in the second).

sion model in table 9.7 indicates that the primary did indeed have a significant positive effect on grassroots organizing.

As in the voting models, these results are derived from logistic regression, with the dependent variable coded one for respondents who participated in PRI meetings and zero otherwise. We find that individuals who voted in the primary were over twice as likely to take part in local party affairs. Those on the losing side in the divisive nomination contest proved to be exceedingly "good sports." On the whole, they were every bit as active as individuals who were early backers of Labastida.

This closer look at the aftereffects of the Mexican primary reminds us that surface appearances can be deceiving. Labastida's remark about the damaging consequences of the internal contest was not warranted. Scholars of Mexican politics have proposed many other factors to account for the PRI loss in 2000.[50] Suffice it to say, the findings from table 9.6, table 9.7, and figure 9.1 point the finger away from the primary.

Table 9.7 The Impact of Primary-Stage Choice on Grassroots Activism for the Institutional Revolutionary Party (PRI) during the General Election Campaign

	b	Exp(b)
Nomination-Stage Choice		
Voted for Labastida in the November primary	.82	2.28**
Voted for another nomination candidate	.82	2.28*
Attended Local Meetings of the PRI, Late 1999–Early 2000	1.03	2.81**
N	1,202	

Note: These are logistic regression coefficients. The dependent variable took on a value of 1 for individuals who reported attending local meetings of the PRI in the final two months of the general election campaign (May–June, 2000), and 0 otherwise. The predictors shown here were also coded on a 0 or 1 scale. * = $p <$ .05; ** = $p < .01$. Voting choices in the two previous national elections and the other controls from Table 9.6 were included when estimating these effects. Pseudo-R^2 = .04.
Source: Mexico 2000 Panel Survey

CONCLUSION

When parties outside of the United States adopt an open primary to select a presidential nominee, they are taking a leap into the dark. Political scientists since Charles Merriam and Louise Overacker's era in the 1920s have warned against giving powers that are this important to voters who might not put the interests of the party first.[51] Since then, and especially since the McGovern-Fraser reforms of the late 1960s, political scientists have devoted a tremendous amount of attention to the American model of candidate selection. Every four years, the process is carefully scrutinized and refined. In striking contrast, practically no comparative investigations have been done on nomination reforms in other presidentialist systems.

Party leaders in these democracies open up the process of candidate selection when alternative schemes are no longer tenable or entail greater risks. It may be awkward or impossible through conventional elite-level deal-making to drop an unpopular incumbent president from the ticket. Primaries offer the possibility of doing this and recruiting a fresh face. This was the motive behind the Bulgarian contest. In other instances (e.g., Argentina or Chile), a party coalition may be so new or shaky that behind-the-scenes norms to resolve internal disagreements have not yet been established. Primary elections consequently become the least objectionable, most legitimate mechanism for conflict resolution. Rival coalition members are free to take their arguments directly to the public. In all of the countries reviewed here, the classic Downsian goal of increasing "electoral market share" loomed large.[52] To one extent or another, party reformers in these six very different political systems believed that an open contest would lead to a larger and more enthusiastic rank-and-file base, and ultimately to greater competitiveness in the general election.

Do presidential primaries live up to these expectations? Since the kind of survey data that has shed so much light on American nominations is available for only one of the cases in table 9.1, our conclusions must be tentative. Regarding the use of primaries to settle disputes over candidate selection, one generalization seems fair: Open campaigns for the presidential nomination draw attention to the various ideological fault lines and warring personalities within the party and probably increase political polarization. There is no necessary logical relationship between an open primary and campaigning that is so aggressive that it threatens to split the party. Yet given the zero-sum nature of the contest—there can be only one nominee at a time—and the overriding need to activate one's supporters, the potential for factional conflict to escalate is great.

Interestingly, however, in no case did the second-place finisher in the primary leave the party during the general-election campaign; all pledged at least lukewarm support for the nominee. As a means to settle intrapartisan conflict over who should carry the banner, primaries thus appear to be decisive. In a departure from Austin Ranney's 1981 observation, the "open party splits" that were so evident when nomination elections were held did not lead to "secessional candidates."

Whether primary elections also rejuvenate the party and make it more competitive remains an open question worthy of much further research. As we have seen, hotly contested primaries can herald general election success. Unfortunately, it is difficult to tell whether these victories represent partisan mandates or more personalized triumphs. In Mexico, our analysis suggests that the Institutional Revolutionary Party primary contributed both to partisanship *and* personalism. The primary forged a lasting personal connection between the nominee and his followers. Yet the mobilization efforts of the losing nomination seekers also gave a lift to the party and its standard bearer. If repeated in future elections, such exercises could be a source of strength and renewal for the party.

Presidential primary elections first sprang from the pressures and ideals of the Progressive Era. For decades they were a quintessentially American phenomenon. This is no longer the case today. While no other democracies have fully adopted the American system in all its complexity, the two core principles of U.S. nomination politics—fierce public contestation and open mass mobilization—have spread internationally. We have much to learn about how "American-style" primaries affect voting behavior, party consolidation, institutional performance, and the quality of democratic governance abroad. This chapter represents a first step in this direction.

NOTES

This chapter was written while I was a Guest Scholar at the Brookings Institution, Governance Studies Program. I thank Margarita Assenova, Lonna Atkeson, Ann Marie Clark,

Ken Janda, Lauri Karvonen, Bill Mayer, and Lee Wilson for helpful feedback. I am also grateful to Alejandro Moreno for sending me the *Reforma* newspaper poll on the 1999 Mexican primary. Joe Bante and Neil Strine provided useful research assistance.

1. Data from the 1992 American National Election Study nicely illustrate this point. Among those who reported taking part in the presidential nomination contest that year, only 7 percent stated that they had contributed funds to one of the major parties during the campaign. In "closed primary" states, where only registered partisans were permitted to vote, and in states where local partisan nominating caucuses were held rather than a primary election, this proportion rises slightly but is still quite low (less than 10 percent). These data are publicly available at the Web site of the Interuniversity Consortium for Political and Social Research in Ann Arbor, MI (http://www.icpsr.umich.edu/).

2. Ernst Christopher Meyer, *Nominating Systems: Direct Primaries Versus Conventions in the United States* (Madison, WI: State Journal Printing Company, 1902), 90.

3. Less formally, of course, party leaders can have an effect on the selection process by funneling resources to their preferred candidates and signaling to others which horse to back. On this point, see Marty Cohen, David Karol, Hans Noel, and John Zaller, "Beating Reform: The Resurgence of Parties in Presidential Nominations, 1980–2000," presented at the annual meeting of the American Political Science Association, August 30–September 2, 2001, San Francisco, CA; and Ronald B. Rapoport, Walter J. Stone, and Alan I. Abramowitz, "Do Endorsements Matter? Group Influence in the 1984 Democratic Caucuses," *American Political Science Review* 85:1 (1991), 193–203.

4. Andrew Hacker, "Does a 'Divisive' Primary Harm a Candidate's Chances?" *American Political Science Review* 59:1 (1965), 105.

5. See Lonna Rae Atkeson, "From the Primaries to the General Election: Does a Divisive Nomination Race Affect a Candidate's Fortunes in the Fall?" in *In Pursuit of the White House 2000*, ed. William G. Mayer (New York: Chatham House), 285–312.

6. André Blais, Louis Massicotte, and Agnieszka Dobrzynska, "Direct Presidential Elections: a World Summary," *Electoral Studies* 16:4 (1997), 441–455. The authors identify thirty-two democratic countries where the head of state is directly elected.

7. Between 1965 and 1974, only one hundred signatures were necessary.

8. Since 1965, anywhere from six to sixteen names have appeared on the first-round presidential ballot. With so many candidates splitting the vote, it is not surprising that elections have all required two steps. For useful comparative treatments of the French electoral system, see James W. Davis, *Leadership Selection in Six Western Democracies* (Westport, CT: Greenwood Press, 1998), chap. 6; Roy Pierce, *Choosing the Chief: Presidential Elections in France and the United States* (Ann Arbor: University of Michigan Press, 1995); Robert Elgie, ed., *Electing the French President* (New York: St. Martin's Press, 1996); and Alan Ware, *Political Parties and Party Systems* (New York: Oxford University Press, 1996).

9. Only a few works seek to place American presidential nomination politics in a comparative perspective. Among these are Austin Ranney, "Candidate Selection," in *Democracy at the Polls: A Comparative Study of Competitive National Elections,* ed. David Butler, Howard R. Penniman, and Austin Ranney (Washington, DC: AEI, 1981), 75–106; Hugh Heclo, "Presidential and Prime Ministerial Selection," in *Perspectives on Presidential Selection,* ed. Donald R. Matthews (Washington, D.C.: Brookings Institution, 1973), 19–48; Carl Baar and Ellen Baar, "Party and Convention Organization and Leadership

Selection in Canada and the United States," in *Perspectives on Presidential Selection*, ed. Donald R. Matthews (Washington, D.C.: Brookings Institution, 1973), 49–84; Leon D. Epstein, *Political Parties in Western Democracies* (New York: Praeger, 1967); Ware, *Political Parties and Party Systems*, chap. 9; Pierce, *Choosing the Chief*; and Davis, *Leadership Selection*. Some of these studies touch on the subject of primary elections, but no systematic research has yet been done on the implications and advisability of open presidential primaries outside of the United States.

10. Larry Diamond and Richard Gunther note that throughout the established Western democracies, confidence in government has plummeted over the last few decades. Citizens are rapidly losing faith in all representative institutions, including political parties. In many emerging democracies outside of the West, citizens are even more skeptical. In seventeen Latin American democracies, for example, only one in five individuals expresses "a lot" or "some" confidence in political parties, while 45 percent voice no confidence at all. Along similar lines, just 20 percent of South Koreans trust political parties; across eleven postcommunist states in Eastern Europe, this drops to 12 percent. See the authors' opening chapter in *Political Parties and Democracy*, ed. Larry Diamond and Richard Gunther (Baltimore: Johns Hopkins University Press, 2001), ix–xxxiv.

11. In the American case, some research suggests that individuals who take part in primary elections and local nominating caucuses come away with a renewed commitment to the political party. See Walter J. Stone, Lonna Rae Atkeson, and Ronald B. Rapoport, "Turning On or Turning Off? Mobilization and Demobilization Effects of Participation in Presidential Nomination Campaigns," *American Journal of Political Science* 36:3 (1992), 665–91; Emmett H. Buell, Jr., "Divisive Primaries and Participation in Fall Presidential Campaigns: A Study of 1984 New Hampshire Primary Activists," *American Politics Quarterly* 14 (1986), 376–90; James A. McCann, "Nomination Politics and Ideological Polarization: Assessing the Attitudinal Effects of Campaign Involvement," *Journal of Politics* 57:1 (1995), 101–20; and James A. McCann, Randall W. Partin, Ronald B. Rapoport, and Walter J. Stone, "Presidential Nomination Campaigns and Party Mobilization: An Assessment of Spillover Effects," *American Journal of Political Science* 40:3 (1996), 756–67.

12. John H. Aldrich, *Why Parties? The Origin and Transformation of Political Parties in America* (Chicago: University of Chicago Press, 1995), 22.

13. This table should not be taken as a complete inventory of all open primary elections held around the world. The ones covered here are the most noteworthy, judging by the amount of attention each received from newspaper reporters and election monitoring organizations. I exclude from consideration presidential primaries where only party functionaries or citizens making financial contributions to the party could take part. Such contests would be very different from the traditional "American" model of presidential candidate selection. It is also worth noting that in parliamentary systems, a trend toward more open nominations for leadership positions is equally apparent. In the 1990s, major parties in Canada, Israel, and Spain conducted special primaries to choose prime ministerial candidates. In each case, observers marveled at the "Americanization" of the contest. The introduction of primary elections in Israel seems to have been particularly consequential. In 1992, Benjamin Netanyahu used the Likud Party primary as a means to cultivate a national following. Some commentators have argued that this reform, while working out quite well for the future prime minister, was disastrous for the party. See Reuven Y. Hazan, "The 1996 Intra-Party Elections in Israel: Adopting Party Primaries," *Electoral Studies* 16:1 (1997), 95–103.

14. This description of the Argentine primary draws from Michael A. May and Carlos Regunaga, "Presidential Election Season Begins," *CSIS Hemisphere 2000*, Series VI, Issue 8, January 19, 1999; "In Perspective," *Oxford Analytica Weekly Column*, November 3, 1999; "Which Candidate for Argentina's Alliance?" *The Economist*, U.S. Edition, November 21, 1998, 37; Mark Falcoff, "Argentina: A New Struggle for Succession," *AEI Latin American Outlook*, September 1998; Mario del Carril, "Classic Menem," *Hemisfile* 10:2 (1999), 6–7; Clifford Krauss, "Two Would-Be Presidents in Argentina Make Corruption an Issue," *New York Times*, November 17, 1998, A12; and Clifford Krauss, "Buenos Aires Mayor to Lead Opposition," *New York Times*, November 30, 1998, A10.

15. In the 1980s, the Judicialist Party began running primary elections to choose its presidential nominee. Participation in these contests, however, was restricted to card-carrying party members, a very small percentage of the electorate.

16. The turnout rates in table 9.1 were calculated from data on *voting age populations* compiled by the International Institute for Democracy and Electoral Assistance (IDEA). The Institute posts this information on its web site: http://www.idea.int/.

17. Will Lester, "Primary Turnout Higher Than in '96 But Still Low," Associated Press report, August 31, 2000. When figuring participation rates, only those states holding both Democratic and Republican primaries were counted.

18. Background information on the Bulgarian primary can be found in *IRI Report on the Bulgarian Primary Election, June 1, 1996* (Washington, D.C.: International Republican Institute, 1996); "Bulgarian Leader Loses Primary," *Financial Times*, June 5, 1996; "Zhelev Bows Out After Defeat in Primaries," *Agence France Presse*, June 5, 1996; "Bulgarian Presidential Election: Final Report," Office for Democratic Institutions and Human Rights (OSCE).

19. The Institute describes its mission as "advancing democracy worldwide" through the principles of "individual liberty, the rule of law, and the entrepreneurial spirit." It is a nonprofit organization formally separated from the Republican Party. Senator John McCain is its current chairman, and many prominent Republicans serve on its board of directors. Its counterpart on the Democratic side is the National Democratic Institute, also based in Washington, D.C. and chaired by former Secretary of State Madeleine K. Albright. Both organizations monitor electoral processes around the world and seek to strengthen parties in developing democracies. The National Democratic Institute had given assistance to Bulgarians in previous elections but was not nearly as involved as the IRI in the 1996 UDF primary.

20. On the Chilean case, see Roberto Espíndola, "Electoral Campaigning and the Consolidation of Democracy in Latin America: The Southern Cone," paper presented at the Workshop on Political Communication, the Mass Media, and the Consolidation of New Democracies, ECPR Joint Sessions of Workshops, March 22–27, 2002, in Torino, Italy; Emma Hughes and Nigel Parsons, "The 1999–2000 Presidential Elections in Chile," *Electoral Studies* 20 (2001), 641–57; Paul E. Sigmund, *The United States and Democracy in Chile* (Baltimore: Johns Hopkins University Press, 1993); "Consternation," *The Economist Newspaper Ltd.*, May 22, 1999; "Primaries' Final Count Gives Lagos Undisputed Victory over Zaldívar," *Global News Wire*, May 31, 1999; and "Socialist Wins Chile's First Presidential Primary," *Agence France Presse*, May 31, 1999.

21. See Pertti Pesonen, "The First Direct Election of Finland's President," *Scandinavian Political Studies* 17:3 (1994), 259–72; "Survey of Finland," *Financial Times*, October

11, 1993, 11; "Without Really Trying," *The Economist Newspaper Ltd.*, June 26, 1993, 58; "Former Premier Sorsa out of the Presidential Contest," *Agence France Presse*, May 27, 1993. In a personal communication, Lauri Karvonen also provided much useful background information on Finnish presidential elections.

22. The notion of "consensual democracy" is discussed in Arend Lijphart, *Patterns of Democracy* (New Haven: Yale University Press, 1999).

23. The best "behind the scenes" look at presidential candidate selection in Mexico under the Institutional Revolutionary Party is Jorge Castañeda's *Perpetuating Power: How Mexican Presidents Were Chosen* (New York: The New Press, 2000). Other sources on the PRI primary are George W. Grayson, "A Guide to the November 7, 1999, PRI Presidential Primary," *Western Hemisphere Election Study Series*, Volume XVII, Study 4, CSIS Americans Program, October, 1999; Kathleen Bruhn, "The Making of the Mexican President, 2000," in *Mexico's Pivotal Democratic Elections: Campaigns, Voting Behavior, and the 2000 Presidential Race*, ed. Jorge I. Domínguez and Chappell Lawson (Stanford, CA: Stanford University Press, forthcoming); James A. McCann, "Primary Priming," in *Mexico's Pivotal Democratic Elections: Campaigns, Voting Behavior, and the 2000 Presidential Race*, ed., Jorge I. Domínguez and Chappell Lawson (Stanford, CA: Stanford University Press, forthcoming); Federico Estévez and Alejandro Poiré, "Campaign Effects and Issue Voting in the 1999 PRI Primary," paper presented at the annual meeting of the Midwest Political Science Association, 2001; "Mexico's Ruling Party to Adopt a More Open System for Picking Candidate," *Agence France Presse*, May 18, 1999; "PRI Ruling Party Tells Rival Candidates to Cool It," *Financial Times Information*, August 6, 1999; John Ward Anderson and Molly Moore, " 'Fantastic Four' Take to the Air, Mexican Ruling Party Sets Precedent with TV Debate in Presidential Race," *Washington Post*, September 9, 1999, A15; Sam Dillon, "A Mexican Debate Shatters Traditions," *New York Times*, September 10, 1999, A10; "Madrazo Slapped with Reprimand on Latest TV Ad," *Novedades Editores*, S.A. de C.V., October 7, 1999; Peter Ward, "Mexico's PRI Could Be About to Open Pandora's Box," *Houston Chronicle*, October 19, 1999, A21; Sam Dillon, "Mexican President Defends Equity of Party's First Primary," *New York Times*, October 25, 1999, A4; "PRI Candidates Ignore Zedillo's Appeals for Calm," *Financial Times Information*, October 26, 1999; Sam Dillon, "Mexican Runs on Both Change and Stability," *New York Times*, November 1, 1999, A10; "PRI Prepares for Primary and Tries to Avoid Rupture," *Financial Times Information*, November 2, 1999; Julia Preston, "Mexican Candidate Plays the Bad Boy," *New York Times*, November 5, 1999, A14; Molly Moore, "In Selling of Candidates, Mexico Tries U.S. Way," *Washington Post*, November 5, 1999, A25; Howard LaFranchi, "Mexico's Political Make-Over," *Christian Science Monitor*, November 9, 1999; Sam Dillon, "Mexican Pollsters Challenge Size of Turnout in the Primary," *New York Times*, November 17, 1999, A10; "Labastida Seeks to Mend Fences with Madrazo," *Financial Times Information*, November 21, 1999.

24. Defining exactly what is meant by "democracy" can be difficult in the study of comparative politics. One common approach to evaluate whether a country is democratic or not is to ask whether certain basic political freedoms are upheld—e.g., are voters free to express themselves at the polls, are parties free to organize and compete, and are the mass media free to report the news? Using these criteria, Mexico's PRI-dominated system would not have been considered fully democratic. But by the mid-1990s, analysts across the board saw the country as firmly moving in this direction.

25. A fuller description of attitudes toward participation in Mexico can be found in Jorge I. Domínguez and James A. McCann, *Democratizing Mexico: Public Opinion and Electoral Choices* (Baltimore: Johns Hopkins University Press, 1996), chapter 2; and James A. McCann, "The Changing Mexican Electorate," in *Governing Mexico: Political Parties and Elections*, ed. Monica Serrano (London: Macmillan/ILAS, 1998).

26. The other two contestants in this primary both had long resumes in politics: Manuel Bartlett, who had been the governor of the state of Puebla and a high-level party official, and Humberto Roque Villanueva, a former national head of the Institutional Revolutionary Party. In spite of their records in politics, neither was able to generate much popular excitement. Throughout the primary campaign, they remained in the second-tier.

27. Grayson, "Guide."

28. Anderson and Moore, "Fantastic Four."

29. In the days after the primary, turnout figures reported by the PRI were called into question. Some of Mexico's leading survey researchers charged that participation rates were inflated. Warren Mitofsky, a New York–based pollster, defended the PRI numbers based on an exit poll he conducted for the Mexican broadcast network *Televisa*. See Dillon, "Mexican Pollsters Challenge Size of Turnout."

30. Madrazo, however, repeated his main campaign theme in his concession speech. "I recognize the tendencies weren't favorable for me but you know the process was never equitable. We fought against the machine and demonstrated it could be done. We're going to continue working within the party in order to create change." This quotation is taken from Dudley Althaus and Michael Riley, "Primary Provides Boost for Mexico's Ruling Party," *Houston Chronicle*, November 9, 1999, A1.

31. This section relies on Roberto Espíndola, "No Change in Uruguay: The 1999 Presidential and Parliamentary Elections," *Electoral Studies* 20 (2001), 649–657; Mads H. Qvortrup, "Uruguay's Constitutional Referendum 8 December 1996," *Electoral Studies* 16 (1997), 549–554; Raul Ronzoni, "Uruguay: Long-Time Rivals Unite to Head Off Left," *Inter-Press Service*, November 10, 1999; "Vázquez, Batlle y Lacalle se impusieron con claridad en las internas de ayer," *La República en la Red*, edición 26/04/99; Espíndola, "Electoral Campaigning and the Consolidation of Democracy in Latin America"; and Constanza Moreira, "Elecciones en Uruguay 1999: Comportamiento Electoral y Cultura Política," paper presented at the XXII International Congress of the Latin American Studies Association, Miami, FL, March 16–18, 2000.

32. In the future, Argentina may also have mandatory presidential primaries. In early 2002, Argentine President Eduardo Duhalde included a call for primaries as part of a much larger reform package to deal with a devastating economic and political crisis. A system of primary elections was not, however, instituted before the 2003 general election in Argentina.

33. Espíndola, "Electoral Campaigning and the Consolidation of Democracy."

34. In a poll conducted by CBS News and the *New York Times* in July of 2000, respondents were asked whether they thought that the "method of nominating presidential candidates has generally, not just this year, produced the best candidates for president." Fifty-five percent of the respondents thought that it did, while 39 percent were critical of the process ($N = 706$). U.S. citizens are much more uniform, however, in their overall assessment of American democracy. An item in the 2000 American National Election Study

asked respondents if on the whole they were "satisfied," "fairly satisfied," "not very satisfied," or "not at all satisfied" with the way democracy works in the United States. Over
80 percent were fully or fairly satisfied, and only 3 percent reported no satisfaction at all
($N = 1,416$). These surveys are available at the Interuniversity Consortium for Political
and Social Research at the University of Michigan (study nos. 8475 and 3120).

35. I am not aware of any polling data on American attitudes toward the growing
"Americanization" of nomination politics abroad. But one item in the 1992 American
National Election Study is suggestive. When asked whether bringing "a democratic form
of government to other nations should be a very important foreign policy goal, a somewhat important goal, or if it is not important at all," the great majority felt at least some
obligation to spread "democracy." One-quarter of the sample thought this should be a
very important goal, and 57 percent saw it as "somewhat important" ($N = 1,044$; data
also available at the ICPSR, study no. 6067).

36. Quoted in Mark Stevenson, "America's Newest Export Industry: Political Advisers," *Associated Press*, January 29, 2000.

37. On this question, see Alan Ware's thoughtful critique of the scholarly literature on
divisive presidential primaries in the United States, "'Divisive' Primaries: The Important
Questions," *British Journal of Political Science* 9:3 (July, 1979), 381–384.

38. Ranney, "Candidate Selection," 97.

39. Partisan officials in some developing democracies have stopped short of sponsoring
open primaries because of this concern. For example, in preparation for the 2002 presidential contest, the governing party in South Korea decided to run what it called "U.S.-
style" primary elections. This was not an accurate characterization, however, in that the
party carefully screened participants. Anyone interested in taking part had to send an
application to the party. The names of the applicants were put into a pool, and 35,000 of
these "ordinary citizens" were chosen through a computerized lottery. The party then
added an equal number of committed party members to this set, and a series of regional
primaries was held. See "South Korea's MDP to Select Presidential Candidate in April,"
Kyodo News Service, January 7, 2002; Paul Shin, "South Korea Ruling Party Adopts U.S.
System," *Associated Press*, January 7, 2002; and Sang-Hun Choe, "Korean Ruling Party
Begins Race for Presidential Nomination," *Associated Press*, February 22, 2002.

40. Donald Green, Bradley Palmquist, and Eric Schicker, *Partisan Hearts and Minds*
(New Haven: Yale University Press, 2002).

41. As mentioned earlier, Uruguay employed a modified "French" system, whereby a
run-off election was conducted if no candidate won a majority or strong plurality on the
day of the election. Similar rules were also used in Argentina, Chile, Bulgaria, and Finland.
In general, the option of a run-off between the top finishers tends to foster a multiparty
system. To have a fighting chance, parties only need to place second in the first round of
the general election; they therefore lose their incentive to join together with other parties
and groups in an attempt to form a majoritarian bloc.

42. Two recent polls are particularly useful: a survey conducted by *Reforma* newspaper
in October of 1999 ($N = 2,531$); and a four-wave panel survey spanning a five-month
period, February–July, 2000 ($N = 2,355$). Respondents in both surveys were randomly
selected from all parts of the country, and interviewing was conducted face-to-face. Alejandro Moreno supervised the administration of these polls. The investigators of the 2000
panel study include Miguel Basañez, Roderic Camp, Wayne Cornelius, Jorge Domínguez,

Federico Estévez, Joseph Klesner, Chappell Lawson (Principal Investigator), Beatriz Magaloni, James McCann, Alejandro Moreno, Pablo Parás, and Alejandro Poiré.

43. Quoted in Estévez and Poiré, "Campaign Effects."

44. In Mexico, federal legislative sessions last three years. As in the United States, elections to the Mexican congress occur halfway through a president's administration.

45. In more formal terms, the model is: *ln* (probability of supporting Labastida in the general election/probability of not supporting Labastida in the general election) = α + β_1 (support for the PRI in the 1994 presidential election) + β_2 (support for the PRI in the 1997 congressional elections) + β_3 (support for Labastida in the open primary election of 1999) + β_4 (support for Roberto Madrazo, Manuel Bartlett, or Humberto Roque—all Labastida opponents—in the open primary) + additional demographic and socioeconomic control variables + residuals. For a good introduction to logistic regression analysis, see Scott W. Menard, *Applied Logistic Regression Analysis*, Quantitative Applications in the Social Sciences, Volume 106 (Thousand Oaks, CA: Sage Publications, 1995).

46. Domínguez and McCann, *Democratizing Mexico*; Jorge I. Domínguez and Alejandro Poiré, eds., *Toward Mexico's Democratization: Parties, Campaigns, Elections, and Public Opinion* (New York: Routledge, 1999).

47. A more extensive logistic regression model of candidate choice appears in McCann, "Primary Priming."

48. By comparison, partisanship is generally more stable in the established Western democracies. See James A. McCann and Chappell Lawson, "An Electorate Adrift? Public Opinion and the Quality of Democracy in Mexico," paper presented at the annual meeting of the American Political Science Association, August 30, 2002; and Eric Schickler and Donald Green, "The Stability of Party Identification in Western Democracies," *Comparative Political Studies* 30 (1997): 450–83.

49. These findings comport well with Lonna Rae Atkeson's analysis of the 1976 and 1980 presidential campaigns in the United States. Using similar kinds of panel survey data, Atkeson shows that Americans who backed a loser in a primary or local caucus upgraded their evaluations of the party nominee over the course of the general election campaign. See her "From the Primaries."

50. See Jorge I. Domínguez and Chappell Lawson, eds., *Mexico's Pivotal Democratic Elections: Campaigns, Voting Behavior, and the 2000 Presidential Race* (Stanford, CA: Stanford University Press, forthcoming).

51. Charles Edward Merriam and Louise Overacker, *Primary Elections* (Chicago: University of Chicago Press, 1928).

52. Anthony Downs, *An Economic Theory of Democracy* (New York: HarperCollins, 1957).

Index

Note: References in *italic* refer to tables or figures.

advertisements: as federal election activity, 45; issue advocacy, 65–66, 71, 155; online, 201, 219–20, 226; television, 225–26; tracking of, 213

Afghanistan, Soviet invasion of, 97

African Americans, 238

AFSCME: and Carter, 178; and Clinton, 186–87; and Dukakis, 185; and financial support to AFL-CIO, 176; and Gore, 188; leadership of, 191; and Kennedy, 179; and McGovern, 175; as PAC, 193; size of, 173

Ahtisaari, Martti, 272

Aldrich, John, 267

Alexander, Lamar: fundraising, 24–25, 57, 59, 60; and John Kasich, 212; results in Iowa, 108, 113; voter knowledge of, *16*, *17*, *18*

Alfonsin, Raul, 269

Alliance, the, 269, 278

Alwin, Patricio, 271

Ambling into History: The Unlikely Odyssey of George W. Bush. See Bruni, Frank

American Federation of Labor (AFL), 162–63

Americans with Disabilities Act, 150

Anderson, Jack, 239

Apple, R. W., 239

Argentina, 269–70, 271, 276, 285

Askew, Ruben, 182

Atwater, Lee, 140, 141, 144, 208

Babbit, Bruce, 184

Baggett, Joan, 141

Baker, James, 92, 149, 151

ballot listing, 26–27, 84, 274

Barbour, Haley, 66

Bartels, Larry, 89

Batlle, Jorge, 275, 276

Bauer, Gary, 113

Bentsen, Lloyd, 98

Bicoastal Blowout. *See* Titanic Tuesday

Biden, Joseph, 184

Bierne, Joseph, 176–77

Bipartisan Campaign Reform Act of 2002 (BCRA), 45–46; consequences of, 68–69; early fundraising, 69; incentives to public funding, 70, 72–75; and issue ads, 155; maximum individual contribution, 67; party support, 70–72; potential for money primary through, 213; solicitation of large gifts, 76; stratifying effect of, 67–68, 76

Blue Smoke and Mirrors. See Germond, Jack W.; Witcover, Jules

Bond, Rich, 147
bonus delegate scheme, 36
Bradley, Bill: and 2000 Iowa caucus, 108; in
   2000 New Hampshire primary, 102; as
   2000 potential union candidate, 188;
   campaigning in Iowa, 112; and large
   donors, 60; performance in the polls
   during invisible primary, 91, 98, 101;
   and polling, 245, 250, 255–56, 259; and
   spending limit, 65; Sweeney's thoughts
   on, 189; use of action kits, 212
Brady, Henry, 20, 89
bridge financing, 66
Broder, David S., 170, 239
Brown, Jerry, *16*, 18, 52, 97, 98, 100, 186
Brown, Ron, 35
Bruni, Frank, 240
Bryan, William Jennings, 163
Buchanan, Pat: as 1991 nomination candidate, 92; and BCRA, 68; and early fundraising, 57, 61; gains from Iowa, 110,
   113; and large donors, 62–63; and
   matching subsidy, 52; performance at
   New Hampshire primary, *103–4*, 106;
   voter knowledge of, *16*, 17, 18
Bulgaria, 270–71, 276, 285
Bush, George H. W.: 1992 quest for reelection, 134; attention to foreign and
   domestic policy, 153–54; competition
   within party during reelection, 143–44;
   delay in campaigning, 135; fundraising
   in 1980, 24; and the "funnel" system,
   151; New Hampshire victory of, 105;
   performance in invisible primary polls,
   90, 91–92; politicization during reelection campaign, 150; and public funds,
   52; and spending limit, 64; staff restructuring during reelection, 148–49
Bush, George W.: advertising, 226; BCRA
   and 2004 fundraising potential, 69;
   Bush-Rather debate, 208; fundraising
   of, 87, 155–56; and "limits to freedom,"
   207, 212; performance in 2000 invisible
   primary polls, 92, 95–96; performance
   in 2000 Iowa caucus, 110; prediction for
   competition in 2004, 261; and press,

236, 237, 238, 241; and private fundraising, 51, 55–56, 60, *61,* 63, 65; and
   public opinion, 245, 255, 259; and
   Republican party supported issue ads,
   66; votes received in 2000 primary

Caddell, Pat, 143, 146
Califano, Joseph, 152
California. *See* Titanic Tuesday
campaign finance, 7, 210, 212. *See also*
   Bipartisan Campaign Reform Act of
   2002 (BCRA); fundraising; public funding; voluntary public funding
campaign manager, 145, *146*
campaign chairman, 145, *146*
campaigns: and front-loading, 21–22; quality of, 21–22
candidates: and contested races, 86; fundraising ability of, *85*; seriousness of,
   83–84
Carter, Jimmy: competition within party
   during reelection, 143–44; demands on
   cabinet members during reelection
   campaign, 152–53; DNC during reelection of, 146; fundraising strategy of,
   23–24; as a late front-runner in 1980,
   96; as a long-shot candidate, 22, 28,
   88–89; and matching funds, 52; in 1976
   New Hampshire primary, 102; politicized decision making during reelection
   campaign, 150; reelection campaign of,
   134, *135,* 180; and region, 37; union
   dissatisfaction with, as president, 179;
   union support of, 177, 178, 193
Ceaser, James, 89
Center for Responsive Politics, 216
Cheney, Dick, 148, 155
Chile, 271, 276, 285
Christian Democratic Party (PDC), 271
Clean Air Act, 150
Clinton, Bill: and Democrat issue advertising effort, 65–66; early fundraising by,
   57; impeachment of, 210–11; issuing of
   executive orders by, 155; and large
   donors, 59, 60, 63; as a late front-runner in 1992 invisible primary, 96,
   97–99; politicized decisions during re-

election campaign, 150–51; and public funds, 52, 53–54; and public opinion, 245; reelection campaign of, 134, *135*; reelection strategy of, 213; reelection warchest in 1996, 144; and spending limit, 64; union support of in 1992, 186, 193; union support of in 1996, 187; voter knowledge of, *16*, 18

Coalition of Parties for Democracy (Concertación de Partidos para la Democracia), 271, 278

Colby, William E., 148

Commission on Party Structure and Delegate Selection. *See* McGovern-Fraser Commission

Committee for the Re-election of the President (CREEP), 138

Committee on Political Education (COPE), 176

Committee on Presidential Nomination. *See* Hunt Commission

communication workers, 176

compliance exemption, 47

Congress of Industrial Organizations (CIO), 163–64

Connelly, John, 54

consensual democracy, in Finland, 271

Cramer, Richard Ben, 240

Cranston, Alan, 182

Crespi, Irving, 251

Crouse, Timothy, 239–40

Cuomo, Mario, 98, 99

Daley, Richard J., 171

Darman, Richard, 151

dateline, definition of, 232

Davis, Richard Harding, 231

de la Rua, Fernando, 269–70

delegate slates, 27–28

democracies, new, 267

Democratic party: issue advertising, 65–66; nomination calendar, 8–9; nomination race of 1972, divisiveness of, 34–35; number of contenders, 31; public funding restrictions, 71–72; support of public funding, 53; white collar/blue collar democrats, 194–95

demographics: change in New Hampshire, 257; study of, by Theodore H. White, 236

Dent, Harry, 134

Dewey, Thomas, 251

DiNatale, Lou, 260

divisive primary hypothesis, 34–35

Dodd, Senator Christopher, 141

Dole, Elizabeth, 95, 113

Dole, Robert: and BCRA, 68; and early fundraising, 57–58; and large donors, 59, 60; performance in 1996 invisible primary polls, 92–93; and public funds, 52, 54, 55; public opinion of, 245; and Republican advertising effort, 66; and spending limit, 65; voter knowledge of, *16*, 18

Dornan, Robert, 54–55

double simultaneous voting, 275

Dukakis, Michael, 18–19, 99, 100–101, 184, 185, 193

Duke, David, 92

Edwards, John, 73, 193

Eisenhower, Dwight, 136

election laws, and polling, 261

electoral college, in Finland, 271, 272

"electoral market share," 285

electoral process, 276

e-mail: basics of, 202, 203–4; G. W. Bush's use of, 215; Forbes' use of, 204; microtargeting in, 201, 220–21; misuse in campaigning, 204, 215

Emmanuel, Rahm, 141

Epso, David, 239

Espindola, Roberto, 276

Euchner, Charles, 139

executive orders, issued during a reelection campaign, *154*, 155

Exley, Zack, 207, 222

expenditures, coordinated and independent, 71

Federal Election Campaign Act of 1974 (FECA), 46–47, 48, 49, 59, 139, 143, 178

Federal Election Commission (FEC), 11,

25; fundraising reports to, 85; statements of candidacy filed within, 83, 135
Fernandez Meijide, Graciela, 269
Ferraro, Geraldine R., 237
Finland, 271–72, 276
Fitzwater, Marlin, 153
Forbes, Malcolm "Steve," 54, 55, 56, 60, 259
Ford, Gerald: competition within party during reelection, 143–44; and the establishment of an independent campaign organization, 138; reelection campaign of, 135, *135*; and regions, 37; and showdown questions, 93–94; staffing changes during reelection campaign, 148
Fournier, Ron, 239
Fox, Vicente, 274
Fraser, Douglas, 180–81
free trade, 275
free-for-all strategy, 165, *166*, 177; 1992 nomination, 186; likelihood in 2004 election, 192. *See also* Labor Coalition Clearinghouse
Frey, Eduardo, 271
Frohnmeyer, John, 150
front-loading: consequences of, 15–33; and the creation of a prohibitive environment, 31; definition of, 2; and the divisive primary hypothesis, 34–35; and "entry fee," 30–31, 35, 37; New Hampshire envy, 9–13; possible benefits of, 33–35; primary calendars before and after, 2–3, *4*, *5*, *6*, 7–8; progression of, 7–8, 38; as a second order effect, 1; solutions for, 35–36; and spending limits, 49; summary measures of, 3, 7, *6*; and voter's decision process, 15, *16*, 18; and voter learning, 18–21
front-runners: advantage of, 22–26, 28; categories of emergence of, 90–101, 111; fate since 1972, *23*; increase in organizational demands upon, 26–28; and the invisible primary, 90; and new delegate selection calendar, 22; and the nomination process, 88–89; and out-

sider breakthrough scenario, 29–30; in regional primaries, 36–37; role in united front strategy, 192
fundraising: early, 56–58, 56, *58*, 61, *219*; exemption, 47; large contributions and, 58–63; lesser-known aspirants and large contributions, 59, 68; maximum contributors and candidate success, 58–60; parties and candidate expenditure ceilings, 65; and personal campaign contributions, limits on, 47, 54. *See also* Bipartisan Campaign Reform Act of 2002 (BCRA); campaign finance; Federal Election Campaign Act of 1974; private funding; public funding; voluntary public funding

Gephardt, Richard: 1992 campaign, 98; 1998 Iowa victory, 105; possibility of union support in 1998, 184–85; possibility of union support in 2000, 188; possibility of union support in 2004, 192, 73; as outspent in 1988 campaign, 25
Germond, Jack W., 240
Glen, John, 95, 108, 182
Gore, Al: and Bipartisan Campaign Reform Act of 2002 (BCRA), 73; and Democrat advertising, 66; and large donors, 60, 63; performance in invisible primary polls in 2000, 90–91; and press, 239, 241; and public matching funds, 52, 55; public opinion of, 245, 250, 255–56, 259; and spending limit, 65; union support of, 112, 188–91; and vote trading, 223; Web site, 217
Gramm, Phil, 17, *16*, 18, 57, 59, 93, 108
grassroots organizing, 26, 284
Gulf War, 87

Hacker, Andrew, 266, 276
Hall, Leonard, 136
Harkin, Tom, *16*, 18, 186
Hart, Gary: and 1984 New Hampshire primary, 102, 113; coverage of, 29; and delegate slates, 27; expected versus actual performance in Iowa caucus,

102, 104, 108, 110; fundraising in 1984,
24; possible union support of, 182, 184;
and public opinion, 99–101; role of
labor in campaign, 183; and voter
learning, 18–19, 20
Hatch, Orrin, 113
Hollings, Ernest, 182
The Hotline, 212
Hume, Brit, 239–40
Humphrey, Hubert, 174. *See also* Meany,
George, endorsement of Hubert Hum-
phrey
Humphries, Robert, 136
Hunt, James B., 180–81
Hunt Commission, 180

Ickes, Harold, 141
incumbent president's campaign:
announcement of, 135; assets in, 133;
cabinet activity in, 152–53; chief of staff
role during, 142; dual roles during, 124,
155; effect on executive branch, 147–55;
effect of FECA on, 139; effect of, on
White House business, 133–34; intra-
party competition, 143–44; and
McGovern-Fraser reforms, 139; outside
advisor roles, 142–43; policy initiative
during, 153–55; politicized decision
making during, 149–51; presidential
travel during, 151–52; recruitment and
strategic planning in, 143; staffing
changes during, 148–49; team recruitment, 143; timing of reelection planning, 134–36, *135*

independent campaign organizations, 139,
144–45
individual donors, 62–63
Institutional Revolutionary Party (PRI),
266, 272, 273, 274, 278, 279–84, 286
International Republican Institute (IRI),
270
Internet campaigning: basics of, 199–207;
and coalition building, 206; current
candidate use of, 204; customer relationship management (CRM), launch-
ing of, 205–6; and databases/database

security, 205, 224–25; and fundraising,
201, 204, 217–18; and news media,
215–17; and online voting, 203; strategies for convention, 224–25; strategies
for invisible primary, 211–14; strategies
for Iowa and New Hampshire, 218–21;
strategies for Super Tuesday, 221–24;
strategies for virtual primary period,
214–15; and television, 225–27; successes and failures of, 207–11; visibility
of, 203, 206. *See also* advertisements,
online; e-mail
invisible primary: 15, 16, 18, 56, 68, 90–
101, 200, 212, 213
issue advocacy ads. *See* advertisements,
issue advocacy
issue advocacy electioneering, 45

Jackson, Henry "Scoop," 23, 174, 178–79
Jackson, Jesse: and matching subsidy, 52;
performance in polls in 2000 invisible
primary, 91, 99, 100, 101; as possible
choice for labor support, 182, 183, 184
Johnson, Lyndon: and advantages of
incumbency, 133; campaign organization for reelection campaign, 136, 137;
performance in New Hampshire primary, 106; reelection campaign of, *135*;
and unions, 169
Johnston, Richard, 20, 89
Jordan, Hamilton, 140, 152
journalism. *See* political journalism

Kasich, Johan, 212
Kemp, Jack, 92–93, 95, 152
Kennedy, Edward M.: failed campaign of,
180; as invisible primary front-runner,
94–95, 97; labor endorsement of, 179;
lack of DNC support in 1979, 144–47
Kennedy, John F., 230, 234, 235
Kennedy, Robert, 169; assassination of,
170–71
Kerrey, Bob, 186, 189; voter knowledge of,
16, 18
Kerry, John, 73, 74–75, 188
Keyes, Alan, 113
key moments, 200

King, John, 239
Kirkland, Lane: and 1988 neutrality, 185; as
    AFL-CIO president, 180; endorsement
    of Hubert Humphrey, 168, 170; and
    solidarity of unions, 183; use of united
    front strategy, 181–82
Kirkpatrick, Jeane, 22
Kissinger, Henry, 148
Klein, Herb, 141
Kraft, 140

LaFollette, Robert, 163
Labastida, Francisco, 274, 278–79, 281–84
Labor Coalition Clearinghouse, 178, 179
labor unions: and 1968 convention,
    169–71; and 1972–1980 nominations,
    174–80; and 1984 nominations,
    180–83; and 1988 nominations,
    184–85; and 1992 nominations,
    185–87; and 2000 nominations,
    188–91; adjustment to nomination
    reforms, 172, 175, 179, 195; and AFL-
    CIO, 164–67, 169, 177; caucus-conven-
    tion nomination system, 167–68; col-
    lective neutrality in the nomination
    process, 165, *166*, 168–69, 177, 178,
    184–85; elite bargaining of leadership,
    168, 172; historical origins of, 162–64;
    internal divisions, 165–67, 174, 177,
    179, 184–85; large union influence and
    nomination process, 168; mid-century
    nomination process, 167; public
    endorsement of candidates and alien-
    ation, 177, 194; predictions for 2004
    nomination strategy; relationship with
    Democratic party, 161, 164. *See also*
    American Federation of Labor (AFL);
    Congress of Industrial Organizations
    (CIO); free-for-all strategy; Kirkland,
    Lane; Labor Coalition Clearinghouse;
    Meany, George; National Labor Rela-
    tions Act; Union of Democratic Forces
    (UDF); United Auto Workers, and
    United Steel Workers; united front
    strategy
Lacalle, Luis Alberto, 275–76
Lagos, Ricardo, 271

Landon, Alf, 247
Lavin, Joaquin, 271
Lieberman, Joseph, 73
Lippmann, Walter, 226
Lugar, Richard, voter knowledge of, *17*, 18

machinists, 176
Madrazo, Roberto, 274, 278, 282
Making of the President. See White, Theo-
    dore H.
Maltese, John Anthony, 139
Marshall, Joshua Micah, 216
McAuliffe, Terry, 71
McCain, John: and aggregate spending
    limit, 63; campaigning in Iowa, 112;
    fundraising of, 87; and large donors, 63;
    and momentum, 89–90; and private
    contributions, 60–61; and public
    matching funds, 52; public opinion, 10,
    245, 255–56, 258, 259; response to criti-
    cism, 223; use of Internet and fund-
    raising, 61, 209, 210; votes received in
    2000 primary, 86
McCarthy, Eugene, 169, 171
McEntee, Gerald, 191
McGinnis, Joe, 240
McGovern, George: as a long-shot candi-
    date, 88; and McGovern-Fraser Com-
    mission, 172; percentage of total
    primary vote received, 35; potential
    union support for, 176, 178; presiden-
    tial nomination of, 174, 175, 176
McGovern–Fraser Commission: 32, 49,
    285; lack of union adjustment to, 175,
    179; and unions 171–72, 173
Meany, George: as AFL-CIO president,
    170; building trade union support of,
    173–74; comparison with Sweeney, 190;
    endorsement of Hubert Humphrey,
    170–71, 181, 190; neutrality in Carter
    campaign, 178, 179; neutrality in
    McGovern-Nixon race, 175–76; per-
    ception of McGovern-Fraser reforms,
    172–73; resignation of, 180
Mears, Walter, 239
Mencken, H. L., 230

Menem, Carlos, 269
Merriam, Charles, 285
Mexico, 272–74, 278, 279. *See also* Institutional Revolutionary Party (PRI)
Mitchell, John, 148
Moe, Terry, 140
momentum, 89–90, 101–2, 111, 209
Mondale, Walter: and delegate slates, 27; endorsement by labor in 1984, 182–83; expected versus actual performance in Iowa caucus, 102, 104, 108; in a front-loaded primary calendar, 29–30; performance in invisible primary polls in 1984, 92, 95; public assessments of, 20; and spending limit, 64
money primary, 56, 60, 212–14, 216
Morris, Dick, 143, 276, 277
motor voter legislation, 258
moveon.org, 210–11
Muskie, Edmund, 106, 174

Nader, Ralph, and vote trading, 223
national conventions, 147
National Council on Public Polls, 261
National Endowment for the Arts, 150
National Labor Relations Act, 163–64; Gore's support of, 189
national party organization, role of in presidential reelection campaigns, 139, 145–47
New Hampshire: demographic change in, 257; polling in, 254–61
Nixon, Richard M.: "Nixon model" of campaigning, 139, 144; reelection campaign of, 134, 135, *135*; staffing changes in reelection campaign, 148; White House directed campaign of, 138; in writing of Theodore White, 234
Nofziger, Lyn, 140
nomination forecasting model, 84, 86, *87*; addition of Iowa caucus and New Hampshire primary, 102; Brady and Johnston model, 89; and declared candidates, 87–88; expectations versus actual performance in Iowa and New Hampshire, 104–6; final vote in New Hampshire is a function of, 108, 110;

indicators in, 84, 85, 86–87; Iowa, impact on New Hampshire, 108, 111, 112; Iowa, statistical significance of, 107–8; mediation effect of New Hampshire, 107; New Hampshire, statistical significance of and impact of, 106–7, 112
nomination process: and candidate withdrawal, 14; characteristics of, 88–90; controversy surrounding, 1; Democrat selection rules, 7; of early states, 11–12; and front-loading, 13–14, 15; purpose of, 84; reforms in, 1; scheduling of, 8–9
non-response rates, 259–61, 262
Nunn, Sam, 98

Office of Communications, 141
Office of Political Affairs (OPA), 140–41, 142
Office of Public Liaison, 141–42
Office of Strategic Initiatives, 155
opensecrets.org. *See* Center for Responsive Politics
opinion leader, 215–17
organized labor. *See* labor unions
Overacker, Louise, 285

Panagakis, Nick, 252–53
party registration, effect on polling in New Hampshire, 254
party unity, 33–35; international, 266
Perot, Ross, 53, 54
Pinochet, Augusto, 271
Pioneers, the, 56, 60
political action committee (PAC), 46
Policy Coordinating Group, 148
political journalism, 229; and beliefs of journalists; 230–32; bias in, 238–39; cannon of, 234–40; and distrust of press, 241; and exhaustive coverage, 232; and female reporters, 240; and gonzo journalism, 237; insecurity of, 232–33; objectivity of, 234; racial makeup of in 1970s, 240; relationship to political science, 233–34; and relationship with politicians, 235, 241–42; reporting style, 234; role in democratic

rule, 230, 242; and spin, 238; use of experts in, 234; use of public opinion research in, 242
political science. *See* political journalism, relationship to political science
polls: accuracy of, 245–46, 251, 260–61; in 2000 New Hampshire primary, 245, 249, 250; in Bulgaria, 270; execution of, 118–19; and data weighting, 251; in gubernatorial and U.S. Senate races, 261; and incumbent rule, 253; and interviews completed, 259–60; and likely voters, 247–48, 251, 262; in Mexico, 273, 278, 279–83; and predicting election outcome, 245; preelection, 245, 246, 247; sampling, 247–49; showdown questions, 93–94; suggestions for, 261–62; timing of, 251–52, 262; and voter lists, 248, 261. *See also* public opinion
Powell, Colin, 93, 95–96
previous primary voters (PPV), 248
primary elections: in Argentina, 269; in Bulgaria, 270; in Chile, 271; decisiveness of, 286; as an international trend, 265, 266, 267; in Mexico, 273; partisanship in, 277–78; in Uruguay, 274–75
private funding, 46, 51, 56–55, 58, 74–75
process stories, 236–37
proportional allocation strategy, 252, 253
public funding: aggregate expenditure ceiling, 47, 49; contribution limits, 50; expenditure ceiling, inadequacy of, 64–65, 66–67; and longer campaigns, 49–51; philosophical opposition to, 54; political consequences associated with, 52–53; and public matching subsidy, 46–47, 50, 51–52, 57; state limits, 47–49
public opinion: influence in New Hampshire and Iowa, 10; of major presidential contenders, 15, 16–17, *16*; monitoring of, 200; and nomination forecasting, 84, 85, *85*, 86–87, 90–91; and voter knowledge, 19–21. *See also* polls

Quayle, Dan, 92–93, 95

random digit dialing (RDD), 248–49, 261, 262
Ranney, Austin, 277, 286
Reagan, Ronald: 1980 performance in invisible primary polls, 92, 93; 1980 performance in New Hampshire primary, 105; and Carter, 180; and matching subsidy, 52; public assessments of, 20; reelection campaign of, 134; and showdown questions, 94; staffing changes in 1984 campaign, 148
refusal conversion, 250
Republican party: Atwater as chairman of, 140; candidates in 2000 race, 31–32; party advertising, 66; and public funding, 54; role in Eisenhower's 1956 election campaign, 136; role in Nixon's campaign, 138; scheduling of primaries and caucuses, 8–9; and support of George H. W. Bush, 147
respondents: contacting, 249–50; in random digit dialing, 248; questions asked to, 50–251
Reuther, Walter, 168–69
Rice, Donna, 100
Robbins, Chauncey, 136
Rockefeller, Nelson, 144
Rogan, James, 211
rolling sample, 252, 256
Roosevelt, Franklin, 163, 247
Roosevelt, James, 9
Roosevelt, Theodore, 133
Rosensteil, Tom, 240
Rubinton, Noel, 22
Rumsfeld, Donald, 148

Sanguinetti, Julio Maria, 276
Schiff, Adam, 211
Schlesinger, James R., 148
The Selling of the President. See McGinnis, Joe
Shafer, Byron, 7
Showtime. See Simon, Roger
Simon, Paul, 184, 186
Simon, Roger, 240
Sixty Second Activist Club, 211
Skinner, Samuel, 148–49

Smothers Brothers Comedy Hour, 208
soft money: ban on, 70–72; BCRA restrictions placed on, 45; and parties, 65, 66, 67
Sorsa, Kalevi, 272
Sosnick, Douglas, 141
Spencer, Stuart, 143
Stans, Maurice H., 148
Stoyanov, Petar, 270, 271
Strange Bedfellows. See Rosensteil, Tom
Sullivan, Andrew, 216
Sununu, John, 148
Super Tuesday, 3, 7, 21, 63, 221–22
Sweeney, John J., 161, 188–90, 191, 194

tarmac campaign. *See* campaigns
Taylor, Maurice, 54
Teeter, Robert, 143
Tehran hostage crisis, 97
telemarketing, and fundraising, 58
television, waning political power of, 201. *See also* Smothers Brothers Comedy Hour
telling detail, 213
Thompson, Hunter S., 237–38
Titanic Tuesday, 8
tracking polls, 252, 259
trial heat questions, 250
Truman, Harry, 136, 251
Trumka, Richard, 191
Tsongas, Paul, 18, *16*, 25, 98, 102, 186, 187
Tutwiler, Margaret, 142

undecided voters: methods for allocating, in polling, 252–53; Web sites aimed at, 222
undeclared voters: and polling in New Hampshire, 254–57
Union of Democratic Forces (UDF), 270, 278
United Auto Workers, and United Steelworkers, 164, 173, 193
unions. *See* labor unions
united front strategy, 165, 166, *166*, 177; in 2000 campaign, 191; past conditions associated with, 191–93; use of by Kirkland, 181

United Steel Workers, and United Auto Workers, 164, 173, 193
University of New Hampshire Survey Center, 260
Uruguay, 274–76

Vasquez, Tabare, 276
Ventura, Jesse: and the Internet, 223; use of e-mail lists by, 209
Vietnam War, 169, 171, 174
Virtual March on Washington, 211
voluntary public funding: campaign spending ceilings and, 46; creation of by FECA, 46
voter participation rates, 22, *33*, 32–33
voter registration: effect on polling in New Hampshire, 257–58; online, 210
voters. *See* undecided voters; undeclared voters
voter turnout: in Argentina, 269; in Bulgaria, 270; in Chile, 271; historical patterns in, 261; in New Hampshire, 254, 258–59
vote trading, 223–24

Wake Us When It's Over. See Germond, Jack W.; Witcover, Jules
walk-up vote, 258
Wallace, Governor George C., 23, 178
Watergate scandal, 139, 178
Wellstone, Paul, 188
What It Takes: The Way to the White House. See Cramer, Richard Ben
White, John, 146
White, Theodore H., 234–36, 237; criticisms of, 235; on Democratic National Convention, 168; on labor's involvement in Humphrey's campaign, 170; on Lyndon Johnson, 133; *Making of the President*, 240; study of demographic patterns, 236
White House: role in presidential reelection campaigns, 139–40, 142; tasks done for reelection, 145
Wilson, Woodrow, 163
Winograd Commission, 144
wire-service news reporting, 239

Witcover, Jules, 240
women, and telephone surveys, 251
Woodcock, Leonard, 178
Wurf, Jerry, 175

Yeutter, Clayton, 141, 148

Zaldivar, Andreas, 271
Zedillo, Ernesto, 274, 278
Zhelev, Zhelyu, 270, 271
Zogby, John, 260

About the Contributors

Andrew E. Busch is an associate professor of political science at the University of Denver, where he teaches American government. He is the author or coauthor of six books on American elections and politics.

Michael Cornfield is an associate research professor at the George Washington University Graduate School of Political Management (GSPM), and Research Director for the school's Institute for Politics, Democracy, and the Internet (www.ipdi.org). He is coeditor of *The Civic Web: Online Politics and Democratic Values* (2002). He writes a monthly column, "The Online Campaigner," for *Campaigns & Elections* magazine. He received his Ph.D. in political science from Harvard University, and has taught online politics, media and politics, and strategy and message development at the GSPM since 1994.

Anthony Corrado is a professor of government at Colby College in Waterville, Maine, and a senior fellow of the Brookings Institution. He currently serves as chair of the American Bar Association Advisory Committee on Election Law and principal investigator of the Coalition to Promote Civic Dialogue on Campaign Finance Reform, which is supported by The Pew Charitable Trusts. His recent publications include *Campaign Finance Reform: A Sourcebook* and *Inside the Campaign Finance Battle*.

Taylor E. Dark III is Associate Dean in the Graduate School of American Studies at Doshisha University in Kyoto, Japan. He is the author of *The Unions and the Democrats: An Enduring Alliance* and has previously published articles on labor unions and politics in the *Journal of Labor Research, Labor History, Political Science Quarterly, Polity,* and *Presidential Studies Quarterly.* He received his Ph.D. in political science from the University of California, Berkeley.

Heitor Gouvêa is a graduate of Colby College in Waterville, Maine, and a research associate of the Coalition to Promote Civic Dialogue on Campaign Finance Reform, sponsored by The Pew Charitable Trusts. He has previously coauthored an article on political party finance published in *The State of the Parties*.

William G. Mayer is an associate professor of political science at Northeastern University. He is the author of four previous books, including *The Changing American Mind* and *The Divided Democrats*. He has also published numerous articles on such topics as public opinion, voting behavior, political parties, and media and politics.

James A. McCann is an associate professor of political science at Purdue University, West Lafayette, Indiana. His research has appeared in several professional journals, including the *American Political Science Review* and the *Journal of Politics*. He is coauthor, with Jorge Dominguez, of *Democratizing Mexico: Public Opinion and Electoral Choices*.

Jonah Seiger is a nationally recognized Internet strategist and pioneer in the field of online public affairs communications. Seiger began organizing online campaigns in 1994 and has managed numerous award-winning efforts on behalf of some of the country's most important corporations, coalitions, and issue groups. In 1997, Seiger co-founded Mindshare Internet Campaigns, LLC, a leading provider of Internet strategy technology development for public affairs. Seiger is currently serving as a visiting fellow with the Institute for Politics, Democracy, and the Internet at the George Washington University.

David M. Shribman is executive editor of the *Pittsburgh Post-Gazette*. He won the Pulitzer Prize in 1995 for his articles on American political culture. A former Washington bureau chief of the *Boston Globe* and national political correspondent of the *Wall Street Journal*, he has also reported from Washington for the *New York Times*, the *Washington Star*, and the *Buffalo Evening News*. He is an adjunct instructor in American Studies at the University of Notre Dame.

Andrew E. Smith is Director of the University of New Hampshire Survey Center and Research Director in the UNH Institute for Policy and Social Science Research. He is the author of several articles on survey methodology and elections. His research focuses on New Hampshire politics, election predictions, and public opinion.

Kathryn Dunn Tenpas is a guest scholar at the Brookings Institution, associate director of the University of Pennsylvania's Washington Semester Program, and author of *Presidents as Candidates: Inside the White House for the Presidential Campaign*. Her articles have appeared in the *Journal of Politics, Political Science Quarterly*, and *Presidential Studies Quarterly*.